Houghton
Mifflin
Harcourt.

HMH Decoding Power: Intensive Reading Instruction

Teacher's Guide

System 1

Program Consultant: Dr. Martha C. Hougen

Printed in the U.S.A.

ISBN 978-0-544-59275-9

4 5 6 7 8 9 10 0607 17

4500669763   C D E F G

Contents

Contents

Contents

Contents

Contents

Contents

Welcome to *HMH Decoding Power*

HMH Decoding Power: Intensive Reading Instruction provides targeted intervention for students who need reteaching and practice in one or more of the key foundational reading skills. The five "systems" of *Decoding Power* provide explicit, sequential, and systematic instruction as well as practice and review in the critical areas of print concepts, letter knowledge, phonological awareness, phonemic awareness, phonics, word recognition, and fluency. The systems include instruction at multiple grade levels, enabling teachers to bring struggling students gradually up to grade level.

Features and Components

Key features of *HMH Decoding Power* include:

- Explicit instructional sessions that follow the steps of Teach/Model, Guided Practice, and Apply.

- Reproducible Practice Pages (for use in the Apply step of most sessions). Most Practice Pages contain connected text with which students can practice reading skills:
  — Phonics Practice Pages at the kindergarten through grade 2 levels contain decodable text (that is, at least 75 percent of the words can be decoded using known sound-spellings, while the remaining words are known high-frequency words).
  — Text passages for cumulative review and fluency practice have Lexile® measures (in grade 2 through 6 levels) that gradually increase. (Lexile® measures are shown in the introduction to the My Progress graph.)

- Regularly spaced cumulative reviews, integrated with fluency practice, to cement learning over time. Students can track their progress through these cumulative reviews on their My Progress graphs.

- Additional predecodable and decodable books (with skill charts) available online, for extended practice.

- Formative assessment and corrective feedback notes in each session to ensure that students understand skills as they are taught.

- Resources such as Alphafriends Cards, Sound/Spelling Cards, Letter Cards, High-Frequency Word Cards, and Handwriting Models.

- Word games and activities for additional hands-on practice.

- Point-of-use language-transfer support to help English learners use what they already know while building the foundations of reading in English. Language-transfer support also points out potential challenges for students of diverse language backgrounds.

- *Intervention Assessments*, for efficient, reliable tools to check that students are progressing toward grade-level achievement at an appropriate pace.
  — These tests are brief enough to administer once every two weeks for students who need close monitoring.
  — Depending on level, the tests assess phonological and phonemic awareness, letter-naming fluency, letter-sound fluency, word-reading fluency, and sentence- and passage-reading fluency.
  — Record forms make placement, monitoring, and exit decisions automatic for teachers and understandable for family members.

Components	Systems				
	K	**1**	**2**	**3**	**4–6**
Teacher's Guide: Instructional sessions as well as hands-on activities and other resources.	√	√	√	√	√
Practice Pages: Reproducible practice pages for applying skills learned in the instructional sessions. (Note that not all sessions use a Practice Page.)	√	√	√	√	√
Handwriting Models: Reproducible pages for practicing letter formation.	√	√	√	√	
Alphafriends Cards: Friendly alphabet characters that help students learn letter names and sounds. Note: Audio of Alphafriends songs is available online.	√	√	√	√	
Sound/Spelling Cards: Cards that help students learn letter-sound relationships and common spelling patterns.	√	√	√	√	√
Letter Cards: A set of cards containing two uppercase and four lowercase cards for each letter of the alphabet.	√	√	√	√	√
High-Frequency Word Cards: Cards that feature high-frequency words and tips for decoding them.	√	√	√	√	√
Intervention Assessments: Tests for checking student progress toward grade-level achievement at an appropriate pace.	√	√	√	√	√
Extended Practice: Additional predecodable and decodable books are available online.	√	√	√	√	√

How the Systems Work

HMH Decoding Power comprises five systems, providing instruction across multiple grade levels to help you target your students' needs:

System K: Instruction and practice at the pre-kindergarten through kindergarten levels in print concepts, letter knowledge, phonological awareness, phonemic awareness, phonics, word recognition, and fluency.

System 1: Instruction and practice at the pre-kindergarten through grade 1 levels in print concepts, letter knowledge, phonological awareness, phonemic awareness, phonics, word recognition, and fluency.

System 2: Instruction and practice at the pre-kindergarten through grade 2 levels in print concepts, letter knowledge, phonological awareness, phonemic awareness, phonics, word recognition, and fluency.

System 3: Instruction and practice at the pre-kindergarten through grade 3 levels in print concepts, letter knowledge, phonological awareness, phonemic awareness, phonics, word recognition, and fluency.

System 4–6: Instruction and practice at the grade 2 through grade 6 levels in phonics and decoding, word recognition, and fluency.

Pacing Suggestions

Suggested pacing for individual sessions is approximately 20–30 minutes. (Some sessions at the pre-kindergarten and kindergarten levels may take as little as 15 minutes.) Note that some sessions are grouped into a cluster; these are the sessions whose numbers end in A, B, C, and so on. It is suggested that these clustered sessions be taught together. This is especially true of clustered sessions in the kindergarten through grade 2 levels, because the decodable text on those sessions' Practice Pages will focus on the phonics skills and high-frequency words taught in that cluster. Suggested pacing for such clustered sessions is approximately 40–60 minutes.

From Good Teacher to Great Teacher

by Martha C. Hougen

Several years ago I read a book that led me to dramatically alter how I conceptualized teaching. The book, *Good to Great*[1] by Jim Collins, discusses how some businesses remain mediocre or good, while other similar companies become great. The "good to great" concept and recent research about teaching and learning converged as I addressed the question, "What makes a great teacher?" Why is it that some teachers enable their students to make significant growth in achievement while students of other teachers may make progress, but not the leaps in achievement that students of the great teachers make? Why are there such wide differences in student achievement in the same schools, same grade, even in classes in the same hall?

I propose that the truly great teachers have mastered high-leverage strategies—ways to teach that produce the most results.[2, 3, 4] Most of these practices can be accomplished by applying five features of effective instruction.[5] These five features can make a good teacher great and turn mediocre student progress into significant student achievement.

1. Explicit Instruction with Modeling

Explicit instruction means being clear in what students are to learn and showing them what they are expected to do. Modeling, including thinking aloud your thought process, is essential for students who may have trouble understanding the concept or skill being taught. Modeling that is clear, concise, and consistent is an essential teacher skill and will reduce student confusion and increase learning.

2. Systematic Instruction with Scaffolding

The sequence in which teachers present new information is crucial. Teachers must be thoughtful about planning, building upon concepts students know. For students who need intervention, this typically requires teachers to ensure students know the prerequisite skills, to break the new skill into smaller skills, and to begin with the concrete and move to the abstract. Scaffolding refers to the practice of providing temporary support until the student has mastered the skill. Scaffolds include such practices as providing starter sentences or partial answers, additional modeling, or using multisensory strategies to reinforce learning.

3. Frequent Opportunities for Responding and Practicing

Great teachers maximize student participation, especially of students who find learning new concepts difficult and who need ample practice in order to master the material. Students need to respond and practice the new skills often. This does not mean more worksheets, but rather more opportunities to manipulate the material in a meaningful way. These opportunities for increased practice and responding are best provided during small-group instruction until the student can practice the skill independently with accuracy.

4. Immediate Corrective and Affirmative Feedback

Feedback that is specific and timely increases student accuracy and learning. The most effective feedback refers to what the student did. For example, a teacher may say to a student who is confusing the letter sounds for *m* and *n*, "You read *nat*. Look at the first letter again. It is the letter *m* and sounds like /m/. Look in the mirror while you say /m/. See how your lips are together? Yes, /m/ is the sound for the letter *m*. Read the word again, slowly. Yes! /m/ /a/ /n/. Now say the word fast. Yes! The word is *man*." This type of feedback is most appropriate in a small-group or one-to-one instruction. Positive and effective ways to provide specific, corrective, and affirmative feedback during whole-class or small-group instruction are provided in this Teacher's Guide.

5. Ongoing Progress Monitoring

Teachers need to be more efficient in their instruction than ever before. In a typical class students vary widely in their skills and instructional needs. Knowing exactly what a student needs to learn helps teachers target their instruction for that student, accelerating student learning in a focused manner. Quick, brief, frequent assessments help teachers plan their instruction to meet the needs of the students. Assessing students' reading fluency, for example, can provide a knowledgeable teacher with a great deal of information about student achievement in reading.

The intervention strategies in the *Decoding Power* systems provide a basis for applying the features of effective instruction. The steps of Teach/Model, Guided Practice, and Apply are explicit and systematic. For example, the reading skills build from phonemic awareness to learning to decode words. The teacher models and is prompted to think aloud for students. Opportunities to practice are provided through Practice Pages as well as games and activities. Each session includes a tip on providing feedback and conducting formative assessment, and the *Intervention Assessments* book provides tools for monitoring students' progress over time.

The resources are available. Now it is up to you, the teacher, to implement the features of effective instruction and become a great teacher for all your students.

Martha C. Hougen, Ph.D., is the Teacher Education Professional Development Leader at the CEEDAR Center, University of Florida. Hougen's recent work focuses on improving preservice teacher education by providing university teacher educators with ongoing professional development and collaborative learning opportunities. She has worked with struggling readers as a general and special education teacher and administrator and as a university faculty member. She consults with state departments, universities, and school districts across the country on teacher education, reading, and special education.

Photo: *Martha C. Hougen © Rice Jackson*

Notes

1. Collins, J. (2001). *Good to Great*. New York: HarperCollins Publishers.
2. Ball, D. L. & Forzani, F. M. (2011, Summer). Building a Common Core for Learning to Teach, and Connecting Professional Learning to Practice. *American Educator*, 35(2), 17–21, 38–39. See also Teaching Works website: http://www.teachingworks.org/.
3. Archer, A. & Hughes, C. (2011). *Explicit Instruction: Effective and Efficient Teaching*. New York: Guilford Press.
4. Rosenshine, B. (2010). *Principles of Instruction*. Brussels, Belgium: The International Academy of Education. Available for download at the International Bureau of Education website:
   http://www.ibe.unesco.org/fileadmin/user_upload/Publications/Educational_Practices/EdPractices_21.pdf
5. Meadows Center for Preventing Education Risk. (2007). *Features of Effective Instruction*. Austin, TX: Texas Education Agency/University of Texas System.

Instructional Sessions

Print Concepts: What Is a Word?

Teach/Model

- Display this row of words:

  Kim   May   José   Maria   Darrell   go   school

- Read each word aloud, scooping your finger under each word as you say it and pausing between words.

- **Say:** *Each group of letters is a word.*

- Scoop your finger under the word *go*. **Say:** *This is a word. The word is* go.

- Scoop your finger under the word *school*. **Say:** *This is a word. The word is* school.

- Scoop your finger under the word *Kim*. **Say:** *This is a name,* Kim.

- Scoop your finger under the name *May*. **Say:** *This is another name,* May.

- Repeat with the names *José, Maria,* and *Darrell*.

- **Say:** *Names are also words. A name is always made of the same letters in the same order.*

- Point to the space between two words. **Say:** *This is a space. That's how we know where one word ends and another starts.*

- Point to each of the spaces while saying the word *space*.

Guided Practice

- Display students' first names with spaces between the names. **Say:** *These are your names. Each name is a word.*

- Point to each name, read it aloud, and have the named student raise his or her hand.

- Point randomly to names and spaces, guiding students to say with you *word* or *space*.

Apply

- Return to the displayed words:

  Kim   May   José   Maria   Darrell   go   school

- Alternate pointing to words and pointing to spaces and have students say *word* or *space*.

- Ask students to point to words and spaces and say *word* or *space*.

- If there is environmental print nearby containing words and spaces, point to the words and spaces and ask students to say *word* or *space*.

Objectives

- Recognize that spoken words are represented in writing by a specific sequence of letters.
- Understand that words in print are separated by spaces.

English Language Support

If students' first language is Spanish, you may want to use concrete words like the following, in addition to students' names: *libro (book), lápiz (pencil), escritorio (desk), mesa (table), silla (chair)*. Write each word in both Spanish and English as you say it aloud and point to the thing it names, and then say: *This is a word (esta es una palabra). We use words to speak and write (utilizamos las palabras para hablar y escribir).*

Formative Assessment and Corrective Feedback

IF a student makes an error, THEN follow this model:

Correct the error.

Guide the student to perform the task correctly by modeling.

Check for understanding by having the student repeat the task.

Reinforce: Make a note to review the skill during the student's next session.

Print Concepts: What Is a Sentence?

Teach/Model

- Display these sentences, with sufficient space between words and sentences:

    We go to school. The school is big.

- Read the first sentence aloud while sliding your finger under the words of the sentence. **Say:** *This is a sentence. A sentence tells us something. It tells us a complete thought.*
- Read the first sentence aloud again, while sliding your finger under the words of the sentence.
- **Say:** *A sentence is made of words. Each group of letters is a word. Here are the words in this sentence.*
- Scoop your finger under each word in the first sentence while saying it aloud.
- **Say:** *There are spaces between the words.*
- Point to each space between words within the sentence and say *space*.
- Read the first sentence aloud again, while sliding your finger under the words of the sentence.
- Repeat the steps above with the second sentence.
- **Say:** *How do we know where a sentence stops and a new sentence starts? Each sentence starts with a capital letter.* Point to the capital letter at the start of the first sentence.
- Point to the period at the end of the first sentence. **Say:** *This is a period. It tells us where the sentence stops.* Repeat with the second sentence.
- Point to the space between the two sentences. **Say:** *There's a space after this period. That's another way we know that one sentence stopped and a new sentence started.*

Guided Practice

- Scoop your finger below the word *school* and read the word aloud. Guide students in answering the question: *Is this a word or a sentence?* Note that it is not a sentence because it doesn't tell a complete thought.
- Slide your finger below the sentence *We go to school* and read the sentence aloud. Guide students in answering the question: *Is this a word or a sentence?* Note that it is a sentence because it tells a complete thought.
- Repeat the steps above, sometimes indicating words and sometimes indicating sentences.
- **Say:** *Where does the first sentence start?* Guide students in identifying the capital *W* in *We*. Repeat for the second sentence.
- **Say:** *Where does the first sentence end?* Guide students in identifying the period. Repeat for the second sentence.

Apply

- Display these sentences, with sufficient space between words and sentences:

    The pencil is red. The book is blue.

- Read each sentence aloud while sliding your finger under the words of the sentences. Repeat.
- Scoop your finger below the word *pencil* and read the word aloud. **Say:** *Is this a word or a sentence?*
- Slide your finger below the sentence *The pencil is red* and read the sentence aloud. **Say:** *Is this a word or a sentence?*
- Repeat the steps above, sometimes indicating words and sometimes indicating sentences.
- Have students identify where each sentence starts and where each sentence ends.

Print Concepts: What Is a Book?

Teach/Model

- Display a book from the classroom or the library. **Say:** *What am I showing you? Yes, it is a book. Look at the book.* Show the front cover. *This is the front cover of the book.*
- Then identify the following features of the front cover. **Say:**

    This is the title of the book. Listen as I read it.

    This is the author of the book. The author wrote the story. Listen as I read the author's name.

    This is the illustrator of the book. The illustrator drew or made the pictures for the book. Listen as I read the illustrator's name.

- Show the back cover. *This is the back cover of the book.* Identify the features on the back cover.
- Show the title page of the book. *This is the title page.* Identify the title, author, and illustrator.
- **Say:** *When we read a book, we start at the front of the book. Look at the pages. The pages are numbered in order.* Turn several pages so students can see how the pages are ordered.
- **Say:** *This is the first page of the story. I start at the top of the page and read from top to bottom. Point to the top and bottom with me.*
- **Say:** *I am at the top of the page, and I always start at the left side and read from left to right. Follow along as I read this sentence from left to right.* Track the text as you read from left to right.
- **Say:** *Let's look at some of the pictures in the book. The words on the page work with the pictures. Together the words and pictures help us understand the story.*

Guided Practice

Display another book from the classroom or the library.

- Point to the front cover and ask students to identify it.
- Point to the title and read it aloud. **Say:** *What part of the book is this?* (title)
- **Say:** *Where is the author's name on the front cover? Point to it. What does the author do?* Read aloud the author's name.
- **Say:** *Where is the illustrator's name on the front cover? Point to it. What does the illustrator do?* Read aloud the illustrator's name.
- Open to the first page of the story. **Say:** *This is where I begin. Where do I start? Show me.*
- **Say:** *Show me how we read from left to right.*

Apply

Have students work with a partner. Give a book to each set of partners.

- **Say:** *Work with your partner and point to the front cover. Point to the title. Point to the author. Point to the illustrator.*
- **Say:** *Work with your partner and point to the back cover? Now find the title page. Point to the title. Point to the author. Point to the illustrator.*
- **Say:** *Turn to the first page of the story. Where do we start reading? Show me the top of the page. Which side of the page do we start on? Show me how we read from left to right. Now show me how we read from top to bottom.*

Objectives

- Understand the concept of a book.
- Recognize front cover, back cover, and title page of a book.
- Understand that pages are read from left to right, top to bottom, and page by page.

Formative Assessment and Corrective Feedback

IF a student makes an error, THEN follow this model:

Correct the error.

Guide the student to perform the task correctly by modeling.

Check for understanding by having the student repeat the task.

Reinforce: Make a note to review the skill during the student's next session.

Print Concepts: Distinguish Letters and Numbers

Objectives

- Recognize that letters are symbols used to make words.
- Recognize that numbers are symbols for amounts.

Formative Assessment and Corrective Feedback

IF a student makes an error, THEN follow this model:

Correct the error.

Guide the student to perform the task correctly by modeling.

Check for understanding by having the student repeat the task.

Reinforce: Make a note to review the skill during the student's next session.

Teach/Model

- Display these rows of letters and numbers:

A	B	C	D	E
1	2	3	4	5

- **Say:** *Look at the rows. The top row contains letters. Letters are used for writing words. These letters are the first letters of the alphabet.* Say the letters aloud and have students repeat. Choose someone to write his or her name and tell which letters s/he used. Point out how the letters in the name represent a word. Repeat with other students.

- **Say:** *The bottom row contains numbers. We use numbers for counting.* Help students identify that numbers are the amount of something by telling how many. Have students count some items (pencils, crayons, books) in the room to tell how many. Choose someone to write the number that tells how old he or she is. Ask other students to write a favorite number or a number they know.

Guided Practice

- Give each student a card. Ask students to write a number or a letter on their card. Gather the cards and place them in a pile. **Say:** *Let's play a game. I will begin by taking a card. I will look at the card to see if it is a letter or a number. Then I will tell whether it is a letter or a number and point to the row that has the same thing.*

- Have students take turns taking a card and telling whether their card has a number or a letter. Then have them point to the matching row.

Apply

- Have students look around the room and find places where they see letters of the alphabet. Have them tell where the letter is and help them name the letter. Repeat the activity, this time having students look for places where they see numbers. Be sure they include things such as a clock or watch.

Letter Knowledge: Letter Names *Aa*

Teach/Model

- Display several letters of the alphabet. **Say:** *These are letters. Letters are used for writing. Letters stand for a sound or sounds. When you put letters together they make words.*

- Display Letter Card *Aa*.

- **Say:** *Let's look at this letter, capital* A. *It has all slanted lines on the side with a short one in the middle, no circles. Capital* A *has a buddy called small, or lowercase,* a. *What lines do you see in the letter* a? (a circle and a straight line)

- Ask students whether their names contain the letter *A* or *a*. Display any student names that contain the letter *A* or *a*. Circle the letters *A* and *a* wherever they appear.

- Look around the room for examples of the letter *A* or *a* (in book titles or other environmental print). Point out an example. Ask students to help you find others.

Guided Practice

- Hold up capital and small Letter Cards *Aa* one at a time. Have students name the letters. Then display Letter Cards *Aa–Cc* in random order. Have students find *A* or *a*. Then have them point to and name the capital *A* and lowercase *a*.

HANDWRITING: WRITING A, a Tell students that they will learn to write capital *A* and lowercase *a*. Write each letter slowly and deliberately as you recite the handwriting rhymes. Have students do the same, using their index fingers to "write" the letters in the air.

Handwriting Rhyme: A

Start at the top, slant

down just a little.

Repeat from the top, and

connect in the middle.

Handwriting Rhyme: a

Start in the middle,

make a circle nice and round.

Go back up a little,

make a straight line down.

- Repeat the handwriting rhymes activity, but this time have students use the Handwriting Models page for *Aa* to practice writing the letters.

Apply

- Have students use Practice Page K.5 to practice the letters *Aa*. Explain that the picture in the upper-left box is the Alphafriend for the letter *a*. Tell students to draw the Alphafriend and its letter in the upper-right box.

- In the lower-left box, have students trace the letters *Aa*. In the lower-right box, have students write the letters *Aa*.

> **Fun with Letters** Optional activities for engaging, hands-on practice are provided in the Resources section.

Objective

- Recognize and write the letters *Aa*.

Materials

- Handwriting Models for Letters *Aa*
- Letter Cards
- Practice Page K.5

Formative Assessment and Corrective Feedback

IF a student has difficulty identifying a previously learned letter, THEN follow this model:

Correct the error. Display the letter and say its name. If students confuse two similar-looking letters (for example, *a* and *o*), point out how the letters differ.

Guide the student to "write" the letter in the air and say its name several times.

Check for understanding by having the student identify the letter from a mix of other previously taught letters.

Reinforce: Make a note to review the letter during the student's next session.

Let's Move!

Have students use play clay to form the letters *A* and *a*.

Letter Knowledge: Letter Names *Bb*

Objectives

- Review letter names *Aa*.
- Recognize and write the letters *Bb*.

Materials

- Handwriting Models for Letters *Bb*
- Letter Cards
- Practice Page K.6

Formative Assessment and Corrective Feedback

IF a student has difficulty identifying a previously learned letter, THEN follow this model:

Correct the error. Display the letter and say its name. If students confuse two similar-looking letters (for example, *b* and *d*), point out how the letters differ.

Guide the student to "write" the letter in the air and say its name several times.

Check for understanding by having the student identify the letter from a mix of other previously taught letters.

Reinforce: Make a note to review the letter during the student's next session.

Let's Move!

Have students use their fingers to "write" the letters *B* and *b* on the back of their hands.

Teach/Model

- Display Letter Card *Bb*.
- **Say:** *This is the letter* B. *Let's look at capital* B. *It has a straight line and two curves. It looks like a stick and two bumps. Capital* B *has a buddy called small, or lowercase,* b. *What lines do you see in the letter* b? *Yes, lowercase* b *has a straight line and just one bump.*
- Ask students whether their names contain the letter *B* or *b*. Display any student names that contain the letter *B* or *b*. Circle the letters *B* and *b* wherever they appear.
- Look around the room for examples of the letter *B* or *b* (in book titles or other environmental print). Point out an example. Ask students to help you find others.

Guided Practice

- Display Letter Cards *Aa–Bb* in random order. Have students find and name *B* or *b*. Then have them point to and name the capital *A* and lowercase *a*.

HANDWRITING: WRITING *B, b* Tell students that they will learn to write capital *B* and small (lowercase) *b*. Write each letter slowly and deliberately as you recite the handwriting rhymes. Have students do the same, using their index fingers to "write" the letters in the air.

Handwriting Rhyme: B

Make a long line down.

Go back to the top.

Curve 'round and 'round

Before you stop!

Handwriting Rhyme: b

Make a long line down.

A circle from the middle,

Nice and round.

Not too big—it's little!

- Repeat the handwriting rhymes activity, but this time have students use the Handwriting Models page for *Bb* to practice writing the letters.

Apply

- Have students use Practice Page K.6 to practice the letters *Bb*. Explain that the picture in the upper-left box is the Alphafriend for the letter *b*. Tell students to draw the Alphafriend and its letter in the upper-right box.
- In the lower-left box, have students trace the letters *Bb*. In the lower-right box, have students write the letters *Bb*.

> **Fun with Letters** Optional activities for engaging, hands-on practice are provided in the Resources section.

Letter Knowledge: Letter Names *Cc*

Teach/Model

- Display Letter Card *Cc*.
- **Say:** *Let's look at capital C. It is almost a circle. It has no straight lines. Capital C has a buddy called small, or lowercase,* c. *Lowercase* c *is almost a circle, too. It looks a lot like its letter buddy.*
- Ask students whether their names contain the letter *C* or *c*. Display any student names that contain the letter *C* or *c*. Circle the letters *C* and *c* wherever they appear.
- Look around for examples of the letter *C* or *c* (in book titles or other environmental print). Point out an example. Ask students to help you find others.

Guided Practice

- Display Letter Cards *Aa–Cc* in random order. Have students find *C* or *c*. Then have them point to and name the other letters.

HANDWRITING: WRITING C, c Tell students that they will learn to write capital *C* and lowercase *c*. Write each letter slowly and deliberately as you recite the handwriting rhymes. Have students do the same, using their index fingers to "write" the letters in the air.

Handwriting Rhyme: C

Start near the top line.

Curve around.

Make a half circle,

nice and round.

Handwriting Rhyme: c

Start near the mid line.

Curve around.

Leave the circle open,

but nice and round.

- Repeat the handwriting rhymes activity, but this time have students use the Handwriting Models page for *Cc* to practice writing the letters.

Apply

- Have students use Practice Page K.7 to practice the letters *Cc*. Explain that the picture in the upper-left box is the Alphafriend for the letter *c*. Tell students to draw the Alphafriend and its letter in the upper-right box.
- In the lower-left box, have students trace the letters *Cc*. In the lower-right box, have students write the letters *Cc*.

> **Fun with Letters** Optional activities for engaging, hands-on practice are provided in the Resources section.

Objectives

- Review letter names *Aa–Bb*.
- Recognize and write the letters *Cc*.

Materials

- Handwriting Models for Letters *Cc*
- Letter Cards
- Practice Page K.7

Formative Assessment and Corrective Feedback

IF a student has difficulty identifying a previously learned letter, THEN follow this model:

Correct the error. Display the letter and say its name. If students confuse two similar-looking letters (for example, *o* and *c*), point out how the letters differ.

Guide the student to "write" the letter in the air and say its name several times.

Check for understanding by having the student identify the letter from a mix of other previously taught letters.

Reinforce: Make a note to review the letter during the student's next session.

Let's Move!

While reciting the handwriting rhymes, perform the actions described in the rhyme to shape your body into the letter *C*. Have students do the same.

Letter Knowledge: Letter Names *Dd*

Objectives

- Review letter names *Aa–Cc*.
- Recognize and write the letters *Dd*.

Materials

- Handwriting Models for Letters *Dd*
- Letter Cards
- Practice Page K.8

Formative Assessment and Corrective Feedback

IF a student has difficulty identifying a previously learned letter, THEN follow this model:

Correct the error. Display the letter and say its name. If students confuse two similar-looking letters (for example, *b* and *d*), point out how the letters differ.

Guide the student to "write" the letter in the air and say its name several times.

Check for understanding by having the student identify the letter from a mix of other previously taught letters.

Reinforce: Make a note to review the letter during the student's next session.

Let's Move!

Have students use their fingers to "write" the letters *D* and *d* on the back of their hands.

Teach/Model

- Display Letter Card *Dd*.
- **Say:** *Let's look at capital* D. *It has a straight line and half of a circle. Capital D has a buddy called small, or lowercase,* d. *Lowercase* d *has a straight line, too. But it has a circle standing next to it.*
- Ask students whether their names contain the letter *D* or *d*. Display any student names that contain the letter *D* or *d*. Circle the letters *D* and *d* wherever they appear.
- Look around for examples of the letter *D* or *d* (in book titles or other environmental print). Point out an example. Ask students to help you find others.

Guided Practice

- Display Letter Cards *Aa–Dd* in random order. Have students find *D* or *d*. Then have them point to and name the other letters.

HANDWRITING: WRITING *D, d* Tell students that they will learn to write capital *D* and lowercase *d*. Write each letter slowly and deliberately as you recite the handwriting rhymes. Have students do the same, using their index fingers to "write" the letters in the air.

Handwriting Rhyme: D

Big *D* starts with a long

line down.

Go back to the top and

curve all the way around.

It's a *D*, a big *D!*

Handwriting Rhyme: d

Start in the middle.

Make a circle nice

and round.

Go up to the top and

come straight down.

It's a *d*, a small *d!*

- Repeat the handwriting rhymes activity, but this time have students use the Handwriting Models page for *Dd* to practice writing the letters.

Apply

- Have students use Practice Page K.8 to practice the letters *Dd*. Explain that the picture in the upper-left box is the Alphafriend for the letter *d*. Tell students to draw the Alphafriend and its letter in the upper-right box.
- In the lower-left box, have students trace the letters *Dd*. In the lower-right box, have students write the letters *Dd*.

Fun with Letters Optional activities for engaging, hands-on practice are provided in the Resources section.

Letter Knowledge: Letter Names *Ee*

Teach/Model

- Display Letter Card *Ee*.
- **Say:** *Let's look at capital* E. *It has all straight lines. One stands up straight. Three more lines stick out. Capital* E *has a buddy called small, or lowercase,* e. *Lowercase* e *is round like a circle, but the circle is open. It has a straight line, too.*
- Ask students whether their names contain the letter *E* or *e*. Display any student names that contain the letter *E* or *e*. Circle the letters *E* and *e* wherever they appear.
- Look around for examples of the letter *E* or *e* (in book titles or other environmental print). Point out an example. Ask students to help you find others.

Guided Practice

- Display Letter Cards *Aa–Ee* in random order. Have students find *E* or *e*. Then have them point to and name the other letters.

HANDWRITING: WRITING *E, e* Tell students that they will learn to write capital *E* and lowercase *e*. Write each letter slowly and deliberately as you recite the handwriting rhymes. Have students do the same, using their index fingers to "write" the letters in the air.

Handwriting Rhyme: E

Make a tall straight line,

then three lines to the side:

top, middle, bottom.

Your big *E* looks fine!

Handwriting Rhyme: e

Go straight across the middle,

then up and around.

Leave the circle open,

but keep it nice and round.

- Repeat the handwriting rhymes activity, but this time have students use the Handwriting Models page for *Ee* to practice writing the letters.

Apply

- Have students use Practice Page K.9 to practice the letters *Ee*. Explain that the picture in the upper-left box is the Alphafriend for the letter *e*. Tell students to draw the Alphafriend and its letter in the upper-right box.
- In the lower-left box, have students trace the letters *Ee*. In the lower-right box, have students write the letters *Ee*.

> **Fun with Letters** Optional activities for engaging, hands-on practice are provided in the Resources section.

Objectives

- Review letter names *Aa–Dd*.
- Recognize and write the letters *Ee*.

Materials

- Handwriting Models for Letters *Ee*
- Letter Cards
- Practice Page K.9

Formative Assessment and Corrective Feedback

IF a student has difficulty identifying a previously learned letter, THEN follow this model:

Correct the error. Display the letter and say its name. If students confuse two similar-looking letters (for example, *e* and *c*), point out how the letters differ.

Guide the student to "write" the letter in the air and say its name several times.

Check for understanding by having the student identify the letter from a mix of other previously taught letters.

Reinforce: Make a note to review the letter during the student's next session.

Let's Move!

Have students use play clay to form the letters *E* and *e*.

Letter Knowledge: Letter Names *Ff*

Objectives

- Review letter names *Aa–Ee*.
- Recognize and write the letters *Ff*.

Materials

- Handwriting Models for Letters *Ff*
- Letter Cards
- Practice Page K.10

Formative Assessment and Corrective Feedback

IF a student has difficulty identifying a previously learned letter, THEN follow this model:

Correct the error. Display the letter and say its name. If students confuse two similar-looking letters (for example, *F* and *E*), point out how the letters differ.

Guide the student to "write" the letter in the air and say its name several times.

Check for understanding by having the student identify the letter from a mix of other previously taught letters.

Reinforce: Make a note to review the letter during the student's next session.

Let's Move!

Have students use their fingers to "write" the letters *F* and *f* on the back of their hands.

Teach/Model

- Display Letter Card *Ff*.
- **Say:** *This is the letter* F. *Let's look at capital* F. *It looks like a capital* E, *but it only has two lines sticking out. Capital* F *has a buddy called small, or lowercase,* f. *Lowercase* f *has a straight line with a curve on top and a short, straight line across.*
- Ask students whether their names contain the letter *F* or *f*. Display any student names that contain the letter *F* or *f*. Circle the letters *F* and *f* wherever they appear.
- Look around for examples of the letter *F* or *f* (in book titles or other environmental print). Point out an example. Ask students to help you find others.

Guided Practice

- Display Letter Cards *Aa–Ff* in random order. Have students find *F* or *f*. Then have them point to and name the other letters.

HANDWRITING: WRITING *F, f* Tell students that they will learn to write capital *F* and lowercase *f*. Write each letter slowly and deliberately as you recite the handwriting rhymes. Have students do the same, using their index fingers to "write" the letters in the air.

Handwriting Rhyme: F

Start at the top

and make a tall, straight line.

Make a line to the side.

Do it one more time.

Handwriting Rhyme: f

Start at the top,

curve round and drop.

Cross the line in the middle

and then you stop.

- Repeat the handwriting rhymes activity, but this time have students use the Handwriting Models page for *Ff* to practice writing the letters.

Apply

- Have students use Practice Page K.10 to practice the letters *Ff*. Explain that the picture in the upper-left box is the Alphafriend for the letter *f*. Tell students to draw the Alphafriend and its letter in the upper-right box.
- In the lower-left box, have students trace the letters *Ff*. In the lower-right box, have students write the letters *Ff*.

> **Fun with Letters** Optional activities for engaging, hands-on practice are provided in the Resources section.

Letter Knowledge: Letter Names *Gg*

Teach/Model

- Display Letter Card *Gg*.

- **Say:** *Let's look at capital G. It looks a lot like capital C, but it has a straight line. Capital G has a buddy called small, or lowercase, g. Lowercase g has a circle and a straight line down that curves back up.*

- Ask students whether their names contain the letter *G* or *g*. Display any student names that contain the letter *G* or *g*. Circle the letters *G* and *g* wherever they appear.

- Look around for examples of the letter *G* or *g* (in book titles or other environmental print). Point out an example. Ask students to help you find others.

Guided Practice

- Display Letter Cards *Aa–Gg* in random order. Have students find *G* or *g*. Then have them point to and name the other letters.

HANDWRITING: WRITING G, g Tell students that they will learn to write capital *G* and lowercase *g*. Write each letter slowly and deliberately as you recite the handwriting rhymes. Have students do the same, using their index fingers to "write" the letters in the air.

Handwriting Rhyme: G

Start at the top and curve

left like a capital C.

Add a short line in the middle

to make capital G.

Handwriting Rhyme: g

Make a small circle in

the middle,

just a little hoop.

Go straight down by the circle and

end with a scoop.

- Repeat the handwriting rhymes activity, but this time have students use the Handwriting Models page for *Gg* to practice writing the letters.

Apply

- Have students use Practice Page K.11 to practice the letters *Gg*. Explain that the picture in the upper-left box is the Alphafriend for the letter *g*. Tell students to draw the Alphafriend and its letter in the upper-right box.

- In the lower-left box, have students trace the letters *Gg*. In the lower-right box, have students write the letters *Gg*.

> **Fun with Letters** Optional activities for engaging, hands-on practice are provided in the Resources section.

Objectives

- Review letter names *Aa–Ff*.
- Recognize and write the letters *Gg*.

Materials

- Handwriting Models for Letters *Gg*
- Letter Cards
- Practice Page K.11

Formative Assessment and Corrective Feedback

IF a student has difficulty identifying a previously learned letter, THEN follow this model:

Correct the error. Display the letter and say its name. If students confuse two similar-looking letters (for example, *G* and *C*), point out how the letters differ.

Guide the student to "write" the letter in the air and say its name several times.

Check for understanding by having the student identify the letter from a mix of other previously taught letters.

Reinforce: Make a note to review the letter during the student's next session.

Let's Move!

Have students pretend they're making footprints to form the shape of the letters *G* and *g*.

Letter Knowledge: Letter Names *Hh*

Objectives

- Review letter names *Aa–Gg*.
- Recognize and write the letters *Hh*.

Materials

- Handwriting Models for Letters *Hh*
- Letter Cards
- Practice Page K.12

Formative Assessment and Corrective Feedback

IF a student has difficulty identifying a previously learned letter, THEN follow this model:

Correct the error. Display the letter and say its name. If students confuse two similar-looking letters (for example, *h* and *n*), point out how the letters differ.

Guide the student to "write" the letter in the air and say its name several times.

Check for understanding by having the student identify the letter from a mix of other previously taught letters.

Reinforce: Make a note to review the letter during the student's next sesssion.

Let's Move!

Have students use their fingers to "write" the letters *H* and *h* on the back of their hands.

Teach/Model

- Display Letter Card *Hh*.
- **Say:** *Let's look at capital* H. *It has three straight lines. Two lines stand up. A short line connects the two. Capital H has a buddy, called small or lowercase,* h. *Lowercase* h *has a straight line and a little hump.*
- Ask students whether their names contain the letter *H* or *h*. Display any student names that contain the letter *H* or *h*. Circle the letters *H* and *h* wherever they appear.
- Look around for examples of the letter *H* or *h* (in book titles or other environmental print). Point out an example. Ask students to help you find others.

Guided Practice

- Display Letter Cards *Aa–Hh* in random order. Have students find *H* or *h*. Then have them point to and name the other letters.

HANDWRITING: WRITING *H, h* Tell students that they will learn to write capital *H* and lowercase *h*. Write each letter slowly and deliberately as you recite the handwriting rhymes. Have students do the same, using their index fingers to "write" the letters in the air.

Handwriting Rhyme: H

Two tall lines standing

next to each other.

Connect them at the middle.

They hold hands with

each other.

Handwriting Rhyme: h

One straight, tall line

and a curvy little bump

Makes a hook like

a little camel's hump.

- Repeat the handwriting rhymes activity, but this time have students use the Handwriting Models page for *Hh* to practice writing the letters.

Apply

- Have students use Practice Page K.12 to practice the letters *Hh*. Explain that the picture in the upper-left box is the Alphafriend for the letter *h*. Tell students to draw the Alphafriend and its letter in the upper-right box.
- In the lower-left box, have students trace the letters *Hh*. In the lower-right box, have students write the letters *Hh*.

> **Fun with Letters** Optional activities for engaging, hands-on practice are provided in the Resources section.

Letter Knowledge: Letter Names *Ii*

Teach/Model

- Display Letter Card *Ii*.
- **Say:** *Let's look at capital* I. *It has a line standing straight. It has two other lines. One is at the top and one is at the bottom. Capital* I *has a buddy called small, or lowercase,* i. *Lowercase* i *has a short, straight line with a little dot above it.*
- Ask students whether their names contain the letter *I* or *i*. Display any student names that contain the letter *I* or *i*. Circle the letters *I* and *i* wherever they appear.
- Look around for examples of the letter *I* or *i* (in book titles or other environmental print). Point out an example. Ask students to help you find others.

Guided Practice

- Display Letter Cards *Aa–Ii* in random order. Have students find *I* or *i*. Then have them point to and name the other letters.

HANDWRITING: WRITING *I, i* Tell students that they will learn to write capital *I* and lowercase *i*. Write each letter slowly and deliberately as you recite the handwriting rhymes. Have students do the same, using their index fingers to "write" the letters in the air.

Handwriting Rhyme: I

Make a long line down

then back up top you go.

Make a short line across

and another down below.

Handwriting Rhyme: i

Straight down for small *i*

and then you stop.

Now put a dot

right on top.

- Repeat the handwriting rhymes activity, but this time have students use the Handwriting Models page for *Ii* to practice writing the letters.

Apply

- Have students use Practice Page K.13 to practice the letters *Ii*. Explain that the picture in the upper-left box is the Alphafriend for the letter *i*. Tell students to draw the Alphafriend and its letter in the upper-right box.
- In the lower-left box, have students trace the letters *Ii*. In the lower-right box, have students write the letters *Ii*.

> **Fun with Letters** Optional activities for engaging, hands-on practice are provided in the Resources section.

Objectives
- Review letter names *Aa–Hh*.
- Recognize and write the letters *Ii*.

Materials
- Handwriting Models for Letters *Ii*
- Letter Cards
- Practice Page K.13

Formative Assessment and Corrective Feedback

IF a student has difficulty identifying a previously learned letter, THEN follow this model:

Correct the error. Display the letter and say its name. If students confuse two similar-looking letters (for example, *I* and *T*), point out how the letters differ.

Guide the student to "write" the letter in the air and say its name several times.

Check for understanding by having the student identify the letter from a mix of other previously taught letters.

Reinforce: Make a note to review the letter during the student's next session.

Let's Move!

Have students pretend they're making footprints to form the shape of the letters *I* and *i*.

Letter Knowledge: Letter Names *Jj*

Session K.14

Objectives

- Review letter names *Aa–Ii*.
- Recognize and write the letters *Jj*.

Materials

- Handwriting Models for Letters *Jj*
- Letter Cards
- Practice Page K.14

Formative Assessment and Corrective Feedback

IF a student has difficulty identifying a previously learned letter, THEN follow this model:

Correct the error. Display the letter and say its name. If students confuse two similar-looking letters (for example *i* and *j*), point out how the letters differ.

Guide the student to "write" the letter in the air and say its name several times.

Check for understanding by having the student identify the letter from a mix of other previously taught letters.

Reinforce: Make a note to review the letter during the student's next session.

Let's Move!

Have students use play clay to form the letters *J* and *j*.

Teach/Model

- Display Letter Card *Jj*.
- **Say:** *This is the letter J. Let's look at capital J. It has a straight line with a little hook at the bottom and a straight line across the top. Capital J has a buddy called small, or lowercase,* j. *Lowercase* j *has a straight line with a little hook at the bottom, too. It has a little dot above it.*
- Ask students whether their names contain the letter *J* or *j*. Display any student names that contain the letter *J* or *j*. Circle the letters *J* and *j* wherever they appear.
- Look around for examples of the letter *J* or *j* (in book titles or other environmental print). Point out an example. Ask students to help you find others.

Guided Practice

- Display Letter Cards *Aa–Jj* in random order. Have students find *J* or *j*. Then have them point to and name the other letters.

HANDWRITING: WRITING *J, j* Tell students that they will learn to write capital *J* and lowercase *j*. Write each letter slowly and deliberately as you recite the handwriting rhymes. Have students do the same, using their index fingers to "write" the letters in the air.

Handwriting Rhyme: J

Down from the top,

then a short curve.

Bring it up a little,

just a little swerve:

It's a big *J*, big *j*!

Handwriting Rhyme: j

Small *j* has

just one line down.

Curve up a little,

add a dot as a crown.

It's a *j*, small *j*, small *j*!

- Repeat the handwriting rhymes activity, but this time have students use the Handwriting Models page for *Jj* to practice writing the letters.

Apply

- Have students use Practice Page K.14 to practice the letters *Jj*. Explain that the picture in the upper-left box is the Alphafriend for the letter *j*. Tell students to draw the Alphafriend and its letter in the upper-right box.
- In the lower-left box, have students trace the letters *Jj*. In the lower-right box, have students write the letters *Jj*.

Fun with Letters Optional activities for engaging, hands-on practice are provided in the Resources section.

Letter Knowledge: Letter Names *Kk*

Teach/Model

- Display Letter Card *Kk*.
- **Say:** *Let's look at capital* K. *It has all straight lines, one straight down and two slanted. Now look at small, or lowercase* k. *It looks almost like capital* K. *But this slanted line on top is shorter than the one in capital* K.
- Ask students whether their names contain the letter *K* or *k*. Display any student names that contain the letter *K* or *k*. Circle the letters *K* and *k* wherever they appear.
- Look around for examples of the letter *K* or *k* (in book titles or other environmental print). Point out an example. Ask students to help you find others.

Guided Practice

- Display Letter Cards *Aa–Kk* in random order. Have students find *K* or *k*. Then have them point to and name the other letters.

HANDWRITING: WRITING *K, k* Tell students that they will learn to write capital *K* and lowercase *k*. Write each letter slowly and deliberately as you recite the handwriting rhymes. Have students do the same, using their index fingers to "write" the letters in the air.

Handwriting Rhyme: K

Make one line,

a tall, straight stick.

Add one arm in a wave

and one leg in a kick:

That's *K*, big *K*, big *K*!

Handwriting Rhyme: k

Make one line,

a tall, straight stick.

Now add a little wave and a little kick:

That's a *k*, a small *k*, a small *k*!

- Repeat the handwriting rhymes activity, but this time have students use the Handwriting Models page for *Kk* to practice writing the letters.

Apply

- Have students use Practice Page K.15 to practice the letters *Kk*. Explain that the picture in the upper-left box is the Alphafriend for the letter *k*. Tell students to draw the Alphafriend and its letter in the upper-right box.
- In the lower-left box, have students trace the letters *Kk*. In the lower right box, have students write the letters *Kk*.

> **Fun with Letters** Optional activities for engaging, hands-on practice are provided in the Resources section.

Objectives

- Review letter names *Aa–Jj*.
- Recognize and write the letters *Kk*.

Materials

- Handwriting Models for Letters *Kk*
- Letter Cards
- Practice Page K.15

Formative Assessment and Corrective Feedback

IF a student has difficulty identifying a previously learned letter, THEN follow this model:

Correct the error. Display the letter and say its name. If students confuse two similar-looking letters (for example, *k* and *l*), point out how the letters differ.

Guide the student to "write" the letter in the air and say its name several times.

Check for understanding by having the student identify the letter from a mix of other previously taught letters.

Reinforce: Make a note to review the letter during the student's next session.

Let's Move!

While reciting the handwriting rhymes, perform the actions described in the rhyme to shape your body into a letter *K*. Have students do the same.

Letter Knowledge: Letter Names *Ll*

Objectives

- Review letter names *Aa–Kk*.
- Recognize and write the letters *Ll*.

Materials

- Handwriting Models for Letters *Ll*
- Letter Cards
- Practice Page K.16

Formative Assessment and Corrective Feedback

IF a student has difficulty identifying a previously learned letter, THEN follow this model:

Correct the error. Display the letter and say its name. If students confuse two similar-looking letters (for example, *L* and *l*), point out how the letters differ.

Guide the student to "write" the letter in the air and say its name several times.

Check for understanding by having the student identify the letter from a mix of other previously taught letters.

Reinforce: Make a note to review the letter during the student's next session.

Let's Move!

While reciting the handwriting rhymes, perform the actions described in the rhyme to shape your body into the lowercase *l*. Have students do the same. Then make the capital *L* with children.

Teach/Model

- Display Letter Card *Ll*.
- **Say:** *This is the letter* L. *Capital* L *is made with one line that stands up straight and one that "lies down" on the line. Now look at small, or lowercase,* l. *Lowercase* l *is just one straight line.*
- Ask students whether their names contain the letter *L* or *l*. Display any student names that contain the letter *L* or *l*. Circle the letters *L* and *l* wherever they appear.
- Look around for examples of the letter *L* or *l* (in book titles or other environmental print). Point out an example. Ask students to help you find others.

Guided Practice

- Display Letter Cards *Aa–Ll* in random order. Have students find *L* or *l*. Then have them point to and name the other letters.

HANDWRITING: WRITING *L, l* Tell students that they will learn to write capital *L* and lowercase *l*. Write each letter slowly and deliberately as you recite the handwriting rhymes. Have students do the same, using their index fingers to "write" the letters in the air.

Handwriting Rhyme: L

Make a tall, straight line

that you start at the top.

Come down to the bottom,

go out, and stop.

Handwriting Rhyme: l

Small *l*

looks like a stick.

Just one straight line.

It's easy and quick.

- Repeat the handwriting rhymes activity, but this time have students use the Handwriting Models page for *Ll* to practice writing the letters.

Apply

- Have students use Practice Page K.16 to practice the letters *Ll*. Explain that the picture in the upper-left box is the Alphafriend for the letter *l*. Tell students to draw the Alphafriend and its letter in the upper-right box.
- In the lower-left box, have students trace the letters *Ll*. In the lower-right box, have students write the letters *Ll*.

Fun with Letters Optional activities for engaging, hands-on practice are provided in the Resources section.

Letter Knowledge: Letter Names *Mm*

Teach/Model

- Display Letter Card *Mm*.
- **Say:** *This is the capital letter* M. *It has straight lines. Look at small, or lowercase,* m. *Lowercase* m *has two little humps.*
- Ask students whether their names contain the letter *M* or *m*. Display any student names that contain the letter *M* or *m*. Circle the letters *M* and *m* wherever they appear.
- Look around for examples of the letter *M* or *m* (in book titles or other environmental print). Point out an example. Ask students to help you find others.

Guided Practice

- Display Letter Cards *Aa–Mm* in random order. Have students find *M* or *m*. Then have them point to and name the other letters.

HANDWRITING: WRITING *M, m* Tell students that they will learn to write capital *M* and lowercase *m*. Write each letter slowly and deliberately as you recite the handwriting rhymes. Have students do the same, using their index fingers to "write" the letters in the air.

Handwriting Rhyme: M

Make a line going down,

then two lines that meet.

Make one more and you're done!

It's very neat.

Handwriting Rhyme: m

Little *m* is short.

Start in the middle.

Make two little hills.

It's not a riddle.

- Repeat the handwriting rhymes activity, but this time have students use the Handwriting Models page for *Mm* to practice writing the letters.

Apply

- Have students use Practice Page K.17 to practice the letters *Mm*. Explain that the picture in the upper-left box is the Alphafriend for the letter *m*. Tell students to draw the Alphafriend and its letter in the upper-right box.
- In the lower-left box, have students trace the letters *Mm*. In the lower-right box, have students write the letters *Mm*.

> **Fun with Letters** Optional activities for engaging, hands-on practice are provided in the Resources section.

Objectives

- Review letter names *Aa–Ll*.
- Recognize and write the letters *Mm*.

Materials

- Handwriting Models for Letters *Mm*
- Letter Cards
- Practice Page K.17

Formative Assessment and Corrective Feedback

IF a student has difficulty identifying a previously learned letter, THEN follow this model:

Correct the error. Display the letter and say its name. If students confuse two similar-looking letters (for example, *m* and *n*), point out how the letters differ.

Guide the student to "write" the letter in the air and say its name several times.

Check for understanding by having the student identify the letter from a mix of other previously taught letters.

Reinforce: Make a note to review the letter during the student's next session.

Let's Move!

Have students use their fingers to "write" the letters *M* and *m* on the back of their hands.

Letter Knowledge: Letter Names *Nn*

Objectives

- Review letter names *Aa–Mm*.
- Recognize and write the letters *Nn*.

Materials

- Handwriting Models for Letters *Nn*
- Letter Cards
- Practice Page K.18

Formative Assessment and Corrective Feedback

IF a student has difficulty identifying a previously learned letter, THEN follow this model:

Correct the error. Display the letter and say its name. If students confuse two similar-looking letters (for example, *N* and *M*), point out how the letters differ.

Guide the student to "write" the letter in the air and say its name several times.

Check for understanding by having the student identify the letter from a mix of other previously taught letters.

Reinforce: Make a note to review the letter during the student's next session.

Let's Move!

Have students pretend they're making footprints to form the shape of the letters *N* and *n*.

Teach/Model

- Display Letter Card *Nn*.
- **Say:** *Let's look at capital* N. *It has straight lines, one straight down, one slanting line, and another straight line. Now look at small, or lowercase,* n. *It has a straight line with one little hump.*
- Ask students whether their names contain the letter *N* or *n*. Display any student names that contain the letter *N* or *n*. Circle the letters *N* and *n* wherever they appear.
- Look around for examples of the letter *N* or *n* (in book titles or other environmental print). Point out an example. Ask students to help you find others.

Guided Practice

- Display Letter Cards *Aa–Nn* in random order. Have students find *N* or *n*. Then have them point to and name the other letters.

HANDWRITING: WRITING *N, n* Tell students that they will learn to write capital *N* and lowercase *n*. Write each letter slowly and deliberately as you recite the handwriting rhymes. Have students do the same, using their index fingers to "write" the letters in the air.

Handwriting Rhyme: *N*

A line that goes down.

Then a slide to the side.

One more line up.

Big *N*, we cried!

Handwriting Rhyme: *n*

Little *N* is short.

One line down at the start.

Then one little hill.

That's the fun part.

- Repeat the handwriting rhymes activity, but this time have students use the Handwriting Models page for *Nn* to practice writing the letters.

Apply

- Have students use Practice Page K.18 to practice the letters *Nn*. Explain that the picture in the upper-left box is the Alphafriend for the letter *n*. Tell students to draw the Alphafriend and its letter in the upper-right box.
- In the lower-left box, have students trace the letters *Nn*. In the lower-right box, have students write the letters *Nn*.

> **Fun with Letters** Optional activities for engaging, hands-on practice are provided in the Resources section.

Letter Knowledge: Letter Names *Oo*

Teach/Model

- Display Letter Card *Oo*.
- **Say:** *Look at capital O. It's round like a circle. Make an o with your fingers. Now look at small, or lowercase, o. It looks just like its letter buddy, but it's smaller.*
- Ask students whether their names contain the letter *O* or *o*. Display any student names that contain the letter *O* or *o*. Circle the letters *O* and *o* wherever they appear.
- Look around for examples of the letter *O* or *o* (in book titles or other environmental print). Point out an example. Ask students to help you find others.

Guided Practice

- Display Letter Cards *Aa–Oo* in random order. Have students find *O* or *o*. Then have them point to and name the other letters.

HANDWRITING: WRITING *O, o* Tell students that they will learn to write capital *O* and lowercase *o*. Write each letter slowly and deliberately as you recite the handwriting rhymes. Have students do the same, using their index fingers to "write" the letters in the air.

Handwriting Rhyme: *O*

Start near the top line, and

curve around.

Make a circle, nice and

round.

Handwriting Rhyme: *o*

Start in the middle to

make small *o*.

Curve around in a

circle, go nice and

slow.

- Repeat the handwriting rhymes activity, but this time have students use the Handwriting Models page for *Oo* to practice writing the letters.

Apply

- Have students use Practice Page K.19 to practice the letters *Oo*. Explain that the picture in the upper-left box is the Alphafriend for the letter *o*. Tell students to draw the Alphafriend and its letter in the upper-right box.
- In the lower-left box, have students trace the letters *Oo*. In the lower-right box, have students write the letters *Oo*.

> **Fun with Letters** Optional activities for engaging, hands-on practice are provided in the Resources section.

Objectives

- Review letter names *Aa–Nn*.
- Recognize and write the letters *Oo*.

Materials

- Handwriting Models for Letters *Oo*
- Letter Cards
- Practice Page K.19

Formative Assessment and Corrective Feedback

IF a student has difficulty identifying a previously learned letter, THEN follow this model:

Correct the error. Display the letter and say its name. If students confuse two similar-looking letters (for example, *O* and *C*), point out how the letters differ.

Guide the student to "write" the letter in the air and say its name several times.

Check for understanding by having the student identify the letter from a mix of other previously taught letters.

Reinforce: Make a note to review the letter during the student's next session.

Let's Move!

While reciting the handwriting rhymes, perform the actions described in the rhyme to shape your arms into the letter *O*. Have students do the same.

Letter Knowledge: Letter Names *Pp*

Objectives

- Review letter names *Aa–Oo*.
- Recognize and write the letters *Pp*.

Materials

- Handwriting Models for Letters *Pp*
- Letter Cards
- Practice Page K.20

Formative Assessment and Corrective Feedback

IF a student has difficulty identifying a previously learned letter, THEN follow this model:

Correct the error. Display the letter and say its name. If students confuse two similar-looking letters (for example, *P* and *B*), point out how the letters differ.

Guide the student to "write" the letter in the air and say its name several times.

Check for understanding by having the student identify the letter from a mix of other previously taught letters.

Reinforce: Make a note to review the letter during the student's next session.

Let's Move!

Have students pretend they're making footprints to form the shape of the letters *P* and *p*.

Teach/Model

- Display Letter Card *Pp*.
- **Say:** *Look at capital* P. *It has a straight line and a round part. Now look at small, or lowercase,* p. *It looks like capital* P, *but it starts in the middle and goes below the bottom line.*
- Ask students whether their names contain the letter *P* or *p*. Display any student names that contain the letter *P* or *p*. Circle the letters *P* and *p* wherever they appear.
- Look around for examples of the letter *P* or *p* (in book titles or other environmental print). Point out an example. Ask students to help you find others.

Guided Practice

- Display Letter Cards *Aa–Pp* in random order. Have students find *P* or *p*. Then have them point to and name the other letters.

HANDWRITING: WRITING *P, p* Tell students that they will learn to write capital *P* and lowercase *p*. Write each letter slowly and deliberately as you recite the handwriting rhymes. Have students do the same, using their index fingers to "write" the letters in the air.

Handwriting Rhyme: *P*

Start at the top and make

a long line down.

Go back to the top and

circle half-way around.

Handwriting Rhyme: *p*

Start in the middle and

make a long line down.

Go back to the middle

and circle half-way

around.

- Repeat the handwriting rhymes activity, but this time have students use the Handwriting Models page for *Pp* to practice writing the letters.

Apply

- Have students use Practice Page K.20 to practice the letters *Pp*. Explain that the picture in the upper-left box is the Alphafriend for the letter *p*. Tell students to draw the Alphafriend and its letter in the upper-right box.
- In the lower-left box, have students trace the letters *Pp*. In the lower-right box, have students write the letters *Pp*.

> **Fun with Letters** Optional activities for engaging, hands-on practice are provided in the Resources section.

Letter Knowledge: Letter Names *Qq*

Teach/Model

- Display Letter Card *Qq*.
- **Say:** *Capital Q looks like capital O, but it has an extra mark. Small, or lowercase, q looks like small p, but the tail is on the other side. We'll have to be careful when we name this letter, so we don't mix it up with small* p.
- Ask students whether their names contain the letter *Q* or *q*. Display any student names that contain the letter *Q* or *q*. Circle the letters *Q* and *q* wherever they appear.
- Look around for examples of the letter *Q* or *q* (in book titles or other environmental print). Point out an example. Ask students to help you find others.

Guided Practice

- Display Letter Cards *Aa–Qq* in random order. Have students find *Q* or *q*. Then have them point to and name the other letters.

  HANDWRITING: WRITING *Q, q* Tell students that they will learn to write capital *Q* and lowercase *q*. Write each letter slowly and deliberately as you recite the handwriting rhymes. Have students do the same, using their index fingers to "write" the letters in the air.

Handwriting Rhyme: Q

Capital *Q* starts like *O*,

nice and fat and round.

But add a little stand-up

stick just so it won't fall

down.

Handwriting Rhyme: q

Start small *q* with a

circle.

Make it very stout.

Then don't forget to

add a tail and curl it

down and out.

- Repeat the handwriting rhymes activity, but this time have students use the Handwriting Models page for *Qq* to practice writing the letters.

Apply

- Have students use Practice Page K.21 to practice the letters *Qq*. Explain that the picture in the upper-left box is the Alphafriend for the letter *q*. Tell students to draw the Alphafriend and its letter in the upper-right box.
- In the lower-left box, have students trace the letters *Qq*. In the lower-right box, have students write the letters *Qq*.

> **Fun with Letters** Optional activities for engaging, hands-on practice are provided in the Resources section.

Objectives

- Review letter names *Aa–Pp*.
- Recognize and write the letters *Qq*.

Materials

- Handwriting Models for Letters *Qq*
- Letter Cards
- Practice Page K.21

Formative Assessment and Corrective Feedback

IF a student has difficulty identifying a previously learned letter, THEN follow this model:

Correct the error. Display the letter and say its name. If students confuse two similar-looking letters (for example, *Q* and *O*), point out how the letters differ.

Guide the student to "write" the letter in the air and say its name several times.

Check for understanding by having the student identify the letter from a mix of other previously taught letters.

Reinforce: Make a note to review the letter during the student's next session.

Let's Move!

Have students use play clay to form the letters *Q* and *q*.

Letter Knowledge: Letter Names *Rr*

Objectives

- Review letter names *Aa–Qq*.
- Recognize and write the letters *Rr*.

Materials

- Handwriting Models for Letters *Rr*
- Letter Cards
- Practice Page K.22

Formative Assessment and Corrective Feedback

IF a student has difficulty identifying a previously learned letter, THEN follow this model:

Correct the error. Display the letter and say its name. If students confuse two similar-looking letters (for example, *R* and *P*), point out how the letters differ.

Guide the student to "write" the letter in the air and say its name several times.

Check for understanding by having the student identify the letter from a mix of other previously taught letters.

Reinforce: Make a note to review the letter during the student's next session.

Let's Move!

Have students use their fingers to "write" the letters *R* and *r* on the back of their hands.

Teach/Model

- Display Letter Card *Rr*.
- **Say:** *Let's look at capital* R. *It has a long straight line and a small curved part. So far it looks like capital* P, *but it has an extra "leg." Now look at small, or lowercase,* r. *It looks different from its letter buddy.*
- Ask students whether their names contain the letter *R* or *r*. Display any student names that contain the letter *R* or *r*. Circle the letters *R* and *r* wherever they appear.
- Look around for examples of the letter *R* or *r* (in book titles or other environmental print). Point out an example. Ask students to help you find others.

Guided Practice

- Display Letter Cards *Aa–Rr* in random order. Have students find *R* or *r*. Then have them point to and name the other letters.

HANDWRITING: WRITING *R, r* Tell students that they will learn to write capital *R* and lowercase *r*. Write each letter slowly and deliberately as you recite the handwriting rhymes. Have students do the same, using their index fingers to "write" the letters in the air.

Handwriting Rhyme: *R*

Make a line down, straight

and tall.

Curve around to the

middle.

A short line out, that's all!

Handwriting Rhyme: *r*

Little *r* is small.

Start in the middle with

a short line.

Curve at the top, that's

all!

- Repeat the handwriting rhymes activity, but this time have students use the Handwriting Models page for *Rr* to practice writing the letters.

Apply

- Have students use Practice Page K.22 to practice the letters *Rr*. Explain that the picture in the upper-left box is the Alphafriend for the letter *r*. Tell students to draw the Alphafriend and its letter in the upper-right box.
- In the lower-left box, have students trace the letters *Rr*. In the lower-right box, have students write the letters *Rr*.

> **Fun with Letters** Optional activities for engaging, hands-on practice are provided in the Resources section.

Letter Knowledge: Letter Names *Ss*

Teach/Model

- Display Letter Card *Ss*.
- **Say:** *Look at capital* S. *It looks like a squiggly line. Let's look at small, or lowercase,* s. *It's just like its letter buddy, only smaller.*
- Ask students whether their names contain the letter *S* or *s*. Display any student names that contain the letter *S* or *s*. Circle the letters *S* and *s* wherever they appear.
- Look around for examples of the letter *S* or *s* (in book titles or other environmental print). Point out an example. Ask students to help you find others.

Guided Practice

- Display Letter Cards *Aa–Ss* in random order. Have students find *S* or *s*. Then have them point to and name the other letters.

HANDWRITING: WRITING S, s Tell students that they will learn to write capital *S* and lowercase *s*. Write each letter slowly and deliberately as you recite the handwriting rhymes. Have students do the same, using their index fingers to "write" the letters in the air.

Handwriting Rhyme: *S*

S looks like a snake, curve

left then right. From top to

bottom, makes it right.

Handwriting Rhyme: *s*

Small *s* looks like a

snake, too. Curve left

then right, that's all

you do.

- Repeat the handwriting rhymes activity, but this time have students use the Handwriting Models page for *Ss* to practice writing the letters.

Apply

- Have students use Practice Page K.23 to practice the letters *Ss*. Explain that the picture in the upper-left box is the Alphafriend for the letter *s*. Tell students to draw the Alphafriend and its letter in the upper-right box.
- In the lower-left box, have students trace the letters *Ss*. In the lower-right box, have students write the letters *Ss*.

Fun with Letters Optional activities for engaging, hands-on practice are provided in the Resources section.

Objectives

- Review letter names *Aa–Rr*.
- Recognize and write the letters *Ss*.

Materials

- Handwriting Models for Letters *Ss*
- Letter Cards
- Practice Page K.23

Formative Assessment and Corrective Feedback

IF a student has difficulty identifying a previously learned letter, THEN follow this model:

Correct the error. Display the letter and say its name. If students confuse two similar-looking letters, point out how the letters differ.

Guide the student to "write" the letter in the air and say its name several times.

Check for understanding by having the student identify the letter from a mix of other previously taught letters.

Reinforce: Make a note to review the letter during the student's next session.

Let's Move!

Have students pretend they're making footprints to form the shape of the letters *S* and *s*.

Letter Knowledge: Letter Names *Tt*

Objectives

- Review letter names *Aa–Ss*.
- Recognize and write the letters *Tt*.

Materials

- Handwriting Models for Letters *Tt*
- Letter Cards
- Practice Page K.24

Formative Assessment and Corrective Feedback

IF a student has difficulty identifying a previously learned letter, THEN follow this model:

Correct the error. Display the letter and say its name. If students confuse two similar-looking letters (for example, *T* and *L*), point out how the letters differ.

Guide the student to "write" the letter in the air and say its name several times.

Check for understanding by having the student identify the letter from a mix of other previously taught letters.

Reinforce: Make a note to review the letter during the student's next session.

Let's Move!

While reciting the handwriting rhymes, perform the actions described in the rhyme to shape your body into the letter *T*. Have students do the same.

Teach/Model

- Display Letter Card *Tt*.
- **Say:** *Look at capital* T. *It has two straight lines. One stands straight up. The other goes across the top. Now look at small, or lowercase,* t. *It's a little bit like its letter buddy, except it has a line across its middle.*
- Ask students whether their names contain the letter *T* or *t*. Display any student names that contain the letter *T* or *t*. Circle the letters *T* and *t* wherever they appear.
- Look around for examples of the letter *T* or *t* (in book titles or other environmental print). Point out an example. Ask students to help you find others.

Guided Practice

- Display Letter Cards *Aa–Tt* in random order. Have students find *T* or *t*. Then have them point to and name the other letters.

HANDWRITING: WRITING *T, t* Tell students that they will learn to write capital *T* and lowercase *t*. Write each letter slowly and deliberately as you recite the handwriting rhymes. Have students do the same, using their index fingers to "write" the letters in the air.

Handwriting Rhyme: *T*

A long line down begins

the *T*.

Draw a straight line across

and a *T* it will be.

Handwriting Rhyme: *t*

Not as tall, straight

down for small *t*.

Cross near the middle, a

t you'll see!

- Repeat the handwriting rhymes activity, but this time have students use the Handwriting Models page for *Tt* to practice writing the letters.

Apply

- Have students use Practice Page K.24 to practice the letters *Tt*. Explain that the picture in the upper-left box is the Alphafriend for the letter *t*. Tell students to draw the Alphafriend and its letter in the upper-right box.
- In the lower-left box, have students trace the letters *Tt*. In the lower-right box, have students write the letters *Tt*.

Fun with Letters Optional activities for engaging, hands-on practice are provided in the Resources section.

Letter Knowledge: Letter Names *Uu*

Teach/Model

- Display Letter Card *Uu*.

- **Say:** *Capital* U *has straight sides and a curve at the bottom. Now look at small, or lowercase,* u. *It looks almost like its letter buddy, only smaller, and one side of the letter is a straight line.*

- Ask students whether their names contain the letter *U* or *u*. Display any student names that contain the letter *U* or *u*. Circle the letters *U* and *u* wherever they appear.

- Look around for examples of the letter *U* or *u* (in book titles or other environmental print). Point out an example. Ask students to help you find others.

Guided Practice

- Display Letter Cards *Aa–Uu* in random order. Have students find *U* or *u*. Then have them point to and name the other letters.

    HANDWRITING: WRITING *U, u* Tell students that they will learn to write capital *U* and lowercase *u*. Write each letter slowly and deliberately as you recite the handwriting rhymes. Have students do the same, using their index fingers to "write" the letters in the air.

    Handwriting Rhyme: *U*

    Make a straight line

    down that you start from

    the top.

    Curve around at the

    bottom, back up and then

    stop!

    Handwriting Rhyme: *u*

    Start in the middle, go

    down and around.

    Back up to the top,

    then a straight line

    down.

- Repeat the handwriting rhymes activity, but this time have students use the Handwriting Models page for *Uu* to practice writing the letters.

Apply

- Have students use Practice Page K.25 to practice the letters *Uu*. Explain that the picture in the upper-left box is the Alphafriend for the letter *u*. Tell students to draw the Alphafriend and its letter in the upper-right box.

- In the lower-left box, have students trace the letters *Uu*. In the lower-right box, have students write the letters *Uu*.

> **Fun with Letters** Optional activities for engaging, hands-on practice are provided in the Resources section.

Objectives

- Review letter names *Aa–Tt*.
- Recognize and write the letters *Uu*.

Materials

- Handwriting Models for Letters *Uu*
- Letter Cards
- Practice Page K.25

Formative Assessment and Corrective Feedback

IF a student has difficulty identifying a previously learned letter, THEN follow this model:

Correct the error. Display the letter and say its name. If students confuse two similar-looking letters (for example, *u* and *n*), point out how the letters differ.

Guide the student to "write" the letter in the air and say its name several times.

Check for understanding by having the student identify the letter from a mix of other previously taught letters.

Reinforce: Make a note to review the letter during the student's next session.

Let's Move!

Have students use their fingers to "write" the letters *U* and *u* on the back of their hands.

Letter Knowledge: Letter Names *Vv*

Objectives

- Review letter names *Aa–Uu*.
- Recognize and write the letters *Vv*.

Materials

- Handwriting Models for Letters *Vv*
- Letter Cards
- Practice Page K.26

Formative Assessment and Corrective Feedback

IF a student has difficulty identifying a previously learned letter, THEN follow this model:

Correct the error. Display the letter and say its name. If students confuse two similar-looking letters (for example, *U* and *V*), point out how the letters differ.

Guide the student to "write" the letter in the air and say its name several times.

Check for understanding by having the student identify the letter from a mix of other previously taught letters.

Reinforce: Make a note to review the letter during the student's next session.

Let's Move!

While reciting the handwriting rhymes, perform the actions described in the rhyme to shape your arms into the letter *V*. Have students do the same.

Teach/Model

- Display Letter Card *Vv*.
- **Say:** *Capital V has two slanted lines. Now look at small, or lowercase, v. It looks like its letter buddy, only smaller.*
- Ask students whether their names contain the letter *V* or *v*. Display any student names that contain the letter *V* or *v*. Circle the letters *V* and *v* wherever they appear.
- Look around for examples of the letter *V* or *v* (in book titles or other environmental print). Point out an example. Ask students to help you find others.

Guided Practice

- Display Letter Cards *Aa–Vv* in random order. Have students find *V* or *v*. Then have them point to and name the other letters.

HANDWRITING: WRITING *V, v* Tell students that they will learn to write capital *V* and lowercase *v*. Write each letter slowly and deliberately as you recite the handwriting rhymes. Have students do the same, using their index fingers to "write" the letters in the air.

Handwriting Rhyme: *V*

Start at the top.

Slant in just a little.

Back up to the top.

Away from the middle.

Handwriting Rhyme: *v*

Little *v*'s lines still meet

in the middle.

It's just like the capital,

only it's little.

- Repeat the handwriting rhymes activity, but this time have students use the Handwriting Models page for *Vv* to practice writing the letters.

Apply

- Have students use Practice Page K.26 to practice the letters *Vv*. Explain that the picture in the upper-left box is the Alphafriend for the letter *v*. Tell students to draw the Alphafriend and its letter in the upper-right box.
- In the lower-left box, have students trace the letters *Vv*. In the lower-right box, have students write the letters *Vv*.

> **Fun with Letters** Optional activities for engaging, hands-on practice are provided in the Resources section.

Letter Knowledge: Letter Names *Ww*

Teach/Model

- Display Letter Card *Ww*.
- **Say:** *Look at capital W. It has straight, slanted lines. Look at small, or lowercase, w. It looks like its letter buddy, only smaller.*
- Ask students whether their names contain the letter *W* or *w*. Display any student names that contain the letter *W* or *w*. Circle the letters *W* and *w* wherever they appear.
- Look around for examples of the letter *W* or *w* (in book titles or other environmental print). Point out an example. Ask students to help you find others.

Guided Practice

- Display Letter Cards *Aa–Ww* in random order. Have students find *W* or *w*. Then have them point to and name the other letters.

HANDWRITING: WRITING W, w Tell students that they will learn to write capital *W* and lowercase *w*. Write each letter slowly and deliberately as you recite the handwriting rhymes. Have students do the same, using their index fingers to "write" the letters in the air.

Handwriting Rhyme: W

Four tall, straight lines

make a capital *W*.

Start high, come down, go

up, then back.

Now one more stroke, and

you're right on track.

Handwriting Rhyme: w

Small *w* looks like its

great big brother.

Down once, go up,

down once again.

Now finish it off and

go up at the end.

- Repeat the handwriting rhymes activity, but this time have students use the Handwriting Models page for *Ww* to practice writing the letters.

Apply

- Have students use Practice Page K.27 to practice the letters *Ww*. Explain that the picture in the upper-left box is the Alphafriend for the letter *w*. Tell students to draw the Alphafriend and its letter in the upper-right box.
- In the lower-left box, have students trace the letters *Ww*. In the lower-right box, have students write the letters *Ww*.

> **Fun with Letters** Optional activities for engaging, hands-on practice are provided in the Resources section.

Objectives

- Review letter names *Aa–Vv*.
- Recognize and write the letters *Ww*.

Materials

- Handwriting Models for Letters *Ww*
- Letter Cards
- Practice Page K.27

Formative Assessment and Corrective Feedback

IF a student has difficulty identifying a previously learned letter, THEN follow this model:

Correct the error. Display the letter and say its name. If students confuse two similar-looking letters (for example, *W* and *V*), point out how the letters differ.

Guide the student to "write" the letter in the air and say its name several times.

Check for understanding by having the student identify the letter from a mix of other previously taught letters.

Reinforce: Make a note to review the letter during the student's next session.

Let's Move!

Have students use play clay to form the letters *W* and *w*.

Letter Knowledge: Letter Names *Xx*

Objectives

- Review letter names *Aa–Ww*.
- Recognize and write the letters *Xx*.

Materials

- Handwriting Models for Letters *Xx*
- Letter Cards
- Practice Page K.28

Formative Assessment and Corrective Feedback

IF a student has difficulty identifying a previously learned letter, THEN follow this model:

Correct the error. Display the letter and say its name. If students confuse two similar-looking letters, point out how the letters differ.

Guide the student to "write" the letter in the air and say its name several times.

Check for understanding by having the student identify the letter from a mix of other previously taught letters.

Reinforce: Make a note to review the letter during the student's next session.

Let's Move!

Have students pretend they're making footprints to form the shape of the letters *X* and *x*.

Teach/Model

- Display Letter Card *Xx*.
- **Say:** *Look at capital* X. *It's made of two slanted lines that cross each other in the middle. Now look at small, or lowercase,* x. *It looks just like its letter buddy, only smaller.*
- Ask students whether their names contain the letter *X* or *x*. Display any student names that contain the letter *X* or *x*. Circle the letters *X* and *x* wherever they appear.
- Look around for examples of the letter *X* or *x* (in book titles or other environmental print). Point out an example. Ask students to help you find others.

Guided Practice

- Display Letter Cards *Aa–Xx* in random order. Have students find *X* or *x*. Then have them point to and name the other letters.

HANDWRITING: WRITING *X, x* Tell students that they will learn to write capital *X* and lowercase *x*. Write each letter slowly and deliberately as you recite the handwriting rhymes. Have students do the same, using their index fingers to "write" the letters in the air.

Handwriting Rhyme: *X*

Tall line leans like a

slanted stick. Another line

crosses quick, quick, quick.

Handwriting Rhyme: *x*

Little *x* isn't hard to do.

The first one slants and

the other one too.

- Repeat the handwriting rhymes activity, but this time have students use the Handwriting Models page for *Xx* to practice writing the letters.

Apply

- Have students use Practice Page K.28 to practice the letters *Xx*. Explain that the picture in the upper-left box is the Alphafriend for the letter *x*. Tell students to draw the Alphafriend and its letter in the upper-right box.
- In the lower-left box, have students trace the letters *Xx*. In the lower-right box, have students write the letters *Xx*.

> **Fun with Letters** Optional activities for engaging, hands-on practice are provided in the Resources section.

Letter Knowledge: Letter Names *Yy*

Teach/Model

- Display Letter Card *Yy*.

- **Say:** *Look at capital* Y. *It's made of straight and slanted lines. The small, or lowercase,* y *looks like its letter buddy, but its tail is slanted and dips down low.*

- Ask students whether their names contain the letter *Y* or *y*. Display any student names that contain the letter *Y* or *y*. Circle the letters *Y* and *y* wherever they appear.

- Look around for examples of the letter *Y* or *y* (in book titles or other environmental print). Point out an example. Ask students to help you find others.

Guided Practice

- Display Letter Cards *Aa–Yy* in random order. Have students find *Y* or *y*. Then have them point to and name the other letters.

HANDWRITING: WRITING *Y, y* Tell students that they will learn to write capital *Y* and lowercase *y*. Write each letter slowly and deliberately as you recite the handwriting rhymes. Have students do the same, using their index fingers to "write" the letters in the air.

Handwriting Rhyme: *Y*

Start at the top line.

Halfway down to the

middle.

Start down once again.

You'll be fit as a fiddle.

Handwriting Rhyme: *y*

Little *y* slants from the

middle line.

Then bring down its

tail, and your *y* will be

fine.

- Repeat the handwriting rhymes activity, but this time have students use the Handwriting Models page for *Yy* to practice writing the letters.

Apply

- Have students use Practice Page K.29 to practice the letters *Yy*. Explain that the picture in the upper-left box is the Alphafriend for the letter *y*. Tell students to draw the Alphafriend and its letter in the upper-right box.

- In the lower-left box, have students trace the letters *Yy*. In the lower-right box, have students write the letters *Yy*.

> **Fun with Letters** Optional activities for engaging, hands-on practice are provided in the Resources section.

Objectives

- Review letter names *Aa–Xx*.
- Recognize and write the letters *Yy*.

Materials

- Handwriting Models for Letters *Yy*
- Letter Cards
- Practice Page K.29

Formative Assessment and Corrective Feedback

IF a student has difficulty identifying a previously learned letter, THEN follow this model:

Correct the error. Display the letter and say its name. If students confuse two similar-looking letters (for example, *V* and *Y*), point out how the letters differ.

Guide the student to "write" the letter in the air and say its name several times.

Check for understanding by having the student identify the letter from a mix of other previously taught letters.

Reinforce: Make a note to review the letter during the student's next session.

Let's Move!

While reciting the handwriting rhymes, perform the actions described in the rhyme to shape your body into the letter *Y*. Have students do the same.

Letter Knowledge: Letter Names *Zz*

Session K.30

Objectives

- Review letter names *Aa–Yy*.
- Recognize and write the letters *Zz*.

Materials

- Handwriting Models for Letters *Zz*
- Letter Cards
- Practice Page K.30

Formative Assessment and Corrective Feedback

IF a student has difficulty identifying a previously learned letter, THEN follow this model:

Correct the error. Display the letter and say its name. If students confuse two similar-looking letters (for example, *N* and *Z*), point out how the letters differ.

Guide the student to "write" the letter in the air and say its name several times.

Check for understanding by having the student identify the letter from a mix of other previously taught letters.

Reinforce: Make a note to review the letter during the student's next session.

Let's Move!

Have students use their fingers to "write" the letters *Z* and *z* on the back of their hands.

Teach/Model

- Display Letter Card *Zz*.
- **Say:** *This is the letter Z. Let's look at capital Z. Capital Z has three straight lines. Let's trace capital Z together. Now look at small, or lowercase, z. Lowercase z has three shorter straight lines. Now let's trace lowercase z.*
- Ask students whether their names contain the letter *Z* or *z*. Display any student names that contain the letter *Z* or *z*. Circle the letters *Z* and *z* wherever they appear.
- Look around for examples of the letter *Z* or *z* (in book titles or other environmental print). Point out an example. Ask students to help you find others.

Guided Practice

- Display Letter Cards *Aa–Zz* in random order. Have students find *Z* or *z*. Then have them point to and name the other letters.

HANDWRITING: WRITING *Z, z* Tell students that they will learn to write capital *Z* and lowercase *z*. Write each letter slowly and deliberately as you recite the handwriting rhymes. Have students do the same, using their index fingers to "write" the letters in the air.

Handwriting Rhyme: *Z*

From the top, zip right

with a line.

Slant down to the left, and

Zip right one more time:

It's a *Z*, big *Z*, big *Z*.

Handwriting Rhyme: *z*

From the middle, zip.

right with a line.

Slant down to the left,

And zip right one more time:

It's *z*, a small *z*, small *z*!

- Repeat the handwriting rhymes activity, but this time have students use the Handwriting Models page for *Zz* to practice writing the letters.

Apply

- Have students use Practice Page K.30 to practice the letters *Zz*. Explain that the picture in the upper-left box is the Alphafriend for the letter *z*. Tell students to draw the Alphafriend and its letter in the upper-right box.
- In the lower-left box, have students trace the letters *Zz*. In the lower-right box, have students write the letters *Zz*.

Fun with Letters Optional activities for engaging, hands-on practice are provided in the Resources section.

Letter Knowledge: Review Letter Names and Order

Teach/Model

- Display the alphabet in capital letters. Sing the "Alphabet Song" with students, pointing to each letter as you sing it. Then display the lowercase letters next to the uppercase letters. Sing the "Alphabet Song" again with students, pointing to the upper- and lowercase of each letter.
- Display Letter Cards in order around the room.
- **Say:** *The letters in the alphabet appear in a certain order. The alphabet starts with the letters* Aa *and ends with the letters* Zz. *Let's say the names of the letters in order from* Aa *to* Zz.

Guided Practice

- As you say the letter name for *A,* slowly trace upper- and lowercase *Aa* and have students "write" the letters in the air.
- Continue tracing a few more letters without saying their names, choosing ones that have been problematic for students. Pose questions: **Say:** *Who can tell me what this letter is? What letter comes after this one in the alphabet?*

HANDWRITING: WRITING *Aa–Zz* Ask students to find the letter that begins their name, point to the Letter Card with that letter, and say the letter name. Ask students to write their name.

Apply

- Take away a few of the letters from the alphabet that you displayed. Guide students to name the ones that are missing and have them write them.
- Play a letter matching game. Give each student a capital or small Letter Card. Have the student holding *A* stand at the front of the room and ask for the student with the lowercase letter buddy to come to the front. Continue through the letters *Zz.*

> **Fun with Letters** Optional activities for engaging, hands-on practice are provided in the Resources section.

Objectives

- Review letter names *Aa–Zz.*
- Review letter order *Aa–Zz.*

Materials

- Handwriting Models for Letters *Aa–Zz*
- Letter Cards

Formative Assessment and Corrective Feedback

IF a student has difficulty identifying a previously learned letter, THEN follow this model:

Correct the error. Display the letter and say its name. If students confuse two similar-looking letters, point out how the letters differ.

Guide the student to "write" the letter in the air and say its name several times.

Check for understanding by having the student identify the letter from a mix of other previously taught letters.

Reinforce: Make a note to review the letter during the student's next session.

Let's Move!

Provide a bag filled with capital and lowercase refrigerator magnet letters. Have students draw a letter and, without looking at it, name it according to its shape.

Phonological Awareness: Words in a Sentence

- Track words in oral sentences.
- Count words in oral sentences.

English Language Support

It's important for English learners to understand the meaning of the words they are using for skills practice. Use visuals, gestures, and context to support student understanding.

Formative Assessment and Corrective Feedback

IF a student makes an error, THEN follow this model:

Correct the error.

Guide the student to perform the task correctly by modeling.

Check for understanding by having the student repeat the task.

Reinforce: Make a note to review the skill during the student's next session.

Teach/Model

- Tell students that you are going to say a sentence. Ask them to say the words in the sentence with you and count each word they say by holding up a finger on one hand.
- **Say:** *I'll do the first one. Listen: The principal is busy. The, principal, is, busy.* (Count each word with your fingers.) Explain that *principal* is a long word, but that it is still just one word. Repeat the sentence and have students count the words with you.
- **Say:** *Let's do it together. Listen: The camera is mine. What words do you hear? The, camera, is, mine.* Repeat the sentence and have students count the words with you. Ask students to raise their hands if they don't understand the number of words.

Guided Practice

- Tell students that now you will say more sentences. Count the number of words in each sentence with students. Have students hold up a finger for each word they say. Use the following sentences:

  Open the door.

  You are nice.

  Sue is very cold.

  This is fun.

  Have a super day.

  We are friends.

Apply

- **Say:** *Listen to the sentence: We will read a book. Repeat the sentence and clap the number of words. How many words are in this sentence?* (5)
- Repeat with these sentences:

  I like to ride my bike.

  Juan went to the park.

  Pam ran a race.

  The ball is big and round.

Phonological Awareness: Blend Syllables

Teach/Model

- **Say:** *Words are made up of parts called syllables. I will say a word in parts. Listen as I say and count the parts:* Da-vid. Count, clapping or tapping twice. **Say:** *Da-vid has two parts or syllables. Now, I'll put the syllables together to say the word:* David.

- Repeat with the word *Ana* and other students' two-syllable names.

Guided Practice

- **Say:** *Now let's put some syllables together. Listen as I say a word in parts:* car-rot. *Say it with me, clapping for each part I say:* car-rot. *We clapped two times because there are two syllables. Now let's put the syllables together. What is the word?* (carrot)

- Continue saying and counting the syllables of a word with students. Then together blend the syllables to say the word. Use these words: *rabbit, hammer, basket, pillow, button, crayon.*

Apply

- Have students practice counting, identifying, and blending syllables in words, using objects in the classroom.

- Point to a table. Pronounce the word *table* in syllables. **Say:** *Ta-ble. How many syllables does the word have? Say it again and clap the number of syllables. Now put the syllables together. What is the word?* (table)

- Repeat with other classroom objects whose names have two syllables:

bookcase	jacket
ruler	tablet
scissors	cubby
pencils	markers
backpack	paper

Objectives

- Count syllables in spoken words.
- Pronounce and blend syllables.

Formative Assessment and Corrective Feedback

IF a student makes an error, THEN follow this model:

Correct the error.

Guide the student to perform the task correctly by modeling.

Check for understanding by having the student repeat the task.

Reinforce: Make a note to review the skill during the student's next session.

Phonological Awareness: Segment Syllables

Objectives

- Segment syllables in spoken words.
- Pronounce and segment syllables.

English Language Support

It's important for English learners to understand the meaning of the words they are using for skills practice. Use visuals, gestures, and context to support student understanding.

Formative Assessment and Corrective Feedback

IF a student makes an error, THEN follow this model:

Correct the error.

Guide the student to perform the task correctly by modeling.

Check for understanding by having the student repeat the task.

Reinforce: Make a note to review the skill during the student's next session.

Teach/Model

- **Say:** *I will say a word. Listen as I say the word:* pencil. *Words are made up of parts called syllables. Now I will say the word in parts:* pen-cil. *The word has two parts or syllables. I can clap out the syllables in the word.* Model clapping the syllables: *pen-cil.*
- Repeat with the word *picnic* and other familiar two-syllable words.

Guided Practice

- **Say:** *Now let's do it together. Listen:* feather. *Say the word, and then say it in parts. Clap as you say each syllable:* feath-er.
- Continue saying other words and having students segment each word into syllables. Use these words: *monkey, tiger, turkey, kitten, giraffe, lion, rabbit.*

Apply

- Have students practice saying and segmenting syllables in words, using objects in the classroom.
- Point to a bookcase. Pronounce the word *bookcase.* **Say:** *Say the word. Now, say the word in parts:* book-case. *Say it again and clap out its syllables. How many syllables does the word have?*
- Continue with other classroom objects whose names have two syllables or whose colors contain two syllables:

table	yellow
button	tablet
markers	cubby
purple	window

Phonological Awareness: Delete Syllables

Teach/Model

- **Say:** *I will say a word. Listen:* kitten. *Remember, words are made up of parts called syllables. I will clap the syllables for* seashell: sea-shell. *Seashell has two parts, or syllables. The first syllable is* sea. *The other syllable is* shell. *Say the syllables with me:* sea-shell. *If I take* sea *away from* seashell, *what syllable is left? The syllable* shell *is left.*

- **Say:** *Listen as I clap the syllables for* cupcake. *Cupcake has two syllables.* Cup-cake. *Say the syllables with me:* cup-cake. *If I take away* cake *from* cupcake, *what syllable is left? The syllable* cup *is left.*

- Repeat with the following words: *picnic, target, sunset, yellow.*

Guided Practice

- **Say:** *Now let's do it together. Listen:* meatball. *Say the word. Let's clap the syllables:* meat-ball. *Now if we take away the syllable* ball, *what will we have left? That's right, the syllable* meat *is left.*

- Continue saying other words and having students remove the first syllable: *cabin, teapot, Sunday, robin.*

- Repeat the practice by having students remove the last syllable: *bedroom, dishpan, baseball, Friday.*

Apply

- Have students practice saying, segmenting, and deleting syllables in words, using familiar items.

- Point to a button. Pronounce the word *button.* **Say:** *Say the word in parts:* but-ton. *Say it again and clap the syllables. Now take away* but *from* button, *what syllable is left?* (ton)

- Continue with these words: *bookcase, cubby, napkin, raincoat.*

- Pronounce the word *tiptoe.* **Say:** *Say the word in parts:* tip-toe. *Say it again and clap the syllables. Now take away* toe *from* tiptoe, *what syllable is left?* (tip)

- Continue with these words: *dustpan, surprise, magnet, oatmeal.*

Objectives

- Pronounce and segment syllables.
- Delete syllables in spoken words.

English Language Support

It's important for English learners to understand the meaning of the words they are using for skills practice. Use visuals, gestures, and context sentences to support student understanding.

Formative Assessment and Corrective Feedback

IF a student makes an error, THEN follow this model:

Correct the error.

Guide the student to perform the task correctly by modeling.

Check for understanding by having the student repeat the task.

Reinforce: Make a note to review the skill during the student's next session.

Phonological Awareness: Recognize Rhyming Words

Objectives

- Pronounce rhyming words.
- Recognize rhyming words.

English Language Support

Some students may have difficulty pronouncing and identifying some English sounds. Isolate the sounds in rhyming word parts and help students listen to and say the sounds.

Formative Assessment and Corrective Feedback

IF a student makes an error, THEN follow this model:

Correct the error.

Guide the student to perform the task correctly by modeling.

Check for understanding by having the student repeat the task.

Reinforce: Make a note to review the skill during the student's next session.

Teach/Model

- **Say:** *Listen as I say two words:* cap, map. *Say the words with me:* cap, map. *The words sound the same at the end. Words that sound alike at the end are called rhyming words. Listen as I say these words:* cap, map, lap. *Say them with me. The words all sound alike at the end. I hear /ăp/ at the end of these words. The words are rhyming words.*

- **Say:** *Listen as I say these words:* cap, map, lap, cat. *The word* cat *does not sound the same at the end, so it is not a rhyming word.*

- Continue with these sets of words and help students recognize words that rhyme:

  cap, lap, map, tap

  cap, lap, map, car

  cap, lap, map, nap

  cap, lap, map, sap

Guided Practice

- Read aloud this sentence, emphasizing the rhyming words: *A duck drives a truck.* **Say:** *Let's say the sentence together. Two words sound alike at the end. Which two words sound alike at the end?* (duck, truck) *That's right.* Duck *and* truck *are rhyming words.*

- Continue with the same procedure with the following sentences:

  A bear has hair.

  A goat drives a boat.

  A cat wears a hat.

  A dog sits on a log.

  A bug is on the rug.

  A fox is in a box.

Apply

- Tell students that you will say a pair of words. Tell them to clap their hands if the words rhyme or fold their hands if the words do not rhyme. Continue with the following word sets:

net, jet	hop, hut
ten, hen	can, pan
cut, zip	bed, red
dog, log	box, fox

Phonological Awareness: Produce Rhyming Words

Teach/Model

- **Say:** *Say these words with me:* cat, hat. *The words sound the same at the end. Listen as I say the word parts:* c-at, h-at. *Say the word parts with me:* c-at, h-at. *Words that sound alike at the end are called rhyming words.*

- **Say:** *I change the beginning sound to /b/. Listen as I say the word parts:* b-at. *Now you say them. The word is* bat. *The words* cat, hat, *and* bat *sound alike at the end. The words are rhyming words.*

- **Say:** *I can make more rhyming words. I can change the beginning sound to /s/. Listen as I say the word parts:* s-at. *Now you say them. The word is* sat. *Sat* rhymes with cat, hat, *and* bat.

- Continue with the following words: *mat, pat, vat.*

Formative Assessment and Corrective Feedback

IF a student makes an error, THEN follow this model:

Correct the error.

Guide the student to perform the task correctly by modeling.

Check for understanding by having the student repeat the task.

Reinforce: Make a note to review the skill during the student's next session.

Guided Practice

- Say the first line of the poem, emphasizing the rhyming words: *Pat had a cat.* **Say:** *Now you say this line. I hear two words that rhyme. What word rhymes with* Pat? (cat)

- Repeat the first line and continue with the other lines. Work with students to complete each line with a rhyming word. Possible examples are given.

    Pat had a cat.

    The cat sat on a _____. (mat)

    The cat had a _____. (bat)

    And it wore a _____. (hat)

Apply

- **Say:** *The words* net *and* jet *rhyme. What other words rhyme with* net *and* jet? Give the following clues as needed.

an animal friend (pet)	someone you know (met)
takes care of animals (vet)	put down in place (set)
can have (get)	used to catch things (net)
allow to do (let)	has water on it (wet)

Phonological Awareness: Categorize Rhyming Words

Objectives

- Recognize rhyming words.
- Categorize rhyming words.

Formative Assessment and Corrective Feedback

IF a student makes an error, THEN follow this model:

Correct the error.

Guide the student to perform the task correctly by modeling.

Check for understanding by having the student repeat the task.

Reinforce: Make a note to review the skill during the student's next session.

Teach/Model

- **Say:** *Listen as I say three words:* cot, dot, can. *Say these words with me:* cot, dot, can. *Remember, rhyming words sound alike at the end.* Cot *and* dot *rhyme because they both end with the same sounds, /ŏt/.* Can *does not rhyme with* cot *and* dot *because it ends with /ăn/.*
- **Say:** *Listen as I say another word:* hot. *Say these words with me:* cot, dot, hot. *These words all sound alike at the end. The words are rhyming words.*
- Continue with the word *bat* and help students recognize that the word *bat* does not rhyme with *cot, dot,* and *hot.* Use these sets of words to continue:

  cot, dot, got,

  cot, hot, job

  cot, hot, lot

Guided Practice

- **Say:** *Now I will say three words. Listen to the words:* mat, can, hat. *Say the words with me:* mat, can, hat. *Which two words rhyme?* (mat, hat)
- Continue with the following word sets:

mix, bug, rug	fox, box, sit
hen, kit, pen	hot, pet, net
jar, nut, hut	pan, fan, top
kit, leg, sit	ran, fun, run

Apply

- Tell students that you are going to say sets of words. Have them tell you the words that rhyme in each set of words.

mat, rat, tan	fill, Bill, fun
hop, hip, pop	net, nut, bet
pat, pit, sit	can, ran, cat
nut, but, cup	pill, pen, Ken

Phonological Awareness: Blend Onset and Rime

Teach/Model

- **Say:** *I'm going to say a word in two parts. Then I will blend the sounds to say the word. Listen: /j/ /ăm/. When I blend /j/ /ăm/, I get* jam.
- Repeat with the word *sit*.

Guided Practice

- **Say:** *Now let's do some together.*
- Pronounce the onset (first sound) and rime (rest of the word, pronounced as a unit) for each of the following words. With students, blend the sounds to say the whole word.

    /g/ /ĕt/ (get)

    /k/ /ăp/ (cap)

    /n/ /ĕt/ (net)

    /d/ /ŭk/ (duck)

    /s/ / ĭx/ (six)

    /d/ /ŏg/ (dog)

Apply

- **Say:** *I'm going to say a word in two parts. You will blend the sounds to say the word.*
- Pronounce the onset and rime for each of the following words. Have students blend the sounds to say the whole word:

    rip

    fix

    wag

    van

    sell

    bed

    doll

    top

Formative Assessment and Corrective Feedback

IF a student makes an error, THEN follow this model:

Correct the error.

Guide the student to perform the task correctly by modeling.

Check for understanding by having the student repeat the task.

Reinforce: Make a note to review the skill during the student's next session.

Phonological Awareness: Segment Onset and Rime

Objective

- Segment onset and rime of single-syllable spoken words.

Formative Assessment and Corrective Feedback

IF a student makes an error, THEN follow this model:

Correct the error.

Guide the student to perform the task correctly by modeling.

Check for understanding by having the student repeat the task.

Reinforce: Make a note to review the skill during the student's next session.

Teach/Model

- **Say:** *I'm going to say a word. Then I will say the word in parts. I'll say the beginning sound and the sounds in the rest of the word. Listen to the word:* cat. *Say the word with me:* cat. *Listen to the parts:* /k/ /ăt/. *Say the parts with me:* /k/ /ăt/.
- Repeat with the following words: *hat, hit, hot, hut.*

Guided Practice

- **Say:** *Now let's do some together.*
- Pronounce the word and then guide students in segmenting the onset (first sound) and rime (rest of the word, pronounced as a unit) for each of the following words:

pet	(/p/ /ĕt/)
map	(/m/ /ăp/)
leg	(/l/ /ĕg/)
rug	(/r/ /ŭg/)
mix	(/m/ /ĭks/)
job	(/j/ /ŏb/)

Apply

- Have students segment the onset and rime in words. **Say:** *I'm going to say a word. I want you to say the beginning sound and then the rest of the word.*

rock (/r/ /ŏk/)	wish (/w/ /ĭsh/)
back (/b/ /ăk/)	tell (/t/ /ĕl/)
hop (/h/ /ŏp/)	pick (/p/ /ĭk/)
luck (/l/ /ŭk/)	cab (/k/ /ăb/)
big (/b/ /ĭg/)	pen (/p/ /ĕn/)

Phonemic Awareness: Isolate Initial Sound

Teach/Model

- **Say:** *Listen to these words:* big, bat. *Let's say the words together. I hear the same sound at the beginning of* big *and* bat. Big *and* bat *both begin with the /b/ sound. Let's say the beginning sound together: /b/-/b/-/b/-/b/.*

- **Say:** *Say this word with me:* bus. *What sound do you hear at the beginning of* bus?

- Continue with these words: *bag, bit, bun.*

- **Say:** *Listen to these words:* sun, sip. *Let's say the words together. I hear the same sound at the beginning of* sun *and* sip. Sun *and* sip *both begin with the /s/ sound. Let's say the beginning sound together: /s/-/s/-/s/-/s/.*

- **Say:** *Say this word with me:* sit. *What sound do you hear at the beginning of* sit?

- Continue with these words: *sat, sub, Sam.*

Guided Practice

- **Say:** *Now let's listen for beginning sounds together. I will say some words:* mat, mop. *Say the words with me. Do you hear the same sound at the beginning of* mat *and* mop? *What is the beginning sound?* (/m/)

- Continue with these word pairs: *fan, fit; log, lap; gas, get; man, map; jet, job; cub, cat.*

Apply

- Tell students that now you will say some more words. They will say *yes* if the sound they hear at the beginning of each word is the same. **Say:** *Listen:* cup, cat. *Do* cup *and* cat *begin with the same sound?* (yes) *What is the sound?* (/k/)

- Continue with *red, rip; dig, Dan; bug, mad; ten, top; hit, hop; lip, sat; pin, pot.*

- **Say:** *Listen:* rope, lamp, salt. *Which word begins with the same sound as* sit? (salt)

- **Say:** *Listen:* big, mine, go. *Which word begins with the same sound as* mat? (mine)

Objectives

- Isolate and pronounce the initial sound in spoken words.

English Language Support

Linguistic Transfer Some English learners (including speakers of Hmong) may have trouble with the /p/ sound. Model pronouncing the sound, and have ELs practice the sound in front of a mirror and then practice pronouncing words such as these: *pat, pet, pan, pot, pin, pup.* Use each word in a brief sentence to reinforce meaning.

Formative Assessment and Corrective Feedback

IF a student makes an error, THEN follow this model:

Correct the error.

Guide the student to perform the task correctly by modeling.

Check for understanding by having the student repeat the task.

Reinforce: Make a note to review the skill during the student's next session.

Phonemic Awareness: Review: Isolate Initial Sound

Objective

- Isolate and pronounce the initial sound in spoken words.

English Language Support

Linguistic Transfer Some students whose first language is Spanish, Vietnamese, Tagalog, or Korean may have trouble with the /j/ sound. Say the sound several times as ELs study your mouth position; students can also practice the sounds in front of a mirror. Then provide extra modeling and practice with words such as *jump, jar, just, joy, joke, jet, jeans,* and *job*. Have students chorally repeat each word after you, then say just the beginning sound, and then say the whole word again. Use each word in a sentence to reinforce meaning.

Formative Assessment and Corrective Feedback

IF a student makes an error, THEN follow this model:

Correct the error.

Guide the student to perform the task correctly by modeling.

Check for understanding by having the student repeat the task.

Reinforce: Make a note to review the skill during the student's next session.

Teach/Model

- Tell students that you will say two words. Have them repeat the words after you. Ask them to raise their hands if the beginning sounds are the same. *Listen to these words:* food, fish. *Let's say the words together. If you hear the same sound at the beginning of* food *and* fish, *raise your hands. I hear the same sound at the beginning of* food *and* fish. Food *and* fish *both begin with the /f/ sound. Let's say the beginning sound together: /f/-/f/-/f/-/f/.*
- Continue with these sets of words.

six, sun	hen, man
pit, pal	boat, leg
dog, dime	top, tape

Guided Practice

- **Say:** *I will say a word. Say the word with me and listen to the beginning sound. Then say the sound you hear at the beginning of the word. Ready? The first word is* moon. *Say the word with me:* moon. *What is the beginning sound?* (/m/)
- Continue with these words:

fan	bus
goat	hop
jeep	corn
door	sun

Apply

- Tell students that now you will say a word and they are to listen to the beginning sound. Then have them say the beginning sound. **Say:** *Listen:* run. *Let's say the beginning sound: /r/-/r/-/r/-/r/.*
- Continue with the following words:

dog	bug	mud
ten	hat	lip
sat	pond	mix
bean	keep	lamp
ball	map	jam

Phonemic Awareness: Isolate Final Sound

Teach/Model

- **Say:** *Listen to this word:* cat. *Let's say the word together. Let's listen for the sound at the end of* cat. *I hear /t/ at the end of* cat. *Let's say the ending sound together: /t/-/t/-/t/-/t/.*
- **Say:** *Listen to this word:* pet. *I hear /t/ at the end of* pet. *Let's say the ending sound together: /t/-/t/-/t/-/t/.* Continue with these words: *nut, jet, kit.*
- **Say:** *Listen to these words:* top, map. *Let's say the words together. I hear the same sound at the end of* top *and* map. *Top and map both end with the /p/ sound. Let's say the ending sound together: /p/-/p/-/p/-/p/.*

Guided Practice

- **Say:** *Now let's listen for ending sounds together. I will say some words:* can, pin. *Say the words with me:* can, pin. *What sound do you hear at the end of* can *and* pin? *(/n/)*
- Continue with these word pairs: *dog, tag; gas, mess; man, nod; hat, jet; cub, cat; fun, pan.*

Apply

- Tell students that now you will say some more words. Have students repeat each word and name the sound they hear at the end.

jam	log	top
lick	ten	hat
lip	sat	pad
quiz	rag	dock
shut	cub	mess

Objective

- Isolate and pronounce the final sound in spoken words.

English Language Support

Linguistic Transfer Before discussing ending sounds with students, have them stand in a line. Develop meaning for the words *beginning* and *ending* by pointing to the first and last students in line. Have students switch positions several times and tell who is at the beginning and who is at the end of the line.

Speakers of Chinese languages may have trouble hearing and producing consonants at the ends of words, or they may add a vowel sound after a final consonant; in Chinese, words usually end with a vowel sound. Provide modeling, and practice segmenting and blending final sounds in words such as *back, bat, sack, sat.* Use each word in a brief sentence to provide a meaningful context.

Formative Assessment and Corrective Feedback

IF a student makes an error, THEN follow this model:

Correct the error.

Guide the student to perform the task correctly by modeling.

Check for understanding by having the student repeat the task.

Reinforce: Make a note to review the skill during the student's next session.

Phonemic Awareness: Review: Isolate Final Sound

Objective

- Isolate and pronounce the final sound in spoken words.

English Language Support

Linguistic Transfer Some ELs may have difficulty hearing and saying words with the /p/ and /t/ ending sounds. Give students practice discriminating these sounds by saying word pairs such as the following: hop/ hog, rat/rap, sat/Sam. Have students raise their hands when they hear the /p/ or /t/ sound at the end of a word. Then have them practice saying the words.

Formative Assessment and Corrective Feedback

IF a student makes an error, THEN follow this model:

Correct the error.

Guide the student to perform the task correctly by modeling.

Check for understanding by having the student repeat the task.

Reinforce: Make a note to review the skill during the student's next session.

Teach/Model

- Model how to identify and isolate the ending sound in words. **Say:** *I'm going to say a word. Listen:* bus. *Say the word with me:* bus. *I hear /s/ at the end of* bus, */s/-/s/-/s/-/s/.*

- **Say:** *Say this word with me:* gas. *I hear /s/ at the end of* gas, */s/-/s/-/s/-/s/.* Continue with these words: *met, clap, yell, log.*

- **Say:** *Listen to these words:* red, bed. *Let's say the words together. I hear /d/ at the end of* red *and* bed. *Say the sound with me, /d/-/d/-/d/-/d/.*

- **Say:** *Say these words with me:* rub, cub. *I hear /b/ at the end of* rub *and* cub. *Say the sound with me, /b/-/b/-/b/-/b/.*

Guided Practice

- **Say:** *Listen as I say a word. Say the word with me and listen to the ending sound. Then say the sound you hear at the end of the word. The first word is* book. *Say the word with me:* book. *What is the ending sound?* (/k/)

- Continue with these words:

sun	beg
web	pad

- **Say:** *Listen as I say a word. Say the word with me and listen to the ending sound.* Tan. *What sound do you hear at the end of* tan? *(/n/) Now I will say two more words. Let's say the words together and listen to the ending sounds:* get, win. *Which word has the same ending sound as* tan? Win *has the same ending sound as* tan, /n/.

- Continue with these words:

  pen: sun, doll

  rip: tug, lap

Apply

- Tell students that now you will say some words and they are to listen to the ending sounds. Have students tell which words have the same ending sounds.

- Continue with these sets of words:

run, pin, vet	van, mop, top
pat, six, get	hid, rod, zip
dot, pot, cub	van, tip, cup

Phonemic Awareness: Isolate Medial Sound

Teach/Model

- Tell students that now they will listen to sounds in the middle of a word. Model how to identify and isolate the middle sound in a word. **Say:** *Listen as I say a word:* cat. *I hear /ă/ in the middle of* cat. *Say the sound with me: /ă/-/ă/-/ă/-/ă/.* If necessary, emphasize the middle sound: *caaat.*
- **Say:** *Listen to the word I say.* Pin. *I hear /ĭ/ in the middle of* pin. *Say the sound with me: /ĭ/-/ĭ/-/ĭ/-/ĭ/.* Continue modeling how to identify and isolate the middle sound in a word, using these words: *wet, job, cup.*

Guided Practice

- **Say:** *Now let's listen for middle sounds together. I will say a word:* can. *Say the word with me:* can. *What sound do you hear in the middle of* can? *Say the sound you hear in the middle of the word.* (/ă/)
- Continue with these words:

pig	tap
sad	jet
pan	bat
fun	box

Apply

- Tell students that now you will say some more words. Have students repeat each word and name the sound they hear in the middle.

map	fan
pin	tack
bag	box
tub	dip
bug	fig
jam	hot

Objective

- Isolate and pronounce the medial sound in spoken words.

English Language Support

Linguistic Transfer Point out to Spanish speakers that the /ă/ sound at the beginning of *apple* is a little different from the sound at the beginning of the word *agua* in Spanish. Have ELs listen carefully as you pronounce words with the /ă/ sound: *apple, at, ad, mat, cat, man, can, pan, pat.* Have students repeat each word, and if they substitute /ŏ/ for /ă/, encourage them to "smile" a little to make the /ă/ sound. Use each word in a brief sentence to reinforce meaning.

Formative Assessment and Corrective Feedback

IF a student makes an error, THEN follow this model:

Correct the error.

Guide the student to perform the task correctly by modeling.

Check for understanding by having the student repeat the task.

Reinforce: Make a note to review the skill during the student's next session.

Phonemic Awareness: Review: Isolate Medial Sound

Objective

- Isolate and pronounce the medial sound in spoken words.

English Language Support

Linguistic Transfer Some English learners, including speakers of Spanish, Korean, Vietnamese, and Tagalog, may need extra practice with the /ĕ/ sound. Have ELs listen carefully as you pronounce words with the /ĕ/ sound: *fed, bet, yet, pep, red, neck.* Have students repeat each word, then vocalize the middle sound, and then say the whole word again. Use each word in a brief sentence to reinforce meaning.

Formative Assessment and Corrective Feedback

IF a student makes an error, THEN follow this model:

Correct the error.

Guide the student to perform the task correctly by modeling.

Check for understanding by having the student repeat the task.

Reinforce: Make a note to review the skill during the student's next session.

Teach/Model

- **Say:** *Listen as I say a word:* tag. *I hear* /ă/ *in the middle of* tag. *Say the sound with me:* /ă/-/ă/-/ă/-/ă/. Continue modeling how to identify and isolate the middle sound in a word, using the following words: *lip, web, rug, hot.*
- **Say:** *Listen to these words:* big, hip. *Let's say the words together. I hear* /ĭ/ *in the middle of* big *and* hip. *Let's say the middle sound together:* /ĭ/-/ĭ/-/ĭ/-/ĭ/.

Guided Practice

- **Say:** *Let's listen for the middle sounds in words. I will say a word. Say the word with me and listen to the sound in the middle of the word. Listen:* cat. *Say the word with me:* cat. *What sound do you hear in the middle of the word?* (/ă/)
- Continue with these words: *bus, tin, top, men, sat, sit, cob, tub, jet.*

Apply

- Tell students that now you will say two words and they are to listen to the middle sounds. Have students name the sound they hear in the middle of each set of words.

hit, pin	can, tap
web, hem	six, tip
dot, nod	fun, mug
bug, cup	hot, job
jam, cat	den, vet

Phonemic Awareness: Identify Phonemes

Teach/Model

- *Listen to this word:* bat. *Let's say the word together. The beginning sound is /b/. Let's say the beginning sound together: /b/-/b/-/b/-/b/.*

- **Say:** *I am going to say a word. Listen:* big. *The sound at the beginning of* big *is /b/. The sound at the beginning of* bat *is /b/. The words begin with the same sound.*

- **Say:** *Listen to the word:* box. *I'm going to say two more words. One of the words has the same beginning sound as* box: bat, fun. *I hear /b/ at the beginning of* box. *I hear /b/ at the beginning of* bat. *I hear /f/ at the beginning of* fun. *So,* bat *and* box *have the same beginning sound, /b/.*

Guided Practice

- **Say:** *Now let's do some together. Let's listen for the words that have the same beginning sound.*

- Pronounce the target word, emphasizing the beginning sound. Then say the pair of words. Work with students to identify the word that has the same beginning sound as the target word.

Target Word	Pairs
zip	zig, bun
cap	rob, cob
top	tag, hug
bed	big, man
dig	rock, dot
pet	pan, fun

Apply

- **Say:** *I'm going to say a word. Listen for the beginning sound. Then I will say two more words. Tell me the word that begins the same as the first word.*

Target Word	Pairs
sun	set, tip
bat	bill, can
pin	pal, hill
net	nod, map
lap	duck, lip
bad	bed, pan

Objective

- Isolate and pronounce the initial sound in spoken words.

English Language Support

It's important for English learners to understand the meaning of the words they are using for skills practice. Use visuals, gestures, and context sentences to support student understanding.

Formative Assessment and Corrective Feedback

IF a student makes an error, THEN follow this model:

Correct the error.

Guide the student to perform the task correctly by modeling.

Check for understanding by having the student repeat the task.

Reinforce: Make a note to review the skill during the student's next session.

Objectives

- Isolate and pronounce the initial sound in spoken words.
- Categorize words by the initial sound in spoken words.

English Language Support

It's important for English learners to understand the meaning of the words they are using for skills practice. Use visuals, gestures, and context sentences to support student understanding.

Formative Assessment and Corrective Feedback

IF a student makes an error, THEN follow this model:

Correct the error.

Guide the student to perform the task correctly by modeling.

Check for understanding by having the student repeat the task.

Reinforce: Make a note to review the skill during the student's next session.

Teach/Model

- **Say:** *Listen to three words:* cat, hat, can. *Let's say the words together. One of the words has a different beginning sound than the others:* cat, hat, can. *Two of these words have the same beginning sound. I hear /k/ at the beginning of* cat *and* can. *I hear /h/ at the beginning of* hat. Hat *begins with a different sound.*

Guided Practice

- **Say:** *Now let's do some together.*
- Pronounce each set of words. Together with students repeat each set of words. Guide students to name the word that has a different beginning sound.

    zip, zap, bun

    cap, cob, rip

    bit, bus, top

    gas, get, sip

    lot, sun, leg

    pat, nod, pick

    dip, Dan, mitt

Apply

- Tell students that you will say three words. Ask them to name the word that has a different beginning sound.

nut, nod, cup	tan, cab, tax
cap, tag, cut	pup, pin, cot
tin, top, cub	mat, nap, mop
dip, lock, log	bit, rip, bed
hat, bus, big	tip, fan, tack
rug, rip, got	duck, dot, hop

Phonemic Awareness: Blend Phonemes

Teach/Model

- **Say:** *Listen to the sounds: /ă/ /t/. Say the sounds with me: /ă/ /t/. I hear two sounds in the word. Watch as I count the sounds with my fingers: /ă/ /t/. I'm going to blend those sounds and say the word: /ă/ /t/,* at. *Say the word with me:* at. *I blended two sounds to make the word* at.

- **Say:** *I am going to say some more sounds that make a word. Listen: /b/ /ă/ /t/. Say the sounds with me. I hear three sounds in this word. I'll count the sounds with my fingers: /b/ /ă/ /t/. Then I'll blend the sounds and say the word: /b/ /ă/ /t/,* bat.

Guided Practice

- **Say:** *Now let's do some together.*
- Guide students to hold up a finger for each sound. Then have students blend the sounds into words.

/t/ /ă/ /p/	(tap)
/f/ /ĭ/ /n/	(fin)
/r/ /ŭ/ /g/	(rug)
/ĭ/ /t/	(it)
/s/ /ĕ/ /t/	(set)
/b/ /ĕ/ /d/	(bed)
/ă/ /t/	(at)

Apply

- Tell students that you will say the sounds for a word that tells about something in the room. They are to blend the sounds and make the word. Then have them point to the item that the word names.
- **Say:** *Listen to the sounds: /p/ /ĕ/ /n/. Blend the sounds to make a word. What is the word?* (pen) *Point to a pen.*
- Continue with the following sounds:

/h/ /ă/ /t/	(hat)
/c/ /ă/ /p/	(cap)
/m/ /ă/ /p/	(map)
/l/ /ĕ/ /g/	(leg)
/k/ /ŭ/ /p/	(cup)
/r/ /ĕ/ /d/	(red)
/b/ /ŏ/ /ks/	(box)

Objective

- Blend phonemes into recognizable words.

English Language Support

It's important for English learners to understand the meaning of the words they are using for skills practice. Use visuals, gestures, and context sentences to support student understanding.

Formative Assessment and Corrective Feedback

IF a student makes an error, THEN follow this model:

Correct the error.

Guide the student to perform the task correctly by modeling.

Check for understanding by having the student repeat the task.

Reinforce: Make a note to review the skill during the student's next session.

Objective

- Blend phonemes into recognizable words.

English Language Support

It's important for English learners to understand the meaning of the words they are using for skills practice. Use visuals, gestures, and context sentences to support student understanding.

Formative Assessment and Corrective Feedback

IF a student makes an error, THEN follow this model:

Correct the error.

Guide the student to perform the task correctly by modeling.

Check for understanding by having the student repeat the task.

Reinforce: Make a note to review the skill during the student's next session.

Phonemic Awareness: Review: Blend Phonemes

Teach/Model

- **Say:** *Listen to the sounds: /i/ /t/. Say the sounds with me: /i/ /t/. I hear two sounds in the word. Watch as I count the sounds with my fingers: /i/ /t/. I'm going to blend those sounds and say the word: /i/ /t/, it. Say the word with me: it. I blended two sounds to make the word it.*
- **Say:** *I am going to say some more sounds that make a word. Listen: /f/ /i/ /t/. Say the sounds with me. I hear three sounds in this word. I'll count the sounds with my fingers: /f/ /i/ /t/. Then I'll blend the sounds and say the word: /f/ /i/ /t/, fit.*

Guided Practice

- **Say:** *Now let's do some together.*
- Guide students to hold up a finger for each sound. Then have them blend the sounds into words.

/ŭ/ /p/	(up)
/r/ /ĕ/ /d/	(red)
/s/ /ă/ /d/	(sad)
/f/ /ŭ/ /n/	(fun)
/h/ /ŏ/ /p/	(hop)
/ĭ/ /z/	(is)
/w/ /ĕ/ /b/	(web)
/h/ /ĭ/ /t/	(hit)

Apply

- Tell students that you will say some sounds. Have them blend the sounds to say the word.

/ă/ /z/	(as)
/p/ /ă/ /d/	(pad)
/b/ /ĭ/ /t/	(bit)
/r/ /ĕ/ /d/	(red)
/ĭ/ /n/	(in)
/h/ /ŏ/ /p/	(hop)
/b/ /ă/ /d/	(bad)
/n/ /ĕ/ /d/	(Ned)
/f/ /ŭ/ /n/	(fun)
/k/ /ĕ/ /n/	(Ken)

Phonemic Awareness: Segment Phonemes

Teach/Model

- **Say:** *Listen as I say a word:* in. *Now I will break the word apart. I will count with my fingers as I say each sound in the word:* /ĭ/ /n/. *There are two sounds in the word* in. *Now say the word and the sounds with me:* in, /ĭ/ /n/.
- **Say:** *Listen as I say a word:* pin. *Now I will break the word apart. I will count with my fingers as I say each sound in the word:* /p/ /ĭ/ /n/. *There are three sounds in the word* pin. *Now say the word and the sounds with me:* pin, /p/ /ĭ/ /n/.

Guided Practice

- **Say:** *Now let's do some together.*
- Guide students to hold up a finger for each sound as they segment the word into sounds.

fit	(/f/ /ĭ/ /t/)
it	(/ĭ/ /t/)
tub	(/t/ /ŭ/ /b/)
bad	(/b/ /ă/ /d/)
rack	(/r/ /ă/ /k/)
pet	(/p/ /ĕ/ /t/)
den	(/d/ /ĕ/ /n/)
bug	(/b/ /ŭ/ /g/)

Apply

- Tell students that you will say a word. Have them segment the sounds in each word.

mix	(/m/ /ĭ/ /ks/)
top	(/t/ /ŏ/ /p/)
cub	(/k/ /ŭ/ /b/)
up	(/ŭ/ /p/)
bed	(/b/ /ĕ/ /d/)
fix	(/f/ /ĭ/ /ks/)
pen	(/p/ /ĕ/ /n/)
rug	(/r/ /ŭ/ /g/)
map	(/m/ /ă/ /p/)
pot	(/p/ /ŏ/ /t/)
man	(/m/ /ă/ /n/)

Objective

- Segment the sounds in spoken words.

English Language Support

Linguistic Transfer Speakers of Spanish, Vietnamese, Tagalog, and Korean may have difficulty with the /ĭ/ sound. Give students additional practice listening and pronouncing words with /ĭ/.

Formative Assessment and Corrective Feedback

IF a student makes an error, THEN follow this model:

Correct the error.

Guide the student to perform the task correctly by modeling.

Check for understanding by having the student repeat the task.

Reinforce: Make a note to review the skill during the student's next session.

Phonemic Awareness: Review: Segment Phonemes

Objective

- Segment the sounds in words.

English Language Support

Speakers of Chinese languages may have trouble hearing and producing consonants at the end of words, or they may add a vowel sound after a final consonant; in Chinese, words usually end with a vowel sound. Provide modeling and practice segmenting final sounds in words such as *back, bat, sack, sat.* Use each word in a brief sentence to provide meaningful context.

Formative Assessment and Corrective Feedback

IF a student makes an error, THEN follow this model:

Correct the error.

Guide the student to perform the task correctly by modeling.

Check for understanding by having the student repeat the task.

Reinforce: Make a note to review the skill during the student's next session.

Teach/Model

- **Say:** *Listen as I say a word:* at. *Now I will break the word apart. I will count with my fingers as I say each sound in the word:* /ă/ /t/. *There are two sounds in the word* at. *Now say the word and the sounds with me:* at, /ă/ /t/.
- **Say:** *Listen as I say a word:* pin. *Now I will break the word apart. I will count with my fingers as I say each sound in the word:* /p/ /ĭ/ /n/. *There are three sounds in the word* pin. *Now say the word and the sounds with me:* pin, /p/ /ĭ/ /n/.

Guided Practice

- **Say:** *Now let's do some together.*
- Guide students to hold up a finger for each sound as they segment the word into sounds.

pet	(/p/ /ĕ/ /t/)
cat	(/k/ /ă/ /t/)
cub	(/k/ /ŭ/ /b/)
cut	(/k/ /ŭ/ /t/)
bus	(/b/ /ŭ/ /s/)

Apply

- Tell students that you will say a word. Have them segment the sounds in each word.

fix	(/f/ /ĭ/ /ks/)
mop	(/m/ /ŏ/ /p/)
tub	(/t/ /ŭ/ /b/)
us	(/ŭ/ /s/)
red	(/r/ /ĕ/ /d/)
mix	(/m/ /ĭ/ /ks/)
ten	(/t/ /ĕ/ /n/)
bug	(/b/ /ŭ/ /g/)
tap	(/t/ /ă/ /p/)
rot	(/r/ /ŏ/ /t/)
fan	(/f/ /ă/ /n/)

Phonemic Awareness: Delete Phonemes

Teach/Model

- **Say:** *Listen as I say the word* cat. *Let's say the word* cat *together. I hear /k/ at the beginning of* cat. *If I take off the /k/ in* cat, *I get a new word:* at. *Say the word with me:* at.

- **Say:** *Listen as I say the word* bus. *Let's say the word* bus *together. I hear /b/ at the beginning of* bus. *If I take off the /b/ in* bus, *I get a new word:* us. *Say the word with me:* us.

- **Say:** *Listen as I say the word* beet. *Let's say the word* beet *together. I hear /t/ at the end of* beet. *If I take off the /t/ in* beet, *I get a new word:* bee. *Say the word with me:* bee.

- **Say:** *Listen as I say the word* bark. *Let's say the word* bark *together. I hear /k/ at the end of* bark. *If I take off the /k/ in* bark, *I get a new word:* bar. *Say the word with me:* bar.

Guided Practice

- **Say:** *Listen to this word:* can. *Let's say the word and listen for the beginning sound. Say the beginning sound with me: /k/. Let's take away the first sound in* can. *What word is made when you take away the /k/ sound in* can? *(/ă/ /n/, an)*

- **Say:** *Let's do a few more together.*

  Say the word band *with me:* band. *If you take off the /b/ sound, what new word do we have? (and)*

  Say the word ball *with me:* ball. *If you take off the /b/ sound, what new word do we have? (all)*

  Say the word mat *with me:* mat. *If you take off the /m/ sound, what new word do we have? (at)*

  Say the word hit *with me:* hit. *If you take off the /h/ sound, what new word do we have? (it)*

  Say the word make *with me:* make. *If you take off the /k/ sound, what new word do we have? (may)*

  Say the word meet *with me:* meet. *If you take off the /t/ sound, what new word do we have? (me)*

Apply

- Have students delete phonemes to produce new words.

  Listen to this word: bit. *If you take off the /b/ sound, what new word do you have? (it)*

  Listen to this word: bat. *If you take off the /b/ sound, what new word do you have? (at)*

  Listen to this word: cup. *If you take off the /k/ sound, what new word do you have? (up)*

  Listen to this word: sit. *If you take off the /s/ sound, what new word do you have? (it)*

  Listen to this word: win. *If you take off the /w/ sound, what new word do you have? (in)*

  Listen to this word: seat. *If you take off the /t/ sound, what new word do you have? (see)*

  Listen to this word: meal. *If you take off the /l/ sound, what new word do you have? (me)*

Objective

- Delete phonemes in words to make new words.

English Language Support

Some students may have difficulty pronouncing and identifying some English sounds and will have difficulty deleting sounds to make new words. Isolate the sounds in the word and then use the sounds to show how a sound is deleted to make a new word.

Formative Assessment and Corrective Feedback

IF a student makes an error, THEN follow this model:

Correct the error.

Guide the student to perform the task correctly by modeling.

Check for understanding by having the student repeat the task.

Reinforce: Make a note to review the skill during the student's next session.

Phonemic Awareness: Add Phonemes

Objective

- Add phonemes in words to make new words.

English Language Support

Some students may have difficulty adding sounds to make new words as well as pronouncing and identifying some English sounds. Isolate the sounds and help students listen to and say the sounds.

Formative Assessment and Corrective Feedback

IF a student makes an error, THEN follow this model:

Correct the error.

Guide the student to perform the task correctly by modeling.

Check for understanding by having the student repeat the task.

Reinforce: Make a note to review the skill during the student's next session.

Teach/Model

- **Say:** *Listen as I say the sounds in the word:* /ă/ /t/. *Let's say the word* at *together:* at. *When I add the* /k/ *sound to the beginning of the word, I make a new word. My new word is* cat. *Let's say the word together:* cat.

- **Say:** *Listen as I say the sounds in the word:* /p/ /ĭ/ /n/. *Let's say the word* pin *together:* pin. *When I add the* /s/ *sound to the beginning of the word, I make a new word. My new word is* spin. *Let's say the word together:* spin.

Guided Practice

- **Say:** *Let's blend the sounds to say this word:* /ă/ /n/. (an) *Let's add a beginning sound to make a new word. What word is made when you add the* /k/ *sound to* an? (can) *What word is made when you add the* /f/ *sound to* an? (fan)

- **Say:** *Let's blend the sounds to say this word:* /l/ /ă/ /p/. (lap) *Let's add a beginning sound to make a new word. What word is made when you add the* /s/ *sound to* lap? (slap) *What word is made when you add the* /s/ *sound to* pit? (spit)

- Continue working with students to add /s/ to the beginning of these words to make new words: *lip, nap, pot.*

Apply

- Have students add phonemes to words to create new words.

    Add the /h/ *sound to* it. *What word did you make?* (hit)

    Add the /p/ *sound to* up. *What word did you make?* (pup)

    Add the /b/ *sound to* lock. *What word did you make?* (block)

    Add the /t/ *sound to* rip. *What word did you make?* (trip)

    Add the /b/ *sound to* ring. *What word did you make?* (bring)

    Add the /f/ *sound to* ox. *What word did you make?* (fox)

Phonemic Awareness: Substitute Phonemes

Teach/Model

- **Say:** *Listen as I say the word* mat. *Let's say the word* mat *together. I can make a new word by changing the beginning sound. I can change the /m/ in* mat *to /k/. My new word is* cat. *Say the new word:* cat.

- **Say:** *Listen as I say the word* pin. *Let's say the word* pin *together. I can make a new word by changing the beginning sound. I can change the /p/ in* pin *to /t/. My new word is* tin. *Say the new word:* tin.

Guided Practice

- **Say:** *Say the word* man *with me:* man. *Let's change the /m/ in* man *to /p/. What new word do we have?* (pan) *Let's make more new words.* Continue with the following:

    Change the /m/ in mat *to /h/. What new word did you make?* (hat)

    Change the /d/ in dig *to /w/. What new word did you make?* (wig)

    Change the /n/ in neck *to /d/. What new word did you make?* (deck)

    Change the /r/ in rush *to /h/. What new word did you make?* (hush)

    Change the /v/ in van *to /r/. What new word did you make?* (ran)

Apply

- Have students change the sound at the beginning of a word to make a new word. Use the following:

    Change the /p/ in pack *to /t/. What new word did you make?* (tack)

    Change the /h/ in hill *to /w/. What new word did you make?* (will)

    Change the /r/ in rug *to /m/. What new word did you make?* (mug)

    Change the /j/ in jet *to /n/. What new word did you make?* (net)

    Change the /m/ in mix *to /s/. What new word did you make?* (six)

    Change the /h/ in hop *to /m/. What new word did you make?* (mop)

    Change the /b/ in bag *to /t/. What new word did you make?* (tag)

    Change the /p/ in pad *to /h/. What new word did you make?* (had)

Objective

- Substitute phonemes in words to make new words.

English Language Support

Some students may have difficulty changing sounds to make new words as well as pronouncing and identifying some English sounds. Isolate the sounds and help students listen to each sound and say the sounds to make the new word.

Formative Assessment and Corrective Feedback

IF a student makes an error, THEN follow this model:

Correct the error.

Guide the student to perform the task correctly by modeling.

Check for understanding by having the student repeat the task.

Reinforce: Make a note to review the skill during the student's next session.

Phonics: Letter/Sound *Mm*

Objectives

- Isolate and pronounce the first sound in words that begin with /m/.
- Learn that *M* and *m* stand for /m/.

Materials

- Alphafriend Cards
- Instructional Routine: Alphafriends
- Practice Page K.56

Phonemic Awareness Warm-up

Display the Alphafriend Card for the letter *m*. Read or sing the "Mimi Mouse" lyrics below and have students echo you line-for-line. Have them listen for the words that start with the sound /m/ and raise their hands when they hear each one.

Mimi Mouse

(tune: This Old Man)

Mimi Mouse. Mimi Mouse.

Minds her manners in the house.

When she sips her milk, she never makes a mess.

Mud pies never stain her dress.

Teach/Model

- Use Instructional Routine: Alphafriends to introduce Mimi Mouse. Display the Mimi Mouse Alphafriend Card with the letter. **Say:** *Say* Mimi Mouse *with me:* Mimi Mouse. *Mimi's letter is the consonant* m. *The letter* m *stands for the /m/ sound, the sound you hear at the beginning of* Mimi *and* mouse.

- Display the words *milk, man, met,* and *mop.* **Say:** *You can hear /m/ at the beginning of these words:* milk, man, met, mop.

- As you pronounce each word, emphasize the /m/ sound as you point to the letter *m* in the word.

Guided Practice

IDENTIFY *m* Display Letter Card *m* and review the sound.

- Say the word *mouse.* Have students say the word *mouse,* say the beginning sound, and point to the Letter Card showing the letter that makes that sound.

- Repeat with the words *milk, met, man, map, mix,* and *mule.*

HANDWRITING: WRITING *M, m* Remind students that they have learned to write the letters that stand for the /m/ sound: capital *M* and lowercase *m.* Write each letter as you recite the handwriting rhymes. Chant each rhyme as students "write" the letter in the air.

Handwriting Rhyme: M

Make a line going down. Then two lines that meet. One more, you're done. It's very neat.

Handwriting Rhyme: m

Little *m* is short. Start in the middle. Make two little hills. It's not a riddle.

Apply

- Distribute Practice Page K.56.

- Have students name the letter. Have them trace and write *Mm* in the spaces provided.

- Guide students to name each picture (chair, mask, monkey, mat, teapot, marble). Have them write *Mm* next to the pictures whose names start with the /m/ sound.

- Ask students to make up and say sentences that have several words starting with the /m/ sound. For example: *The man made a motorcycle.*

Fun with Letters Optional activities for engaging, hands-on practice are provided in the Resources section.

English Language Support

Demonstrate how to make the /m/ sound. Imitate a mooing cow and have students repeat. Some students may have difficulty distinguishing between /m/ and /n/. Have students make the /m/ sound while they trace an imaginary *m* in the air.

Formative Assessment and Corrective Feedback

IF a student makes an error, THEN follow this model:

Correct the error.

Guide the student to perform the task correctly by modeling.

Check for understanding by having the student repeat the task.

Reinforce: Make a note to review the skill during the student's next session.

Phonics: Letter/Sound *Ss*

Objectives

- Isolate and pronounce the first sound in words that begin with /s/.
- Learn that *S* and *s* stand for /s/.

Materials

- Alphafriend Cards
- Instructional Routine: Alphafriends
- Practice Page K.57

Phonemic Awareness Warm-up

Display the Alphafriend Card for the letter *s*. Read or sing the "Sammy Seal" lyrics below and have students echo you line-for-line. Have them listen for the words that start with the sound /s/ and raise their hands when they hear each one.

Sammy Seal

(tune: Yankee Doodle)

Sammy Seal will sail the sea when summer is the season.

Sammy Seal will sail the sea and never need a reason.

Sammy Seal will sail the sea in very sunny weather.

Sammy Seal salutes a seagull as they sail together!

Teach/Model

- Use Instructional Routine: Alphafriends to introduce Sammy Seal. Display the Sammy Seal Alphafriend Card with the letter. **Say:** *Say* Sammy Seal *with me:* Sammy Seal. *Sammy's letter is the consonant* s. *The letter* s *stands for the /s/ sound, the sound you hear at the beginning of* Sammy *and* seal.

- Display the words *Sammy, seal, sea, sun,* and *sail.* **Say:** *You can hear /s/ at the beginning of these words:* sea, sun, sail.

- As you pronounce each word, emphasize the /s/ sound as you point to the letter *s* in the word.

Guided Practice

COMPARE AND REVIEW *m, s* Display Letter Cards *m* and *s* and review the sounds.

- Say the word *sun.* Have students say the word *sun,* say the beginning sound, and point to the Letter Card showing the letter that makes that sound.

- Repeat with the words *sandwich, seal, salt, map, mix,* and *mule.*

HANDWRITING: WRITING *S, s* Remind students that they have learned to write the letters that stand for the /s/ sound: capital *S* and lowercase *s*. Write each letter as you recite the handwriting rhymes. Chant each rhyme as students "write" the letter in the air.

Handwriting Rhyme: S

S looks like a snake, curve left then right. From top to bottom, makes it right.

Handwriting Rhyme: s

Small *s* looks like a snake, too. Curve left then right, that's all you do.

Apply

- Distribute Practice Page K.57.

- Have students name the letter. Have them trace and write *Ss* in the spaces provided.

- Guide students to name each picture (sandwich, tiger, seahorse, sneakers, apple, sock). Have them write *Ss* next to the pictures whose names start with the /s/ sound.

- Ask students to make up and say sentences that have several words starting with the /s/ sound. For example: *Sarah says six sentences.*

> **Fun with Letters** Optional activities for engaging, hands-on practice are provided in the Resources section

Formative Assessment and Corrective Feedback

IF a student makes an error, THEN follow this model:

Correct the error.

Guide the student to perform the task correctly by modeling.

Check for understanding by having the student repeat the task.

Reinforce: Make a note to review the skill during the student's next session.

English Language Support

Demonstrate how to make the /s/ sound. Imitate a hissing cat or whistling wind and have students repeat. Some students may have difficulty distinguishing between /s/ and /z/. Have students make the /s/ sound while they trace an imaginary *s* in the air.

Phonics: Letter/Sound *Aa* (Short *a*)

Objectives

- Isolate and pronounce the sound in words that have /ă/.
- Learn that *A* and *a* stand for /ă/.

Materials

- Alphafriend Cards
- Instructional Routine: Alphafriends
- Practice Page K.58

Phonemic Awareness Warm-up

Display the Alphafriend Card for the letter *a*. Read or sing the "Andy Apple" lyrics below and have students echo you line-for-line. Have them listen for the sound /ă/ at the beginning or in the middle of words and raise their hands when they hear each one.

Andy Apple

(tune: Skip to My Lou)

Andy Apple is an acrobat.

Andy can jump way over his mat.

Ant can catch him, just like that!

Andy Apple is an acrobat.

Teach/Model

- Use Instructional Routine: Alphafriends to introduce Andy Apple. Display the Andy Apple Alphafriend Card with the letter. **Say:** *Say* Andy Apple *with me:* Andy Apple. *Andy's letter is the vowel* a. *One sound the letter* a *stands for is the* /ă/ *sound, the sound you hear at the beginning of* Andy *and* Apple.

- Display the words *am, and,* and *apple*. **Say:** *You can hear* /ă/ *at the beginning of these words:* am, and, apple.

- As you pronounce each word, emphasize the /ă/ sound as you point to the letter *a* in the word.

Guided Practice

COMPARE AND REVIEW *a, m, s* Display Letter Cards *a, m,* and *s* and review the sounds.

- Say the word *ant*. Have students say the word *ant*, say the beginning sound, and point to the Letter Card showing the letter that makes that sound.

- Repeat with the words *salt, map, mix,* and *ax*.

HANDWRITING: WRITING *A, a* Remind students that they have learned to write the letters that stand for the /ă/ sound: capital *A* and lowercase *a*. Write each letter as you recite the handwriting rhymes. Chant each rhyme as students "write" the letter in the air.

Handwriting Rhyme: A

Start at the top, slant down just a little. Repeat from the top, and connect in the middle.

Handwriting Rhyme: a

Start in the middle, make a circle nice and round. Go back up a little, make a straight line down.

Apply

- Distribute Practice Page K.58.

- Have students name the letter. Have them trace and write *Aa* in the spaces provided.

- Guide students to name each picture (mask, ax, book, astronaut, car, alligator). Have them write *Aa* next to the pictures whose names start with the /ă/ sound.

- Ask students to make up and say sentences that have several words starting with the /ă/ sound. For example: *An ant ran after an alligator.*

Fun with Letters Optional activities for engaging, hands-on practice are provided in the Resources section.

English Language Support

Linguistic Transfer Point out to Spanish speakers that the /ă/ sound at the beginning of *apple* is a little different from the sound at the beginning of the word agua in Spanish. Have ELs listen carefully as you pronounce words with the /ă/ sound: *apple, at, ad, mat, cat, man, can, pan, pat*. Have students repeat each word, and if they substitute /ŏ/ for /ă/, encourage them to "smile" a little to make the /ă/ sound. Use each word in a brief sentence to reinforce meaning.

Formative Assessment and Corrective Feedback

IF a student makes an error, THEN follow this model:

Correct the error.

Guide the student to perform the task correctly by modeling.

Check for understanding by having the student repeat the task.

Reinforce: Make a note to review the skill during the student's next session.

Phonics: Letter/Sound *Tt*

Objectives

- Isolate and pronounce the first sound in words that begin with /t/.
- Learn that *T* and *t* stand for /t/.

Materials

- Alphafriend Cards
- Instructional Routine: Alphafriends
- Practice Page K.59

Phonemic Awareness Warm-up

Display the Alphafriend Card for the letter *t*. Read or sing the "Tiggy Tiger" lyrics below and have students echo you line-for-line. Have them listen for the words that start with the sound /t/ and raise their hands when they hear each one.

Tiggy Tiger

(tune: Twinkle, Twinkle Little Star)

Tiggy Tiger can tickle his toes.

Tiggy Tiger can tap his nose.

Tiggy Tiger can turn around.

Tiggy Tiger can touch the ground.

Tiggy Tiger can tie his shoes.

Tiggy Tiger can count by twos.

Teach/Model

- Use Instructional Routine: Alphafriends to introduce Tiggy Tiger. Display the Tiggy Tiger Alphafriend Card with the letter. **Say:** *Say* Tiggy Tiger *with me:* Tiggy Tiger. *Tiggy's letter is the consonant* t. *The letter* t *stands for the /t/ sound, the sound you hear at the beginning of* Tiggy *and* Tiger.
- Display the words *toes, tap, ten,* and *top.* **Say:** *You can hear /t/ at the beginning of these words:* toes, tap, ten, top. As you pronounce each word, emphasize the /t/ sound as you point to the letter *t* in the word.

Guided Practice

COMPARE AND REVIEW *t, s, a* Display Letter Cards *t, s, a* and review their sounds.

- Say the word *ten.* Have students say the word *ten,* say the beginning sound, and point to the Letter Card showing the letter that makes that sound.
- Repeat with the words *tan, ant, seal, ax, salt, tip,* and *apple.*

HANDWRITING: WRITING *T, t* Remind students that they have learned to write the letters that stand for the /t/ sound: capital *T* and lowercase *t*. Write each letter as you recite the handwriting rhymes. Chant each rhyme as students "write" the letter in the air.

Handwriting Rhyme: T

A long line down begins the *T.* Draw a straight line across and a *T* it will be.

Handwriting Rhyme: t

Not as tall, straight down for small *t.* Cross near the middle, a *t* you'll see!

Apply

- Distribute Practice Page K.59.

- Have students name the letter. Have them trace and write *Tt* in the spaces provided.

- Guide students to name each picture (table, window, toaster, teapot, mitten, telephone). Have them write *Tt* next to the pictures whose names start with the /t/ sound.

- Ask students to make up and say sentences that have several words starting with the /t/ sound. For example: *Tiny Tiger has a tall tent.*

> **Fun with Letters** Optional activities for engaging, hands-on practice are provided in the Resources section.

English Language Support

Point out to Spanish speakers that the sound /t/ is the same in Spanish as in English. Encourage students to share words they know in both Spanish and English with the /t/ sound.

Formative Assessment and Corrective Feedback

IF a student makes an error, THEN follow this model:

Correct the error.

Guide the student to perform the task correctly by modeling.

Check for understanding by having the student repeat the task.

Reinforce: Make a note to review the skill during the student's next session.

Objectives

- Isolate and pronounce the first sound in words that begin with /k/.
- Learn that *C* and *c* stand for /k/.

Materials

- Alphafriend Cards
- Instructional Routine: Alphafriends
- Practice Page K.60

Phonics: Letter/Sound *Cc*

Phonemic Awareness Warm-up

Display the Alphafriend Card for the letter *c*. Read or sing the "Callie Cat" lyrics below and have students echo you line-for-line. Have them listen for the words that start with the sound /k/ and raise their hands when they hear each one.

Callie Cat

(tune: Yankee Doodle)

Callie Cat can bake a cake and cover it with candy.

Callie Cat can bake some cornbread. Callie is so handy.

Callie bakes some cupcakes, too. Her cupcakes are so cakey.

Callie bakes some cookies, too. Her cookies are so flakey.

Teach/Model

- Use Instructional Routine: Alphafriends to introduce Callie Cat. Display the Callie Cat Alphafriend Card with the letter. **Say:** *Say* Callie Cat *with me:* Callie Cat. *Callie's letter is the consonant* c. *The letter* c *stands for the /k/ sound, the sound you hear at the beginning of* Callie *and* Cat.
- Display the words *can, cap, cut,* and *cot.* **Say:** *You can hear /k/ at the beginning of these words:* can, cap, cut, cot. *As you pronounce each word, emphasize the /k/ sound as you point to the letter* c *in the word.*

Guided Practice

COMPARE AND REVIEW *c, t, a* Display Letter Cards *c, t,* and *a* and review their sounds.

- Say the word *cow.* Have students say the word *cow,* say the beginning sound, and point to the Letter Card showing the letter that makes that sound.
- Repeat with the words *cut, top, ax, car, ant,* and *ten.*

HANDWRITING: WRITING *C, c* Remind students that they have learned to write the letters that stand for the /k/ sound: capital *C* and lowercase *c.* Write each letter as you recite the handwriting rhymes. Chant each rhyme as students "write" the letter in the air.

Handwriting Rhyme: C

Start near the top line. Curve around. Make a half circle, nice and round.

Handwriting Rhyme: c

Start near the midline. Curve around. Leave the circle open, but nice and round.

Apply

- Distribute Practice Page K.60.

- Have students name the letter. Have them trace and write *Cc* in the spaces provided.

- Guide students to name each picture (camera, book, cow, carrot, gate, cake). Have them write *Cc* next to the pictures whose names start with the /k/ sound.

- Ask students to make up and say sentences that have several words starting with the /k/ sound. For example: *The cute cat had a carrot in a cup.*

> **Fun with Letters** Optional activities for engaging, hands-on practice are provided in the Resources section.

English Language Support

Point out to Spanish speakers that the sound /k/ is the same in Spanish as in English. Encourage students to share words they know in both Spanish and English with the /k/ sound.

Formative Assessment and Corrective Feedback

IF a student makes an error, THEN follow this model:

Correct the error.

Guide the student to perform the task correctly by modeling.

Check for understanding by having the student repeat the task.

Reinforce: Make a note to review the skill during the student's next session.

Phonics: Letter/Sound *Pp*

Objectives

- Isolate and pronounce the first sound in words that begin with /p/.
- Learn that *P* and *p* stand for /p/.

Materials

- Alphafriend Cards
- Instructional Routine: Alphafriends
- Practice Page K.61

Phonemic Awareness Warm-up

Display the Alphafriend Card for the letter *p*. Read or sing the "Pippa Pig" lyrics below and have students echo it line-for-line. Have them listen for the words that start with the sound /p/ and raise their hands when they hear each one. (Audio of Alphafriends songs is available on ThinkCentral.com.)

Pippa Pig

(tune: Hush! Little Baby)

Pippa had a party for Porcupine.

Panda and Penguin came to dine.

Pippa served pizza and pasta, too.

Pieces of peaches and a pickle stew.

Teach/Model

- Use Instructional Routine: Alphafriends to introduce Pippa Pig. Display the Pippa Pig Alphafriend Card with the letter. **Say:** *Say* Pippa Pig *with me:* Pippa Pig. *Pippa's letter is the consonant* p. *The letter* p *stands for the /p/ sound, the sound you hear at the beginning of* Pippa *and* Pig.
- Display the words *Pam, pin, pat, pan.* **Say:** *You can hear /p/ at the beginning of these words:* Pam, pin, pat, pan. As you pronounce each word, emphasize the /p/ sound as you point to the letter *p* in the word.

Guided Practice

COMPARE AND REVIEW *p, t, c* Display Letter Cards *p, t, c* and review their sounds.

- Say the word *pin.* Have students say the word *pin,* say the beginning sound, and point to the Letter Card showing the letter that makes that sound.
- Repeat with the words *tag, pass, can, tan, cow,* and *pen.*

HANDWRITING: WRITING *P, p* Remind students that they have learned to write the letters that stand for the /p/ sound: capital *P* and lowercase *p.* Write each letter as you recite the handwriting rhymes. Chant each rhyme as students "write" the letter in the air.

Handwriting Rhyme: P

Start at the top and make a long line down. Go back to the top and circle half-way around.

Handwriting Rhyme: p

Start in the middle and make a long line down. Go back to the middle and circle half-way around.

Apply

- Distribute Practice Page K.61.

- Have students name the letter. Have them trace and write *Pp* in the spaces provided.

- Guide students to name each picture (pail, wagon, pillow, paintbrush, pie, cow). Have them write *Pp* next to the pictures whose names start with the /p/ sound.

- Ask students to make up and say sentences that have several words starting with the /p/ sound. For example: *Penny picked a puffy peach.*

> **Fun with Letters** Optional activities for engaging, hands-on practice are provided in the Resources section.

English Language Support

Point out to Spanish speakers that the sound /p/ is the same in Spanish as in English. Encourage students to share words they know in both Spanish and English with the /p/ sound.

Formative Assessment and Corrective Feedback

IF a student makes an error, THEN follow this model:

Correct the error.

Guide the student to perform the task correctly by modeling.

Check for understanding by having the student repeat the task.

Reinforce: Make a note to review the skill during the student's next session.

Cumulative Review: Letter/Sounds *m, s, a, t, c,* and *p*

Objectives

- Match letter *m* to /m/.
- Match letter *s* to /s/.
- Match letter *a* to /ă/.
- Match letter *t* to /t/.
- Match letter *c* to /k/.
- Match letter *p* to /p/.

Materials

- Practice Page K.62

Teach/Model

- Remind students that they have learned the sound for *m*. **Say:** *Remember that* m *stands for the /m/ sound.*
- **Say:** *The word* man *starts with* m. *The word* milk *starts with* m.
- Ask students to suggest words they know that start with the sound /m/.
- Remind students that they have learned the sound for *s*. **Say:** *Remember that the letter* s *stands for the /s/ sound.*
- **Say:** *The word* sun *starts with* s. *The word* sat *starts with* s.
- Ask students to suggest words they know that start with the sound /s/.
- Remind students that they have learned the sound for *a*. **Say:** *Remember that the letter* a *can stand for the /ă/ sound.*
- **Say:** *The word* am *starts with* a. *The word* at *starts with* a.
- Ask students to suggest words they know that start with the sound /ă/.
- Remind students that they have learned the sound for *t*. **Say:** *Remember that the letter* t *stands for the /t/ sound.*
- **Say:** *The word* tap *starts with* t. *The word* tall *starts with* t.
- Ask students to suggest words they know that start with the sound /t/.
- Remind students that they have learned the sound for *c*. **Say:** *Remember that the letter* c *can stand for the /k/ sound.*
- **Say:** *The word* cat *starts with* c. *The word* cup *starts with* c.
- Ask students to suggest words they know that start with the sound /k/.
- Remind students that they have learned the sound for *p*. **Say:** *Remember that the letter* p *stands for the /p/ sound.*
- **Say:** *The word* pat *starts with* p. *The word* pick *starts with* p.
- Ask students to suggest words they know that start with the sound /p/.

Guided Practice

- Display the words *man, sun, am, tap, cat,* and *pat.*
- Point to each word and say it. Point to the first letter of the word. **Say:** *What is the letter? What sound does it make?* Guide students to identify the letters and their sounds.

Apply

- Distribute Practice Page K.62.

- Have students name each letter. Have them write *Mm, Ss, Aa, Tt, Cc,* and *Pp* in the spaces provided.

- Ask students to name each picture (mop, sun, ant, cat, table, pencil).

- Next to each picture, have them write the letter for the sound they hear at the beginning of the picture's name.

- After students have finished working with the Practice Page, guide them to track their progress on their My Progress line graphs.

> **Fun with Letters** Optional activities for engaging, hands-on practice are provided in the Resources section.

Formative Assessment and Corrective Feedback

IF a student makes an error, THEN follow this model:

Correct the error.

Guide the student to perform the task correctly by modeling.

Check for understanding by having the student repeat the task.

Reinforce: Make a note to review the word during the student's next session.

High-Frequency Words: *I*

Objective

- Recognize and read high-frequency words.

Materials

- High-Frequency Word Cards

Formative Assessment and Corrective Feedback

IF a student makes an error, THEN follow this model:

Correct the error.

Guide the student to say the word correctly.

Check for understanding by having the student reread the word.

Reinforce: Make a note to review the word during the student's next session.

Teach/Model

- Display the High-Frequency Word Card for *I* and say the word. Tell students that this is a useful word to know, since they will see this word often. Tell students that reading will be easier if they recognize the word.

- Then spell the word aloud as you point to the letter. Explain that *I* is both a word and a letter. Say the word again.

- Use the word in a simple sentence that will provide context. For example: *I am a teacher.*

Guided Practice

Do the following for the high-frequency word:

- Display the High-Frequency Word Card for *I*.

- Ask students to spell the word with you: *I*.

- Have a student take the card and use the word in a sentence. Give clues if needed to construct a sentence.

- Have the student give the card to someone and have that student create a sentence with the word. Continue until many students have used the word in a sentence.

Apply

- Display the High-Frequency Word Card *I*. Have students read the word aloud.

- Have students write the word. Tell them to compare their writing with the word on the card and make corrections if necessary.

- Have students read the word aloud and use it in a sentence.

High-Frequency Words: *like*

Teach/Model

- Display the High-Frequency Word Card for *like* and say the word. Tell students that this is a useful word to know, since they will see this word often. Tell students that reading will be easier if they recognize the word.
- Then spell the word aloud as you point to each letter. Say the word again.
- Use the word in a simple sentence that will provide context. For example: *I like this game.*

Guided Practice

Do the following for the high-frequency word:

- Display the High-Frequency Word Card. Read the word and have students repeat it.
- Note the familiar sound/spelling patterns that are shown on the back of the card. Note as well any unfamiliar and unexpected sound/spellings.
- Blend the word with students.
- Spell the word aloud, pointing to each letter.
- Have students then spell the word aloud as you point to each letter.
- Have students read the word again.

Apply

- Display the High-Frequency Word Cards *I* and *like* in random order. Have students read the words aloud.
- Have students write each word. Tell them to compare their writing with the word on the card and make corrections if necessary.
- Have students read each word aloud and use it in a sentence.

Objective

- Recognize and read high-frequency words.

Materials

- High-Frequency Word Cards

Formative Assessment and Corrective Feedback

IF a student makes an error, THEN follow this model:

Correct the error.

Guide the student to say the word correctly.

Check for understanding by having the student reread the word from among other randomly displayed high-frequency words.

Reinforce: Make a note to review the word during the student's next session.

Objective

- Recognize and read high-frequency words.

Materials

- High-Frequency Word Cards

Formative Assessment and Corrective Feedback

IF a student makes an error, THEN follow this model:

Correct the error.

Guide the student to say the word correctly.

Check for understanding by having the student reread the word from among other randomly displayed high-frequency words.

Reinforce: Make a note to review the word during the student's next session.

High-Frequency Words: *the*

Teach/Model

- Display the High-Frequency Word Card for *the* and say the word. Tell students that this is a useful word to know, since they will see this word often. Tell students that reading will be easier if they recognize the word.
- Then spell the word aloud as you point to each letter. Say the word again.
- Use the word in a simple sentence that will provide context. For example: *The book is heavy.*

Guided Practice

Do the following for the high-frequency word:

- Display the High-Frequency Word Card. Read the word and have students repeat it.
- Note the familiar sound/spelling patterns that are shown on the back of the card. Note as well any unfamiliar and unexpected sound/spellings.
- Blend the word with students.
- Spell the word aloud, pointing to each letter.
- Have students then spell the word aloud as you point to each letter.
- Have students read the word again.

Apply

- Display the High-Frequency Word Cards *the, like,* and *I* in random order. Have students read the words aloud.
- Have students write each word. Tell them to compare their writing with the word on the card and make corrections if necessary.
- Have students read each word aloud and use it in a sentence.

High-Frequency Words: *and*

Teach/Model

- Display the High-Frequency Word Card for *and*. Say the word. Tell students that this is a useful word to know, since they will see this word often. Tell students that reading will be easier if they recognize the word.
- Then spell the word aloud as you point to each letter. Say the word again.
- Use the word in a simple sentence that will provide context. For example: *I like cats and dogs.*

Guided Practice

Do the following for the high-frequency word:

- Display the High-Frequency Word Card. Read the word and have students repeat it.
- Note the familiar sound/spelling patterns that are shown on the back of the card. Note as well any unfamiliar and unexpected sound/spellings.
- Blend the word with students.
- Spell the word aloud, pointing to each letter.
- Have students then spell the word aloud as you point to each letter.
- Have students read the word again.

Apply

- Display the High-Frequency Word Cards *and, the, like,* and *I* in random order. Have students read the words aloud.
- Have students write each word. Tell them to compare their writing with the word on the card and make corrections if necessary.
- Have students read each word aloud and use it in a sentence.

Objective
- Recognize and read high-frequency words.

Materials
- High-Frequency Word Cards

Formative Assessment and Corrective Feedback

IF a student makes an error, THEN follow this model:

Correct the error.

Guide the student to say the word correctly.

Check for understanding by having the student reread the word from among other randomly displayed high-frequency words.

Reinforce: Make a note to review the word during the student's next session.

Objectives

- Read common high-frequency words by sight.

Materials

- High-Frequency Word Cards
- Instructional Routine: High-Frequency Words
- Practice Page K.67

Teach/Model

- Display the high-frequency words: *I, like, the, and.* Remind students that they know these words.
- Use the High-Frequency Word Cards and Instructional Routine: High-Frequency Words to review these words.
- Display this sentence: *I like the dog and the cat.*
- Read the sentence. Then point to the word *I* in the sentence as you read it aloud. Have students say the word.
- Repeat the above step for the words *like, the, and.*
- Read the sentence aloud again, pointing to each high-frequency word as you read it.

Guided Practice

- Display this sentence: *I like the sun and the sky.*
- Read the sentence aloud. Point to each high-frequency word as you read it.
- Point to the word *I* in the sentence. Guide students to say the word as you point to it.
- Repeat with the other high-frequency words in the sentence.
- Display this sentence: *I like the boy and the girl.*
- Read the sentence aloud. Point to each high-frequency word as you read it.
- Point to the word *I* in the sentence. Guide students to say the word as you point to it.
- Repeat with the other high-frequency words in the sentence.

- Distribute Practice Page K.67.
- Have students read the high-frequency words in the box.
- Ask students to read the sentences, including naming the rebus pictures in the sentences.
- Have students choose a high-frequency word from the box to complete each sentence.
- Have students read each completed sentence aloud.
- Ask students to choose a sentence and tell a story about it, using the high-frequency words.
- After students have finished working with the Practice Page, guide them to track their progress on their My Progress line graphs.

Formative Assessment and Corrective Feedback

IF a student makes an error, THEN follow this model:

Correct the error.

Guide the student to perform the task correctly by modeling.

Check for understanding by having the student repeat the task.

Reinforce: Make a note to review the word during the student's next session.

High-Frequency Words: *see*

Objective

- Recognize and read high-frequency words.

Materials

- High-Frequency Word Cards

Formative Assessment and Corrective Feedback

IF a student makes an error, THEN follow this model:

Correct the error.

Guide the student to say the word correctly.

Check for understanding by having the student reread the word from among other randomly displayed high-frequency words.

Reinforce: Make a note to review the word during the student's next session.

Teach/Model

- Display the High-Frequency Word Card for *see* and say the word. Tell students that this is a useful word to know, since they will see this word often. Tell students that reading will be easier if they recognize the word.

- Then spell the word aloud as you point to each letter. Say the word again.

- Use the word in a simple sentence that will provide context. For example: *I see you in the window.*

Guided Practice

Do the following for the high-frequency word:

- Display the High-Frequency Word Card. Read the word and have students repeat it.

- Note the familiar sound/spelling patterns that are shown on the back of the card. Note as well any unfamiliar and unexpected sound/spellings.

- Blend the word with students.

- Spell the word aloud, pointing to each letter.

- Have students then spell the word aloud as you point to each letter.

- Have students read the word again.

Apply

- Display the High-Frequency Word Cards *see, and, the, like,* and *I* in random order. Have students read the words aloud.

- Have students write each word. Tell them to compare their writing with the word on the card and make corrections if necessary.

- Have students read each word aloud and use it in a sentence.

High-Frequency Words: *we*

Teach/Model

- Display the High-Frequency Word Card for *we* and say the word. Tell students that this is a useful word to know, since they will see this word often. Tell students that reading will be easier if they recognize the word.

- Then spell the word aloud as you point to each letter. Say the word again.

- Use the word in a simple sentence that will provide context. For example: *We can go to the park together.*

Guided Practice

Do the following for the high-frequency word:

- Display the High-Frequency Word Card. Read the word and have students repeat it.

- Note the familiar sound/spelling patterns that are shown on the back of the card. Note as well any unfamiliar and unexpected sound/spellings.

- Blend the word with students.

- Spell the word aloud, pointing to each letter.

- Have students then spell the word aloud as you point to each letter.

- Have students read the word again.

Apply

- Display the High-Frequency Word Cards *we, see, and, the, like,* and *I* in random order. Have students read the words aloud.

- Have students write each word. Tell them to compare their writing with the word on the card and make corrections if necessary.

- Have students read each word aloud and use it in a sentence.

Objective

- Recognize and read high-frequency words.

Materials

- High-Frequency Word Cards

Formative Assessment and Corrective Feedback

IF a student makes an error, THEN follow this model:

Correct the error.

Guide the student to say the word correctly.

Check for understanding by having the student reread the word from among other randomly displayed high-frequency words.

Reinforce: Make a note to review the word during the student's next session.

High-Frequency Words: *a*

Objective

- Recognize and read high-frequency words.

Materials

- High-Frequency Word Cards

Formative Assessment and Corrective Feedback

IF a student makes an error, THEN follow this model:

Correct the error.

Guide the student to say the word correctly.

Check for understanding by having the student reread the word from among other randomly displayed high-frequency words.

Reinforce: Make a note to review the word during the student's next session.

Teach/Model

- Display the High-Frequency Word Card for *a* and say the word. Tell students that this is a useful word to know, since they will see this word often. Tell students that reading will be easier if they recognize the word.
- Then spell the word aloud as you point to the letter. Explain that *a* is both a word and a letter. Say the word again.
- Use the word in a simple sentence that will provide context. For example: *We have a cat.*

Guided Practice

Do the following for the high-frequency word:

- Display the High-Frequency Word Card for *a*.
- Ask students to spell the word with you: *a*.
- Have a student take the card and use the word in a sentence. Give clues if needed to construct a sentence.
- Have the student give the card to someone and have that student create a sentence with the word. Continue until many students have used the word in a sentence.

Apply

- Display the High-Frequency Word Cards *a, we, see, and, the, like,* and *I* in random order. Have students read the words aloud.
- Have students write each word. Tell them to compare their writing with the word on the card and make corrections if necessary.
- Have students read each word aloud and use it in a sentence.

High-Frequency Words: *to*

Teach/Model

- Display the High-Frequency Word Card for *to* and say the word. Tell students that this is a useful word to know, since they will see this word often. Tell students that reading will be easier if they recognize the word.
- Then spell the word aloud as you point to each letter. Say the word again.
- Use the word in a simple sentence that will provide context. For example: *We went to the store.*

Guided Practice

Do the following for the high-frequency word:

- Display the High-Frequency Word Card. Read the word and have students repeat it.
- Note the familiar sound/spelling patterns that are shown on the back of the card. Note as well any unfamiliar and unexpected sound/spellings.
- Blend the word with students.
- Spell the word aloud, pointing to each letter.
- Have students then spell the word aloud as you point to each letter.
- Have students read the word again.

Apply

- Display the High-Frequency Word Cards *to, a, we, see, and, the, like,* and *I* in random order. Have students read the words aloud.
- Have students write each word. Tell them to compare their writing with the word on the card and make corrections if necessary.
- Have students read each word aloud and use it in a sentence.

Objective

- Recognize and read high-frequency words.

Materials

- High-Frequency Word Cards

Formative Assessment and Corrective Feedback

IF a student makes an error, THEN follow this model:

Correct the error.

Guide the student to say the word correctly.

Check for understanding by having the student reread the word from among other randomly displayed high-frequency words.

Reinforce: Make a note to review the word during the student's next session.

Cumulative Review: High-Frequency Words *see, we, a, to*

Objectives

- Read common high-frequency words by sight.

Materials

- High-Frequency Word Cards
- Instructional Routine: High-Frequency Words
- Practice Page K.72

Teach/Model

- Display the high-frequency words: *see, we, a, to*. Remind students that they know these words.
- Use the High-Frequency Word Cards and Instructional Routine: High-Frequency Words to review these words.
- Display these sentences: *We see a book. We like to read.*
- Read the first sentence. Then point to the word *We* as you read it aloud. Have students say the word.
- Repeat with the words *see* and *a*.
- Read the sentence aloud again, pointing to each high-frequency word as you read it.
- Read the second sentence. Then point to the word *We* as you read it aloud. Have students say the word.
- Repeat with the word *to*.
- Read the sentence aloud again, pointing to each high-frequency word as you read it.

Guided Practice

- Display this sentence: *We see a park.*
- Read the sentence aloud. Point to each high-frequency word as you read it.
- Point to the word *We* in the sentence. Guide students to say the word as you point to it.
- Repeat with the words *see* and *a*.
- Display this sentence: *We like to play.*
- Read the sentence aloud. Point to each high-frequency word as you read it.
- Point to the word *We* in the sentence. Guide students to say the word as you point to it.
- Repeat with the word *to*.

- Distribute Practice Page K.72.

- Have students read the high-frequency words in the box.

- Ask students to read the sentences, including naming the rebus pictures in the sentences.

- Have students choose a high-frequency word from the box to complete each sentence. Guide students to capitalize *we* at the beginning of the third sentence.

- Have students read the completed sentences aloud.

- Ask students to tell a story about the completed page, using the high-frequency words.

- After students have finished working with the Practice Page, guide them to track their progress on their My Progress line graphs.

Formative Assessment and Corrective Feedback

IF a student makes an error, THEN follow this model:

Correct the error.

Guide the student to perform the task correctly by modeling.

Check for understanding by having the student repeat the task.

Reinforce: Make a note to review the word during the student's next session.

High-Frequency Words: *come, me*

Objective

- Recognize and read high-frequency words.

Materials

- High-Frequency Word Cards

Formative Assessment and Corrective Feedback

IF a student makes an error, THEN follow this model:

Correct the error.

Guide the student to say the word correctly.

Check for understanding by having the student reread the word from among other randomly displayed high-frequency words.

Reinforce: Make a note to review the word during the student's next session.

Teach/Model

- Display the high-frequency word *come*. Tell students that this is a useful word to know, since they will see this word often. Tell students that reading will be easier if they recognize the word.
- Display the High-Frequency Word Card for *come* and say the word. Then spell the word aloud as you point to each letter. Say the word again.
- Use the word in a simple sentence that will provide context. For example: *I can come to your party*.
- Repeat the steps above for the high-frequency word *me*.

Guided Practice

Do the following for each high-frequency word:

- Display the High-Frequency Word Card. Read the word and have students repeat it.
- Note the familiar sound/spelling patterns that are shown on the back of the card. Note as well any unfamiliar and unexpected sound/spellings.
- Blend the word with students.
- Spell the word aloud, pointing to each letter.
- Have students then spell the word aloud as you point to each letter.
- Have students read the word again.

Apply

- Display the High-Frequency Word Cards *come, me, to, a, we,* and *see* in random order. Have students read the words aloud.
- Have students write each word. Tell them to compare their writing with the word on the card and make corrections if necessary.
- Have students read each word aloud and use it in a sentence.

Phonics: Words with Short *a*

Phonemic Awareness Warm-up

- Display the word *sat*. **Say:** *I'm going to say a word. Listen for the sound you hear in the middle. I'll do the first one. Listen:* sat. *What sound do you hear in the middle of* sat? /ă/
- Display the words *fat, cat, Sam, tap,* and *pat*. **Say:** *Now let's do it together. Listen:* fat. *What sound do you hear in the middle of* fat? /ă/ *Now you do it.* Cat? (/ă/).
- Repeat with the words *Sam, tap* and *pat*.

Teach/Model

SOUND/SPELLING Use Instructional Routine: Sound/Spelling Cards to introduce the Sound/Spelling Card for Andy Apple. Name the picture and say the sound. Have students repeat after you. **Say:** *Listen:* Andy, /ă /. *Now you say it.*

- Repeat with *apple*.
- Say the sound and give the spelling. **Say:** Andy Apple *begins with the /ă/ sound. The letter* a *stands for the /ă/ sound at the beginning or in the middle of a word.*

BLENDING Use Letter Cards and Instructional Routine: Sound-by-Sound Blending to model blending the words *at* and *sat*.

Guided Practice

BLENDING Display the words *cat, Pam, pat, am*. Work with students to blend the words, using Instructional Routine: Sound-by-Sound Blending.

PHONICS/DECODING STRATEGY Review the Phonics/Decoding Strategy. Display the sentences below. Call on students to use the strategy to blend one or more words and to read the sentences.

I am Pam.

I pat the cat.

BUILDING AND WRITING WORDS Tell students to follow your directions and build new words with their Letter Cards. Have students start by building the word *sat*.

- **Say**: *Change* s *to* p. *What's the new word?* (pat)
- **Say**: *Change* p *to* c. *What's the new word?* (cat)
- **Say**: *Change* t *to* p. *What's the new word?* (cap)
- **Say**: *Change* c *to* m. *What's the new word?* (map)
- Then have students write each word and read it aloud.

Objectives

- Isolate and pronounce the /ă/ sound in words with short *a*.
- Blend and read words with short *a*.
- Read decodable text that includes words with short *a*.
- Read common high-frequency words by sight.
- Understand that words are separated by spaces in print.

Materials

- Letter Cards
- Sound/Spelling Cards
- Instructional Routine: Sound/Spelling Cards
- Instructional Routine: Sound-by-Sound Blending
- Phonics/Decoding Strategy
- Practice Page K.73B

English Language Support

Linguistic Transfer English learners may have trouble with the short *a* sound. Some languages, such as Khmer, don't have the short *a* sound. Others, such as Russian, might pronounce short *a* like short *e*.

For English learners who have trouble with short *a*, provide extra support and practice with the sound. Guide students in pronouncing the sound by itself. Then guide them in pronouncing one-syllable words with initial short *a*, such as *am* and *ant*, emphasizing the initial short *a* sound in each. Then practice one-syllable words with medial short *a*, such as *cat*, again emphasizing the short *a* sound.

Formative Assessment and Corrective Feedback

IF a student makes an error, THEN follow this model:

Correct the error.

Guide the student to perform the task correctly by modeling.

Check for understanding by having the student repeat the task.

Reinforce: Make a note to review the skill during the student's next session.

- Distribute copies of Practice Page K.73B, which contains decodable story *Pat and Sam*. Point out that the story is made up of several sentences, and each sentence is made of words. Remind students that words are separated by spaces.

- Point out that students have learned the following high-frequency words, which they will also read in the story: *come, me*.

- Review the Sound/Spelling Card for short *a*. Ask students to name the sound for *a*. Tell students that many words in this story have the /ă/ sound.

- Review and model the Phonics/Decoding Strategy using the story title.

- Model fluency and accuracy. Read aloud the first sentence of the story as students follow along. Point out that you do not misread, add, or skip words. Lead them in choral reading the same sentence with fluency and accuracy.

- Have students use what they know about high-frequency words and letter-sound associations to read the story aloud.

> **Fun with Words** Optional activities for engaging, hands-on practice are provided in the Resources section.

High-Frequency Words:
my, with

Teach/Model

- Display the high-frequency word *my*. Tell students that this is a useful word to know, since they will see this word often. Tell students that reading will be easier if they recognize the word.
- Display the High-Frequency Word Card for *my* and say the word. Then spell the word aloud as you point to each letter. Say the word again.
- Use the word in a simple sentence that will provide context. For example: *This is my book.*
- Repeat the steps above for the high-frequency word *with*.

Guided Practice

Do the following for each high-frequency word:

- Display the High-Frequency Word Card. Read the word and have students repeat it.
- Note the familiar sound/spelling patterns that are shown on the back of the card. Note as well any unfamiliar and unexpected sound/spellings.
- Blend the word with students.
- Spell the word aloud, pointing to each letter.
- Have students then spell the word aloud as you point to each letter.
- Have students read the word again.

Apply

- Display the High-Frequency Word Cards *my, with, come,* and *me* in random order. Have students read the words aloud.
- Have students write each word. Tell them to compare their writing with the word on the card and make corrections if necessary.
- Have students read each word aloud and use it in a sentence.

Objective

- Recognize and read high-frequency words.

Materials

- High-Frequency Word Cards

Formative Assessment and Corrective Feedback

IF a student makes an error, THEN follow this model:

Correct the error.

Guide the student to say the word correctly.

Check for understanding by having the student reread the word from among other randomly displayed high-frequency words.

Reinforce: Make a note to review the word during the student's next session.

Phonics: Words with *n*

Objectives

- Isolate and pronounce the /n/ sound in words.
- Blend and read words with /n/.
- Read decodable text that includes words with /n/.
- Read common high-frequency words by sight.

Materials

- Letter Cards
- Sound/Spelling Cards
- Instructional Routine: Sound/Spelling Cards
- Instructional Routine: Sound-by-Sound Blending
- Phonics/Decoding Strategy
- Practice Page K.74B

Phonemic Awareness Warm-up

- **Say:** *I'm going to say a word. Listen for the sound you hear at the beginning of the word. I'll do the first one. Listen:* net. *What sound do you hear at the beginning of* net? /n/
- **Say:** *Now let's do it together. Listen:* not. *What sound do you hear at the beginning of* not? */n/ Now you do it with the word* nut. (/n/)
- Repeat with the words *nap, Ned,* and *Nat.*

Teach/Model

SOUND/SPELLING Use Instructional Routine: Sound/Spelling Cards to introduce the Sound/Spelling Card for Nyle Noodle. Name the picture and say the sound. Have students repeat after you. **Say:** *Listen:* Nyle, /n/. *Now you say it.*

- Repeat with *Noodle.*
- Say the sound and give the spelling. **Say:** Nyle Noodle *begins with the /n/ sound. The letter* n *stands for the /n/ sound at the beginning of* Nyle *and* Noodle.
- Display the words *pan, can, tan,* and *man.* Read each word, and point out the letter *n* at the end. Explain that the letter *n* is last because it stands for the last sound in the word.
- Have students differentiate between words with initial /n/ and words with final /n/. Distribute a Letter Card *n* to each student. **Say:** *I will say some words. If you hear /n/ at the beginning of the word, hold your card in front of you. If you hear /n/ at the end of the word, put your card behind your back.*
- Say the following words: *in, man, not, fun, noodle.*

BLENDING Use Letter Cards and Instructional Routine: Sound-by-Sound Blending to model blending the words *nap* and *can.*

Guided Practice

BLENDING Display the words *nap, Nat, fan,* and *pan.* Work with students to blend the words, using Instructional Routine: Sound-by-Sound Blending.

PHONICS/DECODING STRATEGY Review the Phonics/Decoding Strategy. Display the sentences below. Call on students to use the strategy to blend one or more words and to read the sentences.

> A man can nap.
>
> I see the tan cat.

BUILDING AND WRITING WORDS Tell students to follow your directions and build new words with their Letter Cards. Have students start by building the word *pat.*

- **Say:** *Change* p *to* s. *What's the new word?* (sat)
- **Say:** *Change* s *to* m. *What's the new word?* (mat)
- **Say:** *Change* m *to* c. *What's the new word?* (cat)
- **Say:** *Change* t *to* n. *What's the new word?* (can)
- **Say:** *Change* c *to* m. *What's the new word?* (man)
- Then have students write each word and read it aloud.

Apply

- Distribute copies of Practice Page K.74B, which contains the decodable story *I Can Nap*. Point out that students have learned the following high-frequency words, which they will also read in the story: *my, with*.

- Review the Sound/Spelling Card for *n*. Ask students to name the sound for *n*. Tell them that many words in this story have the /n/ sound.

- Review and model the Phonics/Decoding Strategy using the story title.

- Model fluency and accuracy. Read aloud the first sentence of the story as students follow along. Point out that you do not misread, add, or skip words. Lead students in choral reading the same sentence with fluency and accuracy.

- Have students use what they know about high-frequency words and letter-sound associations to read the story aloud.

Fun with Words Optional activities for engaging, hands-on practice are provided in the Resources section.

English Language Support

Linguistic Transfer Some English learners (including speakers of Cantonese or Mandarin) may have trouble with the /n/ sound. Model pronouncing the sound, and explain that your tongue is touching the roof of your mouth, blocking the air, so the air must come through your nose. Have ELs practice the sound in front of a mirror and then practice pronouncing words such as these: *nap, no, not, nut, net*. Use each word in a brief sentence to reinforce meaning.

Formative Assessment and Corrective Feedback

IF a student makes an error, THEN follow this model:

Correct the error.

Guide the student to perform the task correctly by modeling.

Check that the student understands by having the student repeat the task.

Reinforce: Make a note to review the skill at your next session with the student.

High-Frequency Words: *you, what*

Objective

- Recognize and read high-frequency words.

Materials

- High-Frequency Word Cards

Formative Assessment and Corrective Feedback

IF a student makes an error, THEN follow this model:

Correct the error.

Guide the student to say the word correctly.

Check for understanding by having the student reread the word from among other randomly displayed high-frequency words.

Reinforce: Make a note to review the word during the student's next session.

Teach/Model

- Display the high-frequency word *you*. Tell students that this is a useful word to know, since they will see this word often. Tell students that reading will be easier if they recognize the word.
- Display the High-Frequency Word Card for *you* and say the word. Then spell the word aloud as you point to each letter. Say the word again.
- Use the word in a simple sentence that will provide context. For example: *The gift is for you.*
- Repeat the steps above for the high-frequency word *what*.

Guided Practice

Do the following for each high-frequency word:

- Display the High-Frequency Word Card. Read the word and have students repeat it.
- Note the familiar sound/spelling patterns that are shown on the back of the card. Note as well any unfamiliar and unexpected sound/spellings.
- Blend the word with students.
- Spell the word aloud, pointing to each letter.
- Have students then spell the word aloud as you point to each letter.
- Have students read the word again.

Apply

- Display the High-Frequency Word Cards *you, what, my,* and *with* in random order. Have students read the words aloud.
- Have students write each word. Tell them to compare their writing with the word on the card and make corrections if necessary.
- Have students read each word aloud and use it in a sentence.

Phonics: Words with *f*

Phonemic Awareness Warm-up

- **Say:** *I'm going to say a word. Listen for the sound you hear at the beginning of the word. I'll do the first one. Listen:* fan. *What sound do you hear at the beginning of* fan? (/f/)
- **Say:** *Now let's do it together. Listen:* fun. *What sound do you hear at the beginning of* fun? (/f/) *Now I'm going to say another word. If it begins with the /f/ sound, signal thumbs up.* Demonstrate thumbs up. *If the word doesn't begin with the /f/ sound, signal thumbs down.* Demonstrate thumbs down. *I'll do the first one. Listen:* make. *I hear /m/ at the beginning of* make, *so I signal thumbs down.*
- **Say:** *Now let's do it together. Listen:* fit. *We hear /f/ at the beginning of* fit, *so we signal thumbs up. Now you do it.* Say the following words: *fat, rod, fin, fuss, pin.*

Teach/Model

SOUND/SPELLING Use Instructional Routine: Sound/Spelling Cards to introduce Fifi Fish. Display Alphafriend Card *Fifi Fish* and say the first word. **Say:** *Listen:* Fifi, /f/. *Now you say it.* Have students repeat after you.

- Repeat with *Fish.*
- Say the sound and give the spelling. **Say:** Fifi Fish *begins with the /f/ sound. The letter* f *stands for the /f/ sound at the beginning of* Fifi *and* Fish.

BLENDING Use Letter Cards and Instructional Routine: Sound-by-Sound Blending to model blending the words *fan* and *fat.*

Guided Practice

BLENDING Display the words *fan, pan, nap,* and *fat.* Work with students to blend the words, using Instructional Routine: Sound-by-Sound Blending.

PHONICS/DECODING STRATEGY Review the Phonics/Decoding Strategy. Display the sentences below. Call on students to use the strategy to blend one or more words and to read the sentences.

> The fat cat sat.
>
> We see a fan.

BUILDING AND WRITING WORDS Tell students to follow your directions and build new words with their Letter Cards. Have students start by building the word *cap.*

- **Say:** *Change* c *to* t. *What's the new word?* (tap)
- **Say:** *Change* p *to* n. *What's the new word?* (tan)
- **Say:** *Change* t *to* f. *What's the new word?* (fan)
- **Say:** *Change* n *to* t. *What's the new word?* (fat)
- **Say:** *Change* f *to* s. *What's the new word?* (sat)
- Then have students write each word and read it aloud.

Objectives

- Isolate and pronounce the /f/ sound in words with *f.*
- Blend and read words with /f/.
- Read decodable text that includes words with /f/.
- Read common high-frequency words by sight.

Materials

- Letter Cards
- Sound/Spelling Cards
- Instructional Routine: Sound/Spelling Cards
- Instructional Routine: Sound-by-Sound Blending
- Phonics/Decoding Strategy
- Practice Page K.75B

Apply

English Language Support

Linguistic Transfer Some English learners (including speakers of Hmong, Tagalog, or Korean) may have trouble distinguishing /f/ from /p/. Say both sounds several times as ELs study your mouth positions. Have ELs practice the sounds (in front of a mirror, if possible) and then repeat the word with /f/ in pairs like these: *fun/pun, pin/fin, fine/pine, fan/pan, pill/fill*. Use each word in a brief sentence to reinforce meaning.

Formative Assessment and Corrective Feedback

IF a student makes an error, THEN follow this model:

Correct the error.

Guide the student to perform the task correctly by modeling.

Check for understanding by having the student repeat the task.

Reinforce: Make a note to review the skill during the student's next session.

- Distribute copies of Practice Page K.75B, which contains the decodable story *What Can Fan See?* Point out that students have learned the following high-frequency words, which they will also read in the story: *you, what.*

- Review the Sound/Spelling Card for *f.* Ask students to name the sound for *f.* Tell them that many words in this story have the /f/ sound.

- Review and model the Phonics/Decoding Strategy using the story title.

- Model fluency and accuracy. Read aloud the first sentence of the story as students follow along. Point out that you do not misread, add, or skip words. Lead students in choral reading the same sentence with fluency and accuracy.

- Have students use what they know about high-frequency words and letter-sound associations to read the story aloud.

> **Fun with Words** Optional activities for engaging, hands-on practice are provided in the Resources section.

High-Frequency Words: *are, now*

Teach/Model

- Display the high-frequency word *are*. Tell students that this is a useful word to know, since they will see this word often. Tell students that reading will be easier if they recognize the word.
- Display the High-Frequency Word Card for *are* and say the word. Then spell the word aloud as you point to each letter. Say the word again.
- Use the word in a simple sentence that will provide context. For example: *We are at school.*
- Repeat the steps above for the high-frequency word *now*.

Guided Practice

Do the following for each high-frequency word:

- Display the High-Frequency Word Card. Read the word and have students repeat it.
- Note the familiar sound/spelling patterns that are shown on the back of the card. Note as well any unfamiliar and unexpected sound/spellings.
- Blend the word with students.
- Spell the word aloud, pointing to each letter.
- Have students then spell the word aloud as you point to each letter.
- Have students read the word again.

Apply

- Display the High-Frequency Word Cards *are, now, you,* and *what* in random order. Have students read the words aloud.
- Have students write each word. Tell them to compare their writing with the word on the card and make corrections if necessary.
- Have students read each word aloud and use it in a sentence.

Objective

- Recognize and read high-frequency words.

Materials

- High-Frequency Word Cards

Formative Assessment and Corrective Feedback

IF a student makes an error, THEN follow this model:

Correct the error.

Guide the student to say the word correctly.

Check for understanding by having the student reread the word from among other randomly displayed high-frequency words.

Reinforce: Make a note to review the word during the student's next session.

Phonics: Words with *b*

Objectives

- Isolate and pronounce the /b/ sound.
- Blend and read words with /b/.
- Read decodable text that includes words with /b/.
- Read common high-frequency words by sight.

Materials

- Letter Cards
- Sound/Spelling Cards
- Instructional Routine: Sound/Spelling Cards
- Instructional Routine: Sound-by-Sound Blending
- Phonics/Decoding Strategy
- Practice Page K.76B

Phonemic Awareness Warm-up

- **Say:** *I'm going to say a word. Listen for the sound you hear at the beginning of the word. I'll do the first one. Listen:* bat. *What sound do you hear at the beginning of* bat? (/b/)
- **Say:** *Now let's do it together. Listen:* bag. *What sound do you hear at the beginning of* bag? (/b/) *Now you do it with the word* bad. (/b/)
- Repeat with the words *box, bell, boot,* and *bus.*

Teach/Model

SOUND/SPELLING Use Instructional Routine: Sound/Spelling Cards to introduce the Sound/Spelling Card for Benny Bear. Name the picture and say the sound. Have students repeat after you. **Say:** *Listen:* Benny, /b/. *Now you say it.*

- Repeat with *Bear.*
- Say the sound and give the spelling. **Say:** Benny Bear *begins with the /b/ sound. The letter* b *stands for the /b/ sound at the beginning of* Benny *and* Bear.
- Display the words *rub, tub, dab,* and *sob.* Read each word, and point out the letter *b* at the end. Explain that the letter *b* is last because it stands for the last sound in the word.
- Have students differentiate between words with initial /b/ and words with final /b/. Distribute a Letter Card *b* to each student. **Say:** *I will say some words. If you hear /b/ at the beginning of the word, hold your card in front of you. If you hear /b/ at the end of the word, put your card behind your back.*
  - Say the following words: *cab, rib, bib, bed.*

BLENDING Use Letter Cards and Instructional Routine: Sound-by-Sound Blending to model blending the words *bat* and *cub.*

Guided Practice

BLENDING Display the words *bad, fan, bat,* and *fat.* Work with students to blend the words, using Instructional Routine: Sound-by-Sound Blending.

PHONICS/DECODING STRATEGY Review the Phonics/Decoding Strategy. Display the sentences below. Call on students to use the strategy to blend one or more words and to read the sentences.

> I am at bat.
>
> A cab can come.

BUILDING AND WRITING WORDS Tell students to follow your directions and build new words with their Letter Cards. Have students start by building the word *bat.*

- **Say:** *Change* t *to* n. *What's the new word?* (ban)
- **Say:** *Change* b *to* c. *What's the new word?* (can)
- **Say:** *Change* c *to* p. *What's the new word?* (pan)
- **Say:** *Change* n *to* t. *What's the new word?* (pat)
- **Say:** *Change* p *to* f. *What's the new word?* (fat)
- Then have students write each word and read it aloud.

Apply

- Distribute copies of Practice Page K.76B, which contains the decodable story *At Bat Now*. Point out that students have learned the following high-frequency words, which they will also read in the story: *are, now*.

- Review the Sound/Spelling Card for *b*. Ask students to name the sound for *b*. Tell them that many words in this story have the /b/ sound.

- Review and model the Phonics/Decoding Strategy using the story title.

- Model fluency and accuracy. Read aloud the first sentence of the story as students follow along. Point out that you do not misread, add, or skip words. Lead students in choral reading the same sentence with fluency and accuracy.

- Have students use what they know about high-frequency words and letter-sound associations to read the story aloud.

> **Fun with Words** Optional activities for engaging, hands-on practice are provided in the Resources section.

Point out to Spanish speakers that the sound /b/ is the same in Spanish as in English. Encourage students to share words they know in both Spanish and English with the /b/ sound.

Formative Assessment and Corrective Feedback

IF a student makes an error, THEN follow this model:

Correct the error.

Guide the student to perform the task correctly by modeling.

Check for understanding by having the student repeat the task.

Reinforce: Make a note to review the skill at your next session with the student.

Cumulative Review/Fluency

Teach/Model

Objectives

- Decode words with short vowel *a* and consonants *n, f, b.*
- Read common high-frequency words by sight.
- Read emergent-reader texts with purpose and understanding.

Materials

- High-Frequency Word Cards
- Instructional Routine: High-Frequency Words
- Practice Page K.77

REVIEW

- Remind students they have learned sounds for the consonants *n, f, b.* Review the sounds with the Alphafriend Card for *Nyle Noodle, Fifi Fish,* and *Benny Bear.* Display the cards and review the sounds for each.
- Remind students they have learned the short vowel sound for *a.* Use the Alphafriend Card for *Andy Apple.* Display the vowel and review the short sound for *a.*
- Display these sentences:

  Nan can fan now.

  My cat can nap with you.

  Come see a fat bat.

- Point to the high-frequency words *now, my, you, come,* and *with* and read each one. Remind students that they know these words. Use the High-Frequency Word Cards and Instructional Routine: High-Frequency Words to review these words.

MODEL FLUENCY

- Read the above sentences, focusing on the words in the sentences that contain /n/n, /f/f, /b/b, and short vowel *a.* Model blending the sounds to read the words. Read the first sentence: *Nan can fan now.* Read the words *Nan, can,* and *fan* more slowly, as if sounding them out. Then read the sentence again, this time at a natural pace. Have students read the sentence with you. Continue with the remaining sentences.

Guided Practice

- Tell students they will practice reading. Display the following sentences:

  Cam can bat.

  Nan can fan the cat.

  I can bat now.

- Guide students in reading the sentences aloud. Coach them to sound out each word. Have students go back to any word they read incorrectly. Have students read the text again.

- Have students read aloud the practice text on Practice Page K.77. Explain that the main purpose of reading the text is to practice their reading skills.

- Coach students to use decoding skills and context to self-correct any mistakes they make during reading. They should read the text several times, until they are able to read smoothly and accurately.

- When students have finished the fluency practice, choose a few sentences to review. Have students read each sentence and explain in their own words what it means.

- After students are able to read the text fluently, guide them to track their progress on their My Progress line graphs.

Formative Assessment and Corrective Feedback

IF a student makes an error, THEN follow this model:

Correct the error.

Guide the student to say the word correctly.

Check for understanding by having the student reread the word.

Reinforce: Make a note to review the word during the student's next session.

Objective

- Recognize and read high-frequency words.

Materials

- High-Frequency Word Cards

Formative Assessment and Corrective Feedback

IF a student makes an error, THEN follow this model:

Correct the error.

Guide the student to say the word correctly.

Check for understanding by having the student reread the word from among other randomly displayed high-frequency words.

Reinforce: Make a note to review the word during the student's next session.

High-Frequency Words:
is, how, of, so, many, where

Teach/Model

- Display the high-frequency word *is*. Tell students that this is a useful word to know, since they will see this word often. Tell students that reading will be easier if they recognize the word.
- Display the High-Frequency Word Card for *is* and say the word. Then spell the word aloud as you point to each letter. Say the word again.
- Use the word in a simple sentence that will provide context. For example: *The elephant is big.*

Guided Practice

Do the following for each high-frequency word:

- Display the High-Frequency Word Card. Read the word and have students repeat it.
- Note the familiar sound/spelling patterns that are shown on the back of the card. Note as well any unfamiliar and unexpected sound/spellings.
- Blend the word with students.
- Spell the word aloud, pointing to each letter.
- Have students then spell the word aloud as you point to each letter.
- Have students read the word again.

Apply

- Display the High-Frequency Word Cards in random order. Have students read the words aloud.
- Have students write each word. Tell them to compare their writing with the word on the card and make corrections if necessary.
- Have students read each word aloud and use it in a sentence.

Phonics: Words with Short *i*

Phonemic Awareness Warm-up

- Display the word *bit*. **Say:** *I'm going to say a word. Listen for the sound you hear in the middle. I'll do the first one. Listen:* bit. *What sound do you hear in the middle of* bit? (/ĭ/)
- Display the words *tip, pin, sit, tin,* and *Tim*. **Say:** *Now let's do it together. Listen:* tip. *What sound do you hear in the middle of* tip? (/ĭ/) *Now you do it.* Pin? (/ĭ/)
- Repeat with the words *sit, tin,* and *Tim*.

Teach/Model

SOUND/SPELLING Use Instructional Routine: Sound/Spelling Cards to introduce the Sound/Spelling Card for Iggy Iguana. Name the picture and say the sound. Have students repeat after you. **Say:** *Listen:* Iggy, /ĭ/. *Now you say it.*

- Repeat with *Iguana*.
- Say the sound and give the spelling. **Say:** Iggy Iguana *begins with the* /ĭ/ *sound. The letter* i *stands for the* /ĭ/ *sound at the beginning or in the middle of a word.*

BLENDING Use Letter Cards and Instructional Routine: Sound-by-Sound Blending to model blending the words *in* and *fin*.

Guided Practice

BLENDING Display the words *sit, fit, sip, pit*. Work with students to blend the words, using Instructional Routine: Sound-by-Sound Blending.

PHONICS/DECODING STRATEGY Review the Phonics/Decoding Strategy. Display the sentences below. Call on students to use the strategy to blend one or more words and to read the sentences.

> I sit with my cat.
>
> It is a pin. See the tip?

BUILDING AND WRITING WORDS Tell students to follow your directions and build new words with their Letter Cards. Have students start by building the word *sit*.

- **Say:** *Change* s *to* b. *What's the new word?* (bit)
- **Say:** *Change* b *to* f. *What's the new word?* (fit)
- **Say:** *Change* f *to* p. *What's the new word?* (pit)
- **Say:** *Change* t *to* n. *What's the new word?* (pin)
- Then have students write each word and read it aloud.

Objectives

- Isolate and pronounce the /ĭ/ sound in words with short *i*.
- Blend and read words with short *i*.
- Read decodable text that includes words with short *i*.
- Read common high-frequency words by sight.

Materials

- Letter Cards
- Sound/Spelling Cards
- Instructional Routine: Sound/Spelling Cards
- Instructional Routine: Sound-by-Sound Blending
- Phonics/Decoding Strategy
- Practice Page K.78B

English Language Support

Linguistic Transfer Speakers of Spanish, Tagalog, Korean, Haitian Creole, and Vietnamese may substitute long *e* for /ĭ/, as the /ĭ/ sound is not used in the first language; also, the letter *i* stands for a sound like /ē/ in Spanish. Model the /ĭ/ sound in words like *pit, pin, tip, rip,* and *lip.* Point out that your mouth is more rounded than when you say the /ē/ sound. Have students chorally repeat each word after you, then vocalize the middle sound, and then say the whole word again. Use each word in a sentence to reinforce meaning.

Formative Assessment and Corrective Feedback

IF a student makes an error, THEN follow this model:

Correct the error.

Guide the student to perform the task correctly by modeling.

Check for understanding by having the student repeat the task.

Reinforce: Make a note to review the skill during the student's next session.

Apply

- Distribute copies of Practice Page K.78B, which contains the decodable story *Fit in the Cab.* Point out that the story is made up of several sentences, and each sentence is made of words.

- Point out that students have learned the following high-frequency word, which they will also read in the story: *is.*

- Review the Sound/Spelling Card for short *i.* Ask students to name the sound for *i.* Tell students that many words in this story have the /ĭ/ sound.

- Review and model the Phonics/Decoding Strategy using the story title.

- Model fluency and accuracy. Read aloud the first sentence of the story as students follow along. Point out that you do not misread, add, or skip words. Lead them in choral reading the same sentence with fluency and accuracy.

- Have students use what they know about high-frequency words and letter-sound associations to read the story aloud.

> **Fun with Words** Optional activities for engaging, hands-on practice are provided in the Resources section.

High-Frequency Words:
this, find, from, came, but, on

Teach/Model

- Display the high-frequency words. Tell students that these are useful words to know, since they will see these words often. Tell students that reading will be easier if they recognize these words.
- Display the High-Frequency Word Card for *this* and say the word. Then spell the word aloud as you point to each letter. Say the word again.
- Use the word in a simple sentence that will provide context. For example: *This is my cat.*
- Repeat the steps above with the remaining high-frequency words.

Guided Practice

Do the following for each high-frequency word:

- Display the High-Frequency Word Card. Read the word and have students repeat it.
- Note the familiar sound/spelling patterns that are shown on the back of the card. Note as well any unfamiliar and unexpected sound/spellings.
- Blend the word with students.
- Spell the word aloud, pointing to each letter.
- Have students then spell the word aloud as you point to each letter.
- Have students read the word again.

Apply

- Display the High-Frequency Word Cards in random order. Have students read the words aloud.
- Have students write each word. Tell them to compare their writing with the word on the card and make corrections if necessary.
- Have students read each word aloud and use it in a sentence.

Objective

- Recognize and read high-frequency words.

Materials

- High-Frequency Word Cards

Formative Assessment and Corrective Feedback

IF a student makes an error, THEN follow this model:

Correct the error.

Guide the student to say the word correctly.

Check for understanding by having the student reread the word from among other randomly displayed high-frequency words.

Reinforce: Make a note to review the word during the student's next session.

Objectives

- Isolate and pronounce the /g/ sound in words.
- Blend and read words with /g/.
- Read decodable text that includes words with /g/.
- Read common high-frequency words by sight.

Materials

- Letter Cards
- Sound/Spelling Cards
- Instructional Routine: Sound/Spelling Cards
- Instructional Routine: Sound-by-Sound Blending
- Phonics/Decoding Strategy
- Practice Page K.79B

Phonics: Words with Hard *g*

Phonemic Awareness Warm-up

- **Say:** *I'm going to say a word. Listen for the sound you hear at the beginning of the word. I'll do the first one. Listen:* gas. *What sound do you hear at the beginning of* gas? /g/
- **Say:** *Now let's do it together. Listen:* get. *What sound do you hear at the beginning of* get? /g/ *Now you do it with the word* got. (/g/)
- Repeat with the words *goat, game, gate,* and *give.*

Teach/Model

SOUND/SPELLING Use Instructional Routine: Sound/Spelling Cards to introduce the Sound/Spelling Card for Gertie Goose. Name the picture and say the sound. Have students repeat after you. **Say:** *Listen:* Gertie, /g/. *Now you say it.* Have students repeat after you.

- Repeat with *Goose.*
- Say the sound and give the spelling. **Say:** Gertie Goose *begins with the /g/ sound. The letter* g *stands for the /g/ sound at the beginning of* Gertie *and* Goose.
- **Say:** You can also hear /g/ at the end of a word.
- Display the words *big, tag, dig,* and *bag.* Read each word, and point out the letter *g* at the end. Explain that the letter *g* is last because it stands for the last sound in the word.
- Have students differentiate between words with initial /g/ and words with final /g/. Distribute Letter Card *g* to each student. **Say:** *I will say some words. If you hear /g/ at the beginning of the word, hold your card in front of you. If you hear /g/ at the end of a word, put your card behind your back.*
- Say the following words: *go, wag, gas, gate, dig, bug.*

BLENDING Use Letter Cards and Instructional Routine: Sound-by-Sound Blending to model blending the words *gas* and *get.*

Guided Practice

BLENDING Display the words *fan, got, bag,* and *nap.* Work with students to blend the words, using Instructional Routine: Sound-by-Sound Blending.

PHONICS/DECODING STRATEGY Review the Phonics/Decoding Strategy. Display the sentences below. Call on students to use the strategy to blend one or more words and to read the sentences.

> The gas is in the cab.
> The bag is big.

BUILDING AND WRITING WORDS Tell students to follow your directions and build new words with their Letter Cards. Have students start by building the word *gas.*

- **Say:** *Change* s *to* p. *What's the new word?* (gap)
- **Say:** *Change* g *to* t. *What's the new word?* (tap)
- **Say:** *Change* p *to* g. *What's the new word?* (tag)
- **Say:** *Change* t *to* b. *What's the new word?* (bag)
- **Say:** *Change* b *to* r. *What's the new word?* (rag)
- Then have students write each word and read it aloud.

Apply

- Distribute copies of Practice Page K.79B, which contains the decodable story *Find Big Tim*. Point out that the story is made up of several sentences, and each sentence is made of words.

- Point out that students have learned the following high-frequency words, which they will also read in the story: *find, this*.

- Review the Sound/Spelling Card for *g*. Ask students to name the sound for *g*. Tell them that many words in this story have the /g/ sound.

- Review and model the Phonics/Decoding Strategy using the story title.

- Model fluency and accuracy. Read aloud the first sentence of the story as students follow along. Point out that you do not misread, add, or skip words. Lead students in choral reading the same sentence with fluency and accuracy.

- Have students use what they know about high-frequency words and letter-sound associations to read the story aloud.

Fun with Words Optional activities for engaging, hands-on practice are provided in the Resources section.

English Language Support

Linguistic Transfer Speakers of Chinese languages may have trouble hearing and producing consonants at the ends of words, or they may add a vowel sound after a final consonant; in Chinese, words usually end with a vowel sound. Provide modeling and practice segmenting and blending final sounds in words such as *tag, bat, big, can*. Use each word in a brief sentence to provide a meaningful context.

Formative Assessment and Corrective Feedback

IF a student makes an error, THEN follow this model:

Correct the error.

Guide the student to perform the task correctly by modeling.

Check for understanding by having the student repeat the task.

Reinforce: Make a note to review the skill during the student's next session.

Objective

- Recognize and read high-frequency words.

Materials

- High-Frequency Word Cards

Formative Assessment and Corrective Feedback

IF a student makes an error, THEN follow this model:

Correct the error.

Guide the student to say the word correctly.

Check for understanding by having the student reread the word from among other randomly displayed high-frequency words.

Reinforce: Make a note to review the word during the student's next session.

High-Frequency Words:
will, be, into, that, your, who

Teach/Model

- Display the high-frequency words. Tell students that these are useful words to know, since they will see these words often. Tell students that reading will be easier if they recognize these words.
- Display the High-Frequency Word Card for *will* and say the word. Then spell the word aloud as you point to each letter. Say the word again.
- Use the word in a simple sentence that will provide context. For example: *I will find the bat.*
- Repeat the steps above with the remaining high-frequency words.

Guided Practice

Do the following for each high-frequency word:

- Display the High-Frequency Word Card. Read the word and have students repeat it.
- Note the familiar sound/spelling patterns that are shown on the back of the card. Note as well any unfamiliar and unexpected sound/spellings.
- Blend the word with students.
- Spell the word aloud, pointing to each letter.
- Have students then spell the word aloud as you point to each letter.
- Have students read the word again.

Apply

- Display the High-Frequency Word Cards in random order. Have students read the words aloud.
- Have students write each word. Tell them to compare their writing with the word on the card and make corrections if necessary.
- Have students read each word aloud and use it in a sentence.

Phonics: Words with *r*

Phonemic Awareness Warm-up

- **Say:** *I'm going to say a word. Listen for the sound you hear at the beginning of the word. I'll do the first one. Listen:* ran. *What sound do you hear at the beginning of* ran? */r/*
- **Say:** *Now let's do it together. Listen:* rip. *What sound do you hear at the beginning of* rip? */r/ Now you do it with the word* rag. *(/r/)*
- Repeat with the words *rim, roll, run,* and *rock.*

Teach/Model

SOUND/SPELLING Use Instructional Routine: Sound/Spelling Cards to introduce the Sound/Spelling Card for Reggie Rooster. Name the picture and say the sound. Have students repeat after you. **Say:** *Listen:* Reggie, */r/. Now you say it.*

- Repeat with *Rooster.*
- Say the sound and give the spelling. **Say:** Reggie Rooster *begins with the /r/ sound. The letter* r *stands for the /r/ sound at the beginning of* Reggie *and* Rooster.

BLENDING Use Letter Cards and Instructional Routine: Sound-by-Sound Blending to model blending the words *ran* and *rim.*

Guided Practice

BLENDING Display the words *ram, rip, sip,* and *cap.* Work with students to blend the words, using Instructional Routine: Sound-by-Sound Blending.

PHONICS/DECODING STRATEGY Review the Phonics/Decoding Strategy. Display the sentences below. Call on students to use the strategy to blend one or more words and to read the sentences.

> The big ram ran.
>
> I will rip the rag.

BUILDING AND WRITING WORDS Tell students to follow your directions and build new words with their Letter Cards. Have students start by building the word *ran.*

- **Say:** *Change* n *to* m. *What's the new word?* (ram)
- **Say:** *Change* m *to* g. *What's the new word?* (rag)
- **Say:** *Change* g *to* p. *What's the new word?* (rap)
- **Say:** *Change* p *to* t. *What's the new word?* (rat)
- Then have students write each word and read it aloud.

Objectives

- Isolate and pronounce the /r/ sound in words.
- Blend and read words with /r/r.
- Read decodable text that includes words with /r/r.
- Read common high-frequency words by sight.

Materials

- Letter Cards
- Sound/Spelling Cards
- Instructional Routine: Sound/Spelling Cards
- Instructional Routine: Sound-by-Sound Blending
- Phonics/Decoding Strategy
- Practice Page K.80B

English Language Support

Linguistic Transfer Many English learners (including speakers of Spanish, Cantonese or Mandarin, or Korean) may have trouble with the /r/ sound. Say the sound several times as ELs study your mouth position; point out that your lips are rounded, your throat is vibrating, and the sides of your tongue, but not the tip, are touching your teeth. Have students practice with these words: *rain, right, run, red, rip, rag, ride, road*. Use each word in a brief sentence to reinforce meaning.

Formative Assessment and Corrective Feedback

IF a student makes an error, THEN follow this model:

Correct the error.

Guide the student to perform the task correctly by modeling.

Check for understanding by having the student repeat the task.

Reinforce: Make a note to review the skill during the student's next session.

- Distribute copies of Practice Page K.80B, which contains the decodable story *Who Is It?* Point out that the story is made up of several sentences, and each sentence is made of words.

- Point out that students have learned the following high-frequency words, which they will also read in the story: *be, who, will*.

- Review the Sound/Spelling Card for *r*. Ask students to name the sound for *r*. Tell them that many words in this story have the /r/ sound.

- Review and model the Phonics/Decoding Strategy using the story title.

- Model fluency and accuracy. Read aloud the first sentence of the story as students follow along. Point out that you do not misread, add, or skip words. Lead students in choral reading the same sentence with fluency and accuracy.

- Have students use what they know about high-frequency words and letter-sound associations to read the story aloud.

Fun with Words Optional activities for engaging, hands-on practice are provided in the Resources section.

High-Frequency Words:
go, for, here, they, soon, up

Teach/Model

- Display the high-frequency words. Tell students that these are useful words to know, since they will see these words often. Tell students that reading will be easier if they recognize these words.
- Display the High-Frequency Word Card for *go* and say the word. Then spell the word aloud as you point to each letter. Say the word again.
- Use the word in a simple sentence that will provide context. For example: *We will go to school.*
- Repeat the steps above with the remaining high-frequency words.

Guided Practice

Do the following for each high-frequency word:

- Display the High-Frequency Word Card. Read the word and have students repeat it.
- Note the familiar sound/spelling patterns that are shown on the back of the card. Note as well any unfamiliar and unexpected sound/spellings.
- Blend the word with students.
- Spell the word aloud, pointing to each letter.
- Have students then spell the word aloud as you point to each letter.
- Have students read the word again.

Apply

- Display the High-Frequency Word Cards in random order. Have students read the words aloud.
- Have students write each word. Tell them to compare their writing with the word on the card and make corrections if necessary.
- Have students read each word aloud and use it in a sentence.

Objective

- Recognize and read high-frequency words.

Materials

- High-Frequency Word Cards

Formative Assessment and Corrective Feedback

IF a student makes an error, THEN follow this model:

Correct the error.

Guide the student to say the word correctly.

Check for understanding by having the student reread the word from among other randomly displayed high-frequency words.

Reinforce: Make a note to review the word during the student's next session.

Phonics: Words with *d*

Phonemic Awareness Warm-up

- **Say:** *I'm going to say a word. Listen for the sound you hear at the beginning of the word. I'll do the first one. Listen:* dig. *What sound do you hear at the beginning of* dig? /d/
- **Say:** *Now let's do it together. Listen:* dim. *What sound do you hear at the beginning of* dim? (/d/) Repeat with the words *dip, dime, dirt, dish,* and *dot.*
- **Say:** *I'm going to say a word. Listen for the sound you hear at the end of the word. I'll do the first one. Listen:* bad. *What sound do you hear at the end of* bad? /d/
- **Say:** *Now let's do it together. Listen:* red. *What sound do you hear at the end of* red? (/d/) Repeat with the words *sad, hid, good, mud,* and *lid.*

Teach/Model

SOUND/SPELLING Use Instructional Routine: Sound/Spelling Cards to introduce the Sound Spelling Card for Dudley Duck. Name the picture and say the sound. Have students repeat after you. **Say:** *Listen:* Dudley, /d/. *Now you say it.*

- Repeat with *Duck.*
- Say the sound and give the spelling. **Say:** Dudley Duck *begins with the /d/ sound. The letter* d *stands for the /d/ sound at the beginning of* Dudley *and* Duck.
- **Say:** *You can also hear /d/ at the end of a word.*
- Display the words *bid, lad, rid,* and *mad.* Read each word, and point out the letter *d* at the end. Explain that the letter *d* is last because it stands for the last sound in the word.
- Have students differentiate between words with initial /d/ and words with final /d/. Distribute Letter Card *d* to each student. **Say:** *I will say some words. If you hear /d/ at the beginning of the word, hold your card in front of you. If you hear /d/ at the end of a word, put your card behind your back.*
- Say the following words: *dip, hid, dot, pad, red, dim.*

BLENDING Use Letter Cards and Instructional Routine: Sound-by-Sound Blending to model blending the words *dig* and *dip.*

Guided Practice

BLENDING Display the words *did, pad, dog,* and *dim.* Work with students to blend the words, using Instructional Routine: Sound-by-Sound Blending.

PHONICS/DECODING STRATEGY Review the Phonics/Decoding Strategy. Display the sentences below. Call on students to use the strategy to blend one or more words and to read the sentences.

> Dad can dig.
>
> Did you dig a pit?

BUILDING AND WRITING WORDS Tell students to follow your directions and build new words with their Letter Cards. Have students start by building the word *dig.*

- **Say:** *Change* g *to* p. *What's the new word?* (dip)
- **Say:** *Change* p *to* m. *What's the new word?* (dim)
- **Say:** *Change* m *to* d. *What's the new word?* (did)
- Then have students write each word and read it aloud.

Objectives

- Isolate and pronounce the /d/ sound in words.
- Blend and read words with /d/*d.*
- Read decodable text that includes words with /d/*d.*
- Read common high-frequency words by sight.

Materials

- Letter Cards
- Sound/Spelling Cards
- Instructional Routine: Sound/Spelling Cards
- Instructional Routine: Sound-by-Sound Blending
- Phonics/Decoding Strategy
- Practice Page K.81B

Apply

- Distribute copies of Practice Page K.81B, which contains the decodable story *Dig It Up*. Point out that the story is made up of several sentences, and each sentence is made of words.

- Point out that students have learned the following high-frequency words, which they will also read in the story: *go, here, up*.

- Review the Sound/Spelling Card for *d*. Ask students to name the sound for *d*. Tell them that many words in this story have the /d/ sound.

- Review and model the Phonics/Decoding Strategy using the story title.

- Model fluency and accuracy. Read aloud the first sentence of the story as students follow along. Point out that you do not misread, add, or skip words. Lead students in choral reading the same sentence with fluency and accuracy.

- Have students use what they know about high-frequency words and letter-sound associations to read the story aloud.

Fun with Words Optional activities for engaging, hands-on practice are provided in the Resources section.

English Language Support

Linguistic Transfer Point out to Spanish speakers that the sound /d/ is the same in Spanish as in English. Encourage students to share words they know in both Spanish and English with the /d/ sound.

Formative Assessment and Corrective Feedback

IF a student makes an error, THEN follow this model:

Correct the error.

Guide the student to perform the task correctly by modeling.

Check for understanding by having the student repeat the task.

Reinforce: Make a note to review the skill during the student's next session.

Cumulative Review/Fluency

Objectives

- Decode words with short vowel *i* and consonants *d, g,* and *r.*
- Read common high-frequency words by sight.
- Read emergent-reader texts with purpose and understanding.

Materials

- Sound/Spelling Cards
- High-Frequency Word Cards
- Instructional Routine: High-Frequency Words
- Practice Page K.82

Teach/Model

REVIEW

- Remind students they have learned sounds for the consonants *d, g,* and *r.* Review the sounds with the Sound/Spelling Cards for Dudley Duck, Gertie Goose, and Reggie Rooster. Display the cards and review the sounds for each.
- Remind students they have learned the short vowel sound for *i.* Use the Sound/Spelling Card for Iggy Iguana. Display the card and review the short sound for *i.*
- Display these sentences:

  Come sit in the big rig.

  Dan can dig to find the bag.

  Who will fit the rag into it?

- Point to the high-frequency words *come, find, into, who,* and *will* and read each one. Remind students that they know these words. Use the High-Frequency Word Cards and Instructional Routine: High-Frequency Words to review these words.

MODEL FLUENCY

- Read the above sentences, focusing on the words in the sentences that contain /d/d, /g/g, /r/r, and short vowel *i.* Model blending the sounds to read the words. Read the first sentence: *Come sit in the big rig.* Read the words *sit, big,* and *rig* more slowly, as if sounding them out. Then read the sentence again, this time at a natural pace. Have students read the sentence with you. Continue with the remaining sentences.

Guided Practice

- Tell students they will practice reading. Display the following sentences:

  The big dog ran to see me.

  We can dig in the pit.

  A cat ran to sit on the big mat.

- Guide students in reading the sentences aloud. Coach them to sound out each word. Have students go back to any word they read incorrectly. Have students read the text again.

- Have students read aloud the practice text on Practice Page K.82. Explain that the main purpose of reading the text is to practice their reading skills.

- Coach students to use decoding skills and context to self-correct any mistakes they make during reading. They should read the text several times, until they are able to read smoothly and accurately.

- When students have finished the fluency practice, choose a few sentences to review. Have students read each sentence and explain in their own words what it means.

- After students are able to read the text fluently, guide them to track their progress on their My Progress line graphs.

Formative Assessment and Corrective Feedback

IF a student makes an error, THEN follow this model:

Correct the error.

Guide the student to say the word correctly.

Check for understanding by having the student reread the word.

Reinforce: Make a note to review the word during the student's next session.

High-Frequency Words:
make, play, them, give, say, new

Objective

- Recognize and read high-frequency words.

Materials

- High-Frequency Word Cards

Formative Assessment and Corrective Feedback

IF a student makes an error, THEN follow this model:

Correct the error.

Guide the student to say the word correctly.

Check for understanding by having the student reread the word from among other randomly displayed high-frequency words.

Reinforce: Make a note to review the word during the student's next session.

Teach/Model

- Display the high-frequency words. Tell students that these are useful words to know, since they will see these words often. Tell students that reading will be easier if they recognize these words.
- Display the High-Frequency Word Card for *make* and say the word. Then spell the word aloud as you point to each letter. Say the word again.
- Use the word in a simple sentence that will provide context. For example: *We will make cookies.*
- Repeat the steps above with the remaining high-frequency words.

Guided Practice

Do the following for each high-frequency word:

- Display the High-Frequency Word Card. Read the word and have students repeat it.
- Note the familiar sound/spelling patterns that are shown on the back of the card. Note as well any unfamiliar and unexpected sound/spellings.
- Blend the word with students.
- Spell the word aloud, pointing to each letter.
- Have students then spell the word aloud as you point to each letter.
- Have students read the word again.

Apply

- Display the High-Frequency Word Cards in random order. Have students read the words aloud.
- Have students write each word. Tell them to compare their writing with the word on the card and make corrections if necessary.
- Have students read each word aloud and use it in a sentence.

Phonics: Words with Short *o*

Phonemic Awareness Warm-up

- Display the word *mop*. **Say:** *I'm going to say a word. Listen for the sound you hear in the middle. I'll do the first one. Listen:* mop. *What sound do you hear in the middle of* mop? /ŏ/
- Display the words *cot, top, cob, pot, got,* and *dot*. **Say:** *Now let's do it together. Listen:* cot. *What sound do you hear in the middle of* cot? /ŏ/ *Now you do it.* Top? (/ŏ/)
- Repeat with the words *pot, got,* and *dot*.

Teach/Model

SOUND/SPELLING Use Instructional Routine: Sound/Spelling Cards to introduce the Sound/Spelling Card for Ozzy Octopus. Name the picture and say the sound. Have students repeat after you. **Say:** *Listen:* Ozzy, /ŏ/. *Now you say it.*

- Repeat with *Octopus*.
- Say the sound and give the spelling. **Say:** Ozzy Octopus *begins with the /ŏ/ sound. The letter* o *stands for the /ŏ/ sound at the beginning or in the middle of a word.*

BLENDING Use Letter Cards and Instructional Routine: Sound-by-Sound Blending to model blending the words *on* and *top*.

Guided Practice

BLENDING Display the words *hop, pod, nod, mop*. Work with students to blend the words, using Instructional Routine: Sound-by-Sound Blending.

PHONICS/DECODING STRATEGY Review the Phonics/Decoding Strategy. Display the sentences below. Call on students to use the strategy to blend one or more words and to read the sentences.

> Tom got a mop.
>
> The pot is on the cot.

BUILDING AND WRITING WORDS Tell students to follow your directions and build new words with their Letter Cards. Have students start by building the word *mop*.

- **Say:** *Change* m *to* t. *What's the new word?* (top)
- **Say:** *Change* t *to* h. *What's the new word?* (hop)
- **Say:** *Change* p *to* t. *What's the new word?* (hot)
- **Say:** *Change* h *to* c. *What's the new word?* (cot)
- **Say:** *Change* c *to* d. *What's the new word?* (dot)
- **Say:** *Change* d *to* l. *What's the new word?* (lot)
- **Say:** *Change* l *to* g. *What's the new word?* (got)
- Then have students write each word and read it aloud.

Objectives

- Isolate and pronounce the /ŏ/ sound in words with short *o*.
- Blend and read words with short *o*.
- Read decodable text that includes words with short *o*.
- Read common high-frequency words by sight.

Materials

- Letter Cards
- Sound/Spelling Cards
- Instructional Routine: Sound/Spelling Cards
- Instructional Routine: Sound-by-Sound Blending
- Phonics/Decoding Strategy
- Practice Page K.83B

English Language Support

Linguistic Transfer Students whose first language is Spanish, Tagalog, or Korean may have trouble with the /ŏ/ sound. Have ELs listen carefully as you pronounce words with the /ŏ/ sound: *clock, pot, rock, cot, pop, knock, lock*. Have students repeat each word, then vocalize the middle sound, and then say the whole word again. Use each word in a brief sentence to reinforce meaning.

Formative Assessment and Corrective Feedback

IF a student makes an error, THEN follow this model:

Correct the error.

Guide the student to perform the task correctly by modeling.

Check for understanding by having the student repeat the task.

Reinforce: Make a note to review the skill during the student's next session.

- Distribute copies of Practice Page K.83B, which contains the decodable story *My Dog, Tom*. Point out that the story is made up of several sentences, and each sentence is made of words.

- Point out that students have learned the following high-frequency words, which they will also read in the story: *new, play*.

- Review the Sound/Spelling Card for short *o*. Ask students to name the sound for *o*. Tell students that many words in this story have the /ŏ/ sound.

- Review and model the Phonics/Decoding Strategy using the story title.

- Model fluency and accuracy. Read aloud the first sentence of the story as students follow along. Point out that you do not misread, add, or skip words. Lead them in choral reading the same sentence with fluency and accuracy.

- Have students use what they know about high-frequency words and letter-sound associations to read the story aloud.

> **Fun with Words** Optional activities for engaging, hands-on practice are provided in the Resources section.

High-Frequency Words:
said, good, was, then, ate, could

Teach/Model

- Display the high-frequency words. Tell students that these are useful words to know, since they will see these words often. Tell students that reading will be easier if they recognize these words.
- Display the High-Frequency Word Card for *said* and say the word. Then spell the word aloud as you point to each letter. Say the word again.
- Use the word in a simple sentence that will provide context. For example: *Ron said he will help.*
- Repeat the steps above with the remaining high-frequency words.

Guided Practice

Do the following for each high-frequency word:

- Display the High-Frequency Word Card. Read the word and have students repeat it.
- Note the familiar sound/spelling patterns that are shown on the back of the card. Note as well any unfamiliar and unexpected sound/spellings.
- Blend the word with students.
- Spell the word aloud, pointing to each letter.
- Have students then spell the word aloud as you point to each letter.
- Have students read the word again.

Apply

- Display the High-Frequency Word Cards in random order. Have students read the words aloud.
- Have students write each word. Tell them to compare their writing with the word on the card and make corrections if necessary.
- Have students read each word aloud and use it in a sentence.

Objective

- Recognize and read high-frequency words.

Materials

- High-Frequency Word Cards

Formative Assessment and Corrective Feedback

IF a student makes an error, THEN follow this model:

Correct the error.

Guide the student to say the word correctly.

Check for understanding by having the student reread the word from among other randomly displayed high-frequency words.

Reinforce: Make a note to review the word during the student's next session.

Objectives

- Isolate and pronounce the /ks/ or /j/ sound in words.
- Blend and read words with /ks/x or /j/j.
- Read decodable text that includes words with /ks/x or /j/j.
- Read common high-frequency words by sight.

Materials

- Letter Cards
- Sound/Spelling Cards
- Instructional Routine: Sound/Spelling Cards
- Instructional Routine: Sound-by-Sound Blending
- Phonics/Decoding Strategy
- Practice Page K.84B

Phonics: Words with *x, j*

Phonemic Awareness Warm-up

- **Say:** *I'm going to say a word. Listen for the sound you hear at the beginning of the word. Listen:* x-ray. *What sound do you hear at the beginning of* x-ray? /ks/
- **Say:** *Now let's listen to the sound you hear at the end of the word. Listen:* box. *What sound do you hear at the end of* box? /ks/ *Now you do it with the word* fix. (/ks/)
- Repeat with the words *fox, ax,* and *mix.*
- **Say:** *I'm going to say a word. Listen for the sound you hear at the beginning of the word. I'll do the first one. Listen:* jet. *What sound do you hear at the beginning of* jet? /j/
- **Say:** *Now let's do it together. Listen:* jam. *What sound do you hear at the beginning of* jam? /j/ *Now you do it with the word* job. (/j/)
- Repeat with the words *jar, joke,* and *job.*

Teach/Model

SOUND/SPELLING Use Instructional Routine: Sound/Spelling Cards to introduce the Sound/Spelling Card for Mr. X-Ray. Name the picture and say the sound. Have students repeat after you. **Say:** *Listen:* X-ray, /ks/. *Now you say it.*

- Say the sound and give the spelling. **Say:** X-Ray *has the /ks/ sound in the first part of the word. The letter* x *stands for the /ks/ sound.*
- **Say:** *The letter* x *can also stand for the sound at the end of words. Listen for the sound you hear at the end of the word* ox. *The letter* x *stands for the /ks/ sound at the end of* ox. Ox, /ks/. *Now you say the word.* Have students repeat after you. Repeat with the words *box* and *fix.*
- Repeat with Sound/Spelling Card for Jumping Jill.
- Say the sound and give the spelling. **Say:** Jumping Jill *begins with the /j/ sound. The letter* j *stands for the /j/ sound at the beginning of* Jumping *and* Jill.

BLENDING Use Letter Cards and Instructional Routine: Sound-by-Sound Blending to model blending the words *jet* and *box.*

Guided Practice

BLENDING Display the words *mix, fix, job,* and *jam.* Work with students to blend the words, using Instructional Routine: Sound-by-Sound Blending.

PHONICS/DECODING STRATEGY Review the Phonics/Decoding Strategy. Display the sentences below. Call on students to use the strategy to blend one or more words and to read the sentences.

> My job is to mix jam.
>
> Fox and Ox go for a jog.

BUILDING AND WRITING WORDS Tell students to follow your directions and build new words with their Letter Cards. Have students start by building the word *job.*

- **Say:** *Change* b *to* t. *What's the new word?* (jot)
- **Say:** *Change* t *to* g. *What's the new word?* (jog)
- **Say:** *Change* j *to* b. *What's the new word?* (bog)
- **Say:** *Change* g *to* x. *What's the new word?* (box)
- **Say:** *Change* b *to* f. *What's the new word?* (fox)
- Then have students write each word and read it aloud.

Apply

- Distribute copies of Practice Page K.84B, which contains the decodable story *Will Jan Fix It?* Point out that the story is made up of several sentences, and each sentence is made of words.

- Point out that students have learned the following high-frequency word, which they will also read in the story: *said*.

- Review the Sound/Spelling Cards for *x* and *j*. Ask students to name the sound for *x* and *j*. Tell them that many words in this story have the /ks/ or /j/ sound.

- Review and model the Phonics/Decoding Strategy using the story title.

- Model fluency and accuracy. Read aloud the first sentence of the story as students follow along. Point out that you do not misread, add, or skip words. Lead students in choral reading the same sentence with fluency and accuracy.

- Have students use what they know about high-frequency words and letter-sound associations to read the story aloud.

Fun with Words Optional activities for engaging, hands-on practice are provided in the Resources section.

English Language Support

Linguistic Transfer Some students whose first language is Spanish, Vietnamese, Tagalog, or Korean may have trouble with the /j/ sound. Say the sound several times as ELs study your mouth position; students can also practice the sounds in front of a mirror. Then provide extra modeling and practice with words such as *jump, jar, just, joy, joke, jet, jeans, job*. Have students chorally repeat each word after you, then say just the beginning sound, and then say the whole word again. Use each word in a sentence to reinforce meaning.

Formative Assessment and Corrective Feedback

IF a student makes an error, THEN follow this model:

Correct the error.

Guide the student to perform the task correctly by modeling.

Check for understanding by having the student repeat the task.

Reinforce: Make a note to review the skill during the student's next session.

High-Frequency Words:
she, all, over, her, when, some

Objective

- Recognize and read high-frequency words.

Materials

- High-Frequency Word Cards

Formative Assessment and Corrective Feedback

IF a student makes an error, THEN follow this model:

Correct the error.

Guide the student to say the word correctly.

Check for understanding by having the student reread the word from among other randomly displayed high-frequency words.

Reinforce: Make a note to review the word during the student's next session.

Teach/Model

- Display the high-frequency words. Tell students that these are useful words to know, since they will see these words often. Tell students that reading will be easier if they recognize these words.
- Display the High-Frequency Word Card for *she* and say the word. Then spell the word aloud as you point to each letter. Say the word again.
- Use the word in a simple sentence that will provide context. For example: *She is the new girl.*
- Repeat the steps above with the remaining high-frequency words.

Guided Practice

Do the following for each high-frequency word:

- Display the High-Frequency Word Card. Read the word and have students repeat it.
- Note the familiar sound/spelling patterns that are shown on the back of the card. Note as well any unfamiliar and unexpected sound/spellings.
- Blend the word with students.
- Spell the word aloud, pointing to each letter.
- Have students then spell the word aloud as you point to each letter.
- Have students read the word again.

Apply

- Display the High-Frequency Word Cards in random order. Have students read the words aloud.
- Have students write each word. Tell them to compare their writing with the word on the card and make corrections if necessary.
- Have students read each word aloud and use it in a sentence.

Phonics: Words with Short *e*

Phonemic Awareness Warm-up

- Display the word *jet*. **Say:** *I'm going to say a word. Listen for the sound you hear in the middle. I'll do the first one. Listen:* jet. *What sound do you hear in the middle of* jet? /ĕ/
- Display the words *ten, red, net, pen, bed,* and *men*. **Say:** *Now let's do it together. Listen:* ten. *What sound do you hear in the middle of* ten? /ĕ/ *Now you do it.* Red? (/ĕ/)
- Repeat with the words *net, pen, bed,* and *men*.

Teach/Model

SOUND/SPELLING Use Instructional Routine: Sound/Spelling Cards to introduce the Sound/Spelling Card for Edna Elephant. Name the picture and say the sound. Have students repeat after you. **Say:** *Listen:* Edna, /ĕ/. *Now you say it.*

- Repeat with *Elephant*.
- Say the sound and give the spelling. **Say:** Edna Elephant *begins with the /ĕ/ sound. The letter* e *stands for the /ĕ/ sound at the beginning or in the middle of a word.*

BLENDING Use Letter Cards and Instructional Routine: Sound-by-Sound Blending to model blending the words *met* and *fed*.

Guided Practice

BLENDING Display the words *set, hen, led, pet*. Work with students to blend the words, using Instructional Routine: Sound-by-Sound Blending.

PHONICS/DECODING STRATEGY Review the Phonics/Decoding Strategy. Display the sentences below. Call on students to use the strategy to blend one or more words and to read the sentences.

> We get a red bed.
>
> Ten men see the jet.

BUILDING AND WRITING WORDS Tell students to follow your directions and build new words with their Letter Cards. Have students start by building the word *jet*.

- **Say:** *Change* j *to* s. *What's the new word?* (set)
- **Say:** *Change* s *to* m. *What's the new word?* (met)
- **Say:** *Change* m *to* n. *What's the new word?* (net)
- **Say:** *Change* n *to* w. *What's the new word?* (wet)
- **Say:** *Change* w *to* b. *What's the new word?* (bet)
- **Say:** *Change* b *to* p. *What's the new word?* (pet)
- **Say:** *Change* t *to* n. *What's the new word?* (pen)
- Then have students write each word and read it aloud.

Objectives

- Isolate and pronounce the /ĕ/ sound in words with short *e*.
- Blend and read words with short *e*.
- Read decodable text that includes words with short *e*.
- Read common high-frequency words by sight.

Materials

- Letter Cards
- Sound/Spelling Cards
- Instructional Routine: Sound/Spelling Cards
- Instructional Routine: Sound-by-Sound Blending
- Phonics/Decoding Strategy
- Practice Page K.85B

English Language Support

Linguistic Transfer Some English learners, including speakers of Spanish, Korean, Vietnamese, and Tagalog, may need extra practice with the /ĕ/ sound. Have ELs listen carefully as you pronounce words with the /ĕ/ sound: *fed, bet, yet, pep, red, neck.* Have students repeat each word, then vocalize the middle sound, and then say the whole word again. Use each word in a brief sentence to reinforce meaning.

Formative Assessment and Corrective Feedback

IF a student makes an error, THEN follow this model:

Correct the error.

Guide the student to perform the task correctly by modeling.

Check for understanding by having the student repeat the task.

Reinforce: Make a note to review the skill during the student's next session.

Apply

- Distribute copies of Practice Page K.85B, which contains the decodable story *Jen and Jet*. Point out that the story is made up of several sentences, and each sentence is made of words.

- Point out that students have learned the following high-frequency words, which they will also read in the story: *all, her.*

- Review the Sound/Spelling Card for short *e*. Ask students to name the sound for *e*. Tell students that many words in this story have the /ĕ/ sound.

- Review and model the Phonics/Decoding Strategy using the story title.

- Model fluency and accuracy. Read aloud the first sentence of the story as students follow along. Point out that you do not misread, add, or skip words. Lead them in choral reading the same sentence with fluency and accuracy.

- Have students use what they know about high-frequency words and letter-sound associations to read the story aloud.

> **Fun with Words** Optional activities for engaging, hands-on practice are provided in the Resources section.

High-Frequency Words:
no, he, away, must, by, there

Teach/Model

- Display the high-frequency words. Tell students that these are useful words to know, since they will see these words often. Tell students that reading will be easier if they recognize these words.
- Display the High-Frequency Word Card for *no* and say the word. Then spell the word aloud as you point to each letter. Say the word again.
- Use the word in a simple sentence that will provide context. For example: *There is no cat in the tree.*
- Repeat the steps above with the remaining high-frequency words.

Guided Practice

Do the following for each high-frequency word:

- Display the High-Frequency Word Card. Read the word and have students repeat it.
- Note the familiar sound/spelling patterns that are shown on the back of the card. Note as well any unfamiliar and unexpected sound/spellings.
- Blend the word with students.
- Spell the word aloud, pointing to each letter.
- Have students then spell the word aloud as you point to each letter.
- Have students read the word again.

Apply

- Display the High-Frequency Word Cards in random order. Have students read the words aloud.
- Have students write each word. Tell them to compare their writing with the word on the card and make corrections if necessary.
- Have students read each word aloud and use it in a sentence.

Objective

- Recognize and read high-frequency words.

Materials

- High-Frequency Word Cards

Formative Assessment and Corrective Feedback

IF a student makes an error, THEN follow this model:

Correct the error.

Guide the student to say the word correctly.

Check for understanding by having the student reread the word from among other randomly displayed high-frequency words.

Reinforce: Make a note to review the word during the student's next session.

Phonics: Words with *h, k*

Phonemic Awareness Warm-up

- **Say:** *I'm going to say a word. Listen for the sound you hear at the beginning of the word. Listen:* hat. *What sound do you hear at the beginning of* hat? /h/
- **Say:** *Now let's do it together. Listen:* hug. *What sound do you hear at the beginning of* hug? /h/ *Now you do it with the word* hen. (/h/)
- Repeat with the words *had, hid,* and *hop.*
- **Say:** *I'm going to say a word. Listen for the sound you hear at the beginning of the word. I'll do the first one. Listen:* kit. *What sound do you hear at the beginning of* kit? /k/
- **Say:** *Now let's do it together. Listen:* Ken. *What sound do you hear at the beginning of* Ken? /k/ *Now you do it with the word* Kim. (/k/)
- Repeat with the word *kid.*

Teach/Model

SOUND/SPELLING Use Instructional Routine: Sound/Spelling Cards to introduce the Sound/Spelling Card for Hattie Horse. Name the picture and say the sound. **Say:** *Listen:* Hattie, */h/. Now you say it.*

- Repeat with *Horse.*
- Say the sound and give the spelling. **Say:** Hattie Horse *begins with the /h/ sound. The letter* h *stands for the /h/ sound at the beginning of a word.*
- Repeat with the Sound/Spelling Card for Keely Kangaroo.

BLENDING Use Letter Cards and Instructional Routine: Sound-by-Sound Blending to model blending the words *kit* and *hat.*

Guided Practice

BLENDING Display the words *hop, hot, kid,* and *Ken.* Work with students to blend the words, using Instructional Routine: Sound-by-Sound Blending.

PHONICS/DECODING STRATEGY Review the Phonics/Decoding Strategy. Display the sentences below. Call on students to use the strategy to blend one or more words and to read the sentences.

> Ken hid a hat.
>
> Kim had a kit.

BUILDING AND WRITING WORDS Tell students to follow your directions and build new words with their Letter Cards. Have students start by building the word *hit.*

- **Say:** *Change* t *to* p. *What's the new word?* (hip)
- **Say:** *Change* p *to* m. *What's the new word?* (him)
- **Say:** *Change* h *to* k. *What's the new word?* (Kim)
- **Say:** *Change* m *to* t. *What's the new word?* (kit)
- **Say:** *Change* t *to* d. *What's the new word?* (kid)
- Then have students write each word and read it aloud.

Apply

- Distribute copies of Practice Page K.86B, which contains the decodable story *Kid Hid Here*. Point out that the story is made up of several sentences, and each sentence is made of words.

- Point out that students have learned the following high-frequency words, which they will also read in the story: *by, there*.

- Review the Sound/Spelling Cards for *h* and *k*. Ask students to name the sound for *h* and *k*. Tell them that many words in this story have the /h/ or /k/ sound.

- Review and model the Phonics/Decoding Strategy using the story title.

- Model fluency and accuracy. Read aloud the first sentence of the story as students follow along. Point out that you do not misread, add, or skip words. Lead students in choral reading the same sentence with fluency and accuracy.

- Have students use what they know about high-frequency words and letter-sound associations to read the story aloud.

Fun with Words Optional activities for engaging, hands-on practice are provided in the Resources section.

English Language Support

Linguistic Transfer Students who have reading skill in Spanish may associate the /h/ sound with the letter *j*, as in *jugar* (to play); in Spanish, the letter *h* is silent, as in *hora* (hour). Explain to students that in English, the letter *h* stands for the /h/ sound. Have students practice by repeating words like these after you: *how, hand, hen, hope, hello*. Use each word in a brief sentence to reinforce meaning.

Formative Assessment and Corrective Feedback

IF a student makes an error, THEN follow this model:

Correct the error.

Guide the student to perform the task correctly by modeling.

Check for understanding by having the student repeat the task.

Reinforce: Make a note to review the skill during the student's next session.

Cumulative Review/Fluency

Teach/Model

REVIEW

- Remind students they have learned sounds for the consonants *x, j, h,* and *k.* Review the sounds with the Sound/Spelling Cards for Mr. X-Ray, Jumping Jill, Hattie Horse, and Keely Kangaroo. Display the cards and review the sounds for each.

- Remind students they have learned the short vowel sounds for *o* and *e.* Use the Sound/Spelling Cards for Ozzie Octopus and Edna Elephant. Display the cards and review the short sounds for *o* and *e.*

- Display these sentences:

  The hen is by a box over there.

  A big hen and a fox ran away.

  Jan had a new jet kit.

- Point to the high-frequency words *away, by, new, over,* and *there* and read each one. Remind students that they know these words. Use the High-Frequency Word Cards and Instructional Routine: High-Frequency Words to review these words.

MODEL FLUENCY

- Read the above sentences, focusing on the words in the sentences that contain /ks/*x*, /j/*j*, /h/*h*, /k/*k*, and short vowels *o* and *e.* Model blending the sounds to read the words. Read the first sentence: *The hen is by a box over there.* Read the words *hen* and *box* more slowly, as if sounding them out. Then read the sentence again, this time at a natural pace. Have students read the sentence with you. Continue with the remaining sentences.

Guided Practice

- Tell students they will practice reading. Display the following sentences:

  A pet can hop and hop.

  The jet is on the box.

  A big kit is by the box.

- Guide students in reading the sentences aloud. Coach them to sound out each word. Have students go back to any word they read incorrectly. Have students read the text again.

Objectives

- Decode words with short vowels *o* and *e* and consonants *x, j, h,* and *k.*
- Read common high-frequency words by sight.
- Read emergent-reader texts with purpose and understanding.

Materials

- Sound/Spelling Cards
- High-Frequency Word Cards
- Instructional Routine: High-Frequency Words
- Practice Page K.87

Have students read aloud the practice text on Practice Page K.87.

- Explain that the main purpose of reading the text is to practice their reading skills.

- Coach students to use decoding skills and context to self-correct any mistakes they make during reading. They should read the text several times, until they are able to read smoothly and accurately.

- When students have finished the fluency practice, choose a few sentences to review. Have students read each sentence and explain in their own words what it means.

- After students are able to read the text fluently, guide them to track their progress on their My Progress line graphs.

Formative Assessment and Corrective Feedback

IF a student makes an error, THEN follow this model:

Correct the error.

Guide the student to say the word correctly.

Check for understanding by having the student reread the word.

Reinforce: Make a note to review the word during the student's next session.

Objective

- Recognize and read high-frequency words.

Materials

- High-Frequency Word Cards

Formative Assessment and Corrective Feedback

IF a student makes an error, THEN follow this model:

Correct the error.

Guide the student to say the word correctly.

Check for understanding by having the student reread the word from among other randomly displayed high-frequency words.

Reinforce: Make a note to review the word during the student's next session.

High-Frequency Words: *down, do, went, only, little, just*

Teach/Model

- Display the high-frequency words. Tell students that these are useful words to know, since they will see these words often. Tell students that reading will be easier if they recognize these words.
- Display the High-Frequency Word Card for *down* and say the word. Then spell the word aloud as you point to each letter. Say the word again.
- Use the word in a simple sentence that will provide context. For example: *The cat ran down the hill.*
- Repeat the steps above with the remaining high-frequency words.

Guided Practice

Do the following for each high-frequency word:

- Display the High-Frequency Word Card. Read the word and have students repeat it.
- Note the familiar sound/spelling patterns that are shown on the back of the card. Note as well any unfamiliar and unexpected sound/spellings.
- Blend the word with students.
- Spell the word aloud, pointing to each letter.
- Have students then spell the word aloud as you point to each letter.
- Have students read the word again.

Apply

- Display the High-Frequency Word Cards in random order. Have students read the words aloud.
- Have students write each word. Tell them to compare their writing with the word on the card and make corrections if necessary.
- Have students read each word aloud and use it in a sentence.

Phonics: Words with Short *u*

Phonemic Awareness Warm-up

- Display the word *cup*. **Say:** *I'm going to say a word. Listen for the sound you hear in the middle. I'll do the first one. Listen:* cup. *What sound do you hear in the middle of* cup? /ŭ/
- Display the words *sun, rub, hug, bus, run,* and *bug.* **Say:** *Now let's do it together. Listen:* sun. *What sound do you hear in the middle of* sun? /ŭ/ *Now you do it.* Rub? (/ŭ/)
- Repeat with the words *hug, bus, run,* and *bug.*

Teach/Model

SOUND/SPELLING Use Instructional Routine: Sound/Spelling Cards to introduce the Sound/Spelling Card for Umbie Umbrella. Name the picture and say the sound. Have students repeat after you. **Say:** *Listen:* Umbie, /ŭ/. *Now you say it.*

- Repeat with *Umbrella.*
- Say the sound and give the spelling. **Say:** Umbie Umbrella *begins with the /ŭ/ sound. The letter* u *stands for the /ŭ/ sound at the beginning or in the middle of a word.*

BLENDING Use Letter Cards and Instructional Routine: Sound-by-Sound Blending to model blending the words *up* and *fun.*

Guided Practice

BLENDING Display the words *tub, mud, rug, cut.* Work with students to blend the words, using Instructional Routine: Sound-by-Sound Blending.

PHONICS/DECODING STRATEGY Review the Phonics/Decoding Strategy. Display the sentences below. Call on students to use the strategy to blend one or more words and to read the sentences.

> Gus got mud on the rug.
>
> The cub and the pup had fun.

BUILDING AND WRITING WORDS Tell students to follow your directions and build new words with their Letter Cards. Have students start by building the word *nut.*

- **Say:** *Change* n *to* h. *What's the new word?* (hut)
- **Say:** *Change* h *to* c. *What's the new word?* (cut)
- **Say:** *Change* t *to* p. *What's the new word?* (cup)
- **Say:** *Change* p *to* b. *What's the new word?* (cub)
- **Say:** *Change* c *to* r. *What's the new word?* (rub)
- **Say:** *Change* r *to* t. *What's the new word?* (tub)
- Then have students write each word and read it aloud.

Objectives

- Isolate and pronounce the /ŭ/ sound in words with short *u*.
- Blend and read words with short *u*.
- Read decodable text that includes words with short *u*.
- Read common high-frequency words by sight.

Materials

- Letter Cards
- Sound/Spelling Cards
- Instructional Routine: Sound/Spelling Cards
- Instructional Routine: Sound-by-Sound Blending
- Phonics/Decoding Strategy
- Practice Page K.88B

English Language Support

Linguistic Transfer Students whose first language is Spanish, Chinese, Tagalog, or Korean may have trouble with the /ŭ/ sound. Say the sound several times as ELs study your mouth position; students can also practice the sounds in front of a mirror. Point out that your mouth is more closed for /ŭ/ than for /ŏ/. Then provide extra modeling and practice with words such as *cup, tub, hut, duck, sum,* and *pup;* have students chorally repeat each word after you, then say just the middle sound, and then say the whole word again. Use each word in a sentence to reinforce meaning.

Formative Assessment and Corrective Feedback

IF a student makes an error, THEN follow this model:

Correct the error.

Guide the student to perform the task correctly by modeling.

Check for understanding by having the student repeat the task.

Reinforce: Make a note to review the skill during the student's next session.

Apply

- Distribute copies of Practice Page K.88B, which contains the decodable story *Run for Fun.* Point out that the story is made up of several sentences, and each sentence is made of words.

- Point out that students have learned the following high-frequency words, which they will also read in the story: *down, little, went.*

- Review the Sound/Spelling Card for short *u.* Ask students to name the sound for *u.* Tell students that many words in this story have the /ŭ/ sound.

- Review and model the Phonics/Decoding Strategy using the story title.

- Model fluency and accuracy. Read aloud the first sentence of the story as students follow along. Point out that you do not misread, add, or skip words. Lead them in choral reading the same sentence with fluency and accuracy.

- Have students use what they know about high-frequency words and letter-sound associations to read the story aloud.

Fun with Words Optional activities for engaging, hands-on practice are provided in the Resources section.

High-Frequency Words:
have, help, one, every, ask, walk

Teach/Model

- Display the high-frequency words. Tell students that these are useful words to know, since they will see these words often. Tell students that reading will be easier if they recognize these words.
- Display the High-Frequency Word Card for *have* and say the word. Then spell the word aloud as you point to each letter. Say the word again.
- Use the word in a simple sentence that will provide context. For example: *I have a pet cat.*
- Repeat the steps above with the remaining high-frequency words.

Guided Practice

Do the following for each high-frequency word:

- Display the High-Frequency Word Card. Read the word and have students repeat it.
- Note the familiar sound/spelling patterns that are shown on the back of the card. Note as well any unfamiliar and unexpected sound/spellings.
- Blend the word with students.
- Spell the word aloud, pointing to each letter.
- Have students then spell the word aloud as you point to each letter.
- Have students read the word again.

Apply

- Display the High-Frequency Word Cards in random order. Have students read the words aloud.
- Have students write each word. Tell them to compare their writing with the word on the card and make corrections if necessary.
- Have students read each word aloud and use it in a sentence.

Objective

- Recognize and read high-frequency words.

Materials

- High-Frequency Word Cards

Formative Assessment and Corrective Feedback

IF a student makes an error, THEN follow this model:

Correct the error.

Guide the student to say the word correctly.

Check for understanding by having the student reread the word from among other randomly displayed high-frequency words.

Reinforce: Make a note to review the word during the student's next session.

Objectives

- Isolate and pronounce the /l/ or /w/ sound in words.
- Blend and read words with /l/l or /w/w.
- Read decodable text that includes words with /l/l or /w/w.
- Read common high-frequency words by sight.

Materials

- Letter Cards
- Sound/Spelling Cards
- Instructional Routine: Sound/Spelling Cards
- Instructional Routine: Sound-by-Sound Blending
- Phonics/Decoding Strategy
- Practice Page K.89B

Phonics: Words with *l, w*

Phonemic Awareness Warm-up

- **Say:** *I'm going to say a word. Listen for the sound you hear at the beginning of the word. Listen:* log. *What sound do you hear at the beginning of* log? /l/
- **Say:** *Now let's do it together. Listen:* lit. *What sound do you hear at the beginning of* lit? /l/ *Now you do it with the word* let. (/l/)
- Repeat with the words *like, look,* and *long.*
- **Say:** *I'm going to say a word. Listen for the sound you hear at the beginning of the word. I'll do the first one. Listen:* web. *What sound do you hear at the beginning of* web? /w/
- **Say:** *Now let's do it together. Listen:* win. *What sound do you hear at the beginning of* win? /w/ *Now you do it with the word* wet. (/w/)
- Repeat with the words *we, with,* and *will.*

Teach/Model

SOUND/SPELLING Use Instructional Routine: Sound/Spelling Cards to introduce the Sound/Spelling Card for Larry Lion. Name the picture and say the sound. Say: *Listen:* Larry, /l/. *Now you say it.*

- Repeat with *Lion.*
- Say the sound and give the spelling. **Say:** Larry Lion *begins with the /l/ sound. The letter* l *stands for the /l/ sound at the beginning of a word.*
- Repeat with the Sound/Spelling Card for Willy Worm.

BLENDING Use Letter Cards and Instructional Routine: Sound-by-Sound Blending to model blending the words *log* and *web.*

Guided Practice

BLENDING Display the words *let, win, lid,* and *wet.* Work with students to blend the words, using Instructional Routine: Sound-by-Sound Blending.

PHONICS/DECODING STRATEGY Review the Phonics/Decoding Strategy. Display the sentences below. Call on students to use the strategy to blend one or more words and to read the sentences.

> Let me win a dog.
>
> It is a wet log.

BUILDING AND WRITING WORDS Tell students to follow your directions and build new words with their Letter Cards. Have students start by building the word *web.*

- **Say:** *Change* b *to* d. *What's the new word?* (wed)
- **Say:** *Change* d *to* t. *What's the new word?* (wet)
- **Say:** *Change* w *to* l. *What's the new word?* (let)
- **Say:** *Change* t *to* d. *What's the new word?* (led)
- **Say:** *Change* d *to* g. *What's the new word?* (leg)
- Then have students write each word and read it aloud.

Apply

- Distribute copies of Practice Page K.89B, which contains the decodable story *Win with Wes*. Point out that the story is made up of several sentences, and each sentence is made of words.

- Point out that students have learned the following high-frequency words, which they will also read in the story: *help, walk.*

- Review the Sound/Spelling Cards for *l* and *w*. Ask students to name the sounds for *l* and *w*. Tell them that many words in this story have the /l/ or /w/ sound.

- Review and model the Phonics/Decoding Strategy using the story title.

- Model fluency and accuracy. Read aloud the first sentence of the story as students follow along. Point out that you do not misread, add, or skip words. Lead students in choral reading the same sentence with fluency and accuracy.

- Have students use what they know about high-frequency words and letter-sound associations to read the story aloud.

Fun with Words Optional activities for engaging, hands-on practice are provided in the Resources section.

English Language Support

Linguistic Transfer Some English learners (including speakers of Hmong) may have trouble with the /w/ sound. Model pronouncing the sound, and explain that your tongue is touching the roof of your mouth, blocking the air, so the air must come through your nose. Have ELs practice the sound in front of a mirror and then practice pronouncing words such as these: *will, win, wet, won, wick.* Use each word in a brief sentence to reinforce meaning.

Formative Assessment and Corrective Feedback

IF a student makes an error, THEN follow this model:

Correct the error.

Guide the student to perform the task correctly by modeling.

Check for understanding by having the student repeat the task.

Reinforce: Make a note to review the skill during the student's next session.

Objective

- Recognize and read high-frequency words.

Materials

- High-Frequency Word Cards

Formative Assessment and Corrective Feedback

IF a student makes an error, THEN follow this model:

Correct the error.

Guide the student to say the word correctly.

Check for understanding by having the student reread the word from among other randomly displayed high-frequency words.

Reinforce: Make a note to review the word during the student's next session.

Teach/Model

- Display the high-frequency words. Tell students that these are useful words to know, since they will see these words often. Tell students that reading will be easier if they recognize these words.
- Display the High-Frequency Word Card for *look* and say the word. Then spell the word aloud as you point to each letter. Say the word again.
- Use the word in a simple sentence that will provide context. For example: *Let's look for the lost dog.*
- Repeat the steps above for the remaining high-frequency words.

Guided Practice

Do the following for each high-frequency word:

- Display the High-Frequency Word Card. Read the word and have students repeat it.
- Note the familiar sound/spelling patterns that are shown on the back of the card. Note as well any unfamiliar and unexpected sound/spellings.
- Blend the word with students.
- Spell the word aloud, pointing to each letter.
- Have students then spell the word aloud as you point to each letter.
- Have students read the word again.

Apply

- Display the High-Frequency Word Cards in random order. Have students read the words aloud.
- Have students write each word. Tell them to compare their writing with the word on the card and make corrections if necessary.
- Have students read each word aloud and use it in a sentence.

Phonics: Words with *v, z*

Phonemic Awareness Warm-up

- **Say:** *I'm going to say a word. Listen for the sound you hear at the beginning of the word. Listen:* van. *What sound do you hear at the beginning of* van? /v/
- **Say:** *Now let's do it together. Listen:* vase. *What sound do you hear at the beginning of* vase? /v/ *Now you do it with the word* vine. (/v/)
- Repeat with the words *vet, voice,* and *vest.*
- **Say:** *I'm going to say a word. Listen for the sound you hear at the beginning of the word. I'll do the first one. Listen:* zoo. *What sound do you hear at the beginning of* zoo? /z/
- **Say:** *Now let's do it together. Listen:* zip. *What sound do you hear at the beginning of* zip? /z/ *Now you do it with the word* zone. (/z/)
- Repeat with the words *zig, zap,* and *zest.*

Teach/Model

SOUND/SPELLING Use Instructional Routine: Sound/Spelling Cards to introduce the Sound/Spelling Card for Vinnie Volcano. Name the picture and say the sound. **Say:** *Listen:* Vinnie, */v/. Now you say it.*

- Say the sound and give the spelling. **Say:** Vinnie Volcano *begins with the /v/ sound. The letter* v *stands for the /v/ sound in a word.*
- Repeat with *Volcano.*
- Then introduce the Sound/Spelling Card for Zelda Zebra. Name the picture and say the sound. **Say:** *Listen:* Zelda, */z/. Now you say it.*
- Repeat with *Zebra.*
- Say the sound and give the spelling. **Say:** Zelda Zebra *begins with the /z/ sound. The letter* z *stands for the /z/ sound in a word.*

BLENDING Use Letter Cards and Instructional Routine: Sound-by-Sound Blending to model blending the words *van* and *zip.*

Guided Practice

BLENDING Display the words *vet, Liz, vat,* and *zag.* Work with students to blend the words, using Instructional Routine: Sound-by-Sound Blending.

PHONICS/DECODING STRATEGY Review the Phonics/Decoding Strategy. Display the sentences below. Call on students to use the strategy to blend one or more words and to read the sentences.

> The vet got in a van.
>
> Can Val zip it?

BUILDING AND WRITING WORDS Tell students to follow your directions and build new words with their Letter Cards. Have students start by building the word *van.*

- **Say:** *Change* n *to* t. *What's the new word?* (vat)

Have students start a new activity by building the word *zip.*

- **Say:** *Change* p *to* g. *What's the new word?* (zig)
- Then have students write each word and read it aloud.

Objectives

- Isolate and pronounce the /v/ or /z/ sound in words.
- Blend and read words with /v/v or /z/z.
- Read decodable text that includes words with /v/v or /z/z.
- Read common high-frequency words by sight.

Materials

- Letter Cards
- Sound/Spelling Cards
- Instructional Routine: Sound/Spelling Cards
- Instructional Routine: Sound-by-Sound Blending
- Phonics/Decoding Strategy
- Practice Page K.90B

English Language Support

Linguistic Transfer Some English learners (including speakers of Spanish or Korean) may have trouble distinguishing /v/ from /b/. Cantonese speakers may also have trouble with /v/. Say both sounds several times as ELs study your mouth positions. Have ELs practice the sounds and then repeat the word that starts with /v/ in pairs like these: *van/ban, bet/vet, bat/vat, vote/ boat, very/berry*. Use each word in a brief sentence to reinforce meaning.

Many English learners (including speakers of Spanish, Cantonese or Mandarin, Tagalog, Korean, or Hmong) may have trouble with the /z/ sound. Say the sound several times as ELs study your mouth position; as they imitate the sound, encourage them to feel that their throat is vibrating; point out that this difference between /s/ and /z/. To practice, have ELs repeat the word that starts with /z/ in pairs like these: *zoo/Sue, zip/sip, sap/zap*. Use each word in a brief sentence to reinforce meaning.

Formative Assessment and Corrective Feedback

IF a student makes an error, THEN follow this model:

Correct the error.

Guide the student to perform the task correctly by modeling.

Check for understanding by having the student repeat the task.

Reinforce: Make a note to review the skill during the student's next session.

Apply

- Distribute copies of Practice Page K.90B, which contains the decodable story *Zed the Good Vet*. Point out that the story is made up of several sentences, and each sentence is made of words.

- Point out that students have learned the following high-frequency words, which they will also read in the story: *look, saw*.

- Review the Sound/Spelling Cards for *v* and *z*. Ask students to name the sound for *v* and *z*. Tell them that many words in this story have the /v/ or /z/ sound.

- Review and model the Phonics/Decoding Strategy using the story title.

- Model fluency and accuracy. Read aloud the first sentence of the story as students follow along. Point out that you do not misread, add, or skip words. Lead students in choral reading the same sentence with fluency and accuracy.

- Have students use what they know about high-frequency words and letter-sound associations to read the story aloud.

Fun with Words Optional activities for engaging, hands-on practice are provided in the Resources section.

High-Frequency Words:
off, take, our, day, too, show

Teach/Model

- Display the high-frequency words. Tell students that these are useful words to know, since they will see these words often. Tell students that reading will be easier if they recognize these words.
- Display the High-Frequency Word Card for *off* and say the word. Then spell the word aloud as you point to each letter. Say the word again.
- Use the word in a simple sentence that will provide context. For example: *Bob got off the bus.*
- Repeat the steps above for the remaining high-frequency words.

Guided Practice

Do the following for each high-frequency word:

- Display the High-Frequency Word Card. Read the word and have students repeat it.
- Note the familiar sound/spelling patterns that are shown on the back of the card. Note as well any unfamiliar and unexpected sound/spellings.
- Blend the word with students.
- Spell the word aloud, pointing to each letter.
- Have students then spell the word aloud as you point to each letter.
- Have students read the word again.

Apply

- Display the High-Frequency Word Cards in random order. Have students read the words aloud.
- Have students write each word. Tell them to compare their writing with the word on the card and make corrections if necessary.
- Have students read each word aloud and use it in a sentence.

Formative Assessment and Corrective Feedback

IF a student makes an error, THEN follow this model:

Correct the error.

Guide the student to say the word correctly.

Check for understanding by having the student reread the word from among other randomly displayed high-frequency words.

Reinforce: Make a note to review the word during the student's next session.

Objectives

- Isolate and pronounce the /y/ or /kw/ sound in words.
- Blend and read words with /y/y or /kw/qu.
- Read decodable text that includes words with /y/y or /kw/qu.
- Read common high-frequency words by sight.

Materials

- Letter Cards
- Sound/Spelling Cards
- Instructional Routine: Sound/Spelling Cards
- Instructional Routine: Sound-by-Sound Blending
- Phonics/Decoding Strategy
- Practice Page K.91B

Phonics: Words with *y, qu*

Phonemic Awareness Warm-up

- **Say:** *I'm going to say a word. Listen for the sound you hear at the beginning of the word. Listen:* yet. *What sound do you hear at the beginning of* yet? /y/
- **Say:** *Now let's do it together. Listen:* you. *What sound do you hear at the beginning of* you? /y/ *Now you do it with the word* yard. (/y/)
- Repeat with the words *yes, yell,* and *year.*
- **Say:** *I'm going to say a word. Listen for the sound you hear at the beginning of the word. I'll do the first one. Listen:* quit. *What sound do you hear at the beginning of* quit? /kw/
- **Say:** *Now let's do it together. Listen:* quick. *What sound do you hear at the beginning of* quick? /kw/ *Now you do it with the word* quack. (/kw/)
- Repeat with the words *quick, queen,* and *quiz.*

Teach/Model

SOUND/SPELLING Use Instructional Routine: Sound/Spelling Cards to introduce the Sound/Spelling Card for Yetta Yo-yo. Name the picture and say the sound. **Say:** *Listen:* Yetta, /y/. *Now you say it.*

- Say the sound and give the spelling. **Say:** Yetta Yo-yo *begins with the /y/ sound. The letter* y *stands for the /y/ sound in a word.*
- Repeat with *Yo-yo.*
- Then introduce the Sound/Spelling Card for Queenie Queen. Name the picture and say the sound. **Say:** *Listen:* Queenie, /kw/. *Now you say it.*
- Repeat with *Queen.*

- Say the sound and give the spelling. **Say:** Queenie Queen *begins with the /kw/ sound. The letter* q *along with the letter* u *stand for the /kw/ sound at the beginning of a word.*

BLENDING Use Letter Cards and Instructional Routine: Sound-by-Sound Blending to model blending the words *yet* and *quit.*

Guided Practice

BLENDING Display the words *yip, yam, quiz,* and *yes.* Work with students to blend the words, using Instructional Routine: Sound-by-Sound Blending.

PHONICS/DECODING STRATEGY Review the Phonics/Decoding Strategy. Display the sentences below. Call on students to use the strategy to blend one or more words and to read the sentences.

> Yes, we had a quiz.
>
> The yak had a yam.

BUILDING AND WRITING WORDS Tell students to follow your directions and build new words with their Letter Cards. Have students start by building the word *quit.*

- **Say:** *Change* t *to* z. *What's the new word?* (quiz)

Have students start a new activity by building the word *yes.*

- **Say:** *Change* s *to* t. *What's the new word?* (yet)
- Then have students write each word and read it aloud.

Apply

- Distribute copies of Practice Page K.91B, which contains the decodable story *Who Will Quit?* Point out that the story is made up of several sentences, and each sentence is made of words.
- Point out that students have learned the following high-frequency words, which they will also read in the story: *show, take, too*.
- Review the Sound/Spelling Cards for *y* and *qu*. Ask students to name the sounds for *y* and *qu*. Tell them that many words in this story have the /y/ or /kw/ sound.
- Review and model the Phonics/Decoding Strategy using the story title.
- Model fluency and accuracy. Read aloud the first sentence of the story as students follow along. Point out that you do not misread, add, or skip words. Lead students in choral reading the same sentence with fluency and accuracy.
- Have students use what they know about high-frequency words and letter-sound associations to read the story aloud.

Fun with Words Optional activities for engaging, hands-on practice are provided in the Resources section.

English Language Support

Linguistic Transfer Most Spanish speakers will have little difficulty with the /y/ sound, which is represented by *ll* in Spanish. However, some speakers use a /j/ when they pronounce a word with *y*; for example, /jĕs/ for /yĕs/. Have students try to say the /y/ sound without touching their tongue to the roof of their mouths, practicing with these words: *yes, young, yellow, yesterday*. Use each word in a brief sentence to reinforce meaning.

Students who have reading skill in Spanish may associate the letters *qu* with the /k/ sound, as in the word *que* (/kā/). Point out that in English, the letters *qu* usually stand for the sound /kw/. Have students practice by repeating words like these after you: *queen, quick, quiet, quit*. Use each word in a brief sentence to reinforce meaning.

Formative Assessment and Corrective Feedback

IF a student makes an error, THEN follow this model:

Correct the error.

Guide the student to perform the task correctly by modeling.

Check for understanding by having the student repeat the task.

Reinforce: Make a note to review the skill during the student's next session.

Cumulative Review/Fluency

Objectives

- Decode words with short vowel *u* and consonants *l, w, v, z, y, qu*.
- Read common high-frequency words by sight.
- Read emergent-reader texts with purpose and understanding.

Materials

- Sound/Spelling Cards
- High-Frequency Word Cards
- Instructional Routine: High-Frequency Words
- Practice Page K.92

Teach/Model

REVIEW

- Remind students they have learned sounds for the consonants *l, w, v, z, y, qu*. Review the sounds with the Sound/Spelling Cards for Larry Lion, Willie Worm, Vinnie Volcano, Zelda Zebra, Yetta Yo-Yo, and Queenie Queen. Display the cards and review the sounds for each.
- Remind students they have learned the short vowel sound for *u*. Use the Sound/Spelling Card for Umbie Umbrella. Display the card and review the short sound for *u*.
- Display these sentences:

  A little bug dug in our wet pit.

  One vet let the cat walk over there.

  We have to zip it. We can not just quit.

- Point to the high-frequency words, *have, just, little, one, our*, and *walk* and read each one. Remind students that they know these words. Use the High-Frequency Word Cards and Instructional Routine: High-Frequency Words to review these words.

MODEL FLUENCY

- Read the above sentences, focusing on the words in the sentences that contain /l/*l*, /w/*w*, /v/*v*, /z/*z*, /kw/*qu*, and short vowel *u*. Model blending the sounds to read the words. Read the first sentence: *A little bug dug in our wet pit*. Read the words *bug, dug* and *wet* more slowly, as if sounding them out. Then read the sentence again, this time at a natural pace. Have students read the sentence with you. Continue with the remaining sentences.

Guided Practice

- Tell students they will practice reading. Display the following sentences:

  Zed let me take our van.

  We will not quit yet.

  Ask Len to help with the wet dog.

- Guide students in reading the sentences aloud. Coach them to sound out each word. Have students go back to any word they read incorrectly. Have them sound out the word again. Guide students to look for context clues in surrounding text to help them figure out the word.

Have students read aloud the practice text on Practice Page K.92.

- Explain that the main purpose of reading the text is to practice their reading skills.

- Coach students to use decoding skills to self-correct any mistakes they make during reading. They should read the text several times, until they are able to read smoothly and accurately.

- When students have finished the fluency practice, choose a few sentences to review. Have students read each sentence and explain in their own words what it means.

- After students are able to read the text fluently, guide them to track their progress on their My Progress line graphs.

Formative Assessment and Corrective Feedback

IF a student makes an error, THEN follow this model:

Correct the error.

Guide the student to say the word correctly.

Check for understanding by having the student reread the word.

Reinforce: Make a note to review the word during the student's next session.

Phonics: Words with Short and Long *e*

Objectives

- Isolate and pronounce the /ĕ/ or /ē/ sound in words with short or long *e*.
- Distinguish between the long and short *e* sounds.
- Blend and read words with short and long *e*.
- Read decodable text that includes words with short and long *e*.
- Read common high-frequency words by sight.

Materials

- Letter Cards
- Sound/Spelling Cards
- Instructional Routine: Sound/Spelling Cards
- Instructional Routine: Sound-by-Sound Blending
- Phonics/Decoding Strategy
- Practice Page K.93A

Phonemic Awareness Warm-up

- Display the words *pet* and *Pete*. **Say:** *I'm going to say a word. Listen for the sound you hear in the middle. Listen:* pet. *What sound do you hear in the middle of* pet? /ĕ/ *Yes, that is the short* e *vowel sound.*

- **Say:** *Listen as I say another word. Listen for the sound you hear in the middle. Listen:* Pete. *What sound do you hear in the middle of* Pete? /ē/ *Say the words with me:* pet, Pete. *The middle sound of* pet *is* /ĕ/. *The middle sound of* Pete *is* /ē/.

- **Say:** *Listen as I say some other words. Tell me which word has the* /ē/ *sound. Now let's do it together. Listen:* met/meet. *Which word has the* ē *sound in the middle?* (meet)

- Repeat with these words: *feed/fed, teen/ten, read/red, net/neat, bead/bed, men/mean.*

Teach/Model

SOUND/SPELLING Use Instructional Routine: Sound/Spelling Cards to review the Sound/Spelling Card for Edna Elephant. Name the picture and say the short *e* sound. Have students repeat after you. **Say:** *Listen:* Edna, /ĕ/. *Now you say it.*

- Repeat with *Elephant*.

- Say the sound and give the spelling: **Say:** *Remember that* Edna Elephant *begins with the* /ĕ/ *sound. The letter* e *stands for the* /ĕ/ *sound at the beginning or in the middle of words.*

- Display the Sound/Spelling Card for *eagle*. Name the picture and say the vowel sound. Have students repeat after you. **Say:** *Listen:* eagle, /ē/. *Now you say it.*

- Say the sound and give the spelling: **Say:** Eagle *begins with the* /ē/ *sound. The letter* e *sometimes stands for its name,* /ē/.

BLENDING Use Letter Cards and Instructional Routine: Sound-by-Sound Blending to model blending the word *me* and *we*.

Guided Practice

DISTINGUISH SHORT AND LONG SOUNDS Display Sound/Spelling Cards for Edna Elephant and *eagle*. Say words with the short *e* or long *e* sound at the end or in the middle, such as *he, me, be; pet, set, beg, ten.*

- Have students repeat each word and tell whether they hear /ĕ/ or /ē/. Ask students to sort the words by vowel sound; write each word next to the appropriate Sound/Spelling Card. Then have students blend and read the words.

BLENDING Display the words *be, we, he*. Work with students to blend the words, using Instructional Routine: Sound-by-Sound Blending.

PHONICS/DECODING STRATEGY Review the Phonics/Decoding Strategy. Display the sentences below. Call on students to use the strategy to blend one or more words and to read the sentences.

> We get ten men.
>
> He can get a jet.

BUILDING AND WRITING WORDS Tell students to follow your directions and build new words with their Letter Cards. Have students start by building the word *we*.

- **Say:** *Change* w *to* m. *What's the new word?* (me)
- **Say:** *Change* m *to* b. *What's the new word?* (be)
- **Say:** *Change* b *to* h. *What's the new word?* (he)
- Then have students write each word and read it aloud.

Apply

- Distribute copies of Practice Page K.93A, which contains the decodable story *We Can Have Fun*. Point out that the story is made up of several sentences, and each sentence is made of words.

- Point out that students have learned the following high-frequency words, which they will also read in the story: *a, and, go, have, into, look, said, see, take, the, there, to*.

- Review the Sound/Spelling Cards for short *e* and long *e*. Ask students to name the sounds for short *e* and long *e*. Tell students that many words in this story have the /ĕ/ or /ē/ sound.

- Review and model the Phonics/Decoding Strategy using the story title.

- Model fluency and accuracy. Read aloud the first sentence of the story as students follow along. Point out that you do not misread, add, or skip words. Lead them in choral reading the same sentence with fluency and accuracy.

- Have students use what they know about high-frequency words and letter-sound associations to read the story aloud.

Fun with Words Optional activities for engaging, hands-on practice are provided in the Resources section.

English Language Support

Linguistic Transfer Provide extra practice with the English vowel sounds. Display the Sound/Spelling Cards for Edna Elephant and *eagle*. Say the words, emphasizing the target vowel sound. English learners may need extra practice with the /ĕ/ sound. Have ELs listen carefully as you pronounce words with the /ĕ/ sound: *bed, yes, yet, pen, ten, red*. Have students repeat each word. Then vocalize the middle sound and say the whole word again. Use each word in a brief sentence to reinforce meaning. For the /ē/ sound, have students suggest words that rhyme with *feed* and have them name the middle sound. Continue the activity with *meet*.

Formative Assessment and Corrective Feedback

IF a student makes an error, THEN follow this model:

Correct the error.

Guide the student to perform the task correctly by modeling.

Check for understanding by having the student repeat the task.

Reinforce: Make a note to review the skill during the student's next session.

Objectives

- Isolate and pronounce the /ĭ/ or /ī/ sound in words with short or long *i*.
- Distinguish between the long and short *i* sounds.
- Blend and read words with short and long *i*.
- Read decodable text that includes words with short and long *i*.
- Read common high-frequency words by sight.

Materials

- Letter Cards
- Sound/Spelling Cards
- High-Frequency Word Card: I
- Instructional Routine: Sound/Spelling Cards
- Instructional Routine: Sound-by-Sound Blending
- Phonics/Decoding Strategy
- Practice Page K.93B

Phonics: Words with Short and Long *i*

Phonemic Awareness Warm-up

- Display the words *kit* and *kite*. **Say:** *I'm going to say a word. Listen for the sound you hear in the middle. Listen:* kit. *What sound do you hear in the middle of* kit? /ĭ/ *Yes, that is the short* i *vowel sound.*
- **Say:** *Listen as I say another word. Listen for the sound you hear in the middle. Listen:* kite. *What sound do you hear in the middle of* kite? /ī/ *Say the words with me:* kit, kite. *The middle sound of* kit *is* /ĭ/. *The middle sound of* kite *is* /ī/.
- **Say:** *Listen as I say some other words. Tell me which word has the* /ī/ *sound. Now let's do it together. Listen:* pin/pine. *Which word has the* /ī/ *sound in the middle?* (pine)
- Repeat with these words: *rid/ride, dime/dim, time/Tim, bit/bite, hide/hid, fin/fine.*

Teach/Model

SOUND/SPELLING Use Instructional Routine: Sound/Spelling Cards to review the Sound/Spelling Card for Iggy Iguana. Name the picture and say the short *i* sound. Have students repeat after you. **Say:** *Listen:* Iggy, /ĭ/. *Now you say it.*

- Repeat with *Iguana.*
- Say the sound and give the spelling: **Say:** *Remember that* Iggy Iguana *begins with the* /ĭ/ *sound. The letter* i *stands for the* /ĭ/ *sound at the beginning or in the middle of words.*
- Display the Sound Spelling Card for *ice cream.* Name the picture and say the vowel sound. Have students repeat after you. **Say:** *Listen:* ice cream, /ī/. *Now you say it.*
- Say the sound and give the spelling: **Say:** Ice *begins with the* /ī/ *sound. The letter* i *sometimes stands for its name,* /ī/.
- Point to the i_e pattern. **Say:** *When you come to a word that has an* i, *and then any consonant, and then an* e *at the end, the* i *will usually stand for* /ī/. *In these words, the* e *doesn't stand for any sound. It just tells you that* i *will stand for its long sound.*
- Point out that the High-Frequency Word *I* is an example of the letter *i* standing for the sound /ī/. Display the High-Frequency Word Card and have students read the word.

BLENDING Use Letter Cards and Instructional Routine: Sound-by-Sound Blending to model blending the words *hi* and *kite*. Point out that the word *kite* has the silent *e* at the end of the word so that the vowel stands for the long vowel sound.

Guided Practice

DISTINGUISH SHORT AND LONG SOUNDS Display Sound/Spelling Cards for Iggy Iguana and *ice cream.* Say words with the short *i* or long *i* sound at the end or in the middle, such as *sit, him, sip, big, lid, bin; hi, I, size, line, rice, bite.*

- Have students repeat each word and tell whether they hear /ĭ/ or /ī/. Ask students to sort the words by vowel sound; write each word next to the appropriate Sound/Spelling Card. Then have students blend and read the words.

BLENDING Display the words *hi, line, bite.* Work with students to blend the words, using Instructional Routine: Sound-by-Sound Blending.

PHONICS/DECODING STRATEGY Review the Phonics/Decoding Strategy. Display the sentences below. Call on students to use the strategy to blend one or more words and to read the sentences.

> We can ride the big bike.
>
> Mike hid the kite in a pile.

BUILDING AND WRITING WORDS Tell students to follow your directions and build new words with their Letter Cards. Have students start by building the word *fine*.

- **Say:** *Change* f *to* p. *What's the new word?* (pine)
- **Say:** *Change* p *to* l. *What's the new word?* (line)
- **Say:** *Change* n *to* k. *What's the new word?* (like)
- **Say:** *Change* l *to* b. *What's the new word?* (bike)
- **Say:** *Change* k *to* t. *What's the new word?* (bite)
- Then have students write each word and read it aloud.

Apply

- Distribute copies of Practice Page K.93B, which contains the decodable story *What I Like*. Point out that the story is made up of several sentences, and each sentence is made of words.

- Point out that students have learned the following high-frequency words, which they will also read in the story: *a, by, do, from, have, help, my, put, the, to, what, will, you.*

- Review the Sound/Spelling Cards for short *i* and long *i*. Ask students to name the sounds for short *i* and long *i*. Tell students that many words in this story have the /ĭ/ or /ī/ sound.

- Review and model the Phonics/Decoding Strategy using the story title.

- Model fluency and accuracy. Read aloud the first sentence of the story as students follow along. Point out that you do not misread, add, or skip words. Lead them in choral reading the same sentence with fluency and accuracy.

- Have students use what they know about high-frequency words and letter-sound associations to read the story aloud.

> **Fun with Words** Optional activities for engaging, hands-on practice are provided in the Resources section.

English Language Support

Linguistic Transfer Speakers of Spanish, Tagalog, Korean, Haitian Creole, and Vietnamese may substitute long *e* for /ĭ/, as the /ĭ/ sound is not used in their first language; also, the letter *i* stands for a sound like /ē/ in Spanish. Model the /ĭ/ sound in words like *hit, him, did, six,* and *fix*. Point out that your mouth is more rounded than when you say the /ē/ sound. Have students repeat each word. Then vocalize the middle sound and say the whole word again. Use each word in a brief sentence to reinforce meaning. For the /ī/ sound, have students suggest words that rhyme with *time* and have them name the middle sound. Continue the activity with *fine*.

Formative Assessment and Corrective Feedback

IF a student makes an error, THEN follow this model:

Correct the error.

Guide the student to perform the task correctly by modeling.

Check for understanding by having the student repeat the task.

Reinforce: Make a note to review the skill during the student's next session.

Objectives

- Isolate and pronounce the /ŏ/ or /ō/ sound in words with short or long *o*.
- Distinguish between the long and short *o* sounds.
- Blend and read words with short or long *o*.
- Read decodable text that includes words with short or long *o*.
- Read common high-frequency words by sight.

Materials

- Letter Cards
- Sound/Spelling Cards
- Instructional Routine: Sound/Spelling Cards
- Instructional Routine: Sound-by-Sound Blending
- Phonics/Decoding Strategy
- Practice Page K.94A

Phonemic Awareness Warm-up

- Display the words *not* and *note*. **Say:** *I'm going to say a word. Listen for the sound you hear in the middle. Listen:* not. *What sound do you hear in the middle of* not? */ŏ/ Yes, that is the short* o *vowel sound.*

- **Say:** *Listen as I say another word. Listen for the sound you hear in the middle. Listen:* note. *What sound do you hear in the middle of* note? */ō/ Say the words with me:* not, note. *The middle sound of* not *is /ŏ/. The middle sound of* note *is /ō/.*

- **Say:** *Listen as I say some other words. Tell me which word has the /ō/ sound. Now let's do it together. Listen:* hop/hope. *Which word has the /ō/ sound in the middle?* (hope)

- Repeat with these words: *rod/rode, code/cod, mope/mop, tot/tote.*

Teach/Model

SOUND/SPELLING Use Instructional Routine: Sound/Spelling Cards to review the Sound/Spelling Card for Ozzie Octopus. Name the picture and say the short *o* sound. Have students repeat after you. **Say:** *Listen: Ozzie, /ŏ/. Now you say it.*

- Repeat with *Octopus*.

- Say the sound and give the spelling: **Say:** *Remember that* Ozzie Octopus *begins with the /ŏ/ sound. The letter* o *stands for the /ŏ/ sound at the beginning or in the middle of words.*

- Display the Sound/Spelling Card for *ocean*. Name the picture and say the vowel sound. Have students repeat after you. **Say:** *Listen:* ocean, */ō/. Now you say it.*

- Say the sound and give the spelling: **Say:** Ocean *begins with the /ō/ sound. The letter* o *sometimes stands for its name, /ō/.*

- Point to the o_e pattern. **Say:** *When you come to a word that has an* o, *and then any consonant, and then an* e *at the end, the* o *will usually stand for /ō/. In these words, the* e *doesn't stand for any sound. It just tells you that* o *will stand for its long sound.*

BLENDING Use Letter Cards and Instructional Routine: Sound-by-Sound Blending to model blending the word *pole*. Point out that the word *pole* has the silent *e* at the end of the word so that the vowel stands for the long vowel sound.

Guided Practice

DISTINGUISH SHORT AND LONG SOUNDS Display Sound/Spelling Cards for Ozzie Octopus and *ocean*. Say words with the short *o* or long *o* sound in the middle, such as *pot, rod, log; rode, hope, bone.*

- Have students repeat each word and tell whether they hear /ŏ/ or /ō/. Ask students to sort the words by vowel sound; write each word next to the appropriate Sound/Spelling Card. Then have students blend and read the words.

BLENDING Display the words *no, go, robe, so, bone*. Work with students to blend the words, using Instructional Routine: Sound-by-Sound Blending.

PHONICS/DECODING STRATEGY Review the Phonics/Decoding Strategy. Display the sentences below. Call on students to use the strategy to blend one or more words and to read the sentences.

Go to the home by the pole.

The hole by the rope is so big.

BUILDING AND WRITING WORDS Tell students to follow your directions and build new words with their Letter Cards. Have students start by building the word *rope*.

- **Say:** *Change* p *to* b. *What's the new word?* (robe)
- **Say:** *Change* b *to* d. *What's the new word?* (rode)
- **Say:** *Change* r *to* c. *What's the new word?* (code)
- **Say:** *Change* d *to* n. *What's the new word?* (cone)
- **Say:** *Change* c *to* b. *What's the new word?* (bone)
- Then have students write each word and read it aloud.

Apply

- Distribute copies of Practice Page K.94A, which contains the decodable story *Getting a Dog*. Point out that the story is made up of several sentences, and each sentence is made of words.
- Point out that students have learned the following high-frequency words, which they will also read in the story: *a, is, my, say, the, to, too, walk, will.*
- Review the Sound/Spelling Cards for short *o* and long *o*. Ask students to name the sounds for short *o* and long *o*. Tell students that many words in this story have the /ŏ/ or /ō/ sound.
- Review and model the Phonics/Decoding Strategy using the story title.
- Model fluency and accuracy. Read aloud the first sentence of the story as students follow along. Point out that you do not misread, add, or skip words. Lead them in choral reading the same sentence with fluency and accuracy.
- Have students use what they know about high-frequency words and letter-sound associations to read the story aloud.

> **Fun with Words** Optional activities for engaging, hands-on practice are provided in the Resources section.

English Language Support

Linguistic Transfer Students whose first language is Spanish, Tagalog, or Korean may have trouble with the /ŏ/ sound. Have ELs listen carefully as you pronounce words with the /ŏ/ sound: *clock, pot, rock, cot, pop, knock, lock.* Have students repeat each word, then vocalize the middle sound, and then say the whole word again. Use each word in a brief sentence to reinforce meaning. For the /ō/ sound, have students suggest words that rhyme with *tote* and have them name the middle sound. Continue the activity with *mope*.

Formative Assessment and Corrective Feedback

IF a student makes an error, THEN follow this model:

Correct the error.

Guide the student to perform the task correctly by modeling.

Check for understanding by having the student repeat the task.

Reinforce: Make a note to review the skill during the student's next session.

Phonics: Words with Short and Long *a*

Objectives

- Isolate and pronounce the /ă/ or /ā/ sound in words with short or long *a*.
- Distinguish between the long and short *a* sounds.
- Blend and read words with short and long *a*.
- Read decodable text that includes words with short and long *a*.
- Read common high-frequency words by sight.

Materials

- Letter Cards
- Sound/Spelling Cards
- Instructional Routine: Sound/Spelling Cards
- Instructional Routine: Sound-by-Sound Blending
- Phonics/Decoding Strategy
- Practice Page K.94B

Phonemic Awareness Warm-up

- Display the words *tap* and *tape*. **Say:** *I'm going to say a word. Listen for the sound you hear in the middle. Listen:* tap. *What sound do you hear in the middle of* tap? /ă/ *Yes, that is the short* a *vowel sound.*
- **Say:** *Listen as I say another word. Listen for the sound you hear in the middle. Listen:* tape. *What sound do you hear in the middle of* tape? /ā/ *Say the words with me:* tap, tape. *The middle sound of* tap *is /ă/. The middle sound of* tape *is /ā/.*
- **Say:** *Listen as I say some other words. Tell me which word has the /ā/ sound. Now let's do it together. Listen:* cap/cape. *Which word has the /ā/ sound in the middle?* (cape)
- Repeat with these words: *can/cane, tame/tam, mane/man, mat/mate.*

Teach/Model

SOUND/SPELLING Use Instructional Routine: Sound/Spelling Cards to review the Sound/Spelling Card for Andy Apple. Name the picture and say the short *a* sound. Have students repeat after you. **Say:** *Listen:* Andy, /ă/. *Now you say it.*

- Repeat with *Apple*.
- Say the sound and give the spelling: **Say:** *Remember that* Andy Apple *begins with the /ă/ sound. The letter* a *stands for the /ă/ sound at the beginning or in the middle of words.*
- Display the Sound/Spelling Card for *acorn*. Name the picture and say vowel sound. Have students repeat after you. **Say:** *Listen:* acorn, /ā/. *Now you say it.*
- Say the sound and give the spelling: **Say:** Acorn *begins with the /ā/ sound. The letter* a *sometimes stands for its name, /ā/.*
- Point to the *a_e* pattern. **Say:** *When you come to a word that has an* a, *and then any consonant, and then an* e *at the end, the* a *will usually stand for /ā/. In these words, the* e *doesn't stand for any sound. It just tells you that* a *will stand for its long sound.*

BLENDING Use Letter Cards and Instructional Routine: Sound-by-Sound Blending to model blending the word *ate* and *make*. Point out that the words have the silent *e* at the end of the word so that the vowel stands for the long vowel sound.

Guided Practice

DISTINGUISH SHORT AND LONG SOUNDS Display Sound/Spelling Cards for Andy Apple and *acorn*. Say words with the short *a* or long *a* sound at the beginning or in the middle, such as *at, sad, man; lane, made, cape, fake.*

- Have students repeat each word and tell whether they hear /ă/ or /ā/. Ask students to sort the words by vowel sound; write each word next to the appropriate Sound/Spelling Card. Then have students blend and read the words.

BLENDING Display the words *rake, sale, lane, take.* Work with students to blend the words, using Instructional Routine: Sound-by-Sound Blending.

PHONICS/DECODING STRATEGY Review the Phonics/Decoding Strategy. Display the sentences below. Call on students to use the strategy to blend one or more words and to read the sentences.

> Will Jane help me make a cape?
>
> The game is by the gate at the lake.

BUILDING AND WRITING WORDS Tell students to follow your directions and build new words with their Letter Cards. Have students start by building the word *bake*.

- **Say:** *Change b to m. What's the new word?* (make)
- **Say:** *Change m to t. What's the new word?* (take)
- **Say:** *Change t to r. What's the new word?* (rake)
- **Say:** *Change r to l. What's the new word?* (lake)
- **Say:** *Change l to c. What's the new word?* (cake)
- Then have students write each word and read it aloud.

Apply

- Distribute copies of Practice Page K.94B, which contains the decodable story *Fun at the Lake*. Point out that the story is made up of several sentences, and each sentence is made of words.

- Point out that students have learned the following high-frequency words, which they will also read in the story: *a, and, is, said, see, the, to, too.*

- Review the Sound/Spelling Cards for short *a* and long *a*. Ask students to name the sounds for short *a* and long *a*. Tell students that many words in this story have the /ă/ or /ā/ sound.

- Review and model the Phonics/Decoding Strategy using the story title.

- Model fluency and accuracy. Read aloud the first sentence of the story as students follow along. Point out that you do not misread, add, or skip words. Lead them in choral reading the same sentence with fluency and accuracy.

- Have students use what they know about high-frequency words and letter-sound associations to read the story aloud.

> **Fun with Words** Optional activities for engaging, hands-on practice are provided in the Resources section.

English Language Support

Linguistic Transfer Have Spanish speakers listen carefully as you pronounce words with the /ă/ sound: *apple, at, ad, mat, cat, man, can, pan, pat.* Have students repeat each word, and if they substitute /ŏ/ for /ă/, encourage them to "smile" a little to make the /ă/ sound. Use each word in a brief sentence to reinforce meaning. For the /ā/ sound, have students suggest words that rhyme with *bake* and have them name the middle sound. Continue the activity with *cane*.

Formative Assessment and Corrective Feedback

IF a student makes an error, THEN follow this model:

Correct the error.

Guide the student to perform the task correctly by modeling.

Check for understanding by having the student repeat the task.

Reinforce: Make a note to review the skill during the student's next session.

Phonics: Words with Short and Long *u*

Objectives

- Isolate and pronounce the /ŭ/ or /yōō/ sound in words with short or long *u*.
- Distinguish between the long and short *u* sounds.
- Blend and read words with short and long *u*.
- Read decodable text that includes words with short or long *u*.
- Read common high-frequency words by sight.

Materials

- Letter Cards
- Sound/Spelling Cards
- Instructional Routine: Sound/Spelling Cards
- Instructional Routine: Sound-by-Sound Blending
- Phonics/Decoding Strategy
- Practice Page K.94C

Phonemic Awareness Warm-up

- Display the words *hug* and *huge*. **Say:** *I'm going to say a word. Listen for the sound you hear in the middle. Listen:* hug. *What sound do you hear in the middle of* hug? /ŭ/ *Yes, that is the short* u *vowel sound.*
- **Say:** *Listen as I say another word. Listen for the sound you hear in the middle. Listen:* huge. *What sound do you hear in the middle of* huge? /yōō/ *Say the words with me:* hug, huge. *The middle sound of* hug *is /ŭ/. The middle sound of* huge *is /yōō/.*
- **Say:** *Listen as I say some other words. Tell me which word has the /yōō/ sound. Now let's do it together. Listen:* cut/cute. *Which word has the /yōō/ sound in the middle?* (cute)
- Repeat with these words: *cub/cube, tube/tub.*

Teach/Model

SOUND/SPELLING Use Instructional Routine: Sound/Spelling Cards to review the Sound/Spelling Card for Umbie Umbrella. Name the picture and say the short *u* sound. Have students repeat after you. Say: *Listen:* Umbie, /ŭ/. *Now you say it.*

- Repeat with *Umbrella.*
- Display the Sound/Spelling Card for *uniform*. Name the picture and say the vowel sound. Have students repeat after you. **Say:** *Listen:* uniform, /yōō/. *Now you say it.*
- Say the sound and give the spelling: **Say:** Uniform *begins with the /yōō/ sound. The letter* u *sometimes stands for its name, /yōō/.*
- Point to the *u_e* pattern. **Say:** *When you come to a word that has a* u, *and then any consonant, and then an* e *at the end, the* u *will usually stand for /yōō/. In these words, the* e *doesn't stand for any sound. It just tells you that* u *will stand for its long sound.*

BLENDING Use Letter Cards and Instructional Routine: Sound-by-Sound Blending to model blending the word *cute* and *June*. Point out that the words have the silent *e* at the end of the word so that the vowel stands for the long vowel sound.

Guided Practice

DISTINGUISH SHORT AND LONG SOUNDS Display Sound/Spelling Cards for Umbie Umbrella and *uniform*. Say words with the short *u* or long *u* sound in the middle, such as *cup, fun, bud; huge, dune, duke.*

- Have students repeat each word and tell whether they hear /ŭ/ or /yōō/. Ask students to sort the words by vowel sound; write each word next to the appropriate Sound/Spelling Card. Then have students blend and read the words.

BLENDING Display the words *tube, cube, huge, mule.* Work with students to blend the words, using Instructional Routine: Sound-by-Sound Blending.

PHONICS/DECODING STRATEGY Review the Phonics/Decoding Strategy. Display the sentences below. Call on students to use the strategy to blend one or more words and to read the sentences.

> The cute mule is huge.
>
> The fuse is like a cube.

BUILDING AND WRITING WORDS Tell students to follow your directions and build new words with their Letter Cards. Have students start by building the word *cute*.

- **Say:** *Change* t *to* b. *What's the new word?* (cube)
- **Say:** *Change* c *to* t. *What's the new word?* (tube)
- **Say:** *Change* b *to* n. *What's the new word?* (tune)
- Then have students write each word and read it aloud.

Apply

- Distribute copies of Practice Page K.94C, which contains the decodable story *A Rule for Pup*. Point out that the story is made up of several sentences, and each sentence is made of words.
- Point out that students have learned the following high-frequency words, which they will also read in the story: *a, and, do, good, is, now, the*.
- Review the Sound/Spelling Cards for short *u* and long *u*. Ask students to name the sounds for short *u* and long *u*. Tell students that many words in this story have the /ŭ/ or /yo͞o/ sound.
- Review and model the Phonics/Decoding Strategy using the story title.
- Model fluency and accuracy. Read aloud the first sentence of the story as students follow along. Point out that you do not misread, add, or skip words. Lead them in choral reading the same sentence with fluency and accuracy.
- Have students use what they know about high-frequency words and letter-sound associations to read the story aloud.

> **Fun with Words** Optional activities for engaging, hands-on practice are provided in the Resources section.

English Language Support

Linguistic Transfer Students whose first language is Spanish, Chinese, Tagalog, or Korean may have trouble with the /ŭ/ sound. Say the sound several times as ELs study your mouth position; students can also practice the sounds in front of a mirror. Point out that your mouth is more closed for /ŭ/ than for /ŏ/. Then provide extra modeling and practice with words such as *cup, tub, but, duck, gum,* and *pup*. Have students chorally repeat each word after you, then say just the middle sound, and then say the whole word again. Use each word in a sentence to reinforce meaning. Continue with the long *u* sound in *cute, cube, huge,* and *mule*.

Formative Assessment and Corrective Feedback

IF a student makes an error, THEN follow this model:

Correct the error.

Guide the student to perform the task correctly by modeling.

Check for understanding by having the student repeat the task.

Reinforce: Make a note to review the skill during the student's next session.

Cumulative Review/Fluency

- Decode words with long and short vowels *a, e, i, o, u.*
- Read common high-frequency words by sight.
- Read emergent-reader texts with purpose and understanding.

Materials

- Sound/Spelling Cards
- High-Frequency Word Cards
- Instructional Routine: High-Frequency Words
- Practice Page K.95

Teach/Model

REVIEW

- Remind students they have learned the long sounds for the vowels *a, e, i, o, u.* Review the long sounds with the Sound/Spelling Cards for *acorn, eagle, ice cream, ocean,* and *uniform.* Display the cards and review the long vowel sounds for each.

- Remind students they have learned the short vowel sounds for *a, e, i, o, u.* Use the Sound/Spelling Cards for Andy Apple, Edna Elephant, Izzy Iguana, Ozzy Octopus, and Umbie Umbrella. Display the vowels and review the short sounds for *a, e, i, o,* and *u.*

- Display these sentences:

  The cute mule dug a hole down in the pit.

  Pete had a kit to make a big kite.

  Zeke must put on a cap and a cape to ride the bike.

- Point to the high-frequency words *a, down, must, put, to,* and *the* and read each one. Remind students that they know these words. Use the High-Frequency Word Cards and Instructional Routine: High-Frequency Words to review these words.

MODEL FLUENCY

- Read the above sentences, focusing on the words in the sentences that contain long and short vowels *a, e, i, o, u.* Model blending the sounds to read the words. Read the first sentence: *The cute mule dug a hole down in the pit.* Read the words *cute, mule, dug, hole,* and *pit* more slowly, as if sounding them out. Then read the sentence again, this time at a natural pace. Have students read the sentence with you. Continue with the remaining sentences.

Guided Practice

- Tell students they will practice reading. Display the following sentences:

  The rope is by the big tube.

  I will take a ride to the lake.

  Pete rode his bike by the huge pole.

- Guide students in reading the sentences aloud. Coach them to sound out each word. Have students go back to any word they read incorrectly. Have them sound out the word again. Guide students to look for context clues in surrounding text to help them figure out the word.

Have students read aloud the practice text on Practice Page K.95.

- Explain that the main purpose of reading the text is to practice their reading skills.

- Coach students to use decoding skills and context to self-correct any mistakes they make during reading. They should read the text several times, until they are able to read smoothly and accurately.

- When students have finished the fluency practice, choose a few sentences to review. Have students read each sentence and explain in their own words what it means.

- After students are able to read the text fluently, guide them to track their progress on their My Progress line graphs.

Formative Assessment and Corrective Feedback

IF a student makes an error, THEN follow this model:

Correct the error.

Guide the student to say the word correctly.

Check for understanding by having the student reread the word.

Reinforce: Make a note to review the word during the student's next session.

High-Frequency Words:
I, to, like, a, see, the, we, go, is, are

Teach/Model

- Display the high-frequency words. Tell students that these are useful words to know since they will see these words often. Tell them that reading will be easier if they recognize these words.
- Display the High-Frequency Word Card for *I* and say the word. Then spell the word aloud as you point to the letter. Say the word again.
- Use the word in a simple sentence that will provide context. For example: *I am a teacher.*
- Repeat the steps above with the remaining high-frequency words.

Guided Practice

Do the following for each high-frequency word:

- Display the High-Frequency Word Card. Read the word and have students repeat it.
- Note the familiar sound/spelling patterns that are shown on the back of the card. Note as well any unfamiliar and unexpected sound/spellings.
- Blend the word with students.
- Spell the word aloud, pointing to each letter.
- Have students then spell the word aloud as you point to each letter.
- Have students read the word again.

Apply

- Display the High-Frequency Word Cards in random order. Have students read the words aloud.
- Have students write each word. Tell them to compare their writing with the word on the card and make corrections if necessary.
- Have students read each word aloud and use it in a sentence.

Objectives

- Recognize and read high-frequency words.

Materials

- High-Frequency Word Cards

Formative Assessment and Corrective Feedback

IF a student makes an error, THEN follow this model:

Correct the error.

Guide the student to say the word correctly.

Check for understanding by having the student reread the word from among other randomly displayed high-frequency words.

Reinforce: Make a note to review the word during the student's next session.

Objectives

- Isolate initial and final phonemes in spoken single-syllable words.

Formative Assessment and Corrective Feedback

IF a student makes an error, THEN follow this model:

Correct the error.

Guide the student to perform the task correctly by modeling.

Check for understanding by having the student repeat the task.

Reinforce: Make a note to review the skill during the student's next session.

Teach/Model

- **Say:** *I'm going to say a word. The word is* cap. *Now I'm going to say some words that rhyme with cap. Listen:* cap, tap, map, lap, rap. *The words rhyme because they all end with the same sounds, /ăp/.*

- Repeat with the word *bat* and the rhyming words *cat, mat, fat, hat,* and *rat.* Explain that the words rhyme because they have the same ending sounds, /ăt/.

Guided Practice

- **Say:** *Now I'm going to say a word and together we're going to say some words that rhyme with the word I say.*

- Say each of the following words and with students say words that rhyme. At the end of each set, ask students how the words are alike. (They have the same ending sounds.) Help students identify those sounds.

    bed (fed, led, Ned, red, Ted)

    dig (big, fig, jig, pig, rig, wig)

    hot (cot, dot, got, jot, lot, not, pot)

    mug (bug, dug, hug, jug, rug, tug)

Apply

- **Say:** *I'm going to say two words. You'll tell me if they rhyme. Then you'll explain how you know. Let's do the first two pairs of words together. Listen:* man, can. *Do these words rhyme?* (Yes.) *Why do they rhyme?* (They have the same ending sounds, /ăn/.) *Listen:* ten, tag. *Do these two words rhyme?* (No.) *Why don't they rhyme?* (They have different ending sounds, /ĕn/ and /ăg/.)

- Say each of the following word pairs and ask students to tell whether or not the words rhyme and how they know.

    lake, cake (yes; /āk/)   *home, roam* (yes; /ōm/)

    fun, fan (no; /ŭn/ and /ăn/)   *will, fill* (yes; /ĭl/)

    get, jet (yes; /ĕt/)   *leg, lean* (no; /ĕg/ and /ēn/)

Phonics: Review: Short *a*; Consonants *m, s, t, c*

Phonemic Awareness Warm-up

- **Say:** *Listen as I say some sounds: /m/ /ă/ /p/. Let's blend the sounds to say a word: /m/ /ă/ /p/,* map.
- Guide students to blend the sounds to say these words: /s/ /ă/ /d/, *sad;* /g/ /ă/ /s/, *gas;* /p/ /ă/ /t/, *pat.*
- **Say:** *Say this word and listen for the sounds in it:* bag. *Say each sound with me and then say the word: /b/ /ă/ /g/,* bag.
- Guide students to segment the sounds in these words: *tan, cap, bat, pan.*

Teach/Model

- Display the Sound/Spelling Card for *apple*. Name the picture and say the beginning sound. Have students repeat after you. **Say:** *Listen:* apple, /ă/. *Now you say it.*
- Say the sound and give the spelling. **Say:** Apple *begins with the sound /ă/. The letter* a *stands for the sound /ă/. This sound is called the short* a *sound.*
- Display the Sound/Spelling Card for *mouse* and review /m/ *m.*
- Write and read *am.* **Say:** *This is the word* am. *The letter* a *stands for the sound /ă/ in* am. *The letter* m *stands for the sound /m/ in* am. *Read with me: /ă/ /m/, /ăm/,* am.
- Repeat the routine for *s, t,* and *c* using the Sound/Spelling Cards for *sock, tiger,* and *cat* and the words *sat, mat,* and *cat.*

Guided Practice

BLENDING Display the words in Rows 1 and 2 below. Using Instructional Routine: Sound-by-Sound Blending, work with students to blend each word.

| 1. am | at | Sam | sat |
| 2. cat | Cam | Mac | mat |

DECODING Display the sentences below. Call on students to read the sentences.

- I go to see Sam.
- Sam is a cat.
- Sam the cat sat.

BUILDING AND WRITING WORDS Display the Letter Cards *a, m, s, t,* and *c.* Build the word *am.* **Say:** *The letter* a *stands for the first sound, /ă/. The letter* m *stands for the last sound, /m/.*

- Guide students to identify sounds in the following words and build them with Letter Cards: *at, cat, mat, sat, Sam, Mac.*
- Have students write each word and read it aloud.

Objectives

- Review the sound-spelling correspondences for short *a* and consonants *m, s, t,* and *c.*
- Blend sounds in spoken single-syllable words with /ă/, /m/, /s/, /t/, and /k/.
- Blend, build, and decode regularly spelled one-syllable words with *a, m, s, t,* and *c.*
- Read on-level text with fluency and accuracy.

Materials

- Sound/Spelling Cards
- Instructional Routine: Sound-by-Sound Blending
- Letter Cards
- Practice Page 1.1C

English Language Support

Linguistic Transfer Point out to Spanish speakers that the sounds /m/, /s/, /t/, and /k/ spelled *c* are the same in Spanish as in English. Students with reading skill in Spanish should also be told that they can use their knowledge of Spanish to help them read words with these sounds in English, as the sounds are often spelled the same. Work with students to spell words with the sounds /m/, /s/, /t/, and /k/ spelled *c* in both languages.

Formative Assessment and Corrective Feedback

IF a student makes an error, THEN follow this model:

Correct the error.

Guide the student to perform the task correctly by modeling.

Check for understanding by having the student repeat the task.

Reinforce: Make a note to review the skill during the student's next session.

Apply

- Distribute copies of Practice Page 1.1C, which contains the decodable story *Mac Cat, Sam Cat.* Tell students that many words in this story have *a, m, s, t,* or *c.* Point out that students have learned the following high-frequency words, which they will also read in the story: *I, see, we, like, the.*

- Read aloud the first sentence of the story as students follow along. Point out that you do not misread, add, or skip words when you read. Lead students in reading the same sentence with fluency and accuracy.

- Have students read the passage silently and then aloud. Remind them to track the words from left to right. When they come to the end of a line, they should sweep their hand down to the beginning of the next line and continue reading.

- Review basic features of print by asking students to point to the first word of a sentence, to identify a capital letter at the beginning of a sentence, and to identify end punctuation.

- When students have finished reading the text, choose a few sentences to review. Have students read each sentence and explain in their own words what it means.

Fun with Words Optional activities for engaging, hands-on practice are provided in the Resources section.

High-Frequency Words:
play, be, and, help, with, you

Teach/Model

- Display the high-frequency words. Tell students that these are useful words to know, since they will see these words often. Tell students that reading will be easier if they recognize these words.
- Display the High-Frequency Word Card for *play* and say the word. Then spell the word aloud as you point to each letter. Say the word again.
- Use the word in a simple sentence that will provide context. For example: *The children play a game.*
- Repeat the steps above with the remaining high-frequency words.

Guided Practice

Do the following for each high-frequency word:

- Display the High-Frequency Word Card. Read the word and have students repeat it.
- Note the familiar sound/spelling patterns that are shown on the back of the card. Note as well any unfamiliar and unexpected sound/spellings.
- Blend the word with students.
- Spell the word aloud, pointing to each letter.
- Have students then spell the word aloud as you point to each letter.
- Have students read the word again.

Apply

- Display the High-Frequency Word Cards in random order. Have students read the words aloud.
- Have students write each word. Tell them to compare their writing with the word on the card and make corrections if necessary.
- Have students read each word aloud and use it in a sentence.

Objectives

- Recognize and read high-frequency words.

Materials

- High-Frequency Word Cards

Formative Assessment and Corrective Feedback

IF a student makes an error, THEN follow this model:

Correct the error.

Guide the student to say the word correctly.

Check for understanding by having the student reread the word from among other randomly displayed high-frequency words.

Reinforce: Make a note to review the word during the student's next session.

Phonics: Review: Consonants *n, d, p, f*

Objectives

- Learn the sound-spelling correspondences for consonants *n, d, p,* and *f.*
- Blend sounds in spoken single-syllable words with /n/, /d/, /p/, and /f/.
- Blend, build, and decode regularly spelled one-syllable words with *n, d, p,* and *f.*
- Read on-level text with fluency and accuracy.

Materials

- Sound/Spelling Cards
- Instructional Routine: Sound-by-Sound Blending
- Letter Cards
- Practice Page 1.2B

Phonological Awareness Warm-up

- **Say:** *I'll say a word, and then you'll say a word that rhymes and begins with the sound I name. Listen: The word is* pan. *Say a word that rhymes with* pan *and begins with /f/.* (fan)
- Continue with these words and sounds: *Nan,* /t/ (tan); *dad,* /p/ (pad); *nap,* /m/ (map).
- Have students generate additional rhyming words that end with -*an,* -*ad,* or -*ap* (Dan, can, man, ran; mad, sad, bad, had; cap, sap, tap, gap, lap).

Teach/Model

- Display the Sound/Spelling Card for *noodles.* Name the picture and say the beginning sound. Have students repeat after you. **Say:** *Listen:* noodles, /n/. *Now you say it.*
- Say the sound and give the spelling. **Say:** Noodles *begins with the sound /n/. The letter* n *stands for the sound /n/ at the beginning, middle, or end of a word.*
- Write and read *man.* **Say:** *This is the word* man. *The letter* m *stands for the sound /m/ in* man. *The letter* a *stands for the sound /ă/ in* man. *The letter* n *stands for the sound /n/ in* man. *Read with me:* /m/ /ă/, /mă/ /n/, /măn/, man.
- Repeat the routine for *d, p,* and *f* using the Sound/Spelling Cards *duck, pig,* and *fish.*

Guided Practice

BLENDING Display the words in Rows 1, 2, and 3 below. Using Instructional Routine: Sound-by-Sound Blending, work with students to blend each word.

1. dad	cap	Dan	nap	fat
2. fan	mat	sad	Nan	pad
3. Sam	pan	pat	mad	sat

DECODING Display the sentences below. Call on students to read the sentences.

- Pam can tap and pat the cat.
- Dad can see the fat cat.

BUILDING AND WRITING WORDS Have partners take turns using Letter Cards to build and read words with *n, p, f,* and *d,* such as *dad, Dan, fan, nap,* and *pad.*

- After reading a word, each partner uses the word in a sentence.
- Then partners write each word and read it aloud.

Apply

- Distribute copies of Practice Page 1.2B, which contains the decodable story *Be a Fan!* Tell students that many words in this story have *n, d, p,* or *f*. Point out that students have learned the following high-frequency words, which they will also read in the story: *be, you.*

- Read aloud the first three sentences of the story as students follow along. Point out that you do not misread, add, or skip words when you read. Lead students in reading the same sentences with fluency and accuracy.

- Have students read the passage silently and then aloud. Remind them to track the words from left to right. When they come to the end of a line, they should sweep their hand down to the beginning of the next line and continue reading.

- Review basic features of print by asking students to point to the first word of a sentence, to identify a capital letter at the beginning of a sentence, and to identify end punctuation.

- When students have finished reading the text, choose a few sentences to review. You may want to focus on sentences that include words containing the target phonics elements. Have students read each sentence and explain in their own words what it means.

> **Fun with Words** Optional activities for engaging, hands-on practice are provided in the Resources section.

English Language Support

Linguistic Transfer Point out to Spanish speakers that the sounds /n/, /d/, and /p/ are the same in Spanish as in English. Students with reading skill in Spanish should also be told that they can use their knowledge of Spanish to help them read words with these sounds in English, as the sounds are often spelled the same. Work with students to spell words with the /n/, /d/, and /p/ sounds in both languages.

Formative Assessment and Corrective Feedback

IF a student makes an error, THEN follow this model:

Correct the error.

Guide the student to perform the task correctly by modeling.

Check for understanding by having the student repeat the task.

Reinforce: Make a note to review the skill during the student's next session.

Objectives

- Recognize and read high-frequency words.

Materials

- High-Frequency Word Cards

Formative Assessment and Corrective Feedback

IF a student makes an error, THEN follow this model:

Correct the error.

Guide the student to say the word correctly.

Check for understanding by having the student reread the word from among other randomly displayed high-frequency words.

Reinforce: Make a note to review the word during the student's next session.

High-Frequency Words:
for, what, have, he, look, too

Teach/Model

- Display the high-frequency words. Tell students that these are useful words to know since they will see these words often. Tell them that reading will be easier if they recognize these words.
- Display the High-Frequency Word Card for *for* and say the word. Then spell the word aloud as you point to each letter. Say the word again.
- Use the word in a simple sentence that will provide context. For example: *The gift is for my mom.*
- Repeat the steps above with the remaining high-frequency words.

Guided Practice

Do the following for each high-frequency word:

- Display the High-Frequency Word Card. Read the word and have students repeat it.
- Note the familiar sound/spelling patterns that are shown on the back of the card. Note as well any unfamiliar and unexpected sound/spellings.
- Blend the word with students.
- Spell the word aloud, pointing to each letter.
- Have students then spell the word aloud as you point to each letter.
- Have students read the word again.

Apply

- Display the High-Frequency Word Cards in random order. Have students read the words aloud.
- Have students write each word. Tell them to compare their writing with the word on the card and make corrections if necessary.
- Have students read each word aloud and use it in a sentence.

Phonics: Review: Short *i*

Phonemic Awareness Warm-up

- Guide students to listen for and blend the short *i* sound, /ĭ/, in words. **Say:** *I'll blend the sounds in a word, and then you say the word. I'll do it first. Listen:* pin. *The first sound is /p/. The middle sound is /ĭ/. The last sound is /n/. /p/ /ĭ/, /n/,* pin.

- **Say:** *Now let's try one together. The word is* sit. *What sound do you hear at the beginning?* (/s/) *In the middle?* (/ĭ/) *At the end?* (/t/) *Blend the sounds. What is the word?* (sit) *Now you listen and blend:* /t/ /ĭ/ /p/ (tip), /d/ /ĭ/ /d/ (did), /f/ /ĭ/ /t/ (fit).

Teach/Model

- Display the Sound/Spelling Card for *igloo*. Name the picture and say the beginning sound. Have students repeat after you. **Say:** *Listen:* igloo, /ĭ/. *Now you say it.*

- Say the sound and give the spelling. **Say:** Igloo *begins with the sound /ĭ/. The letter i stands for the sound /ĭ/ at the beginning or middle of a word. This sound is called the short i sound.*

- Write and read *fin.* **Say:** *This is the word* fin. *The letter f stands for the sound /f/ at the beginning of* fin. *The letter i stands for the sound /ĭ/ in the middle of* fin. *The letter n stands for the sound /n/ at the end of* fin. *Read with me: /f/ /ĭ/, /fĭ/ /n/, /fĭn/,* fin.

Guided Practice

BLENDING Display the words in Rows 1, 2, and 3 below. Using Instructional Routine: Sound-by-Sound Blending, work with students to blend each word.

1. pit	in	if	dip	it
2. pad	Tim	man	nip	did
3. sit	cap	fit	sat	pin

DECODING Display the sentences below. Call on students to read the sentences.

- The pan is for Tim.

- He did sit with Dad.

BUILDING AND WRITING WORDS Model using Letter Cards to build the word *tin.* **Say:** *The letter t stands for the first sound, /t/. The letter i stands for the middle sound, /ĭ/. The letter n stands for the last sound, /n/.* Then write the word. Repeat for the words *fin* and *pin.* Point out that *tin, fin,* and *pin* belong to the same word family because they end with the same letters (-in) and sounds (/ĭ/ /n/).

- Guide students to identify sounds in the following words and build them with Letter Cards: *pit, fit, sit, dip, nip, tip, sip.*

- Have students write each word and read it aloud.

- Have students group the words into two word families (-it and -ip).

Objectives

- Review the sound-spelling correspondence for short *i*.
- Blend sounds in spoken single-syllable words with /ĭ/.
- Blend, build, and decode regularly spelled one-syllable words with *i*.
- Read on-level text with fluency and accuracy.

Materials

- Sound/Spelling Cards
- Instructional Routine: Sound-by-Sound Blending
- Letter Cards
- Practice Page 1.3B

English Language Support

Linguistic Transfer Speakers of Spanish, Tagalog, Korean, Haitian Creole, and Vietnamese may substitute long *e* for short *i* because /i/ is not used in the first language. Also, the letter *i* stands for a sound like /ē/ in Spanish. Model /i/ in words such as *pit, pin, tip, sip,* and *dip.* Point out that your mouth is more rounded than when you say /ē/. Have students chorally repeat each word after you, vocalize the middle sound, and then say the whole word again. Use each word in a sentence to reinforce meaning. Remind students that using standard English pronunciation can help them remember how to spell words.

Formative Assessment and Corrective Feedback

IF a student makes an error, THEN follow this model:

Correct the error.

Guide the student to perform the task correctly by modeling.

Check for understanding by having the student repeat the task.

Reinforce: Make a note to review the skill during the student's next session.

- Distribute copies of Practice Page 1.3B, which contains the decodable story *What Can Fit?* Tell students that many words in this story have short *i* spelled *i.* Point out that students have learned the following high-frequency words, which they will also read in the story: *what, for.*

- Read aloud the first two sentences of the story as students follow along. Point out that you do not misread, add, or skip words when you read. Lead students in reading the same sentences with fluency and accuracy.

- Have students read the passage silently and then aloud. Remind them to track the words from left to right. When they come to the end of a line, they should sweep their hand down to the beginning of the next line and continue reading.

- When students have finished reading the text, choose a few sentences to review. Have students read each sentence and explain in their own words what it means.

> **Fun with Words** Optional activities for engaging, hands-on practice are provided in the Resources section.

Phonics: Consonants *r, h, s* /z/

Phonemic Awareness Warm-up

- **Say:** *Let's play a game. I'll say the sounds in a word one at a time. Then you blend the sounds to say the word. I'll do the first one. Listen: /r/ /i/ /p/,* rip.
- **Say:** *Now let's try one together. Listen: /h/ /i/ /m/. Blend the sounds. What is the word?* (him)
- Repeat with these words: *is, rat, ham, rid, has, rim.*

Teach/Model

- Display the Sound/Spelling Card for *rooster*. Name the picture and say the beginning sound. Have students repeat after you. **Say:** *Listen:* rooster, */r/. Now you say it.*
- Say the sound and give the spelling. **Say:** Rooster *begins with the sound /r/. The letter* r *stands for the sound /r/ at the beginning, middle, or end of a word.*
- Repeat the routine for *h* and *s* /z/ using the Sound/Spelling Cards for *horse* and *zebra.*
- Write and read *his.* **Say:** *This is the word* his*. The letter* h *stands for the sound /h/ at the beginning. The letter* i *stands for the sound /ĭ/ in the middle. The letter* s *stands for the sound /z/ at the end. Read with me: /h/ /ĭ/ /z/,* his.

Guided Practice

BLENDING Display the words in Rows 1, 2, and 3 below. Using Instructional Routine: Sound-by-Sound Blending, work with students to blend each word.

1. is	rip	his	has	rat
2. hip	fan	ran	him	rap
3. rid	had	Tim	as	fit

DECODING Display the sentences below. Call on students to read the sentences.

- Tad has hid the mat, too.
- Look at the big rip in his hat.

BUILDING AND WRITING WORDS Display the Letter Cards *h, i,* and *m.* Build the word *him.* **Say:** *The letter* h *stands for the first sound /h/. The letter* i *stands for the /ĭ/ sound. The letter* m *stands for the last sound, /m/.* Have partners take turns using Letter Cards to build and read words with *r, h,* and *s* /z/.

- Guide students to identify sounds in the following words and build them with Letter Cards: *rim, hit, rap, had, is, has.*
- Have students write each word and read it aloud.

Objectives

- Learn the sound-spelling correspondences for consonants *r, h,* and *s* /z/.
- Blend sounds in spoken single-syllable words with /r/, /h/, and /z/.
- Blend, build, and decode regularly spelled one-syllable words with *r, h,* and *s* /z/.
- Read on-level text with fluency and accuracy.

Materials

- Sound/Spelling Cards
- Instructional Routine: Sound-by-Sound Blending
- Letter Cards
- Practice Page 1.3C

English Language Support

Linguistic Transfer Students who have reading skill in Spanish may associate the /h/ sound with the letter *j*, as in *jugar* (to play). In Spanish, the letter *h* is silent, as in *hora* (hour). Explain to students that in English, the letter *h* stands for the /h/ sound. Have students practice by repeating words such as these after you: *how, hand, hen, hope, hello.* Use each word in a brief sentence to reinforce meaning.

Formative Assessment and Corrective Feedback

IF a student makes an error, THEN follow this model:

Correct the error.

Guide the student to perform the task correctly by modeling.

Check for understanding by having the student repeat the task.

Reinforce: Make a note to review the skill during the student's next session.

- Distribute copies of Practice Page 1.3C, which contains the decodable story *Ran, Ran, Ran!* Tell students that many words in this story have *r, h,* or *s* with the /z/ sound. Point out that students have learned the following high-frequency words, which they will also read in the story: *too, he.*

- Read aloud the first two sentences of the story as students follow along. Point out that you do not misread, add, or skip words when you read. Lead students in reading the same sentences with fluency and accuracy.

- Have students read the passage silently and then aloud. Remind them to track the words from left to right. When they come to the end of a line, they should sweep their hand down to the beginning of the next line and continue reading.

- When students have finished reading the text, choose a few sentences to review. You may want to focus on sentences that include words containing the target phonics elements. Have students read each sentence and explain in their own words what it means.

Fun with Words Optional activities for engaging, hands-on practice are provided in the Resources section.

Phonics: Consonants *b, g*

Phonemic Awareness Warm-up

- Guide students to listen for and blend words with the short *i* sound, /ĭ/. **Say:** *I'll blend the sounds in a word, and then you say the word. I'll do it first. Listen: The first sound is /b/. The middle sound is /ĭ/. The last sound is /b/. /b/ /ĭ/ /b/,* bib.

- **Say:** *Now let's try one together. Listen: /d/ /ĭ/ /g/. Let's blend the sounds. What is the word?* (dig) *Now you listen and blend: /r/ /ĭ/ /b/* (rib), */b/ /ĭ/ /t/* (bit), */f/ /ĭ/ /g/* (fig).

Teach/Model

- Display the Sound/Spelling Card for *bear*. Name the picture and say the beginning sound. Have students repeat after you. **Say:** *Listen:* bear, */b/. Now you say it.*

- Say the sound and give the spelling. **Say:** Bear *begins with the sound /b/. The letter* b *stands for the sound /b/ at the beginning, middle, or end of a word.*

- Write and read *big*. **Say:** *This is the word* big. *The letter* b *stands for the sound /b/ in* big. *The letter* i *stands for the sound /ĭ/ in* big. *The letter* g *stands for the sound /g/ in* big. *Read with me: /b/ /ĭ/ /bĭ/ /g/ /bĭg/,* big.

- Repeat the routine for *g* using the Sound/Spelling Card for *goose*.

Guided Practice

BLENDING Display the words in Rows 1, 2, and 3 below. Using Instructional Routine: Sound-by-Sound Blending, work with students to blend each word.

1. big	dig	gas	gap	his
2. tag	bib	fin	rib	bat
3. fat	bin	sip	if	tap

DECODING Display the sentences below. Call on students to read the sentences.

- Look at Tad dig and dig.

- I have a big bat.

BUILDING AND WRITING WORDS Have partners take turns using Letter Cards to build and read words with *b* and *g*, such as *big, gap, rib, tag,* and *bib*.

- After reading a word, each partner uses the word in a sentence.

- Then have partners write each word and read it aloud.

Objectives

- Learn the sound-spelling correspondences for consonants *b* and *g*.
- Blend sounds in single-syllable words with /b/ and /g/.
- Blend, build, and decode regularly spelled one-syllable words with *b, g,* and *i*.
- Read on-level text with fluency and accuracy.

Materials

- Sound/Spelling Cards
- Instructional Routine: Sound-by-Sound Blending
- Letter Cards
- Practice Page 1.3D

English Language Support

Linguistic Transfer Point out to Spanish speakers that the sound /b/ is the same in Spanish as in English. Students with reading skill in Spanish should also be told that they can use their knowledge of Spanish to help them read words with this sound in English, as the sound is often spelled the same. Work with students to spell several words with the /b/ sound in both languages.

Formative Assessment and Corrective Feedback

IF a student makes an error, THEN follow this model:

Correct the error.

Guide the student to perform the task correctly by modeling.

Check for understanding by having the student repeat the task.

Reinforce: Make a note to review the skill during the student's next session.

- Distribute copies of Practice Page 1.3D, which contains the decodable story *A Big, Fat Fig*. Tell students that many words in this story have *b* or *g*. Point out that students have learned the following high-frequency words, which they will also read in the story: *have, he, too.*

- Read aloud the first two sentences of the story as students follow along. Point out that you do not misread, add, or skip words when you read. Lead students in reading the same sentences with fluency and accuracy.

- Have students read the passage silently and then aloud. Remind them to track the words from left to right. When they come to the end of a line, they should sweep their hand down to the beginning of the next line and continue reading.

- When students have finished reading the text, choose a few sentences to review. You may want to focus on sentences that include words containing the target phonics elements. Have students read each sentence and explain in their own words what it means.

Fun with Words Optional activities for engaging, hands-on practice are provided in the Resources section.

High-Frequency Words:
do, find, funny, sing, no, they

Teach/Model

- Display the high-frequency words. Tell students that these are useful words to know since they will see these words often. Tell them that reading will be easier if they recognize these words.

- Display the High-Frequency Word Card for *do* and say the word. Then spell the word aloud as you point to each letter. Say the word again.

- Use the word in a simple sentence that will provide context. For example: *They do their work well.*

- Repeat the steps above with the remaining high-frequency words.

Guided Practice

Do the following for each high-frequency word:

- Display the High-Frequency Word Card. Read the word and have students repeat it.

- Note the familiar sound/spelling patterns that are shown on the back of the card. Note as well any unfamiliar and unexpected sound/spellings.

- Blend the word with students.

- Spell the word aloud, pointing to each letter.

- Have students then spell the word aloud as you point to each letter.

- Have students read the word again.

Apply

- Display the High-Frequency Word Cards in random order. Have students read the words.

- Have students write each word. Tell them to compare their writing with the word on the card and make corrections if necessary.

- Have students read each word aloud and use it in a sentence.

Objectives

- Recognize and read high-frequency words.

Materials

- High-Frequency Word Cards

Formative Assessment and Corrective Feedback

IF a student makes an error, THEN follow this model:

Correct the error.

Guide the student to say the word correctly.

Check for understanding by having the student reread the word from among other randomly displayed high-frequency words.

Reinforce: Make a note to review the word during the student's next session.

Phonics: Review: Short *o*

Phonemic Awareness Warm-up

- Guide students to listen for and blend the short *o* sound, /ŏ/, in words. **Say:** *I'll say each sound in a word. Then I'll blend the sounds together to say the word. Listen: The first sound is /d/. The middle sound is /ŏ/. The last sound is /t/. /d/ /ŏ/ /t/,* dot.
- **Say:** *Now let's try one together. Listen: /m/ /ŏ/ /p/. Blend the sounds:* mop. *What is the word?* (mop) *Now you listen and blend: /n/ /ŏ/ /d/* (nod), */p/ /ŏ/ /p/* (pop), */h/ /ŏ/ /t/* (hot).

Teach/Model

- Display the Sound/Spelling Card for *ostrich*. Name the picture and say the beginning sound. Have students repeat after you. **Say:** *Listen:* ostrich, */ŏ/. Now you say it.*
- Say the sound and give the spelling. **Say:** Ostrich *begins with the sound /ŏ/. The letter* o *can stand for the sound /ŏ/. This sound is called the short* o *sound.*
- Write and read *not.* **Say:** *This is the word* not. *The letter* n *stands for the sound /n/ at the beginning of* not. *The letter* o *stands for the sound /ŏ/ in the middle of* not. *The letter* t *stands for the sound /t/ at the end of* not. *Read with me: /n/ /ŏ/, /nŏ/ /t/, /nŏt/* not.

Guided Practice

BLENDING Display the words in Rows 1, 2, and 3 below. Using Instructional Routine: Sound-by-Sound Blending, work with students to blend each word.

1. Mom	hop	rob	cot	on
2. got	sob	Tom	bog	pot
3. ran	his	hot	gap	rim

DECODING Display the sentences below. Call on students to read the sentences.

- Mom and Ron can not sing.
- Tom can find a big pot.

BUILDING AND WRITING WORDS Model, using Letter Cards, how to spell the word *hot.* **Say:** *The letter* h *stands for the first sound, /h/. The letter* o *stands for the middle sound, /ŏ/. The letter* t *stands for the last sound, /t/.* Then write the word. Repeat for the words *cot.* Point out that *hot* and *cot* belong to the same word family because they end with the same letters (-ot) and sounds (/ŏ/, /t/).

- Guide students to identify sounds in the following words and build them with Letter Cards: *dot, hop, nod, pot, rob.*
- Have students write each word and read it aloud.

Apply

- Distribute copies of Practice Page 1.4B, which contains the decodable story *Dot and Bob*. Tell students that many words in this story have short *o* spelled *o*. Point out that students have learned the following high-frequency words, which they will also read in the story: *do, find, no, they*.

- Read aloud the first four sentences of the story as students follow along. Point out that you do not misread, add, or skip words when you read. Lead students in reading the same sentences with fluency and accuracy.

- Have students read the passage silently and then aloud. Remind them to track the words from left to right. When they come to the end of a line, they should sweep their hand down to the beginning of the next line and continue reading.

- When students have finished reading the text, review a few sentences. You may want to focus on sentences that include words containing the target phonics element. Have students read each sentence and explain in their own words what it means.

Fun with Words Optional activities for engaging, hands-on practice are provided in the Resources section.

English Language Support

Linguistic Transfer Students whose first language is Spanish, Tagalog, or Korean may have difficulty with the /ŏ/ sound. Have students listen carefully as you say words with /ŏ/: *rob, got, pop, nod, mom, cot, hop*. Ask students to repeat each word, vocalize the middle sound, and say the whole word again. Use each word in a brief sentence to reinforce meaning.

Formative Assessment and Corrective Feedback

IF a student makes an error, THEN follow this model:

Correct the error.

Guide the student to perform the task correctly by modeling.

Check for understanding by having the student repeat the task.

Reinforce: Make a note to review the skill during the student's next session.

Phonics: Consonants *l, x*

Objectives

- Learn the sound-spelling correspondences for consonants *l* and *x*.
- Blend sounds in spoken single-syllable words with /l/ and /ks/.
- Blend, build, and decode regularly spelled one-syllable words with *l* and *x*.
- Read on-level text with fluency and accuracy.

Materials

- Sound/Spelling Cards
- Instructional Routine: Sound-by-Sound Blending
- Letter Cards
- Practice Page 1.4C

Phonemic Awareness Warm-up

- **Say:** *Let's play a game. I'll say the sounds in a word one at a time. Then you blend the sounds to say the word. I'll do the first one. Listen: /l/ /ŏ/ /t/,* lot.
- **Say:** *Now let's try one together. Listen: /f/ /ĭ/ /ks/. Blend the sounds. What is the word?* (fix)
- Repeat with these words: *tax, lad, fox, mix, not, lip, lot, box.*

Teach/Model

- Display the Sound/Spelling Card *lion*. Name the picture and say the beginning sound. Have students repeat after you. **Say:** *Listen:* lion, */l/. Now you say it.*
- Say the sound and give the spelling. **Say:** Lion *begins with the sound /l/. The letter* l *stands for the sound /l/ at the beginning, middle, or end of a word.*
- Repeat the routine for *x* using the Sound/Spelling Card *fox*.
- Write and read *box*. **Say:** *This is the word* box. *The letter* b *stands for the sound /b/ at the beginning. The letter* o *stands for the sound /ŏ/ in the middle. The letter* x *stands for the sound /ks/ at the end. Read with me: /b/ /ŏ/, /bŏ/ /ks/, /bŏks/,* box.

Guided Practice

BLENDING Display the words in Rows 1, 2, and 3 below. Using Instructional Routine: Sound-by-Sound Blending, work with students to blend each word.

1. tax	lap	ox	lot	six
2. fix	sax	lid	big	top
3. fox	is	Max	has	dot

DECODING Display the sentences below. Call on students to read the sentences.

- Lon and Max sit on a lap.
- They sit in a box, too.

BUILDING AND WRITING WORDS Model how to spell the word box. **Say:** *The letter* b *stands for the first sound. The next sound is /ŏ/. I know that* o *stands for /ŏ/. The last sound is /ks/.*

- Guide students to identify sounds in the following words and build them with Letter Cards: *lab, six, lid, tax, lot, fox, pal.*
- Then have students write each word and read it aloud.

Apply

- Distribute copies of Practice Page 1.4C, which contains the decodable story *Lil Fox and Lon Ox*. Tell students that many words in this story have *l* or *x*. Point out that students have learned the following high-frequency words, which they will also read in the story: *do, no, sing*.

- Read aloud the first two sentences of the story as students follow along. Point out that you do not misread, add, or skip words when you read. Lead students in reading the same sentences with fluency and accuracy.

- Have students read the passage silently and then aloud. Remind them to track the words from left to right. When they come to the end of a line, they should sweep their hand down to the beginning of the next line and continue reading.

- When students have finished reading the text, choose a few sentences to review. You may want to focus on sentences that include words containing the target phonics elements. Have students read each sentence and explain in their own words what it means.

> **Fun with Words** Optional activities for engaging, hands-on practice are provided in the Resources section.

Formative Assessment and Corrective Feedback

IF a student makes an error, THEN follow this model:

Correct the error.

Guide the student to perform the task correctly by modeling.

Check for understanding by having the student repeat the task.

Reinforce: Make a note to review the skill during the student's next session.

Phonics: Inflection -s

Objectives

- Learn the sound-spelling correspondences for inflectional ending -s.
- Blend sounds in spoken single-syllable words with final /s/ and /z/.
- Blend, build, and decode regularly spelled one-syllable words with inflectional ending -s.
- Read on-level text with fluency and accuracy.

Materials

- Sound/Spelling Cards
- Instructional Routine: Sound-by-Sound Blending
- Letter Cards
- Practice Page 1.4D

Phonemic Awareness Warm-up

- **Say:** *I'll blend the sounds in a word and then you say the word. I'll do it first. Listen:* pot. *The first sound is /p/. The middle sound is /ŏ/. The last sound is /t/. /p/ /ŏ/ /t/,* pot.
- Have students listen and blend the sounds in these words: *lid, top, cat, pan, wig.*
- Guide students to add /s/ or /z/ to the end of each word. *Now we're going to add the sound /s/ or /z/ to the end of a word to make a new word. Listen:* pot. *Add /s/ to the end, and the word is* pots. *Now you do it.* Lid. *Add /z/.* (lids) Top. *Add /s/.* (tops) Cat. *Add /s/.* (cats) Pan. *Add /z/.* (pans) Wig. *Add /z/.* (wigs)

Teach/Model

- Tell students that the letter *s* can have two sounds. Display the Sound/Spelling Card for *seal.* Name the picture and say the beginning sound. Have students repeat after you. **Say:** *Listen:* seal, /s/. *Now you say it.*
- Display the Sound/Spelling card for *zebra.* **Say:** *Listen:* zebra, /z/. *Now you say it. The letter* s *can stand for the sound /s/ or the sound /z/ at the end of words.*
- Write and read *rod.* Say each sound. **Say:** *Read with me: /r/ /ŏ/, /rŏ/ /d/, /rŏd/,* rod. *What letter do we add to the end of the word* rod *to make the word* rods? (s) *What sound do you hear at the end of* rods? (/z/)

Guided Practice

BLENDING Display the words in Rows 1, 2, and 3 below. Using Instructional Routine: Sound-by-Sound Blending, work with students to blend each word.

1. pots	tops	lids	dots	hats
2. tags	taps	cats	rats	fins
3. pins	figs	pigs	hips	caps

DECODING Display the sentences below. Call on individuals to blend one or more words and to read the sentences.

- Bob has six dots on his cap.
- Find the funny tags on the cots.

BUILDING AND WRITING WORDS Model how to spell the word mops. **Say:** *The letter* m *stands for the first sound. The next sound is /ŏ/. I know* o *stands for /ŏ/. The next sound is /p/. The letter* p *stands for /p/. The last sound is /s/. I know the letter* s *stands for /s/.*

- Guide students to identify sounds in the following words and build them with Letter Cards: *pals, lips, bats, pods, bins, cobs,* and *rags.*
- Then have students write each word and read it aloud.

Apply

- Distribute copies of Practice Page 1.4D, which contains the decodable story *What Is Funny?* Tell students that many words in this story end with *-s*. Point out that students have learned the following high-frequency words, which they will also read in the story: *funny, sing, they.*

- Read aloud the first two sentences of the story as students follow along. Point out that you do not misread, add, or skip words when you read. Lead students in reading the same sentences with fluency and accuracy.

- Have students read the passage silently and then aloud. Remind them to track the words from left to right. When they come to the end of a line, they should sweep their hand down to the beginning of the next line and continue reading.

- When students have finished reading the text, choose a few sentences to review. You may want to focus on sentences that include words containing the target phonics element. Have students read each sentence and explain in their own words what it means.

> **Fun with Words** Optional activities for engaging, hands-on practice are provided in the Resources section.

Formative Assessment and Corrective Feedback

IF a student makes an error, THEN follow this model:

Correct the error.

Guide the student to perform the task correctly by modeling.

Check for understanding by having the student repeat the task.

Reinforce: Make a note to review the skill during the student's next session.

Objectives

- Recognize and read high-frequency words.

Materials

- High-Frequency Word Cards

Formative Assessment and Corrective Feedback

IF a student makes an error, THEN follow this model:

Correct the error.

Guide the student to say the word correctly.

Check for understanding by having the student reread the word from among other randomly displayed high-frequency words.

Reinforce: Make a note to review the word during the student's next session.

High-Frequency Words:
all, does, here, me, my, who

Teach/Model

- Display the high-frequency words. Tell students that these are useful words to know since they will see these words often. Tell them that reading will be easier if they recognize these words.
- Display the High-Frequency Word Card for *all* and say the word. Then spell the word aloud as you point to each letter. Say the word again.
- Use the word in a simple sentence that will provide context. For example: *All animals need food and water.*
- Repeat the steps above with the remaining high-frequency words.

Guided Practice

Do the following for each high-frequency word:

- Display the High-Frequency Word Card. Read the word and have students repeat it.
- Note the familiar sound/spelling patterns that are shown on the back of the card. Note as well any unfamiliar and unexpected sound/spellings.
- Blend the word with students.
- Spell the word aloud, pointing to each letter.
- Have students then spell the word aloud as you point to each letter.
- Have students read the word again.

Apply

- Display the High-Frequency Word Cards in random order. Have students read the words.
- Have students write each word. Tell them to compare their writing with the word on the card and make corrections if necessary.
- Have students read each word aloud and use it in a sentence.

Phonics: Review: Short *e*

Phonemic Awareness Warm-up

- Guide students to listen for and blend the short *e* sound, /ĕ/, in words. **Say:** *I'll blend the sounds in a word, and then you say the word. I'll do it first. Listen:* bed. *The first sound is /b/. The middle sound is /ĕ/. The last sound is /d/. /b/ /ĕ/ /d/,* bed.
- **Say:** *Now let's try one together. The word is* set. *What sound do you hear at the beginning?* (/s/) *in the middle?* (/ĕ/) *at the end?* (/t/) *Blend the sounds. What is the word?* (set) *Now you listen and blend:* /m/ /ĕ/ /n/ (men), /p/ /ĕ/ /g/ (peg), /l/ /ĕ/ /d/ (led).

Teach/Model

- Display the Sound/Spelling Card *elephant*. Name the picture and say the beginning sound. Have students repeat after you. **Say:** *Listen:* elephant, /ĕ/. *Now you say it.*
- Say the sound and give the spelling. **Say:** *Elephant begins with the sound /ĕ/. The letter* e *can stand for the sound /ĕ/. This sound is called the short* e *sound.*
- Write and read *let*. **Say:** *This is the word* let. *The letter* l *stands for the sound /l/ at the beginning of* let. *The letter* e *stands for the sound /ĕ/ in the middle of* let. *The letter* t *stands for the sound /t/ at the end of* let. *Read with me:* /l/ /ĕ/, /lĕ/ /t/, /lĕt/, let.

Guided Practice

BLENDING Display the words in Rows 1, 2, and 3 below. Using Instructional Routine: Sound-by-Sound Blending, work with students to blend each word.

1. bed	pet	hen	Meg	lip
2. fox	hem	net	Len	red
3. Rob	tax	not	peg	den

DECODING Display the sentences below. Call on students to read the sentences.

- Who met Ted and his hens?
- I fed all my pets at ten.

BUILDING AND WRITING WORDS Model how to spell the word *pet*. **Say:** *The letters* p, e, t *stand for the sounds /p/ /ĕ/ /t/.* Then write the word. Repeat for the words *bet* and *let*. Point out that *pet, bet,* and *let* belong to the same word family because they end with the same letters (-et) and sounds (/ĕ/ /t/).

- Guide students to identify sounds in the following words and build them with Letter Cards: *met, set, net, get, hen, pen, den, ten, men.*
- Have students write each word and read it aloud.
- Have students group the words into two word families (-et and -en).

Objectives

- Review the sound-spelling correspondence for short *e*.
- Blend sounds in spoken single-syllable words with /ĕ/.
- Blend, build, and decode regularly spelled one-syllable words with *e*.
- Read on-level text with fluency and accuracy.

Materials

- Sound/Spelling Cards
- Instructional Routine: Sound-by-Sound Blending
- Letter Cards
- Practice Page 1.5B

English Language Support

Linguistic Transfer Some English learners, including speakers of Spanish, Korean, Vietnamese, and Tagalog, may need extra practice with the /ĕ/ sound. Have students listen carefully as you say words with /ĕ/: *fed, bet, den, pep, red, net.* Have students repeat each word, vocalize the middle sound, and say the whole word again. Use each word in a brief sentence to reinforce meaning.

Formative Assessment and Corrective Feedback

IF a student makes an error, THEN follow this model:

Correct the error.

Guide the student to perform the task correctly by modeling.

Check for understanding by having the student repeat the task.

Reinforce: Make a note to review the skill during the student's next session.

- Distribute copies of Practice Page 1.5B, which contains the decodable story *Pals.* Tell students that many words in this story have short *e* spelled *e.* Point out that students have learned the following high-frequency words, which they will also read in the story: *all, me, who.*

- Read aloud the first two sentences of the story as students follow along. Point out that you do not misread, add, or skip words when you read. Lead students in reading the same sentences with fluency and accuracy.

- Have students read the passage silently and then aloud. Remind them to track the words from left to right. When they come to the end of a line, they should sweep their hand down to the beginning of the next line and continue reading.

- When students have finished reading the text, review a few sentences. You may want to focus on sentences that include words containing the target phonics element. Have students read each sentence and explain in their own words what it means.

Fun with Words Optional activities for engaging, hands-on practice are provided in the Resources section.

Phonics: Consonants *k, v, j, y, w*

Objectives

- Learn the sound-spelling correspondences for consonants *k, v, j, y,* and *w.*
- Blend sounds in spoken single-syllable words with /k/, /v/, /j/, /y/, and /w/.
- Blend, build, and decode regularly spelled one-syllable words with *k, v, j, y,* and *w.*
- Read on-level text with fluency and accuracy.

Materials

- Sound/Spelling Cards
- Instructional Routine: Sound-by-Sound Blending
- Letter Cards
- Practice Page 1.5C

Phonemic Awareness Warm-up

- **Say:** *Let's play a game. I'll say the sounds in a word one at a time. Then you blend the sounds to say the word. I'll do the first one. Listen: /j/ /ĕ/ /t/,* jet.
- **Say:** *Now let's try one together. Listen: /w/ /ă/ /g/. Blend the sounds. What is the word?* (wag)
- Repeat with these words: *yes, kit, jog, van, web.*

Teach/Model

- Display the Sound/Spelling Card for *kangaroo.* Name the picture and say the beginning sound. Have students repeat after you. **Say:** *Listen:* kangaroo, */k/. Now you say it.*
- Say the sound and give the spelling. **Say:** Kangaroo *begins with the sound /k/. The letter* k *stands for the sound /k/ at the beginning, middle, or end of a word.*
- Repeat the routine for *v, j, y,* and *w* using the Sound/Spelling Cards for *volcano, jump, yo-yo,* and *worm.*
- Write and read *yak.* **Say:** *This is the word* yak. *The letter* y *stands for the sound /y/ at the beginning. The letter* a *stands for the sound /ă/ in the middle. The letter* k *stands for the sound /k/ at the end. Read with me: /y/ /ă/, /yă/ /k/, /yăk/,* yak.

Guided Practice

BLENDING Display the words in Rows 1, 2, and 3 below. Using Instructional Routine: Sound-by-Sound Blending, work with students to blend each word.

1. Ken	vet	Kip	yes	wag
2. van	web	yam	Jim	wet
3. win	jet	kits	yet	jig

DECODING Display the sentences below. Call on individuals to blend one or more words and to read the sentences.

- Did Val fix the wig for me yet?
- Kids can win a jet in a kit.

BUILDING AND WRITING WORDS Model how to spell the word *kit.* **Say:** *The letter* k *stands for the first sound. The next sound is /ĭ/. I know* i *stands for /ĭ/. The last sound is /t/. I know the letter* t *stands for /t/.*

- Guide students to identify sounds in the following words and build them with Letter Cards: *Ken, kid, vet, Dev, jab, jot, yam, yip, wax, wed.*
- Then have students write each word and read it aloud.

English Language Support

Linguistic Transfer Most Spanish speakers will have little difficulty with the /y/ sound, which is represented by the letters *ll* in Spanish. However, some speakers use a /j/ sound when they pronounce a word with *y*, for example, /jes/ for /yes/. Have students say the /y/ sound without touching their tongue to the roof of their mouth as they practice these words: *yes, yet, yam, yap, yip, young, yellow.* Use each word in a brief sentence to reinforce meaning.

Formative Assessment and Corrective Feedback

IF a student makes an error, THEN follow this model:

Correct the error.

Guide the student to perform the task correctly by modeling.

Check for understanding by having the student repeat the task.

Reinforce: Make a note to review the skill during the student's next session.

- Distribute copies of Practice Page 1.5C, which contains the decodable story *The Big Win*. Tell students that many words in this story have *k, v, j, y,* or *w.* Point out that students have learned the following high-frequency words, which they will also read in the story: *all, does, here.*

- Read aloud the first four sentences of the story as students follow along. Point out that you do not misread, add, or skip words when you read. Lead students in reading the same sentences with fluency and accuracy.

- Have students read the passage silently and then aloud. Remind them to track the words from left to right. When they come to the end of a line, they should sweep their hand down to the beginning of the next line and continue reading.

- When students have finished reading the text, choose a few sentences to review. You may want to focus on sentences that include words containing the target phonics elements. Have students read each sentence and explain in their own words what it means.

> **Fun with Words** Optional activities for engaging, hands-on practice are provided in the Resources section.

High-Frequency Words:
friend, full, good, hold, many, pull

Teach/Model

- Display the high-frequency words. Tell students that these are useful words to know since they will see these words often. Tell them that reading will be easier if they recognize these words.
- Display the High-Frequency Word Card for *friend* and say the word. Then spell the word aloud as you point to each letter. Say the word again.
- Use the word in a simple sentence that will provide context. For example: *A good friend is careful with your toys.*
- Repeat the steps above with the remaining high-frequency words.

Guided Practice

Do the following for each high-frequency word:

- Display the High-Frequency Word Card. Read the word and have students repeat it.
- Note the familiar sound/spelling patterns that are shown on the back of the card. Note as well any unfamiliar and unexpected sound/spellings.
- Blend the word with students.
- Spell the word aloud, pointing to each letter.
- Have students then spell the word aloud as you point to each letter.
- Have students read the word again.

Apply

- Display the High-Frequency Word Cards in random order. Have students read the words.
- Have students write each word. Tell them to compare their writing with the word on the card and make corrections if necessary.
- Have students read each word aloud and use it in a sentence.

Objectives

- Recognize and read high-frequency words.

Materials

- High-Frequency Word Cards

Formative Assessment and Corrective Feedback

IF a student makes an error, THEN follow this model:

Correct the error.

Guide the student to say the word correctly.

Check for understanding by having the student reread the word from among other randomly displayed high-frequency words.

Reinforce: Make a note to review the word during the student's next session.

Phonics: Review: Short *u*

Objectives

- Review the sound-spelling correspondence for short *u*.
- Blend sounds in spoken single-syllable words with /ŭ/.
- Blend, build, and decode regularly spelled one-syllable words with *u*.
- Read on-level text with fluency and accuracy.

Materials

- Sound/Spelling Cards
- Instructional Routine: Sound-by-Sound Blending
- Letter Cards
- Practice Page 1.6B

Phonemic Awareness Warm-up

- Guide students to listen for and blend the short *u* sound, /ŭ/, in words. **Say:** *I'll say the sounds in a word. Then you say them. Listen: /m/ /ŭ/ /g/. The first sound is /m/. The middle sound is /ŭ/. The last sound is /g/. When we blend the sounds together, we say* mug.
- **Say:** *Now let's try one together. Listen: /r/ /ŭ/ /b/. Say the sounds. Then blend the sounds together. What is the word?* (rub) Repeat for the words *nut, bug, cup,* and *hum.*
- **Say:** *Let's add the sound /s/ or /z/ to the end of a word to make a new word. Listen:* mug. *Add /z/ to the end. The word is* mugs. *Now you do it.* Rub. *Add /z/.* (rubs) Nut. *Add /s/.* (nuts) Bug. *Add /z/.* (bugs) Cup. *Add /s/.* (cups) Hum. *Add /z/.* (hums)

Teach/Model

- Display the Sound/Spelling Card for *umbrella*. Name the picture and say the beginning sound. Have students repeat after you. **Say:** *Listen:* umbrella, */ŭ/. Now you say it.*
- Say the sound and give the spelling. **Say:** Umbrella *begins with the sound /ŭ/. The letter* u *stands for the sound /ŭ/. This sound is called the short* u *sound.*
- Write and read *sun.* **Say:** *This is the word* sun. *The letter* s *stands for the sound /s/ at the beginning of* sun. *The letter* u *stands for the sound /ŭ/ in the middle of* sun. *The letter* n *stands for the sound /n/ at the end of* sun. *Read with me: /s/ /ŭ/, /s/ŭ/ /n/, /sŭn/,* sun.

Guided Practice

BLENDING Display the words in Rows 1, 2, and 3 below. Using Instructional Routine: Sound-by-Sound Blending, work with students to blend each word.

1. Gus	mud	bus	jug	tub
2. yak	Kip	pet	van	cup
3. sum	web	jig	hut	Bud

DECODING Display the sentences below. Call on individuals to blend one or more words and to read the sentences.

- Gus has many bugs in a cup.
- Look at the good pup on the rug.

BUILDING AND WRITING WORDS Model how to spell the word *run.* **Say:** *The letter* r *stands for the first sound, /r/. The letter* u *stands for the middle sound, /ŭ/. The letter* n *stands for the last sound, /n/.*

- Guide students to identify sounds in the following words and build them with Letter Cards: *sub, bun, hut, dug, pup.*
- Have students write each word and read it aloud.

Apply

- Distribute copies of Practice Page 1.6B, which contains the decodable story *Yum! Yum!* Tell students that many words in this story have short *u* spelled *u*. Point out that students have learned the following high-frequency words, which they will also read in the story: *full, gold, hold, many.*

- Read aloud the first two sentences of the story as students follow along. Point out that you do not misread, add, or skip words when you read. Lead students in reading the same sentences with fluency and accuracy.

- Have students read the passage silently and then aloud. Remind them to track the words from left to right. When they come to the end of a line, they should sweep their hand down to the beginning of the next line and continue reading.

- When students have finished reading the text, review a few sentences. Have students read each sentence and explain in their own words what it means.

> **Fun with Words** Optional activities for engaging, hands-on practice are provided in the Resources section.

English Language Support

Linguistic Transfer Students whose first language is Spanish, Chinese, Tagalog, or Korean may have difficulty with the /ŭ/ sound. Say the sound several times and point out that your mouth is more closed for /ŭ/ than for /ŏ/. Provide extra modeling and practice with words such as *cup, tub, but, yum, fun, bus,* and *rug.* Have students chorally repeat each word, vocalize the middle sound, and say the whole word again. Use each word in a brief sentence to reinforce meaning.

Formative Assessment and Corrective Feedback

IF a student makes an error, THEN follow this model:

Correct the error.

Guide the student to perform the task correctly by modeling.

Check for understanding by having the student repeat the task.

Reinforce: Make a note to review the skill during the student's next session.

Objectives

- Learn the sound-spelling correspondences for consonants *qu* and *z*.
- Blend sounds in spoken single-syllable words with /kw/ and /z/.
- Blend, build, and decode regularly spelled one-syllable words with *qu* and *z*.
- Read on-level text with fluency and accuracy.

Materials

- Sound/Spelling Cards
- Instructional Routine: Sound-by-Sound Blending
- Letter Cards
- Practice Page 1.6C

Phonics: Consonants *qu, z*

Phonemic Awareness Warm-up

- Guide students to listen for words that end with the sound /z/. **Say:** *I'll say some words. Listen to the sound at the end of each word: buzz, quiz, fizz. Each word ends with /z/. Now I will say two words. Listen for the word that ends with /z/. Listen: prize, quit. The word* prize *ends with /z/.*
- **Say:** *Now let's try one together. Listen: ox, is. Which word ends with /z/?* (is) *Listen and name the word that ends with /z/:* sight, size (size); him, has (has); doze, dot (doze).

Teach/Model

- Display the Sound/Spelling Card for *queen*. Name the picture and say the beginning sound. Have students repeat after you. **Say:** *Listen:* queen, /kw/. *Now you say it.*
- Say the sound and give the spelling. **Say:** Queen *begins with the sound /kw/. The letters* qu *stand for the sound /kw/ at the beginning or in the middle of a word.*
- Display the card for *zebra*. Name the picture and say the beginning sound. Have students repeat after you **Say:** *Listen:* zebra, /z/. *Now you say it.*
- Write and read *quiz*. **Say:** *This is the word* quiz. *The letters* qu *stand for the sound /kw/ in* quiz. *The letter* i *stands for the sound /i/ in* quiz. *The letter* z *stands for the sound /z/ in* quiz. *Read with me: /kw/ /ĭ/, /kwĭ/ /z/, /kwĭz/,* quiz.

Guided Practice

BLENDING Display the words in Rows 1, 2, and 3 below. Using Instructional Routine: Sound-by-Sound Blending, work with students to blend each word.

1. quit	pup	zig	dug	zag
2. set	sun	fun	rug	zip
3. yet	quiz	yak	pet	Ken

DECODING Display the sentences below. Call on individuals to blend one or more words and to read the sentences.

- Liz the pup zig and zags in the pen.
- My dog Zip is a good friend with Quip the cat.

BUILDING AND WRITING WORDS Model how to spell the word quit. **Say:** *The letters* qu *stand for the first sound. The next sound is /ĭ/. I know the letter* i *stands for the sound. The last sound is /t/. The letter* t *stands for /t/.*

- Guide students to identify sounds in the following words and build them with Letter Cards: *zip, quiz, zig, zag.*
- Then have students write each word and read it aloud.

Apply

- Distribute copies of Practice Page 1.6C, which contains the decodable story *Quin*. Tell students that many words in this story have *qu* or *z*. Point out that students have learned the following high-frequency words, which they will also read in the story: *good, many, pull.*

- Read aloud the first three sentences of the story as students follow along. Point out that you do not misread, add, or skip words when you read. Lead students in reading the same sentences with fluency and accuracy.

- Have students read the passage silently and then aloud. Remind them to track the words from left to right. When they come to the end of a line, they should sweep their hand down to the beginning of the next line and continue reading.

- When students have finished reading the text, choose a few sentences to review. You may want to focus on sentences that include words containing the target phonics elements. Have students read each sentence and explain in their own words what it means.

> **Fun with Words** Optional activities for engaging, hands-on practice are provided in the Resources section.

English Language Support

Linguistic Transfer Students who have reading skill in Spanish may associate the letters *qu* with the /k/ sound, as in the word *que* (/kā/). Point out that in English, the letters *qu* usually stand for the sound /kw/. Have students practice by repeating words such as the following after you: *queen, quick, quiet, quit, quack, quarter.* Use each word in a brief sentence to reinforce meaning.

Formative Assessment and Corrective Feedback

IF a student makes an error, THEN follow this model:

Correct the error.

Guide the student to perform the task correctly by modeling.

Check for understanding by having the student repeat the task.

Reinforce: Make a note to review the skill during the student's next session.

Cumulative Review/Fluency

Objectives

- Decode words with short vowels, consonants, and inflection -*s*.
- Recognize and read high-frequency words.
- Read on-level text with purpose and understanding.
- Read on-level text orally with accuracy on successive readings.
- Use context to confirm or self-correct word recognition and understanding, rereading as necessary.

Materials

- High-Frequency Word Cards
- Instructional Routine: High-Frequency Words
- Practice Page 1.7

Teach/Model

REVIEW

- Remind students they have learned sounds for all consonants. Display consonants and review the sounds for each. Keep in mind that students have learned the hard sounds for *c* and *g*. They've learned the /s/ and /z/ sounds for *s*.
- Remind students they have learned the short vowel sounds for *a, e, i, o,* and *u*. Display the vowels and review the short sounds for each.
- Display these sentences:

    Gus is my friend.

    Gus has a red bag.

    His red bag can hold lots.

- Point to the high-frequency words *is, my, friend, a,* and *hold* and read each one. Remind students that they know these words. Use the High-Frequency Word Cards and Instructional Routine: High-Frequency Words to review these words.

MODEL FLUENCY

- Explain that good readers don't skip hard parts. They take their time, go back, and correct themselves. That way, they understand the words they are reading and what they mean.
- Then read the sentences, pointing to each word as you read it slowly. Read the following sentence with an error: **Say:** *Gus has a red dag.* Point to the word *bag.* **Say:** *I read this word as* dag. *But that doesn't make sense. So I'm going to try again. /b/ /ă/ /g/. Bag. The first letter is* b, *not* d. *I also looked for clues in the text. I recognize the word* hold *in the next sentence. A bag can hold things. Now it makes sense.*
- Reread the sentence with no mistakes, pointing to the words as you read them.

Guided Practice

- Tell students they will practice reading. Display the following sentences:

    Wes has big pots.

    Wes can mix a lot.

    I did not help Wes yet.

- Guide students in reading the sentences aloud. Coach them to sound out each word. Have students go back to any word they read incorrectly. Remind them that sometimes letters can be pronounced in more than one way, and have them sound out the word again. Guide students to look for context clues in surrounding text to help them figure out the word.
- Have students read the sentences again.

- Have students read aloud the practice text on Practice Page 1.7.

- Explain that the main purpose of reading the text is to practice their reading skills.

- Coach students to use decoding skills and context to self-correct any mistakes they make during reading. They should read the text several times, until they are able to read smoothly and accurately.

- When students have finished the fluency practice, choose a few sentences to review. Have students read each sentence and explain in their own words what it means.

- After students are able to read the text fluently, guide them to track their progress on their My Progress line graphs.

Formative Assessment and Corrective Feedback

IF a student makes an error, THEN follow this model:

Correct the error.

Guide the student to say the word correctly.

Check for understanding by having the student reread the word.

Reinforce: Make a note to review the word during the student's next session.

- Recognize and read high-frequency words.

Materials

- High-Frequency Word Cards

Formative Assessment and Corrective Feedback

IF a student makes an error, THEN follow this model:

Correct the error.

Guide the student to say the word correctly.

Check for understanding by having the student reread the word from among other randomly displayed high-frequency words.

Reinforce: Make a note to review the word during the student's next session.

High-Frequency Words:
away, call, come, every, hear, said

Teach/Model

- Display the high-frequency words. Tell students that these are useful words to know since they will see these words often. Tell them that reading will be easier if they recognize these words.

- Display the High-Frequency Word Card for *away* and say the word. Then spell the word aloud as you point to each letter. Say the word again.

- Use the word in a simple sentence that will provide context. For example: *We waved as they drove away.*

- Repeat the steps above with the remaining high-frequency words.

Guided Practice

Do the following for each high-frequency word:

- Display the High-Frequency Word Card. Read the word and have students repeat it.

- Note the familiar sound/spelling patterns that are shown on the back of the card. Note as well any unfamiliar and unexpected sound/spellings.

- Blend the word with students.

- Spell the word aloud, pointing to each letter.

- Have students then spell the word aloud as you point to each letter.

- Have students read the word again.

Apply

- Display the High-Frequency Word Cards in random order. Have students read the words aloud.

- Have students write each word. Tell them to compare their writing with the word on the card and make corrections if necessary.

- Have students read each word aloud and use it in a sentence.

Phonics: Review: Words with Short *a*

Phonemic Awareness Warm-up

- Guide students to listen for the middle sound in words with short *a*. **Say:** *I'll say a word. Then you say it. Listen:* wax. *The first sound in* wax *is /w/.* Wax *has the vowel sound /ă/ in the middle. The ending sound in* wax *is /ks/. Listen and say* wax.

- **Say:** *Now let's do some more. Say each word sound by sound after me and tell me if it has the sound /ă/ in the middle, like* wax. *Listen:* bag (yes), yet (no), sob (no), jam (yes), nut (no), van (yes), zip (no).

Teach/Model

- Display the Sound/Spelling Card for *apple*. Name the picture and say the beginning sound. Have students repeat after you. **Say:** *Listen:* apple, */ă/. Now you say it.*

- Say the sound and give the spelling. **Say:** *Remember,* apple *begins with the sound /ă/. The letter* a *stands for the sound /ă/. This sound is called short* a.

- Display and read *pal*. **Say:** *This is the word* pal. *The letter* p *stands for the sound /p/ at the beginning. The letter* a *stands for the sound /ă/ in the middle. The letter* l *stands for the sound /l/ at the end. Read with me: /p/ /ă/, /pă/ /l/, /păl/,* pal.

Guided Practice

BLENDING Display the words in Rows 1, 2, and 3 below. Using Instructional Routine: Sound-by-Sound Blending, work with students to blend each word.

1. tab	mad	den	yam	gas
2. bud	wag	sun	hid	pad
3. win	cab	nap	web	got

DECODING Display the sentences below. Call on individuals to blend one or more words and to read the sentences.

> Pat said, "The map is in my bag."
>
> Call a cab to come get Sam.

BUILDING AND WRITING WORDS Model how to spell the word *has*. **Say:** *The letter* h *stands for the first sound, /h/. The letter* a *stands for the middle sound, /ă/. The letter* s *stands for the last sound, /z/.*

- Guide students to identify sounds in the following words and build them with Letter Cards: *cap, nag, tan, sat, bad, lab.*

- Have students write each word and read it aloud.

Session 1.8B

Objectives

- Review the sound-spelling correspondence for short *a*.
- Segment sounds in spoken single-syllable words with /ă/.
- Blend, build, and decode regularly spelled one-syllable words with *a*.
- Read on-level text with fluency and accuracy.

Materials

- Sound/Spelling Cards
- Instructional Routine: Sound-by-Sound Blending
- Letter Cards
- Practice Page 1.8B

Formative Assessment and Corrective Feedback

IF a student makes an error, THEN follow this model:

Correct the error.

Guide the student to perform the task correctly by modeling.

Check for understanding by having the student repeat the task.

Reinforce. Make a note to review the skill during the student's next session.

Apply

- Distribute copies of Practice Page 1.8B, which contains the decodable story *Pam and the Bag.* Tell students that many words in this story have short *a.* Point out that students have learned the following high-frequency words, which they will also read in the story: *call, come, said.*

- Read aloud the first two sentences of the story as students follow along. Point out that you do not misread, add, or skip words. Lead students in reading the same sentences with fluency and accuracy.

- Have students read the passage silently and then aloud. Remind them to track the words from left to right. When they come to the end of a line, they should sweep their hand down to the beginning of the next line and continue reading.

- When students have finished reading the text, choose a few sentences to review. You may want to focus on sentences that include words containing the target phonics skill. Have students read each sentence and explain in their own words what it means.

Fun with Words Optional activities for engaging, hands-on practice are provided in the Resources section.

Phonics: Words with Double Final Consonants

Objectives

- Learn the sound-spelling correspondences for double final consonants.
- Segment sounds in spoken single-syllable words with final /d/, /f/, /g/, /l/, /s/, /t/, and /z/.
- Blend, build, and decode regularly spelled one-syllable words with double final consonants.
- Read on-level text with fluency and accuracy.

Materials

- Sound/Spelling Cards
- Instructional Routine: Sound-by-Sound Blending
- Letter Cards
- Practice Page 1.8C

Phonemic Awareness Warm-up

- **Say:** *Let's play a game. I'll say the sounds in a word one at a time. Then you blend the sounds to say the word. I'll do the first one. Listen: /v/ /ă/ /n/,* van.
- **Say:** *Now let's try one together. Listen: /t/ /ă/ /g/. Blend the sounds. What is the word?* (tag)
- Repeat with these words: *jam, rot, will, add, mess.*

Teach/Model

- Display the Sound/Spelling Card for *duck*. Name the picture and say the beginning sound. Have students repeat after you. **Say:** *Listen:* duck, */d/. Now you say it.*
- Say the sound and give the spelling. **Say:** Duck *begins with the sound /d/.* Point to the letters *dd* on the card. Explain that the letters *dd* at the end of a word stand for the /d/ sound.
- **Say:** *Some words have two of the same consonants at the end.* Write and read the word *add.* Point to *dd* at the end. **Say:** *The letters* dd *stand for the /d/ sound at the end of* add. Repeat with the words *mess, off,* and *will.*

Guided Practice

BLENDING Display the words in Rows 1, 2, and 3 below. Using Instructional Routine: Sound-by-Sound Blending, work with students to blend each word.

1. egg	bus	add	Matt	hill
2. miss	well	jog	puff	quit
3. Tess	doll	buzz	wed	sat

DECODING Display the sentences below. Call on individuals to blend one or more words and to read the sentences.

- Matt will hear if you yell.
- Tess can run up every hill.

BUILDING AND WRITING WORDS Model how to spell the word *well.* **Say:** *The letter* w *stands for the first sound. The next sound is /ĕ/. I know* e *stands for /ĕ/. The last sound is /l/. The double consonants* ll *stand for this /l/.*

- Guide students to identify sounds in the following words and build them with Letter Cards: *puff, jazz, mitt, kiss, odd, yell.*
- Then have students write each word and read it aloud.

Formative Assessment and Corrective Feedback

IF a student makes an error, THEN follow this model:

Correct the error.

Guide the student to perform the task correctly by modeling.

Check for understanding by having the student repeat the task.

Reinforce: Make a note to review the skill during the student's next session.

- Distribute copies of Practice Page 1.8C, which contains the decodable story *Tess and Finn*. Tell students that many words in this story have double final consonants. Point out that students have learned the following high-frequency words, which they will also read in the story: *call, said.*

- Read aloud the first two sentences of the story as students follow along. Point out that you do not misread, add, or skip words. Lead students in reading the same sentences with fluency and accuracy.

- Have students read the passage silently and then aloud. Remind them to track the words from left to right. When they come to the end of a line, they should sweep their hand down to the beginning of the next line and continue reading.

- When students have finished reading the text, choose a few sentences to review. You may want to focus on sentences that include words containing the target phonics skill. Have students read each sentence and explain in their own words what it means.

> **Fun with Words** Optional activities for engaging, hands-on practice are provided in the Resources section.

Phonics: Words with *ck*

Phonemic Awareness Warm-up

- Guide students to listen for the ending sounds in words. **Say:** *I'll say a word. Then you say it. Listen:* back. *The first sound in* back *is /b/. The next sound is /ă/. The ending sound in* back *is /k/. Listen and say* back.

- **Say:** *Now let's do some more. Say each word sound by sound after me and tell me if it has the /k/ sound at the end, like* back. *Listen:* neck (yes), kit (no), tug (no), sick (yes), lock (yes), duck (yes), nod (no).

Teach/Model

- Display the Sound/Spelling Card for *cat*. Name the picture and say the beginning sound. Have students repeat after you. **Say:** *Listen:* cat, */k/. Now you say it.*

- Say the sound and give the spelling. **Say:** *Cat begins with the sound /k/.* Point to the letters *ck* on the Sound/Spelling Card. **Say:** *The letters* ck *at the end of a word stand for the /k/ sound.*

- Display and read *back.* **Say:** *This is the word* back. Point out the *ck* spelling. **Say:** *The letters* ck *stand for the sound /k/ in* back. Repeat with the words *neck, sick, lock,* and *duck.*

Guided Practice

BLENDING Display the words in Rows 1, 2, and 3 below. Using Instructional Routine: Sound-by-Sound Blending, work with students to blend each word.

1. Jack	sock	fuss	tack	luck
2. fill	box	peck	buzz	sell
3. duck	hem	quack	wig	rock

DECODING Display the sentences below. Call on individuals to blend one or more words and to read the sentences.

> Rick will pack his bag and go away.
>
> Did you hear a duck quack in the sack?

BUILDING AND WRITING WORDS Model how to spell the word *sack.* Say: *The letter* s *stands for the first sound. The next sound is /ă/. I know the letter* a *stands for /ă/. The last sound is /k/. I know that* ck *together stands for /k/.* Repeat for the word *pack.* Point out that *sack* and *pack* belong to the same word family because they end with the same letters (-*ack*) and sounds (/ă/ /k/).

- Guide students to identify sounds in other words in the -*ack* word family and build them with Letter Cards: *back, lack, rack, tack.*

- Then have students write each word and read it aloud.

Objectives

- Learn the sound-spelling correspondence for *ck*.
- Segment sounds in spoken single-syllable words with final /k/.
- Blend, build, and decode regularly spelled one-syllable words with *ck*.
- Read on-level text with fluency and accuracy.

Materials

- Sound/Spelling Cards
- Instructional Routine: Sound-by-Sound Blending
- Letter Cards
- Practice Page 1.8D

Apply

- Distribute copies of Practice Page 1.8D, which contains the decodable story *Ducks Quack*. Tell students that many words in this story end with *ck*. Point out that students have learned the following high-frequency words, which they will also read in the story: *every, hear*.

- Read aloud the first three sentences of the story as students follow along. Point out that you do not misread, add, or skip words. Lead students in reading the same sentences with fluency and accuracy.

- Have students read the passage silently and then aloud. Remind them to track the words from left to right. When they come to the end of a line, they should sweep their hand down to the beginning of the next line and continue reading.

- When students have finished reading the text, choose a few sentences to review. You may want to focus on sentences that include words containing the target phonics skill. Have students read each sentence and explain in their own words what it means.

> **Fun with Words** Optional activities for engaging, hands-on practice are provided in the Resources section.

English Language Support

Linguistic Transfer Speakers of Chinese languages may have trouble hearing and producing consonants at the ends of words, or they may add a vowel sound after a consonant. In Chinese, words usually end with a vowel sound. Provide modeling and practice segmenting and blending final sounds in words such as *rack, ram, rap, rat; peck, peg, pen, pet; sick, sip, sit, six;* and *buck, bud, bug, bus.* Use each word in a brief sentence to provide a meaningful context.

Formative Assessment and Corrective Feedback

IF a student makes an error, THEN follow this model:

Correct the error.

Guide the student to perform the task correctly by modeling.

Check for understanding by having the student repeat the task.

Reinforce: Make a note to review the skill during the student's next session.

High-Frequency Words:
animal, how, make, of, some, why

Teach/Model

- Display the high-frequency words. Tell students that these are useful words to know since they will see these words often. Tell them that reading will be easier if they recognize these words.
- Display the High-Frequency Word Card for *animal* and say the word. Then spell the word aloud as you point to each letter. Say the word again.
- Use the word in a simple sentence that will provide context. For example: *A bird is a kind of animal.*
- Repeat the steps above with the remaining high-frequency words.

Guided Practice

Do the following for each high-frequency word:

- Display the High-Frequency Word Card. Read the word and have students repeat it.
- Note the familiar sound/spelling patterns that are shown on the back of the card. Note as well any unfamiliar and unexpected sound/spellings.
- Blend the word with students.
- Spell the word aloud, pointing to each letter.
- Have students then spell the word aloud as you point to each letter.
- Have students read the word again.

Apply

- Display the High-Frequency Word Cards in random order. Have students read the words aloud.
- Have students write each word. Tell them to compare their writing with the word on the card and make corrections if necessary.
- Have students read each word aloud and use it in a sentence.

Objectives

- Recognize and read high-frequency words.

Materials

- High-Frequency Word Cards

Formative Assessment and Corrective Feedback

IF a student makes an error, THEN follow this model:

Correct the error.

Guide the student to say the word correctly.

Check for understanding by having the student reread the word from among other randomly displayed high-frequency words.

Reinforce: Make a note to review the word during the student's next session.

Phonics: Review: Words with Short *i*

Objectives

- Review the sound-spelling correspondence for short *i*.
- Segment sounds in spoken single-syllable words with /ĭ/.
- Blend, build, and decode regularly spelled one-syllable words with *i*.
- Read on-level text with fluency and accuracy.

Materials

- Sound/Spelling Cards
- Instructional Routine: Sound-by-Sound Blending
- Letter Cards
- Practice Page 1.9B

Phonemic Awareness Warm-up

- Guide students to listen for the middle sound in words with short *i*. **Say:** *I'll say a word. Then you say it. Listen:* rip. *The first sound in* rip *is /r/.* Rip *has the /ĭ/ sound in the middle. The ending sound in* rip *is /p/. Listen and say* rip.
- **Say:** *Now let's do some more. Say each word sound by sound after me and tell me if it has the sound /ĭ/ in the middle, like* pit. *Listen:* big (yes), set (no), rob (no), him (yes), cut (no), fin (yes), tap (no).

Teach/Model

- Display the Sound/Spelling Card for *igloo*. Name the picture and say the beginning sound. Have students repeat after you. **Say:** *Listen:* igloo, /ĭ/. *Now you say it.*
- Say the sound and give the spelling. **Say:** *Remember,* igloo *begins with the sound /ĭ/. The letter* i *stands for the sound /ĭ/. This sound is called the short i sound.*
- Display and read *zip*. **Say:** *This is the word* zip. *The letter* z *stands for the sound /z/ at the beginning. The letter* i *stands for the sound /ĭ/ in the middle. The letter* p *stands for the sound /p/ at the end. Read with me: /z/ /ĭ/, /zĭ/ /p/, /zĭp/,* zip.

Guided Practice

BLENDING Display the words in Rows 1, 2, and 3 below. Using Instructional Routine: Sound-by-Sound Blending, work with students to blend each word.

1. rim	did	fuzz	pick	hill
2. pass	will	his	dock	tuck
3. lick	vet	quack	bell	miss

DECODING Display the sentences below. Call on individuals to blend one or more words and to read the sentences.

Why did Bill pick some yams?

How will Nick get up the hill?

BUILDING AND WRITING WORDS Model how to spell the word *sip*. **Say:** *The letter* s *stands for the first sound. The next sound is /ĭ/. I know* i *stands for /ĭ/. The letter* p *stands for the last sound /p/.* Repeat for the word *hip*. Point out that *sip* and *hip* belong to the same word family because they end with the same letters (*-ip*) and sounds (/ĭ/ /p/).

- Guide students to identify sounds in other words in the *-ip* word family and build them with Letter Cards: *dip, lip, nip, rip, sip, tip, zip.*
- Then have students write each word and read it aloud.

Apply

- Distribute copies of Practice Page 1.9B, which contains the decodable story *Big Jobs*. Tell students that many words in this story have the short *i* sound. Point out that students have learned the following high-frequency words, which they will also read in the story: *make, of, some, why.*

- Read aloud the first two sentences of the story as students follow along. Point out that you do not misread, add, or skip words. Lead students in reading the same sentences with fluency and accuracy.

- Have students read the passage silently and then aloud. Remind them to track the words from left to right. When they come to the end of a line, they should sweep their hand down to the beginning of the next line and continue reading.

- When students have finished reading the text, choose a few sentences to review. You may want to focus on sentences that include words containing the target phonics skill. Have students read each sentence and explain in their own words what it means.

Fun with Words Optional activities for engaging, hands-on practice are provided in the Resources section.

Formative Assessment and Corrective Feedback

IF a student makes an error, THEN follow this model:

Correct the error.

Guide the student to perform the task correctly by modeling.

Check for understanding by having the student repeat the task.

Reinforce: Make a note to review the skill during the student's next session.

Phonics: Blends with *r*

Objectives

- Learn the sound-spelling correspondences for blends with *r*.
- Segment sounds in spoken single-syllable words with blends with /r/.
- Blend, build, and decode regularly spelled one-syllable words with blends with *r*.
- Read on-level text with fluency and accuracy.

Materials

- Sound/Spelling Cards
- Instructional Routine: Sound-by-Sound Blending
- Letter Cards
- Practice Page 1.9C

Phonemic Awareness Warm-up

- **Say:** *I'll say a word. Then you say the sounds that make up the word. Listen: The word is* rip. *Let's say the sounds: /r/ /ĭ/ /p/. The word has three sounds. Now you do it. The next word is* trip. *Say the sounds in* trip. *(/t/ /r/ /ĭ/ /p/) How many sounds do you hear in* trip? *(4)*
- **Say:** *I'll say some more words. Tell me how many sounds you hear in each word:* rim (3), brim (4), rag (3), brag (4), rot (3), trot (4), rib (3), crib (4), rid (3), grid (4).

Teach/Model

- Display the Sound/Spelling Card for *goose*. Name the picture and say the beginning sound. Have students repeat after you. **Say:** *Listen:* goose, */g/. Now you say it.* Repeat with the Sound/Spelling Card for *rooster*.
- Say the sounds and give the spellings. **Say:** *When* g *and* r *are side by side in a word, we say them together and their sounds blend together, /g/ /r/. Say it with me: /g/ /r/.* Have students say and spell the blend three times. Repeat with *br, cr, dr, fr, pr,* and *tr*.
- Display and read *grin*. **Say:** *This is the word* grin. *The letters* g *and* r *stand for the sounds /g/ and /r/. The letter* i *stands for the sound /ĭ/. The letter* n *stands for the sound /n/. Read with me: /g/ /r/, /gr/, /gr/ /ĭ/, /grĭ/ /n/, /grĭn/,* grin.

Guided Practice

BLENDING Display the words in Rows 1, 2, and 3 below. Using Instructional Routine: Sound-by-Sound Blending, work with students to blend each word.

1. crab	drop	trip	brim	drum
2. buck	tell	grin	press	drag
3. trim	frog	pass	grill	trap

DECODING Display the sentences below. Call on individuals to blend one or more words and to read the sentences.

Why did Brad grin at the frog?

How did Greg make a brim for his cap?

BUILDING AND WRITING WORDS Model how to spell the word *drop*. **Say:** *The letter* d *stands for the first sound. The next sound is /r/. The letter* r *stands for /r/. I hear /ŏ/ next. The letter* o *stands for the short o sound. The last sound is /p/. I know the letter* p *stands for /p/.*

- Guide students to identify sounds in the following words and build them with Letter Cards: *bran, crack, drill, frizz, grab, prod, truck.*
- Then have students write each word and read it aloud.

Apply

- Distribute copies of Practice Page 1.9C, which contains the decodable story *A Bag for Brad*. Tell students that many words in this story have blends with *r*. Point out that students have learned the following high-frequency words, which they will also read in the story: *animal, how, of*.

- Read aloud the first three sentences of the story as students follow along. Point out that you do not misread, add, or skip words. Lead students in reading the same sentences with fluency and accuracy.

- Have students read the passage silently and then aloud. Remind them to track the words from left to right. When they come to the end of a line, they should sweep their hand down to the beginning of the next line and continue reading.

- When students have finished reading the text, choose a few sentences to review. You may want to focus on sentences that include words containing the target phonics skill. Have students read each sentence and explain in their own words what it means.

Fun with Words Optional activities for engaging, hands-on practice are provided in the Resources section.

English Language Support

Linguistic Transfer Speakers of Cantonese and other Chinese languages, Spanish, and Vietnamese may have trouble hearing and producing consonant blends such as /br/, /kr/, /dr/, /fr/, /gr/, /pr/, and /tr/. Provide extended modeling and practice with segmenting and blending the sounds in each consonant blend in words such as *brim, crab, dress, frog, grip, prop,* and *track*. Use each word in a brief sentence to provide a meaningful context.

Formative Assessment and Corrective Feedback

IF a student makes an error, THEN follow this model:

Correct the error.

Guide the student to perform the task correctly by modeling.

Check for understanding by having the student repeat the task.

Reinforce: Make a note to review the skill during the student's next session.

Objectives

- Recognize and read high-frequency words.

Materials

- High-Frequency Word Cards

Formative Assessment and Corrective Feedback

IF a student makes an error, THEN follow this model:

Correct the error.

Guide the student to say the word correctly.

Check for understanding by having the student reread the word from among other randomly displayed high-frequency words.

Reinforce: Make a note to review the word during the student's next session.

High-Frequency Words:
her, now, our, she, today, would

Teach/Model

- Display the high-frequency words. Tell students that these are useful words to know since they will see these words often. Tell them that reading will be easier if they recognize these words.
- Display the High-Frequency Word Card for *her* and say the word. Then spell the word aloud as you point to each letter. Say the word again.
- Use the word in a simple sentence that will provide context. For example: *The girl put on her coat.*
- Repeat the steps above with the remaining high-frequency words.

Guided Practice

Do the following for each high-frequency word:

- Display the High-Frequency Word Card. Read the word and have students repeat it.
- Note the familiar sound/spelling patterns that are shown on the back of the card. Note as well any unfamiliar and unexpected sound/spellings.
- Blend the word with students.
- Spell the word aloud, pointing to each letter.
- Have students then spell the word aloud as you point to each letter.
- Have students read the word again.

Apply

- Display the High-Frequency Word Cards in random order. Have students read the words aloud.
- Have students write each word. Tell them to compare their writing with the word on the card and make corrections if necessary.
- Have students read each word aloud and use it in a sentence.

Phonics: Review: Words with Short *o*

Phonemic Awareness Warm-up

- Guide students to listen for the middle sound in words with short *o*. **Say:** *I'll say a word. Then you say it. Listen:* box. *The first sound in* box *is /b/.* Box *has the short* o *vowel sound, /ŏ/, in the middle. The ending sound in* box *is /ks/. Listen and say* box.

- **Say:** *Now let's do some more. Say each word sound by sound after me and tell me if it has the sound /ŏ/ in the middle, like* box. *Listen:* lock (yes), drag (no), sum (no), doll (yes), miss (no), trot (yes), peck (no).

Teach/Model

- Display the Sound/Spelling Card for *ostrich*. Name the picture and say the beginning sound. Have students repeat after you. **Say:** *Listen:* ostrich, */ŏ/. Now you say it.*

- Say the sound and give the spelling. **Say:** *Remember,* ostrich *begins with the sound /ŏ/. The letter* o *stands for the sound /ŏ/, the short* o *sound.*

- Display and read *jog*. **Say:** *This is the word* jog. *The letter* j *stands for the sound /j/ at the beginning. The letter* o *stands for the sound /ŏ/ in the middle. The letter* g *stands for the sound /g/ at the end. Read with me: /j/ /ŏ/, /jŏ/ /g/, /jŏg/,* jog.

Guided Practice

BLENDING Display the words in Rows 1, 2, and 3 below. Using Instructional Routine: Sound-by-Sound Blending, work with students to blend each word.

1. lock	rob	drop	got	brim
2. crab	trip	sock	prod	dull
3. well	crack	fox	trot	drum

DECODING Display the sentences below. Call on individuals to blend one or more words and to read the sentences.

The fox would not hop in our box.

She and her mom got on top of the rock.

BUILDING AND WRITING WORDS Model how to spell the word *rock*. **Say:** *The letter* r *stands for the first sound. The next sound is /ŏ/, the short* o *sound. I know* o *stands for that sound. The letters* ck *stand for the sound /k/ at the end of the word.* Repeat for the word *dock*. Point out that *rock* and *dock* belong to the same word family because they end with the same letters (-*ock*) and sounds (/ŏ/ /k/).

- Guide students to identify sounds in other words in the -*ock* word family and build them with Letter Cards: *lock, mock, sock*.

- Then have students write each word and read it aloud.

- Segment sounds in spoken single-syllable words with /ŏ/.
- Review the sound-spelling correspondence for short *o*.
- Blend, build, and decode regularly spelled one-syllable words with *o*.
- Read on-level text with fluency and accuracy.

Materials

- Sound/Spelling Cards
- Instructional Routine: Sound-by-Sound Blending
- Letter Cards
- Practice Page 1.10B

Formative Assessment and Corrective Feedback

IF a student makes an error, THEN follow this model:

Correct the error.

Guide the student to perform the task correctly by modeling.

Check for understanding by having the student repeat the task.

Reinforce: Make a note to review the skill during the student's next session.

- Distribute copies of Practice Page 1.10B, which contains the decodable story *Fox and Frog*. Tell students that many words in this story have short *o*. Point out that students have learned the following high-frequency words, which they will also read in the story: *her, now, today*.

- Read aloud the first three sentences of the story as students follow along. Point out that you do not misread, add, or skip words. Lead students in reading the same sentences with fluency and accuracy.

- Have students read the passage silently and then aloud. Remind them to track the words from left to right. When they come to the end of a line, they should sweep their hand down to the beginning of the next line and continue reading.

- When students have finished reading the text, choose a few sentences to review. You may want to focus on sentences that include words containing the target phonics skill. Have students read each sentence and explain in their own words what it means.

> **Fun with Words** Optional activities for engaging, hands-on practice are provided in the Resources section.

Phonics: Blends with *l*

Phonemic Awareness Warm-up

- Guide students to listen for the middle sound in words. **Say:** *I'll say a word. Then you say what vowel sound you hear in the middle. I'll do it first. The word is* plot. *Listen to the sounds:* /p/ /l/ /ŏ/ /t/. *The vowel sound in the middle is /ŏ/.*

- **Say:** *Now let's try one together. The word is* flag. *Let's say the sounds:* /f/ /l/ /ă/ /g/. *The vowel sound in the middle is /ă/. Now you do it. The word is* clip. *Say the sounds:* /c/ /l/ /ĭ/ /p/. *What vowel sound do you hear in the middle?* (/ĭ/) *I'll say some more words. Listen and tell me the vowel sound you hear in the middle of each word:* plan (/ă/), flip (/ĭ/), clock (/ŏ/), plum (/ŭ/), sled (/ĕ/).

Teach/Model

- Display the Sound/Spelling Card for *seal*. Name the picture and say the beginning sound. Have students repeat after you. **Say:** *Listen:* seal, /s/. *Now you say it.* Repeat with the Sound/Spelling Card for *lion*.

- Say the sounds and give the spellings. **Say:** *When* s *and* l *are side by side in a word, we say them together and their sounds blend together,* /s/ /l/. *Say it with me:* /s/ /l/. Have students say and spell the blend three times. Repeat with *bl, cl, fl,* and *pl*.

- Display and read *slam*. **Say:** *This is the word* slam. *The letters* s *and* l *stand for the sounds /s/ and /l/ in* slam. *We blend /s/ and /l/ together when we say* slam. *The letter* a *stands for the sound /ă/ in* slam. *The letter* m *stands for the sound /m/ in* slam. *Read with me:* /s/ /l/, /sl/, /sl/ /ă/, /slă/ /m/, /slăm/, slam.

Guided Practice

BLENDING Display the words in Rows 1, 2, and 3 below. Using Instructional Routine: Sound-by-Sound Blending, work with students to blend each word.

1. plan	glass	plop	grip	clock
2. brim	flip	cram	slot	clip
3. black	frog	flag	slop	track

DECODING Display the sentences below. Call on individuals to blend one or more words and to read the sentences.

She is glad her black sled slid well.

Today our class plans to get glass blocks.

BUILDING AND WRITING WORDS Model how to spell the word *block*. **Say:** *The letter* b *stands for the first sound. The letter* l *stands for the next sound I hear. The next sound is /ŏ/. The letter* o *stands for /ŏ/. I know that* ck *together stand for /k/.*

- Guide students to identify sounds in the following words and build them with Letter Cards: *block, club, flap, glad, plug, slim.*

- Then have students write each word and read it aloud.

Objectives

- Segment sounds in spoken single-syllable words with blends with *l*.
- Learn the sound-spelling correspondences for blends with *l*.
- Blend, build, and decode regularly spelled one-syllable words with blends with *l*.
- Read on-level text with fluency and accuracy.

Materials

- Sound/Spelling Cards
- Instructional Routine: Sound-by-Sound Blending
- Letter Cards
- Practice Page 1.10C

English Language Support

Linguistic Transfer Speakers of Cantonese and other Chinese languages, Spanish, and Vietnamese may have trouble hearing and producing consonant blends such as /bl/, /kl/, /fl/, /gl/, /pl/, and /sl/. Provide extended modeling and practice with segmenting and blending the sounds in each consonant blend in words such as *black, clip, flat, glass, plot,* and *slap*. Use each word in a brief sentence to provide a meaningful context.

Formative Assessment and Corrective Feedback

IF a student makes an error, THEN follow this model:

Correct the error.

Guide the student to perform the task correctly by modeling.

Check for understanding by having the student repeat the task.

Reinforce: Make a note to review the skill during the student's next session.

Apply

- Distribute copies of Practice Page 1.10C, which contains the decodable story *Go, Sled Club!* Tell students that many words in this story have blends with *l*. Point out that students have learned the following high-frequency words, which they will also read in the story: *her, now, our, she.*

- Read aloud the first two sentences of the story as students follow along. Point out that you do not misread, add, or skip words. Lead students in reading the same sentences with fluency and accuracy.

- Have students read the passage silently and then aloud. Remind them to track the words from left to right. When they come to the end of a line, they should sweep their hand down to the beginning of the next line and continue reading.

- When students have finished reading the text, choose a few sentences to review. You may want to focus on sentences that include words containing the target phonics skill. Have students read each sentence and explain in their own words what it means.

> **Fun with Words** Optional activities for engaging, hands-on practice are provided in the Resources section.

High-Frequency Words:
after, draw, pictures, read, was, write

Teach/Model

- Display the high-frequency words. Tell students that these are useful words to know since they will see these words often. Tell them that reading will be easier if they recognize these words.
- Display the High-Frequency Word Card for *after* and say the word. Then spell the word aloud as you point to each letter. Say the word again.
- Use the word in a simple sentence that will provide context. For example: *We went to the park after lunch.*
- Repeat the steps above with the remaining high-frequency words.

Guided Practice

Do the following for each high-frequency word:

- Display the High-Frequency Word Card. Read the word and have students repeat it.
- Note the familiar sound/spelling patterns that are shown on the back of the card. Note as well any unfamiliar and unexpected sound/spellings.
- Blend the word with students.
- Spell the word aloud, pointing to each letter.
- Have students then spell the word aloud as you point to each letter.
- Have students read the word again.

Apply

- Display the High-Frequency Word Cards in random order. Have students read the words aloud.
- Have students write each word. Tell them to compare their writing with the word on the card and make corrections if necessary.
- Have students read each word aloud and use it in a sentence.

Objectives

- Recognize and read high-frequency words.

Materials

- High-Frequency Word Cards

Formative Assessment and Corrective Feedback

IF a student makes an error, THEN follow this model:

Correct the error.

Guide the student to say the word correctly.

Check for understanding by having the student reread the word from among other randomly displayed high-frequency words.

Reinforce: Make a note to review the word during the student's next session.

Objectives

- Segment sounds in spoken single-syllable words with blends with s.
- Learn the sound-spelling correspondences for blends with s.
- Blend, build, and decode regularly spelled one-syllable words with blends with s.
- Read on-level text with fluency and accuracy.

Materials

- Sound/Spelling Cards
- Instructional Routine: Sound-by-Sound Blending
- Letter Cards
- Practice Page 1.11B

Phonics: Blends with s

Phonemic Awareness Warm-up

- **Say:** *I'll say a word and then say the sounds in it. The word is* stem. *The sounds are /s/ /t/ /ĕ/ /m/. The vowel sound in the middle is /ĕ/. The word has four sounds.*
- **Say:** *Now let's try one together. The word is* sled. *Let's say the sounds: /s/ /l/ /ĕ/ /d/. What is the vowel sound in the middle? (/ĕ/) How many sounds do you hear? (4) Now you do it. The word is* split. *Say the sounds. (/s/ /p/ /l/ /ĭ/ /t/) What is the vowel sound in the middle? (/ĭ/) How many sounds do you hear? (5)*
- **Say:** *I'll say some more words. Listen and tell me what vowel sound and how many sounds you hear in each word:* stop *(/ŏ/; 4),* strip *(/ĭ/; 5),* spell *(/ĕ/; 4),* scrap *(/ă/; 5).*

Teach/Model

- Display the Sound/Spelling Card for *seal*. Name the picture and say the beginning sound. Have students repeat after you. **Say:** *Listen:* seal, */s/. Now you say it.* Repeat with the Sound/Spelling Card for *tiger*.
- Say the sounds and give the spellings. **Say:** *When* s *and* t *are side by side in a word, we say them together and their sounds blend together, /s/ /t/. Say it with me: /s/ /t/.* Have students say and spell the blend three times. Repeat with *sk, sm, sw*, and the three-letter blend *str*.
- Display and read *stem*. **Say:** *This is the word* stem. *The letters* s *and* t *stand for the sounds /s/ and /t/ in* stem. *We blend /s/ and /t/ together when we say* stem. *The letter* e *stands for the sound /ĕ/ in* stem. *The letter* m *stands for the sound /m/ in* stem. *Read with me: /s/ /t/, /st/, /st/ /ĕ/, /stĕ/ /m/, /stem/,* stem.

Guided Practice

BLENDING Display the words in Rows 1, 2, and 3 below. Using Instructional Routine: Sound-by-Sound Blending, work with students to blend each word.

1. step	sled	swim	scrap	strap
2. still	smell	sniff	skip	scan
3. snug	swam	slam	spell	slip

DECODING Display the sentences below. Call on individuals to blend one or more words and to read the sentences.

Stan will skip and spin after a snack.

Was the stick too stiff to snap and split?

BUILDING AND WRITING WORDS Model how to spell the word *swim*. **Say:** *The letter* s *stands for the first sound. The letter* w *stands for the next sound. The next sound is /ĭ/. I know* i *stands for /ĭ/. The last sound is /m/. I know* m *stands for /m/.*

- Guide students to identify sounds in the following words and build them with Letter Cards: *stack, spell, snag, smock, slot, scrap, strum*.
- Then have students write each word and read it aloud.

Apply

- Distribute copies of Practice Page 1.11B, which contains the decodable story *Stan and Fran*. Tell students that many words in this story have blends with *s*. Point out that students have learned the following high-frequency words, which they will also read in the story: *draw, pictures*.

- Read aloud the first two sentences of the story as students follow along. Point out that you do not misread, add, or skip words. Lead students in reading the same sentences with fluency and accuracy.

- Have students read the passage silently and then aloud. Remind them to track the words from left to right. When they come to the end of a line, they should sweep their hand down to the beginning of the next line and continue reading.

- When students have finished reading the text, choose a few sentences to review. You may want to focus on sentences that include words containing the target phonics skill. Have students read each sentence and explain in their own words what it means.

Fun with Words Optional activities for engaging, hands-on practice are provided in the Resources section.

English Language Support

Linguistic Transfer Students whose first language is Spanish may add a vowel sound before initial consonant blends such as /st/: *ehstudent*. In Spanish, consonants do not usually cluster in a syllable, so students may add the vowel sound to create another syllable. Have them practice making a continuant /ssss/ and then blending the next consonant sound at the beginning of words such as *spot, step, skin, swell, scuff, smack, snap,* and *slip*.

Formative Assessment and Corrective Feedback

IF a student makes an error, THEN follow this model:

Correct the error.

Guide the student to perform the task correctly by modeling.

Check for understanding by having the student repeat the task.

Reinforce: Make a note to review the skill during the student's next session.

High-Frequency Words:
eat, give, one, put, small, take

Objectives

- Recognize and read high-frequency words.

Materials

- High-Frequency Word Cards

Formative Assessment and Corrective Feedback

IF a student makes an error, THEN follow this model:

Correct the error.

Guide the student to say the word correctly.

Check for understanding by having the student reread the word from among other randomly displayed high-frequency words.

Reinforce: Make a note to review the word during the student's next session.

Teach/Model

- Display the high-frequency words. Tell students that these are useful words to know since they will see these words often. Tell them that reading will be easier if they recognize these words.
- Display the High-Frequency Word Card for *eat* and say the word. Then spell the word aloud as you point to each letter. Say the word again.
- Use the word in a simple sentence that will provide context. For example: *Many people eat cereal for breakfast.*
- Repeat the steps above with the remaining high-frequency words.

Guided Practice

Do the following for each high-frequency word:

- Display the High-Frequency Word Card. Read the word and have students repeat it.
- Note the familiar sound/spelling patterns that are shown on the back of the card. Note as well any unfamiliar and unexpected sound/spellings.
- Blend the word with students.
- Spell the word aloud, pointing to each letter.
- Have students then spell the word aloud as you point to each letter.
- Have students read the word again.

Apply

- Display the High-Frequency Word Cards in random order. Have students read the words aloud.
- Have students write each word. Tell them to compare their writing with the word on the card and make corrections if necessary.
- Have students read each word aloud and use it in a sentence.

Phonics: Review: Words with Short *u*

Phonemic Awareness Warm-up

- Guide students to listen for the middle sound in words with short *u*. **Say:** *I'll say a word. Then you say it. Listen:* buzz. *The first sound in* buzz *is /b/.* Buzz *has the /ŭ/ sound in the middle. The ending sound in* buzz *is /z/. Listen and say* buzz.

- **Say:** *Now let's do some more. Say each word sound by sound after me and tell me if it has the sound /ŭ/ in the middle. Listen:* club (yes), still (no), drop (no), truck (yes), press (no), snug (yes), glad (no).

Teach/Model

- Display the Sound/Spelling Card for *umbrella*. Name the picture and say the beginning sound. Have students repeat after you. **Say:** *Listen:* umbrella, */ŭ/. Now you say it.*

- Say the sound and give the spelling. **Say:** *Remember,* umbrella *begins with the sound /ŭ/. The letter* u *stands for the sound /ŭ/. This sound is called the short* u *sound.*

- Display and read *plum*. **Say:** *This is the word* plum. *The letters* p *and* l *stand for the sounds /p/ and /l/ at the beginning. The letter* u *stands for the sound /ŭ/ in the middle. The letter* m *stands for the sound /m/ at the end. Read with me: /p/ /l/, /pl/, /pl/ /ŭ/, /plŭ/ /m/, /plŭm/,* plum.

Guided Practice

BLENDING Display the words in Rows 1, 2, and 3 below. Using Instructional Routine: Sound-by-Sound Blending, work with students to blend each word.

1. dull	plug	buck	fuss	stop
2. grub	drill	skid	drum	neck
3. clam	plus	tuck	grass	lots

DECODING Display the sentences below. Call on individuals to blend one or more words and to read the sentences.

> Gus will give one of us a plum.
>
> Ducks eat small bugs in the mud.

BUILDING AND WRITING WORDS Model using Letter Cards to build the word *duck*. **Say:** *The letter* d *stands for the first sound, /d/. The letter* u *stands for the middle sound, /ŭ/. The letters* ck *stand for the last sound, /k/.*

- Guide students to identify sounds in the following words and build them with Letter Cards: *tub, mud, rug, cuff, luck, snub, strum.*

- Have students write each word and read it aloud.

Objectives
- Review the sound-spelling correspondence for short *u*.
- Segment sounds in spoken single-syllable words with short *u*.
- Blend, build, and decode regularly spelled one-syllable words with *u*.
- Read on-level text with fluency and accuracy.

Materials
- Sound/Spelling Cards
- Instructional Routine: Sound-by-Sound Blending
- Letter Cards
- Practice Page 1.12B

Formative Assessment and Corrective Feedback

IF a student makes an error, THEN follow this model:

Correct the error.

Guide the student to perform the task correctly by modeling.

Check for understanding by having the student repeat the task.

Reinforce: Make a note to review the skill during the student's next session.

Apply

- Distribute copies of Practice Page 1.12B, which contains the decodable story *Run, Huck!* Tell students that many words in this story have short *u*. Point out that students have learned the following high-frequency words, which they will also read in the story: *eat, one, put, take.*

- Read aloud the first three sentences of the story as students follow along. Point out that you do not misread, add, or skip words. Lead students in reading the same sentences with fluency and accuracy.

- Have students read the passage silently and then aloud. Remind them to track the words from left to right. When they come to the end of a line, they should sweep their hand down to the beginning of the next line and continue reading.

- When students have finished reading the text, choose a few sentences to review. You may want to focus on sentences that include words containing the target phonics skill. Have students read each sentence and explain in their own words what it means.

> **Fun with Words** Optional activities for engaging, hands-on practice are provided in the Resources section.

Phonics: Final Blends

Phonemic Awareness Warm-up

- **Say:** *I'll say a word and then say the sounds in it. The word is* bend. *The sounds are /b/ /ĕ/ /n/ /d/. The vowel sound in the middle is /ĕ/. The word has four sounds.*

- **Say:** *Now let's try one together. The word is* hunt. *Let's say the sounds: /h/ /ŭ/ /n/ /t/. What is the vowel sound in the middle?* (/ŭ/) *How many sounds do you hear?* (4) *Now you do it. The word is* lump. *Say the sounds.* (/l/ /ŭ/ /m/ /p/) *What is the vowel sound in the middle?* (/ŭ/) *How many sounds do you hear?* (4)

- **Say:** *I'll say some more words. Listen and tell me what vowel sound and how many sounds you hear in each word:* stamp (/ă/; 5), send (/ĕ/; 4), pond (/ŏ/; 4), splint (/ĭ/; 5).

Teach/Model

- Display the Sound/Spelling Card for *noodles*. Name the picture and say the beginning sound. Have students repeat after you. **Say:** *Listen:* noodles, /n/. *Now you say it.* Repeat with the Sound/Spelling Card for *duck*.

- Say the sounds and give the spellings. **Say:** *When* n *and* d *are side by side in a word, we say them together and their sounds blend together, /n/ /d/. Say it with me: /n/ /d/.* Have students say and spell the blend three times.

- Display and read *bend*. **Say:** *This is the word* bend. *The letter* b *stands for the sound /b/ in* bend. *The letter* e *stands for the sound /ĕ/ in* bend. *The letter* n *stands for the sound /n/. The letter* d *stands for the sound /d/ in* bend. *Read with me: /b/ /ĕ/, /bĕ/, /bĕ/ /n/, /bĕn/ /d/, /bĕnd/* bend.

- Repeat the routine for *nt* and *mp* using the words *hunt* and *lump*.

Guided Practice

BLENDING Display the words in Rows 1, 2, and 3 below. Using Instructional Routine: Sound-by-Sound Blending, work with students to blend each word.

1. bump	stunt	mend	camp	ant
2. stop	smack	dent	stand	jump
3. lamp	strap	mint	snug	band

DECODING Display the sentences below. Call on individuals to blend one or more words and to read the sentences.

> Grant put up a tent at camp.
>
> She will take a lamp to the desk.

BUILDING AND WRITING WORDS Display the words *jump* and *pump* and have students read each word. Ask which letters are the same in each word. Remind students that words that end with the same letters and sounds belong to the same word family. Underline *ump* as students reread the words.

- Guide students to identify sounds in the following words and build them with Letter Cards: *stump, bump, lump, plump.*

- Then have students write each word and read it aloud.

Objectives

- Segment sounds in spoken single-syllable words with final blends.
- Learn the sound-spelling correspondence for common final blends.
- Blend, build, and decode regularly spelled one-syllable words with final blends.
- Read on-level text with fluency and accuracy.

Materials

- Sound/Spelling Cards
- Instructional Routine: Sound-by-Sound Blending
- Letter Cards
- Practice Page 1.12C

English Language Support

Linguistic Transfer Spanish speakers may have trouble with final consonant blends. They may add a vowel sound to make another syllable, or they may drop the last consonant: /kep/ /et/ or /kep/ for /kept/. Have students practice saying one consonant sound and then blending the other consonant sound at the end of words such as *jump, hand, went, fast,* and *ask.*

Formative Assessment and Corrective Feedback

IF a student makes an error, THEN follow this model:

Correct the error.

Guide the student to perform the task correctly by modeling.

Check for understanding by having the student repeat the task.

Reinforce: Make a note to review the skill during the student's next session.

Apply

- Distribute copies of Practice Page 1.12C, which contains the decodable story *Find Scamp.* Tell students that many words in this story have final blends. Point out that students have learned the following high-frequency words, which they will also read in the story: *one, small, take.*

- Read aloud the first four sentences of the story as students follow along. Point out that you do not misread, add, or skip words. Lead students in reading the same sentences with fluency and accuracy.

- Have students read the passage silently and then aloud. Remind them to track the words from left to right. When they come to the end of a line, they should sweep their hand down to the beginning of the next line and continue reading.

- When students have finished reading the text, choose a few sentences to review. You may want to focus on sentences that include words containing the target phonics skill. Have students read each sentence and explain in their own words what it means.

> **Fun with Words** Optional activities for engaging, hands-on practice are provided in the Resources section.

Cumulative Review/Fluency

Teach/Model

REVIEW

- Remind students they have learned the short vowel sounds for *a, i, o,* and *u.* Display the vowels and review the short sound for each.

- Remind students they have learned sounds for double final consonants, *ck,* blends at the ends of words, and blends with *r, l,* and *s* at the beginnings of words. Display the consonants and blends and review the sounds for each.

- Display these sentences:

    Jack will swim at camp.

    Will Jill take pictures of us?

    Brad will make a clock.

- Point to the high-frequency words *take, pictures, of,* and *make* and read each one. Remind students that they know these words. Use the High-Frequency Word Cards and Instructional Routine: High-Frequency Words to review these words.

MODEL FLUENCY

- Explain that good readers don't skip hard parts. They take their time, go back, and correct themselves. That way, they understand the words they are reading and what the words mean.

- Read the sentences, pointing to each word as you read it slowly. Read the following sentence with an error: **Say:** *Brad will make a cluck.* Point to the word *clock.* **Say:** *I read this word as* cluck, *but that doesn't make sense. I'm going to try again: /k/ /l/ /ŏ/ /k/,* clock. *The vowel is o /ŏ/, not u /ŭ/. I also looked for clues in the text. Brad is making something. He can't make a cluck, but he can make a clock. Now it makes sense.*

- Reread the sentence with no mistakes, pointing to the words as you read them.

Guided Practice

- Tell students they will practice reading. Display the following sentences:

    Brin and her mom make a plan.

    Brin will pick a small plant.

    Her mom will put it in a pot.

- Guide students in reading the sentences aloud. Coach them to sound out each word. Have students go back to any word they read incorrectly. Remind them that sometimes letters can be pronounced in more than one way, and have them sound out the word again. Guide students to look for context clues in surrounding text to help them figure out the word.

- Have students read the sentences again.

Objectives

- Decode words with short vowels, final consonants, and blends.
- Recognize and read high-frequency words.
- Read on-level text with purpose and understanding.
- Read on-level text orally with accuracy on successive readings.
- Use context to confirm or self-correct word recognition and understanding, rereading as necessary.

Materials

- High-Frequency Word Cards
- Instructional Routine: High-Frequency Words
- Practice Page 1.13

Formative Assessment and Corrective Feedback

IF a student makes an error, THEN follow this model:

Correct the error.

Guide the student to say the word correctly.

Check for understanding by having the student reread the word.

Reinforce: Make a note to review the word during the student's next session.

- Have students read aloud the practice text on Practice Page 1.13.

- Explain that the main purpose of reading the text is to practice their reading skills.

- Coach students to use decoding skills and context to self-correct any mistakes they make during reading. They should read the text several times, until they are able to read smoothly and accurately.

- When students have finished the fluency practice, choose a few sentences to review. Have students read each sentence and explain in their own words what it means.

- After students are able to read the text fluently, guide them to track their progress on their My Progress line graphs.

High-Frequency Words:
blue, cold, far, little, live, their, water, where

Teach/Model

- Display the high-frequency words. Tell students that these are useful words to know since they will see these words often. Tell them that reading will be easier if they recognize these words.
- Display the High-Frequency Word Card for *blue* and say the word. Then spell the word aloud as you point to each letter. Say the word again.
- Use the word in a simple sentence that will provide context. For example: *Her favorite color is blue.*
- Repeat the steps above with the remaining high-frequency words.

Guided Practice

Do the following for each high-frequency word:

- Display the High-Frequency Word Card. Read the word and have students repeat it.
- Note the familiar sound/spelling patterns that are shown on the back of the card. Note as well any unfamiliar and unexpected sound/spellings.
- Blend the word with students.
- Spell the word aloud, pointing to each letter.
- Have students then spell the word aloud as you point to each letter.
- Have students read the word again.

Apply

- Display the High-Frequency Word Cards in random order. Have students read the words aloud.
- Have students write each word. Tell them to compare their writing with the word on the card and make corrections if necessary.
- Have students read each word aloud and use it in a sentence.

Objectives

- Recognize and read high-frequency words.

Materials

- High-Frequency Word Cards

Formative Assessment and Corrective Feedback

IF a student makes an error, THEN follow this model:

Correct the error.

Guide the student to say the word correctly.

Check for understanding by having the student reread the word from among other randomly displayed high-frequency words.

Reinforce: Make a note to review the word during the student's next session.

Phonics: Digraph *th*

Phonemic Awareness Warm-up

Objectives

- Blend and segment sounds in spoken single-syllable words with digraph *th*.
- Learn the sound-spelling correspondence for digraph *th*.
- Blend, build, and decode regularly spelled one-syllable words with digraph *th*.
- Read on-level text with fluency and accuracy.

Materials

- Sound/Spelling Cards
- Instructional Routine: Sound-by-Sound Blending
- Letter Cards
- Practice Page 1.14B

- **Say:** *Listen as I blend some sounds to say a word: /th/ /ĭ/ /k/. The word is* thick. *Listen again: /p/ /ă/ /th/. The word is* path.
- **Say:** *Now let's do it together. Listen. Blend the sounds: /th/ /ĭ/ /n/. What is the word?* (thin) *Now you listen, blend the sounds, and tell me each word: /b/ /ă/ /th/* (bath), */w/ /ĭ/ /th/* (with), */th/ /ŭ/ /m/* (thumb).
- Reverse the process, segmenting instead of blending. Use the same words but in random order.

Teach/Model

- Display the Sound/Spelling Card for *thumb*. Name the picture and say the beginning sound. Have students repeat after you. **Say:** *Listen:* thumb, */th/. Now you say it.*
- Say the sound and give the spelling. **Say:** Thumb *begins with the sound /th/. The letters* th *stand for the sound /th/ at the beginning, middle, or end of a word.*
- Write and read *thin*. **Say:** *This is the word* thin. *The letters* th *stand for the beginning sound /th/. The letter* i *stands for the middle sound /ĭ/. The letter* n *stands for the ending sound /n/. Read with me: /th/ /ĭ/, /thĭ/ /n/, /thĭn/,* thin.
- Write and read *bath*. **Say:** *This is the word* bath. *The letter* b *stands for the beginning sound /b/. The letter* a *stands for the middle sound /ă/. The letters* th *stand for the ending sound /th/. Read with me: /b/ /ă/, /bă/ /th/, /băth/,* bath.
- Repeat with the words *thick* and *with*.

Guided Practice

BLENDING Display the words in Rows 1 and 2 below. Using Instructional Routine: Sound-by-Sound Blending, work with students to blend each word.

1. math	thick	thin	with	bath
2. jump	path	thump	scrap	Beth

DECODING Display the sentences below. Call on students to blend one or more words and to read the sentences.

- The water in the bath got cold.
- He had on a thick blue hat.
- How far does the path go?

BUILDING AND WRITING WORDS Model how to build the word *thick* with Letter Cards.
Say: *The first sound is /th/. The letters* th *stand for the sound /th/. The next sound is /ĭ/. I know* i *stands for /ĭ/. The last sound is /k/. I know that the letters* ck *usually stand for final /k/.*

- Guide students to identify sounds in the following words and build them with Letter Cards: *thin, bath, thump, with, Beth, math, path.*
- Have students write each word and read it aloud.

Apply

- Distribute copies of Practice Page 1.14B, which contains the decodable story *The Path to Blue Pond*. Tell students that many words in this story begin or end with the letters *th*. Point out that students have learned the following high-frequency words, which they will also read in the story: *blue, far, live, their, where.*

- Read aloud the first three sentences of the story as students follow along. Point out that you do not misread, add, or skip words. Lead students in reading the same sentences with fluency and accuracy.

- Have students read the passage silently and then aloud. Remind them to track the words from left to right. When they come to the end of a line, they should sweep their hand down to the beginning of the next line and continue reading.

- When students have finished reading the text, choose a few sentences to review. You may want to focus on sentences that include words containing the target phonics skill. Have students read each sentence and explain in their own words what it means.

Fun with Words Optional activities for engaging, hands-on practice are provided in the Resources section.

English Language Support

Linguistic Transfer Many English learners (including speakers of Spanish, Vietnamese, Cantonese or Mandarin, Tagalog, Korean, Haitian Creole, or Hmong) have trouble with the /th/ sound, and some may substitute /d/. Model saying /th/, pointing out that your tongue is between your teeth. Have students practice the /th/ sound and then repeat the word with /th/ in pairs such as these: *thin/din, die/thigh, thaw/paw, pink/think, bad/bath, path/pad, math/mad.* Use each word in a brief sentence to reinforce meaning.

Formative Assessment and Corrective Feedback

IF a student makes an error, THEN follow this model:

Correct the error.

Guide the student to perform the task correctly by modeling.

Check for understanding by having the student repeat the task.

Reinforce: Make a note to review the skill during the student's next session.

Phonics: Base Words and Endings -s, -es, -ed, -ing

Objectives

- Blend and segment sounds in spoken single-syllable words.
- Blend, build, and decode regularly spelled one-syllable words with inflectional endings -s, -es, -ed, and -ing.
- Recognize that inflectional endings -s and -ed stand for different sounds.
- Read on-level text with fluency and accuracy.

Materials

- Letter Cards
- Instructional Routine: Sound-by-Sound Blending
- Practice Page 1.14C

Phonemic Awareness Warm-up

- **Say:** *Listen as I blend some sounds to say a word:* /r/ /ŭ/ /n/ /z/, *runs. I'll do another one. Listen:* /j/ /ŭ/ /m/ /p/ /t/, *jumped. Let's do this one together. Listen to tell me what word I get when I blend the sounds:* /r/ /ĕ/ /n/ /t/ /s/. (rents)
- Reverse the process to segment phonemes. **Say:** *Listen to tell me the sounds that make up the word* fished. *The sounds are* /f/ /ĭ/ /sh/ /t/. *Now you try. Tell me the sounds in the word* claps. (/k/ /l/ /ă/ /p/ /s/)

Teach/Model

- **Say:** *Sometimes action words, or verbs, have letters added at the end. These added letters tell when the action happens.*
- Display Letter Cards *j, u, m, p*. Read the word: *jump*. Add Letter Card *s* at the end. Blend the new word: /j/ /ŭ/ /m/ /p/ /s/, jumps. Have students repeat the word. Remind them that *-s* can stand for /s/ or /z/ at the end of an action word. Use *jumps* in a sentence: *Jan jumps up and down*.
- Replace Letter Card *s* with Letter Cards *e, d*. Blend the new word: /j/ /ŭ/ /m/ /p/ /t/, jumped. Have students repeat the word. Explain that *-ed* can stand for /t/, /d/, or /ed/ at the end of an action word. Use *jumped* in a sentence: *Jan jumped up and down*.
- Replace Letter Cards *e, d* with Letter Cards *i, n, g*. Blend the new word and have students repeat it. Use *jumping* in a sentence: *Jan is jumping up and down*.
- Repeat the routine with Letter Cards to build the words *miss, misses, missed,* and *missing*.

Guided Practice

BLENDING Display the words in Rows 1 and 2 below. Using Instructional Routine: Sound-by-Sound Blending, work with students to blend each word.

| 1. clicks | thumped | telling | missed | bumps |
| 2. passes | asked | sits | resting | ticking |

DECODING Display the sentences below. Call on individuals to blend one or more words and to read the sentences.

- My friend is packing a big blue bag.
- Beth runs and jumps if she is cold.
- Big and little ducks rested on the water.

BUILDING AND WRITING WORDS Model using Letter Cards to build the word *camps*. **Say:** *The letter* c *stands for the first sound,* /k/. *The letter* a *stands for* /ă/. *The next sound is* /m/. *The letter* m *stands for that sound. The letter* p *stands for* /p/. *The last sound is* /s/. *The letter* s *stands for that sound.*

- Guide students to identify sounds in the following words and build them with Letter Cards: *misses, standing, planted, asks, dumped, sending*.
- Have students write each word and read it aloud.

Apply

- Distribute copies of Practice Page 1.14C, which contains the decodable story *The Little Duck*. Tell students that many words in this story end with *-s, -es, -ed,* or *-ing.* Point out that students have learned the following high-frequency words, which they will also read in the story: *far, little, where.*

- Read aloud the first three sentences of the story as students follow along. Point out that you do not misread, add, or skip words. Lead students in reading the same sentences with fluency and accuracy.

- Have students read the passage silently and then aloud. Remind them to track the words from left to right. When they come to the end of a line, they should sweep their hand down to the beginning of the next line and continue reading.

- When students have finished reading the text, choose a few sentences to review. You may want to focus on sentences that include words containing the target phonics skill. Have students read each sentence and explain in their own words what it means.

> **Fun with Words** Optional activities for engaging, hands-on practice are provided in the Resources section.

Formative Assessment and Corrective Feedback

IF a student makes an error, THEN follow this model:

Correct the error.

Guide the student to perform the task correctly by modeling.

Check for understanding by having the student repeat the task.

Reinforce: Make a note to review the skill during the student's next session.

Objectives

- Recognize and read high-frequency words.

Materials

- High-Frequency Word Cards

Formative Assessment and Corrective Feedback

IF a student makes an error, THEN follow this model:

Correct the error.

Guide the student to say the word correctly.

Check for understanding by having the student reread the word from among other randomly displayed high-frequency words.

Reinforce: Make a note to review the word during the student's next session.

High-Frequency Words:
been, brown, know, never, off, out, own, very

Teach/Model

- Display the high-frequency words. Tell students that these are useful words to know since they will see these words often. Tell them that reading will be easier if they recognize these words.
- Display the High-Frequency Word Card for *been* and say the word. Then spell the word aloud as you point to each letter. Say the word again.
- Use the word in a simple sentence that will provide context. For example: *Cal has been to the fair several times.*
- Repeat the steps above with the remaining high-frequency words.

Guided Practice

Do the following for each high-frequency word:

- Display the High-Frequency Word Card. Read the word and have students repeat it.
- Note the familiar sound/spelling patterns that are shown on the back of the card. Note as well any unfamiliar and unexpected sound/spellings.
- Blend the word with students.
- Spell the word aloud, pointing to each letter.
- Have students then spell the word aloud as you point to each letter.
- Have students read the word again.

Apply

- Display the High-Frequency Word Cards in random order. Have students read the words aloud.
- Have students write each word. Tell them to compare their writing with the word on the card and make corrections if necessary.
- Have students read each word aloud and use it in a sentence.

Phonemic Awareness: Substitute Initial Phonemes

Teach/Model

- **Say:** *Today we're going to change the first sound in a word to make a new word. For example,* bat *begins with the /b/ sound. The first sound in* bat *is /b/.*

- Say the word *bat,* emphasizing the /b/ sound. **Say:** *Listen:* bat.

- **Say:** *Now I'll change the /b/ sound to /s/. Listen: /s/ /ă/ /t/,* sat. *Say it with me:* sat. *I changed the first sound /b/ to /s/ and made the word* sat.

- **Say:** *Now I'll change the /b/ sound in* bat *to /m/. Listen: /m/ /ă/ /t/,* mat. *Say it with me:* mat. *I changed the first sound /b/ to /m/ and made the word* mat. *Let's keep going.*

Guided Practice

- **Say:** *We're going to change the beginning sounds in words to make new words. For example, what is the first sound in* den? *(/d/) Good. Now let's change the first sound in* den *to /t/. Listen: /t/ /ĕ/ /n/. What is the word?* (ten) *Good! Let's try some more.*

- Continue with the words shown below.

Change the . . .	Result
/g/ in *get* to /m/	met
/b/ in *bun* to /r/	run
/t/ in *tan* to /p/	pan
/j/ in *jump* to /l/	lump
/n/ in *nest* to /b/	best
/f/ in *fin* to /th/	thin
/th/ in *thick* to /kw/	quick
/m/ in *mop* to /ch/	chop

Apply

Have students practice substituting initial phonemes, using the words below. **Say:**

- *Change the /r/ in* rich *to /d/. What is the word?* (ditch)
- *Change the /ch/ in* chain *to /r/. What is the word?* (rain)
- *Change the /n/ in* neck *to /ch/. What is the word?* (check)
- *Change the /d/ in* dance *to /ch/. What is the word?* (chance)
- *Change the /l/ in* lump *to /th/. What is the word?* (thump)
- *Change the /m/ in* mud *to /th/. What is the word?* (thud)
- *Change the first sound in* top *to /ch/. What is the word?* (chop)
- *Change the first sound in* match *to /p/. What is the word?* (patch)
- *Change the first sound in* pin *to /ch/. What is the word?* (chin)
- *Change the first sound in* cat *to /ch/. What is the word?* (chat)

Objectives

- Isolate and substitute the initial sounds in spoken single-syllable words.

English Language Support

Linguistic Transfer Point out to Spanish speakers that many of the initial sounds they are isolating and replacing in the activities are the same in Spanish as in English. Encourage students to share words they know in both Spanish and English that begin with sounds such as /b/, /d/, /l/, /m/, /n/, /p/, /t/, and /ch/.

Formative Assessment and Corrective Feedback

IF a student makes an error, THEN follow this model:

Correct the error.

Guide the student to perform the task correctly by modeling.

Check for understanding by having the student repeat the task.

Reinforce: Make a note to review the skill during the student's next session.

Phonics: Digraphs *ch, tch*

Objectives

- Blend and segment sounds in spoken single-syllable words.
- Learn the sound-spelling correspondence for digraphs *ch, tch*.
- Blend, build, and decode regularly spelled one-syllable words with digraphs *ch* and *tch*.
- Read on-level text with fluency and accuracy.

Materials

- Sound/Spelling Cards
- Instructional Routine: Sound-by-Sound Blending
- Letter Cards
- Practice Page 1.15C

Phonemic Awareness Warm-up

- **Say:** *Listen as I blend sounds to say a word: /h/ /ĭ/ /p/. I'll say the sounds again.* Repeat the sounds. **Say:** *The word is* hip. *I'll do another one. Listen: /ch/ /ĭ/ /p/. The word is* chip.

- **Say:** *Now let's do it together. What word do I get when I blend these sounds? Listen: /ch/ /ĭ/ /n/. What is the word?* (chin) *Now you listen, blend the sounds, and tell me each word: /h/ /ŏ/ /p/* (hop), */ch/ /ŏ/ /p/* (chop), */p/ /ĭ/ /n/ /ch/* (pinch).

- Reverse the process, segmenting instead of blending. Use the same words but in random order.

Teach/Model

- Display the Sound/Spelling Card for *chick*. Name the picture and say the beginning sound. Have students repeat after you. **Say:** *Listen:* chick, */ch/. Now you say it.*

- Say the sound and give the spelling. **Say:** Chick *begins with the sound /ch/. The letters* ch *stand for the sound /ch/ at the beginning, middle, or end of a word.*

- Write and read *chin.* **Say:** *This is the word* chin. *The letters* ch *stand for the beginning sound /ch/. The letter* i *stands for the middle sound /ĭ/. The letter* n *stands for the ending sound /n/. Read with me: /ch/ /ĭ/, /chĭ/, /chĭn/,* chin.

- Write and read *match.* **Say:** *This is the word* match. *The letter* m *stands for the beginning sound /m/. The letter* a *stands for the middle sound /ă/. The letters* tch *stand for the ending sound /ch/. Read with me: /m/ /ă/, /mă/, /măch/,* match.

- Repeat with the words *chop, pinch,* and *hatch.*

Guided Practice

BLENDING Display the words in Rows 1 and 2 below. Using Instructional Routine: Sound-by-Sound Blending, work with students to blend each word.

1. chip	chop	chin	match	bench
2. rich	chat	itch	check	such

DECODING Display the sentences below. Call on individuals to blend one or more words and to read the sentences.

- The brown chimp sat on a branch.
- The hen can see her own chick hatch.
- I know Chuck can catch my pitch.

BUILDING AND WRITING WORDS Model how to spell the word *batch.* **Say:** *The letter* b *stands for the first sound. The next sound is /ă/. The letter* a *stands for /ă/. The letters* tch *stand for the sound /ch/. Repeat for the word* catch. *Point out that* batch *and* catch *belong to the same word family because they end with the same letters (-atch) and sounds (/ă/ /ch/).*

- Guide students to identify sounds in other words in the *-atch* word family and build them with Letter Cards: *hatch, latch, match, patch, snatch, scratch.*

- Have students write each word and read it aloud.

Apply

- Distribute copies of Practice Page 1.15C, which contains the decodable story *A Dog Called Chip*. Tell students that many words in this story begin or end with the letters *ch*. Point out that students have learned the following high-frequency words, which they will also read in the story: *brown, own, very*.

- Read aloud the first four sentences of the story as students follow along. Point out that you do not misread, add, or skip words. Lead students in reading the same sentences with fluency and accuracy.

- Have students read the passage silently and then aloud. Remind them to track the words from left to right. When they come to the end of a line, they should sweep their hand down to the beginning of the next line and continue reading.

- When students have finished reading the text, choose a few sentences to review. You may want to focus on sentences that include words containing the target phonics skill. Have students read each sentence and explain in their own words what it means.

> **Fun with Words** Optional activities for engaging, hands-on practice are provided in the Resources section.

IF a student makes an error, THEN follow this model:

Correct the error.

Guide the student to perform the task correctly by modeling.

Check for understanding by having the student repeat the task.

Reinforce: Make a note to review the skill during the student's next session.

Phonics: Possessive 's

Objectives

- Blend, build, and decode regularly spelled one-syllable words with possessive 's.
- Learn how to use an apostrophe when writing possessives.
- Read on-level text with fluency and accuracy.

Materials

- Sound/Spelling Cards
- Instructional Routine: Sound-by-Sound Blending
- Letter Cards
- Practice Page 1.15D

Phonemic Awareness Warm-up

- **Say:** *Listen as I say a word:* sun. *What is the first sound in* sun? (/s/) *If I change the first sound /s/ to /b/, I get the word* bun. *Let's say some more words together. Listen to the word:* hop. *What word do I get if I change the first sound to /ch/?* (chop)
- Repeat the process with these word pairs: *cat, hat; Sam, jam; less, mess; pick, sick.*

Teach/Model

- **Say:** *Sometimes a noun has a letter added at the end to tell us more about the word. When an s is added, it can make the word plural. When a special mark called an apostrophe is added before the s, it shows that the noun owns something.*
- Write the words *cat, cats,* and *cat's* on the board. Point to *cats* and *cat's.* **Say:** *These words have s added at the end, but they mean different things.* Circle the apostrophe in *cat's.* **Say:** *This mark means the cat owns something.* Read each word and have students repeat after you.
- Write *Chad's* on the board. Show and read Sound/Spelling Card for *seal* to review sounds for *s.* Remind students that an *s* can sound like /s/ as in *cat's* or like /z/ as in *Chad's.*
- Use the word *cat's* in a sentence: *My cat's food dish is empty.* Have students repeat /k/ /ă/ /t/ /s/ with you.

Guided Practice

BLENDING Display the words in Rows 1 and 2 below. Using Instructional Routine: Sound-by-Sound Blending, work with students to blend each word.

| 1. Seth's | ant's | mom's | plant's | chick's |
| 2. rug's | batch | limping | jumps | check |

DECODING Display the sentences below. Call on individuals to blend one or more words and to read the sentences.

- Beth's sister is very rich.
- My friend's cat is brown.
- Never fill up a plant's pot.

BUILDING AND WRITING WORDS Model how to spell the possessive *chick's.* **Say:** *The letters* ch *stand for the first sound, /th/. The next sound is /ĭ/. The letter* i *stands for that sound. The letters* ck *stand for the sound /k/. The letter* s *stands for the last sound, /s/, but I put an apostrophe before the* s.

- Guide students to identify sounds in the following words and build them with Letter Cards: *Beth's, Chip's, band's, fox's, sun's, truck's.*
- Have students write each word and read it aloud.

Apply

- Distribute copies of Practice Page 1.15D, which contains the decodable story *Champs at Catch*. Tell students that many words in this story have 's. Point out that students have learned the following high-frequency words, which they will also read in the story: *been, know, own, very*.

- Read aloud the first two sentences of the story as students follow along. Point out that you do not misread, add, or skip words. Lead students in reading the same sentences with fluency and accuracy.

- Have students read the passage silently and then aloud. Remind them to track the words from left to right. When they come to the end of a line, they should sweep their hand down to the beginning of the next line and continue reading.

- When students have finished reading the text, choose a few sentences to review. You may want to focus on sentences that include words containing the target phonics skill. Have students read each sentence and explain in their own words what it means.

> **Fun with Words** Optional activities for engaging, hands-on practice are provided in the Resources section.

IF a student makes an error, THEN follow this model:

Correct the error.

Guide the student to perform the task correctly by modeling.

Check for understanding by having the student repeat the task.

Reinforce: Make a note to review the skill during the student's next session.

Objectives

- Recognize and read high-frequency words.

Materials

- High-Frequency Word Cards

Formative Assessment and Corrective Feedback

IF a student makes an error, THEN follow this model:

Correct the error.

Guide the student to say the word correctly.

Check for understanding by having the student reread the word from among other randomly displayed high-frequency words.

Reinforce: Make a note to review the word during the student's next session.

High-Frequency Words:
down, fall, goes, green, grow, new, open, yellow

Teach/Model

- Display the high-frequency words. Tell students that these are useful words to know, since they will see these words often. Tell students that reading will be easier if they recognize these words.

- Display the High-Frequency Word Card for *down* and say the word. Then spell the word aloud as you point to each letter. Say the word again.

- Use the word in a simple sentence that will provide context. For example: *Rain falls down.*

- Repeat the steps above with the remaining high-frequency words.

Guided Practice

Do the following for each high-frequency word:

- Display the High-Frequency Word Card. Read the word and have students repeat it.

- Note the familiar sound/spelling patterns that are shown on the back of the card. Note as well any unfamiliar and unexpected sound/spellings.

- Blend the word with students.

- Spell the word aloud, pointing to each letter.

- Have students then spell the word aloud as you point to each letter.

- Have students read the word again.

Apply

- Display the High-Frequency Word Cards in random order. Have students read the words aloud.

- Have students write each word. Tell them to compare their writing with the word on the card and make corrections if necessary.

- Have students read each word aloud and use it in a sentence.

Phonemic Awareness: Substitute Initial Phonemes

Teach/Model

- **Say:** *Today we're going to change the first sound in a word to make a new word. For example,* pick *starts with the /p/ sound. The first sound in* pick *is /p/.*
- Say the word *pick,* emphasizing the /p/ sound. **Say:** *Listen:* pick.
- **Say:** *Now I'll change the /p/ sound to /s/. Listen: /s/ /ĭ/ /k/. Sick. Say it with me: sick. I changed the first sound /p/ to /s/ and made the word* sick.
- **Say:** *Now I'll change the /p/ in* pick *to /ch/. Listen: /ch/ /ĭ/ /k/. Chick. Say it with me: chick. I changed the first sound /p/ to /ch/ and made the word* chick. *Let's keep going.*

Guided Practice

- **Say:** *We're going to change the sounds in words to make new words. For example, what is the first sound in* sip? *(/s/) Good. Now let's change the first sound in* sip *to /z/. Listen: /z/ /ĭ/ /p /. What is the word? (*zip*) Good! Let's try some more.*
- Continue with the words shown below.

Change the . . .	Result
/s/ in *sock* to /r/	rock
/r/ in *rock* to /d/	dock
/l/ in *lid* to /d/	did
/b/ in *but* to /sh/	shut
/s/ in *sip* to /hw/	whip
/th/ in *thin* to /ch/	chin
/l/ in *lock* to /sh/	shock
/s/ in *sick* to /th/	thick

Apply

Have students practice substituting initial phonemes, using the words below. **Say:**

- *Change the /d/ in* dish *to /w/. What is the word?* (wish)
- *Change the /th/ in* that *to /ch/. What is the word?* (chat)
- *Change the /m/ in* mix *to /f/. What is the word?* (fix)
- *Change the /b/ in* but *to /sh/. What is the word?* (shut)
- *Change the /h/ in* hop *to /sh/. What is the word?* (shop)
- *Change the /h/ in* hen *to /hw/. What is the word?* (when)
- *Change the first sound in* top *to /sh/. What is the word?* (shop)
- *Change the first sound in* hip *to /ch/. What is the word?* (chip)
- *Change the first sound in* well *to /sh/. What is the word?* (shell)
- *Change the first sound in* tone *to /f/. What is the word?* (phone)

Objectives

- Isolate and substitute the initial sound in spoken single-syllable words.

English Language Support

Linguistic Transfer Many English learners, including those who speak Spanish and several Asian languages, may have trouble with the sounds /hw/ and /th/ (as in *thick*). In addition, speakers of Spanish, Vietnamese, and Cantonese may substitute /ch/ or /s/ for /sh/. Say each sound several times as students study your mouth position. Have students practice the sounds in front of a mirror. Then provide extra modeling and practice with words starting with those sounds, including *ship, shell, shop, thick, thin, thought, whip, whale, when.*

Formative Assessment and Corrective Feedback

IF a student makes an error, THEN follow this model:

Correct the error.

Guide the student to perform the task correctly by modeling.

Check for understanding by having the student repeat the task.

Reinforce: Make a note to review the skill during the student's next session.

Phonics: Digraphs *sh, wh, ph*

Objectives

- Learn the sound-spelling correspondences for digraphs *sh, wh, ph*.
- Blend and segment words with digraphs *sh, wh, ph*.
- Blend, build, and decode regularly spelled one-syllable words with digraphs *sh, wh, ph*.
- Read on-level text with fluency and accuracy.

Materials

- Sound/Spelling Cards
- Instructional Routine: Sound-by-Sound Blending
- Letter Cards
- Practice Page 1.16C

Phonemic Awareness Warm-up

- **Say:** *Listen as I blend some sounds to say a word: /sh/ / ĭ / /p/. The word is* ship. *Listen again. /sh/ / ĭ / /p/,* ship.
- Repeat with the words *whale* and *phone*.
- **Say:** *Now let's do it together. Listen. Blend the sounds: /f/ /ĭ / /sh/. What is the word?* (fish) *Now you blend the sounds, and tell me each word. /hw/ / ĭ / /p/* (whip), */d/ / ă / /sh/* dash, */g/ /r/ / ă / /f/* (graph), */hw/ / ĕ / /n/* (when).
- Repeat with these words: *rush, shell, which*.
- Reverse the process, segmenting instead of blending. Use the same words, but in random order.

Teach/Model

- Display the Sound/Spelling Card for *sheep*. Name the picture and say the beginning sound. Have students repeat after you. **Say:** *Listen:* sheep, /sh/. *Now you say it.*
- Say the sound and give the spelling. **Say:** Sheep *begins with the sound /sh/. The letters* sh *can stand for the sound /sh/ at the beginning, middle, or end of a word.*
- Display the card for *whale*. Name the picture and say the beginning sound. Have students repeat after you. **Say:** *Listen:* whale, /hw/. *Now you say it.*
- Say the sound and give the spelling. **Say:** Whale *begins with the sound /hw/. The letters* wh *can stand for the sound /hw/ at the beginning or middle of a word.*
- Write and read *graph*. Point out the *ph* spelling at the end of *graph*. **Say:** Graph *ends with the sound /f/.*
- Display the card for *fish*. **Say:** *The letters* ph *can stand for the sound /f/ at the beginning, middle, or end of a word.*
- Repeat with the words *fish, elephant,* and *wheel*.

Guided Practice

BLENDING Display the words in Rows 1 and 2 below. Using Instructional Routine: Sound-by-Sound Blending, work with students to blend each word.

| 1. fish | when | whip | graph | shop |
| 2. what | shell | which | ship | path |

DECODING Display the three sentences below. Call on individuals to blend one or more words and to read the sentences.

- What can a math whiz do?
- Look at the graphs in the shop.
- Which shell did Seth rush to find?

BUILDING AND WRITING WORDS Model how to spell the word *rush*. **Say:** *The letter* r *stands for the first sound, /r/. The next sound is /ŭ/. I know* u *stands for /ŭ/. The last sound is /sh/. I know that* s *and* h *together stand for /sh/.*

- Guide students to identify sounds in the following words and build them with Letter Cards: *shop, shut, dish, crash, whiz, graph*.
- Then have students write each word and read it aloud.

Apply

- Distribute copies of Practice Page 1.16C, which contains decodable story *Phil's Wish*. Tell students that many words in this story have *sh, wh,* or *ph*. Point out that students have learned the following high-frequency words, which they will also read in the story: *down, fall, new*.

- Read aloud the first two sentences of the story as students follow along. Point out that you do not misread, add, or skip words. Lead them in reading the same sentences with fluency and accuracy.

- Have students read the passage silently, and then aloud. Remind students to track the words from left to right. When they come to the end of a line, they should sweep their hand down to the beginning of the next line and continue reading.

- When students have finished reading the text, choose a few sentences to review. You may want to focus on sentences that include words containing the target phonics skill. Have students read each sentence and explain in their own words what it means.

Fun with Words Optional activities for engaging, hands-on practice are provided in the Resources section.

English Language Support

Linguistic Transfer Students who speak Spanish or Vietnamese might have trouble distinguishing between the sound /sh/ and the sound /ch/. Say both sounds several times as students study your mouth positions. Have students practice the /sh/ sound, and then practice these word pairs: *ship/chip, sheep/cheap, dish/ditch*.

Formative Assessment and Corrective Feedback

IF a student makes an error, THEN follow this model:

Correct the error.

Guide the student to perform the task correctly by modeling.

Check for understanding by having the student repeat the task.

Reinforce: Make a note to review the skill during the student's next session.

Phonics: Contractions with 's, n't

Objectives

- Blend, build, and decode contractions with 's and n't.
- Learn how to use apostrophes when writing contractions.
- Read on-level text with fluency and accuracy.

Materials

- Letter Cards
- Instructional Routine: Sound-by-Sound Blending
- Practice Page 1.16D

Phonemic Awareness Warm-up

- **Say:** *Listen as I blend some sounds to say a word: /hw/ /ĭ/ /ch/. Which. Now you try. Blend these sounds: /f/ /l/ /ă/ /sh/. What is the word?* (flash) Repeat with *dish, whale, shock,* and *when.*
- **Say:** *Now tell the sounds that make up the word* Phil. (/f/ /ĭ/ /l/) Repeat with *shape, graph, white,* and *dish.*

Teach/Model

- **Say:** *A contraction is a shorter, more informal way of saying two words together. The words* is *and* not *can sometimes be combined with other words. When this happens, an apostrophe takes the place of missing letters.*
- Use Letter Cards to build the words *has not.* Read the words. Model forming the contraction *hasn't.* **Say:** *I know a shorter way to say* has not. *I replace the letter* o *in* not *with an apostrophe to make the word* hasn't. Display the Letter Cards, remove the *o* card, and add an apostrophe between the *n* and the *t.* Have students read the word. Use *hasn't* in a sentence: *She hasn't gone to the zoo.* Repeat with the words *was not* and *wasn't.*
- Use Letter Cards to build the words *it is.* Read the words. Model forming the contraction *it's.* **Say:** *I know a shorter way to say* it is. *I replace the letter* i *in* is *with an apostrophe to make the word* it's. Display the Letter Cards, remove the *i* card, and add an apostrophe between the *t* and the *s.* Have students read the word. Use *it's* in a sentence: *It's a hot, sunny day.* Repeat with the words *that is* and *that's.*

Guided Practice

BLENDING Display the words in Rows 1 and 2 below. Using Instructional Routine: Sound-by-Sound Blending, work with students to blend each word.

1. hadn't	wasn't	it's	that's	didn't
2. he's	graph	don't	splash	when

DECODING Display the sentences below. Call on individuals to blend one or more words and to read the sentences.

- Chet didn't fall down.
- That's my yellow fish.
- She isn't at the new shop.

BUILDING AND WRITING WORDS Model how to spell the contraction *can't.* **Say:** *The letter* c *stands for the first sound, /k/. The next sound is /ă/. I know the letter* a *stands for the sound /ă/. The letter* n *stands for the sound /n/. The last sound is /t/. The letter* t *stands for /t/. I also know to put an apostrophe between the* n *and the* t.

- Guide students to identify sounds in the following words and build them with Letter Cards: *it's, that's, hasn't, hadn't, didn't.* Remind students to put an apostrophe in each contraction.
- Have students write each contraction and read it aloud.

Apply

- Distribute copies of Practice Page 1.16D, which contains the decodable story *The Gift*. Tell students that many words in this story are contractions with *'s* and *n't*. Point out that students have learned the following high-frequency words, which they will also read in the story: *green, grow, new, open.*

- Read aloud the first three sentences of the story as students follow along. Point out that you do not misread, add, or skip words. Lead students in reading the same sentences with fluency and accuracy.

- Have students read the passage silently and then aloud. Remind them to track the words from left to right. When they come to the end of a line, they should sweep their hand down to the beginning of the next line and continue reading.

- When students have finished reading the text, choose a few sentences to review. You may want to focus on sentences that include words containing the target phonics skill. Have students read each sentence and explain in their own words what it means.

> **Fun with Words**   Optional activities for engaging, hands-on practice are provided in the Resources section.

Formative Assessment and Corrective Feedback

IF a student makes an error, THEN follow this model:

Correct the error.

Guide the student to perform the task correctly by modeling.

Check for understanding by having the student repeat the task.

Reinforce: Make a note to review the skill during the student's next session.

Objectives

- Recognize and read high-frequency words.

Materials

- High-Frequency Word Cards

Formative Assessment and Corrective Feedback

IF a student makes an error, THEN follow this model:

Correct the error.

Guide the student to say the word correctly.

Check for understanding by having the student reread the word from among other randomly displayed high-frequency words.

Reinforce: Make a note to review the word during the student's next session.

High-Frequency Words:
four, five, into, over, starts, three, two, watch

Teach/Model

- Display the high-frequency words. Tell students that these are useful words to know since they will see these words often. Tell them that reading will be easier if they recognize these words.
- Display the High-Frequency Word Card for *four* and say the word. Then spell the word aloud as you point to each letter. Say the word again.
- Use the word in a simple sentence that will provide context. For example: *Four is the number after three.*
- Repeat the steps above with the remaining high-frequency words.

Guided Practice

Do the following for each high-frequency word:

- Display the High-Frequency Word Card. Read the word and have students repeat it.
- Note the familiar sound/spelling patterns that are shown on the back of the card. Note as well any unfamiliar and unexpected sound/spellings.
- Blend the word with students.
- Spell the word aloud, pointing to each letter.
- Have students then spell the word aloud as you point to each letter.
- Have students read the word again.

Apply

- Display the High-Frequency Word Cards in random order. Have students read the words.
- Have students write each word. Tell them to compare their writing with the word on the card and make corrections if necessary.
- Have students read each word aloud and use it in a sentence.

Phonemic Awareness: Substitute Medial Phonemes

Teach/Model

- **Say:** *Today we're going to change the vowel sound in a word to make a new word. For example, the word* cat *has the short a vowel sound. The middle sound in* cat *is /ă/.*

- Say the word *cat*, emphasizing the short *a* sound. **Say:** *Listen:* cat.

- **Say:** *Now I'll change the /ă/ sound to /ŏ/. Listen: /k/ /ŏ/ /t/,* cot. *Say it with me:* cot. *I changed the vowel sound /ă/ in* cat *to /ŏ/ and made the word* cot.

- **Say:** *Now I'll change the /ŏ/ sound in* cot *to /ŭ/. Listen: /k/ /ŭ/ /t/,* cut. *Say it with me:* cut. *I changed the vowel sound /ŏ/ in* cot *to /ŭ/ and made the word* cut. *Let's keep going.*

Guided Practice

- **Say:** *We're going to change the vowel sounds in words to make new words. For example, what is the vowel sound in* tap? *(/ă/) Good. Now let's change the vowel sound in* tap *to /ā/. Listen: /t/ /ā/ /p/. What is the word?* (tape) *Good! Let's try some more.*

- Continue with the words shown below.

Change the . . .	Result
/ă/ in *lack* to /ŭ/	luck
/ĭ/ in *sick* to /ŏ/	sock
/ă/ in *pan* to /ĕ/	pen
/ŏ/ in *shop* to /ā/	shape
/ŭ/ in *hut* to /ĭ/	hit
/ă/ in *tack* to /ā/	take
/ĕ/ in *peck* to /ĭ/	pick
/ă/ in *can* to /ā/	cane

Apply

Have students practice substituting medial phonemes, using the words below. **Say:**

- *Change the /ă/ in* cap *to /ā/. What is the word?* (cape)
- *Change the /ĭ/ in* chip *to /ŏ/. What is the word?* (chop)
- *Change the /ă/ in* quack *to /ā/. What is the word?* (quake)
- *Change the /ŭ/ in* bunch *to /ĕ/. What is the word?* (bench)
- *Change the /ā/ in* glade *to /ă/. What is the word?* (glad)
- *Change the /ă/ in* lamp *to /ĭ/. What is the word?* (limp)
- *Change the /ā/ in* made *to /ă/. What is the word?* (mad)
- *Change the /ŭ/ in* run *to /ă/. What is the word?* (ran)
- *Change the /ă/ in* back *to /ā/. What is the word?* (bake)
- *Change the /ă/ in* ran *to /ā/. What is the word?* (rain)

Objectives

- Isolate and substitute the medial sounds in spoken single-syllable words.

Formative Assessment and Corrective Feedback

IF a student makes an error, THEN follow this model:

Correct the error.

Guide the student to perform the task correctly by modeling.

Check for understanding by having the student repeat the task.

Reinforce: Make a note to review the skill during the student's next session.

Phonics: Long *a* (CVC*e*)

Objectives

- Isolate medial sounds in spoken single-syllable words.
- Learn the sound-spelling correspondence for long *a* (CVC*e*).
- Blend, build, and decode regularly spelled one-syllable words with *a_e*.
- Read on-level text with fluency and accuracy.

Materials

- Sound/Spelling Cards
- Instructional Routine: Sound-by-Sound Blending
- Letter Cards
- Practice Page 1.17C

Phonemic Awareness Warm-up

- Guide students to listen for the middle sounds in words. **Say:** *I'm going to say a word. Listen for the middle sound. The word is* tack, /t/ /ă/ /k/. *The middle sound is* /ă/. *Let's do another one:* gate, /g/ /ā/ /t/. *The middle sound is* /ā/.
- **Say:** *Now you try. Listen:* pick. *What is the middle sound in* pick? (/ĭ/) *Repeat with these words:* shop (/ŏ/), mate (/ā/), bet (/ĕ/), lane (/ā/), sand (/ă/).

Teach/Model

- Display the Sound/Spelling Card for *acorn*. Name the picture and say the beginning sound. Have students repeat after you. **Say:** *Listen:* acorn, /ā/. *Now you say it.*
- Point to the *a_e* spelling pattern. **Say:** *When you see the letter* a *followed by a consonant and an* e, *the letter* a *will often stand for the long* a *sound,* /ā/.
- Write and read *made*. Cover the *e*. Read *mad*, pointing out the /ă/ sound. Uncover the *e* and point out the *a-consonant-e* pattern. Have students read *made*. Repeat with the words *pane* and *tape*.
- List *bake* and *take* on the board and have students read each word. Ask them which three letters are the same in both words. (ake) **Say:** Bake *and* take *belong to the same word family because they end with the same letters and sounds.* Guide students to offer more *-ake* words such as *cake, fake, lake, make, rake,* and *wake*. List them on the board and have students read them.

Guided Practice

BLENDING Display the words in Rows 1 and 2 below. Using Instructional Routine: Sound-by-Sound Blending, work with students to blend each word.

1. take	plane	gave	made	lane
2. shake	crash	chase	whale	whip

DECODING Display the sentences below. Call on individuals to blend one or more words and to read the sentences.

- Dave gave him five grapes.
- Watch me eat Jake's cake.
- Kate jumped into the lake.

BUILDING AND WRITING WORDS Model how to build the word *chase* with Letter Cards. **Say:** *The letters* ch *stand for the first sound,* /ch/. *The next sound is* /ā/. *I know that* a *followed by a consonant and* e *can stand for* /ā/. *The last sound is* /s/. *The letter* s *can stand for the* /s/ *sound.*

- Guide students to identify sounds in the following words and build them with Letter Cards: *make, late, gave, cake, wave.*
- Have students write each word and read it aloud.

Apply

- Distribute copies of Practice Page 1.17C, which contains the decodable story *Singing Whales*. Tell students that many words in this story have the *a*-consonant-*e* pattern, which often stands for the long *a* sound. Point out that students have learned the following high-frequency words, which they will also read in the story: *five, four, three, two, watch.*

- Read aloud the first four sentences of the story as students follow along. Point out that you do not misread, add, or skip words. Lead students in reading the same sentences with fluency and accuracy.

- Have students read the passage silently and then aloud. Remind them to track the words from left to right. When they come to the end of a line, they should sweep their hand down to the beginning of the next line and continue reading.

- When students have finished reading the text, choose a few sentences to review. You may want to focus on sentences that include words containing the target phonics skill. Have students read each sentence and explain in their own words what it means.

> **Fun with Words** Optional activities for engaging, hands-on practice are provided in the Resources section.

English Language Support

Linguistic Transfer Students with reading skill in Spanish may tend to use the letter *e* to represent the long *a* sound in English because the letter *e* in Spanish stands for the sound /ā/. Explain to students that in English, the /ā/ sound is usually spelled with the letter *a* plus another letter, such as *e*, as in *cane, fade, lake, name,* and *tape*. Provide additional CVC*e* example words for practice, and use each word in a brief sentence to reinforce meaning.

Formative Assessment and Corrective Feedback

IF a student makes an error, THEN follow this model:

Correct the error.

Guide the student to perform the task correctly by modeling.

Check for understanding by having the student repeat the task.

Reinforce: Make a note to review the skill during the student's next session.

Phonics: Soft *c, g, dge*

Objectives

- Isolate the medial vowel sound in spoken single-syllable words.
- Learn the sound-spelling correspondences for soft *c, g,* and *dge*.
- Blend, build, and decode regularly spelled one-syllable words with soft *c, g,* and *dge*.
- Read on-level text with fluency and accuracy.

Materials

- Sound/Spelling Cards
- Instructional Routine: Sound-by-Sound Blending
- Letter Cards
- Practice Page 1.17D

Phonemic Awareness Warm-up

- **Say:** *I'll say a word and you say the vowel sound you hear in the word. Listen:* bake. *Do you hear the vowel sound? The vowel sound is /ā/.*

- **Say:** *Let's do some together. Listen:* stack. *The vowel sound is /ă/. Listen:* stage. *The vowel sound is /ā/. Now let's do more:* mat (/ă/), date (/ā/), plant (/ă/), badge (/ă/), trace (/ā/), last (/ă/), page (/ā/).

Teach/Model

- Display the Sound/Spelling card for *seal*. Point to each spelling and say /s/. Explain that *c* can stand for the sound /s/ in some words. Write the word *race*. Read the word. Say the ending sound /s/ and give the spelling. **Say:** *The word* race *ends with /s/. The letter* c *stands for /s/ at the end of* race.

- Display the Sound/Spelling card for *jump*. Point to each spelling and say /j/. Explain that *g* and *dge* can stand for the sound /j/ in some words. Write the words *cage* and *badge*. Read the words. Say the ending sound /j/ in each word and give the spellings. **Say:** *The word* cage *ends with /j/. The letter* g *stands for /j/ at the end of* cage. *The word* badge *ends with /j/. The letters* dge *stand for /j/ at the end of* badge.

- Write *lace* and *trace* on the board and have students read each word. Ask them which three letters are the same in both words. (ace) **Say:** Lace *and* trace *belong to the same word family because they end with the same letters and sounds.* Guide students to think of more *-ace* words, such as *face, pace, place, race,* and *space*. Write them on the board and have students read them.

Guided Practice

BLENDING Display the words in Rows 1 and 2 below. Using Instructional Routine: Sound-by-Sound Blending, work with students to blend each word.

1. lace	cage	badge	space	place
2. page	fudge	bridge	gem	cell

DECODING Display the sentences below. Call on individuals to blend one or more words to read the sentences.

- The judge will watch the race.
- Grace got three blue gems.
- My run starts on that ridge.

BUILDING AND WRITING WORDS Model how to build the word *budge* with Letter Cards. **Say:** *The letter* b *stands for the beginning /b/ sound. The vowel sound is /ŭ/ spelled* u. *The letters* dge *stand for the ending /j/ sound.*

- Guide students to identify sounds in the following words and build them with Letter Cards: *place, gem, cage, space, stage, cent, dodge, ledge*.
- Have students write each word and read it aloud.

Apply

- Distribute copies of Practice Page 1.17D, which contains the decodable story *Watching Races*. Tell students that many words in this story have soft *c, g,* or *dge*. Point out that students have learned the following high-frequency words, which they will also read in the story: *four, into, over, starts, two, watch.*

- Read aloud the first five sentences of the story as students follow along. Point out that you do not misread, add, or skip words. Lead students in reading the same sentences with fluency and accuracy.

- Have students read the passage silently and then aloud. Remind them to track the words from left to right. When they come to the end of a line, they should sweep their hand down to the beginning of the next line and continue reading.

- When students have finished reading the text, choose a few sentences to review. You may want to focus on sentences that include words containing the target phonics skill. Have students read each sentence and explain in their own words what it means.

> **Fun with Words** Optional activities for engaging, hands-on practice are provided in the Resources section.

Formative Assessment and Corrective Feedback

IF a student makes an error, THEN follow this model:

Correct the error.

Guide the student to perform the task correctly by modeling.

Check for understanding by having the student repeat the task.

Reinforce: Make a note to review the skill during the student's next session.

Objectives

- Recognize and read high-frequency words.

Materials

- High-Frequency Word Cards

Formative Assessment and Corrective Feedback

IF a student makes an error, THEN follow this model:

Correct the error.

Guide the student to say the word correctly.

Check for understanding by having the student reread the word from among other randomly displayed high-frequency words.

Reinforce: Make a note to review the word during the student's next session.

High-Frequency Words:
bird, both, eyes, fly, long, or, those, walk

Teach/Model

- Display the high-frequency words. Tell students that these are useful words to know since they will see these words often. Tell them that reading will be easier if they recognize these words.
- Display the High-Frequency Word Card for *bird* and say the word. Then spell the word aloud as you point to each letter. Say the word again.
- Use the word in a simple sentence that will provide context. For example: *That bird has shiny green feathers.*
- Repeat the steps above with the remaining high-frequency words.

Guided Practice

Do the following for each high-frequency word:

- Display the High-Frequency Word Card. Read the word and have students repeat it.
- Note the familiar sound/spelling patterns that are shown on the back of the card. Note as well any unfamiliar and unexpected sound/spellings.
- Blend the word with students.
- Spell the word aloud, pointing to each letter.
- Have students then spell the word aloud as you point to each letter.
- Have students read the word again.

Apply

- Display the High-Frequency Word Cards in random order. Have students read the words.
- Have students write each word. Tell them to compare their writing with the word on the card and make corrections if necessary.
- Have students read each word aloud and use it in a sentence.

Phonemic Awareness: Review: Substitute Medial Phonemes

Teach/Model

- **Say:** *Today we're going to change the vowel sound in a word to make a new word. Listen to the word:* mad. *The middle sound in* mad *is /ă/.*

- Say the word *mad*, emphasizing the /ă/ sound. **Say:** *Listen:* mad.

- **Say:** *Now I'll change the /ă/ sound to /ŭ/. Listen: /m/ /ŭ/ /d/,* mud. *Say it with me:* mud. *I changed the vowel sound /ă/ in* mad *to /ŭ/ and made the word* mud.

- **Say:** *Now I'll change the /ŭ/ sound in* mud *to /ā/. Listen: /m/ /ā/ /d/,* made. *Say it with me:* made. *I changed the vowel sound /ŭ/ in* mud *to /ā/ and made the word* made. *Let's keep going.*

Guided Practice

- **Say:** *We're going to change the vowel sounds in words to make new words. For example, what is the vowel sound in* cap? *(/ă/) Good. Now let's change the vowel sound in* cap *to /ā/. Listen: /k/ /ā/ /p/. What is the word?* (cape) *Good! Let's try some more.*

- Continue with the words shown below.

Change the . . .	Result
/ă/ in hat to /ĭ/	hit
/ĭ/ in kit to /ī/	kite
/ā/ in tape to /ă/	tap
/ā/ in lake to /ī/	like
/ŭ/ in duck to /ŏ/	dock
/ŏ/ in dock to /ě/	deck
/ĭ/ in sit to /ī/	sight
/ī/ in sight to /ă/	sat

Apply

Have students practice substituting medial phonemes, using the words below. **Say:**

- *Change the /ĭ/ in* lit *to /ī/. What is the word?* (light)
- *Change the /ī/ in* light *to /ā/. What is the word?* (late)
- *Change the /ă/ in* bat *to /ī/. What is the word?* (bite)
- *Change the /ī/ in* kite *to /ŭ/. What is the word?* (cut)
- *Change the /ĭ/ in* fin *to /ī/. What is the word?* (fine)
- *Change the /ī/ in* right *to /ā/. What is the word?* (rate)
- *Change the /ă/ in* clam *to /ī/. What is the word?* (climb)
- *Change the /ī/ in* climb *to /ā/. What is the word?* (claim)
- *Change the /ā/ in* gave *to /ĭ/. What is the word?* (give)

Objectives

- Isolate and substitute the medial sounds in spoken single-syllable words.

Formative Assessment and Corrective Feedback

IF a student makes an error, THEN follow this model:

Correct the error.

Guide the student to perform the task correctly by modeling.

Check for understanding by having the student repeat the task.

Reinforce: Make a note to review the skill during the student's next session.

Phonics: Long *i* (CVC*e*)

Objectives

- Isolate and pronounce the medial vowel sound in spoken single-syllable words.
- Learn the sound-spelling correspondence for long *i* (CVC*e*).
- Blend, build, and decode regularly spelled one-syllable words with *i_e*.
- Read on-level text with fluency and accuracy.

Materials

- Sound/Spelling Cards
- Instructional Routine: Sound-by-Sound Blending
- Letter Cards
- Practice Page 1.18C

Phonemic Awareness Warm-up

- Guide students to listen for the middle sounds in words. **Say:** *I'm going to say a word. Listen for the middle sound. The word is* kit, /k/ /ĭ/ /t/. *The middle sound is* /ĭ/. *Let's do another one:* ride, /r/ /ī/ /d/. *The middle sound is* /ī/.
- **Say:** *Now you do it. Listen:* like. *What is the middle sound in* like? (/ī/) *Repeat with these words:* time (/ī/), pack (/ă/), mine (/ī/), fit (/ĭ/), map (/ă/), bike (/ī/).

Teach/Model

- Display the Sound/Spelling Card for *ice cream*. Name the picture and say the beginning sound. Have students repeat after you. **Say:** *Listen:* ice cream, /ī/. *Now you say it.*
- Point to the *i_e* spelling pattern. **Say:** *When you see the letter* i *followed by a consonant and an* e, *the letter* i *will often stand for the long* i *sound,* /ī/.
- Write and read *hide*. Cover the *e*. Read *hid*, pointing out the /ĭ/ sound. Uncover the *e* and point out the *i*-consonant-*e* pattern. Have students read *hide*. Repeat with the word pairs *slid/slide* and *rid/ride*.
- List *fine* and *mine* on the board and have students read each word. Ask them which three letters are the same in both words. (ine) **Say:** *Fine* and *mine* belong to the same word family because they end with the same letters and sounds. Guide students to offer more -ine words, such as *dine, line, nine, pine, vine, shine,* and *whine*. List them on the board and have students read them. Repeat for -ite, using words such as *bite, kite, quite,* and *white*.

Guided Practice

BLENDING Display the words in Rows 1 and 2 below. Using Instructional Routine: Sound-by-Sound Blending, work with students to blend each word.

1. time	bite	slide	kite	dime
2. chime	chase	shine	press	white

DECODING Display the sentences below. Call on individuals to blend one or more words and to read the sentences.

- Mike and I had time for a walk.
- The bike ride was nine miles long.
- Giles can fly a kite over the pines.

BUILDING AND WRITING WORDS Model how to build the word *drive* with Letter Cards.
Say: *The letters* d *and* r *stand for the beginning sounds,* /d/ *and* /r/. *The next sound is* /ī/. *I know that* i *followed by a consonant and* e *can stand for* /ī/. *The last sound is* /v/. *The letter* v *stands for the* /v/ *sound. At the end I add the* e.

- Guide students to identify sounds in the following words and build them with Letter Cards: *like, kite, time, spine, glide, smile*.
- Have students write each word and read it aloud.

Apply

- Distribute copies of Practice Page 1.18C, which contains the decodable story *The Long Ride*. Tell students that many words in this story have the *i*-consonant-*e* pattern, which can stand for the long *i* sound. Point out that students have learned the following high-frequency words, which they will also read in the story: *both, long, or.*

- Read aloud the first four sentences of the story as students follow along. Point out that you do not misread, add, or skip words. Lead students in reading the same sentences with fluency and accuracy.

- Have students read the passage silently and then aloud. Remind them to track the words from left to right. When they come to the end of a line, they should sweep their hand down to the beginning of the next line and continue reading.

- When students have finished reading the text, choose a few sentences to review. You may want to focus on sentences that include words containing the target phonics skill. Have students read each sentence and explain in their own words what it means.

> **Fun with Words** Optional activities for engaging, hands-on practice are provided in the Resources section.

Formative Assessment and Corrective Feedback

IF a student makes an error, THEN follow this model:

Correct the error.

Guide the student to perform the task correctly by modeling.

Check for understanding by having the student repeat the task.

Reinforce: Make a note to review the skill during the student's next session.

Phonics: Digraphs *kn, wr, gn, mb*

Objectives

- Learn the sound-spelling correspondences for digraphs *kn, wr, gn, mb*.
- Substitute medial sounds in spoken words.
- Blend, build, and decode regularly spelled one-syllable words with digraphs *kn, wr, gn, mb*.
- Read on-level text with fluency and accuracy.

Materials

- Sound/Spelling Cards
- Instructional Routine: Sound-by-Sound Blending
- Letter Cards
- Practice Page 1.18D

Phonemic Awareness Warm-up

- **Say:** *I'm going to say a word and then change its middle sound to make a new word. Listen:* bake. *What word do I get if I change /ā/ to /ī/?* Bike.
- **Say:** *Now you try. Listen:* sick. *What word do I get if I change /ĭ/ to /ŏ/?* (sock) *Continue with these words:* rash, rush; tick, tack; like, lock; pin, pine; ripe, rip.

Teach/Model

- Display the Sound/Spelling Card for *noodles* to review /n/. Say *noodles* and say the beginning sound /n/. Point to the *kn* and *gn* spellings on the card. Explain that these letter combinations can stand for the /n/ sound. Write *knock* and *gnat* on the board and read each word. Circle *kn* and *gn* and say /n/. Reread the words and have students repeat.
- Display the Sound/Spelling Card for *rooster* to review /r/. Say *rooster* and say the beginning sound /r/. Point to the *wr* spelling on the card. Explain that this letter combination can stand for the /r/ sound. Write *wren* on the board and read it. Circle *wr* and say /r/. Reread the word and have students repeat.
- Display the Sound/Spelling Card for *mouse* to review /m/. Say *mouse* and say the beginning sound /m/. Point to the *mb* spelling on the card. Explain that this letter combination can stand for the /m/ sound. Write *numb* on the board and read it. Circle *mb* and say /m/. Reread the word and have students repeat.

Guided Practice

BLENDING Display the words in Rows 1 and 2 below. Using Instructional Routine: Sound-by-Sound Blending, work with students to blend each word.

1. knock	gnash	wrist	thumb	knot
2. lamb	judge	wren	place	gnat

DECODING Display the sentences below. Call on individuals to blend one or more words and to read the sentences.

- Gnats land and walk on my wrist.
- Use the knife to cut both knots.
- A wren can fly with a crumb.

BUILDING AND WRITING WORDS Model how to spell the word *lamb* with Letter Cards.
Say: *The letter* l *stands for the beginning sound /l/. The next sound is /ă/. I know that* a *stands for /ă/. The last sound is /m/. The letters* mb *stand for the /m/ sound in* lamb.

- Guide students to identify sounds in the following words and build them with Letter Cards: *knock, write, gnat, thumb, wrap, knit*.
- Have students write each word and read it aloud.

Apply

- Distribute copies of Practice Page 1.18D, which contains the decodable story *Go Fly a Kite*. Tell students that some words in this story begin with *kn* or *wr*. Point out that students have learned the following high-frequency words, which they will also read in the story: *bird, fly, or*.

- Read aloud the first four sentences of the story as students follow along. Point out that you do not misread, add, or skip words when you read. Lead students in reading the same sentences with fluency and accuracy.

- Have students read the passage silently and then aloud. Remind them to track the words from left to right. When they come to the end of a line, they should sweep their hand down to the beginning of the next line and continue reading.

- When students have finished reading the text, choose a few sentences to review. You may want to focus on sentences that include words containing the target phonics skill. Have students read each sentence and explain in their own words what it means.

Fun with Words Optional activities for engaging, hands-on practice are provided in the Resources section.

English Language Support

Linguistic Transfer Some English learners (including speakers of Cantonese or Mandarin) may have trouble with the /n/ sound. Model saying the sound. Explain that your tongue is touching the roof of your mouth, blocking the air so that it must come through your nose. Have students practice the sound in front of a mirror and then practice saying words such as these: *knack, gnat, know, sign, knee, gnaw, knob, gnash*. Use each word in a brief sentence to reinforce meaning.

Formative Assessment and Corrective Feedback

IF a student makes an error, THEN follow this model:

Correct the error.

Guide the student to perform the task correctly by modeling.

Check for understanding by having the student repeat the task.

Reinforce: Make a note to review the skill during the student's next session.

Cumulative Review/Fluency

Teach/Model

Objectives

- Decode words with long vowels, consonant digraphs, endings, and soft consonants; possessives; and contractions.
- Recognize and read high-frequency words.
- Read on-level text with purpose and understanding.
- Read on-level text orally with accuracy, appropriate rate, and expression on successive readings.
- Use context to confirm or self-correct word recognition and understanding, rereading as necessary.

Materials

- High-Frequency Word Cards
- Instructional Routine: High-Frequency Words
- Practice Page 1.19

REVIEW

- Remind students they have learned soft sounds for *c, g,* and *dge;* sounds for digraphs *th, ch, tch, sh, wh, ph, kn, wr, gn,* and *mb;* and long *a* and *i* vowel sounds spelled CVCe. Display the consonants, digraphs, and vowels and review the sound for each.
- Remind students they have learned sounds for the endings *-s, -es, -ed,* and *-ing;* possessive *'s;* and *'s* and *n't* in contractions. Display the various endings and review the sound or sounds for each.
- Display these sentences:

  The line on Mike's graph goes down.

  Why didn't the white cat chase that bird?

  Cold water makes Madge's face numb.

- Point to the high-frequency words *goes, down, bird, cold,* and *water* and read each one. Remind students that they know these words. Use the High-Frequency Word Cards and Instructional Routine: High-Frequency Words to review these words.

MODEL FLUENCY

- Explain that good readers don't skip hard parts. They take their time, go back, and correct themselves. That way, they understand the words they are reading and what the words mean.
- Read the sentences, pointing to each word as you read it slowly. Read the following sentence with an error: **Say:** *Cold water makes Madge's face nub.* Point to the word *numb.* **Say:** *I read this word as* nub, *but that doesn't make sense. I'm going to try again: /n/ /ŭ/ /m/,* numb. *The letters* mb *stand for the /m/ sound, not the /b/ sound. I also looked for clues in the text. Cold can make something feel numb, or have no feeling. Now it makes sense.*
- Reread the sentences with no mistakes. Model reading with expression and at a natural rate. Point out that you read aloud in a natural way: not too slowly and not too quickly. Note that your voice rose up at the end of the question.

Guided Practice

- Tell students they will practice reading. Display the following sentences:

  Five wrens ate gnats in Dad's pines.

  Where is Miles dashing to at such a pace?

  Kate isn't the one who knocked over the cage!

- Guide students in reading the sentences aloud. Coach them to sound out each word. Have students go back to any word they read incorrectly. Remind them that sometimes letters can be pronounced in more than one way, and have them sound out the word again. Guide students to look for context clues in surrounding text to help them figure out the word.
- Guide students to read the text again. Coach them to read at a natural rate and to use expression when reading questions or exclamations.

Apply

- Have students read aloud the practice text on Practice Page 1.19.

- Explain that the main purpose of reading the text is to practice their reading skills.

- Coach students to use decoding skills and context to self-correct any mistakes they make during reading. They should read the text several times until they are able to read smoothly and accurately with expression and at a natural rate.

- When students have finished the fluency practice, choose a few sentences to review. Have students read each sentence and explain in their own words what it means.

- After students are able to read the text fluently, guide them to track their progress on their My Progress line graphs.

Formative Assessment and Corrective Feedback

IF a student makes an error, THEN follow this model:

Correct the error.

Guide the student to say the word correctly.

Check for understanding by having the student reread the word.

Reinforce: Make a note to review the word during the student's next session.

Objectives

- Recognize and read high-frequency words.

Materials

- High-Frequency Word Cards

Formative Assessment and Corrective Feedback

IF a student makes an error, THEN follow this model:

Correct the error.

Guide the student to say the word correctly.

Check for understanding by having the student reread the word from among other randomly displayed high-frequency words.

Reinforce: Make a note to review the word during the student's next session.

High-Frequency Words: *around, because, before, bring, carry, light, show, think*

Teach/Model

- Display the high-frequency words. Tell students that these are useful words to know since they will see these words often. Tell them that reading will be easier if they recognize these words.
- Display the High-Frequency Word Card for *around* and say the word. Then spell the word aloud as you point to each letter. Say the word again.
- Use the word in a simple sentence that will provide context. For example: *The squirrels ran around the tree.*
- Repeat the steps above with the remaining high-frequency words.

Guided Practice

Do the following for each high-frequency word:

- Display the High-Frequency Word Card. Read the word and have students repeat it.
- Note the familiar sound/spelling patterns that are shown on the back of the card. Note as well any unfamiliar and unexpected sound/spellings.
- Blend the word with students.
- Spell the word aloud, pointing to each letter.
- Have students then spell the word aloud as you point to each letter.
- Have students read the word again.

Apply

- Display the High-Frequency Word Cards in random order. Have students read the words.
- Have students write each word. Tell them to compare their writing with the word on the card and make corrections if necessary.
- Have students read each word aloud and use it in a sentence.

Phonemic Awareness: Substitute Final Phonemes

- Isolate and substitute the final sounds in spoken single-syllable words.

Teach/Model

- **Say:** *Today we're going to change the last sound in a word to make a new word. For example, the word* dig *ends with the /g/ sound. The last sound in* dig *is /g/.*

- Say the word *dig*, emphasizing the /g/ sound. **Say:** *Listen:* dig.

- **Say:** *Now I'll change the /g/ sound in* dig *to /p/. Listen: /d/ /ĭ/ /p/,* dip. *Say it with me:* dip. *I changed the last sound /g/ in* dig *to /p/ and made the word* dip.

- **Say:** *Now I'll change the /g/ sound in* dig *to /m/. Listen: /d/ /ĭ/ /m/,* dim. *Say it with me:* dim. *I changed the last sound /g/ in* dig *to /m/ and made the word* dim. *Let's keep going.*

Guided Practice

- **Say:** *We're going to change the last sounds in words to make new words. For example, what is the sound at the end of* bat? *(/t/) Good. Now let's change the last sound in* bat *to /g/. Listen: /b/ /ă/ /g/. What is the word?* (bag) *Good! Let's try some more.*

- Continue with the words shown below.

Change the . . .	Result
/g/ in bug to /d/	bud
/sh/ in fish to /n/	fin
/n/ in cane to /v/	cave
/th/ in math to /p/	map
/k/ in like to /t/	light
/b/ in grab to /f/	graph
/l/ in mill to /s/	miss
/s/ in pass to /th/	path

English Language Support

Speakers of Chinese languages may have trouble hearing and producing consonants at the ends of words, or they may add a vowel sound after a final consonant; in Chinese, words usually end with a vowel sound. Provide modeling and practice segmenting and blending final sounds in words such as *back, bat, sack, sat.* Use each word in a brief sentence to provide a meaningful context.

Formative Assessment and Corrective Feedback

IF a student makes an error, THEN follow this model:

Correct the error.

Guide the student to perform the task correctly by modeling.

Check for understanding by having the student repeat the task.

Reinforce: Make a note to review the skill during the student's next session.

Apply

Have students practice substituting final phonemes, using the words below. **Say:**

- *Change the /t/ in* hat *to /v/. What is the word?* (have)

- *Change the /g/ in* mug *to /ch/. What is the word?* (much)

- *Change the /j/ in* cage *to /k/. What is the word?* (cake)

- *Change the /k/ in* knock *to /t/. What is the word?* (knot)

- *Change the /n/ in* mine *to /s/. What is the word?* (mice)

- *Change the /sh/ in* wish *to /th/. What is the word?* (with)

- *Change the last sound in* lamb *to /ch/. What is the word?* (latch)

- *Change the last sound in* fuss *to /j/. What is the word?* (fudge)

- *Change the last sound in* gave *to /m/. What is the word?* (game)

- *Change the last sound in* price *to /d/. What is the word?* (pride)

Phonics: Long *o* (CV, CVC*e*)

Objectives

- Learn the sound-spelling correspondences for long *o* (CV, CVC*e*).
- Substitute medial sounds in spoken words.
- Distinguish long and short *o*.
- Blend, build, and decode regularly spelled one-syllable words with _o, o_e.
- Read on-level text with fluency and accuracy.

Materials

- Sound/Spelling Cards
- Instructional Routine: Sound-by-Sound Blending
- Letter Cards
- Practice Page 1.20C

Phonemic Awareness Warm-up

- **Say:** *I'll change the middle vowel sound in a word. Listen:* not. *The middle sound is /ŏ/. Listen again:* note. *The middle sound is /ō/.*

- **Say:** *Now let's do it together. Listen:* hop, hope. *Which word has the /ō/ sound?* (hope) *Now you change the middle vowel sound in each word I say to the /ō/ sound:* rob (robe), rod (rode), ten (tone), hill (hole), pack (poke), bun (bone).

- Guide students to distinguish long and short vowel sounds. **Say:** *When I say a word with the long* o *sound, /ō/, form an* o *with your thumb and index finger. When I say a word with the short* o *sound, /ŏ/, keep your hand in your lap.* Say the following word pairs, emphasizing the vowel sound: *hop/hope, got/goat, mope/mop, sock/soak, coat/cot.*

Teach/Model

- Display the Sound/Spelling Card for *ocean*. Name the picture and say the beginning sound. Have students repeat after you. **Say:** *Listen:* ocean, /ō/. *Now you say it.*

- Point to the o_e spelling pattern. **Say:** *When you see the letter* o *followed by a consonant and an* e, *the letter* o *will often stand for the long* o *sound, /ō/.*

- Write and read *hope*. Cover the *e*. Read *hop*, pointing out the /ŏ/ sound. Uncover the *e* and point out the *o*-consonant-*e* pattern. Have students read *hope*. Repeat with *not* and *note*.

- Write and read *so*. Point to the letter *o*. **Say:** *This is the word* so. *The letter* o *stands for the /ō/ sound.* Repeat with *no* and *go*.

Guided Practice

BLENDING Display the words in Rows 1 and 2 below. Using Instructional Routine: Sound-by-Sound Blending, work with students to blend each word.

| 1. note | hope | go | stove | broke |
| 2. wrote | judge | robe | shades | so |

DECODING Display the sentences below. Guide students to blend one or more words and to read the sentences.

- Who do you think broke the stove?
- She hopes to show her new robe.
- Close the shades before we go home.

BUILDING AND WRITING WORDS Model how to spell the word *joke* with Letter Cards. **Say:** *The letter* j *stands for the first sound /j/. The next sound is /ō/. I know that* o *followed by a consonant and* e *can stand for /ō/. The letter* k *stands for the last sound /k/. At the end I add the* e.

- Guide students to identify sounds in the following words and build them with Letter Cards: *go, so, hot, top, pole, dome, vote, bone.*

- Have students write each word and read it aloud.

Apply

- Distribute copies of Practice Page 1.20C, which contains the decodable story *Jake and the Joke*. Tell students that many words in this story have *o* or the *o*-consonant-*e* pattern, which can stand for the long *o* sound. Point out that students have learned the following high-frequency words, which they will also read in the story: *around, before, bring*.

- Read aloud the first two sentences of the story as students follow along. Point out that you do not misread, add, or skip words when you read. Lead students in reading the same sentences with fluency and accuracy.

- Have students read the passage silently and then aloud. Remind them to track the words from left to right. When they come to the end of a line, they should sweep their hand down to the beginning of the next line and continue reading.

- When students have finished reading the text, choose a few sentences to review. You may want to focus on sentences that include words containing the target phonics skill. Have students read each sentence and explain in their own words what it means.

Fun with Words Optional activities for engaging, hands-on practice are provided in the Resources section.

English Language Support

Linguistic Transfer Point out to Spanish speakers that the sound /ō/ is the same in Spanish as in English. Students with reading skills in Spanish should also be told that they can use their knowledge of Spanish to help them read words with this sound in English as the sound is often spelled the same. Work with students to spell several words with the /ō/ sound in both languages.

Formative Assessment and Corrective Feedback

IF a student makes an error, THEN follow this model:

Correct the error.

Guide the student to perform the task correctly by modeling.

Check for understanding by having the student repeat the task.

Reinforce: Make a note to review the skill during the student's next session.

Phonics: Long *u* (CVC*e*)

Objectives

- Learn the sound-spelling correspondence for long *u* (CVC*e*).
- Substitute medial sounds in spoken words.
- Distinguish long and short *u*.
- Blend and decode regularly spelled one-syllable words with *u_e*.
- Read on-level text with fluency and accuracy.

Materials

- Sound/Spelling Cards
- Instructional Routine: Sound-by-Sound Blending
- Letter Cards
- Practice Page 1.20D

Phonemic Awareness Warm-up

- **Say:** *I'll change the middle vowel sound in a word. Listen:* cub. *The middle sound is /ŭ/. Listen again:* cube. *The middle sound is /ū/.*
- **Say:** *Now let's do it together. Listen:* cut, cute. *Which word has the /ū/ sound?* (cute)
- Guide students to distinguish long and short vowel sounds. **Say:** *When I say a word with the long* u *sound, /ū/, form a letter* u *with your thumb and index finger. When I say a word with the short* u *sound, /ŭ/, keep your hand in your lap.* Say the following word pairs, emphasizing the vowel sound in each word: *tub/tube; mull/mule; us/use; hug/huge.*

Teach/Model

- Display the Sound/Spelling Card for *uniform*. Name the picture and say the beginning sound. Have students repeat after you. **Say:** *Listen:* uniform, /ū/. *Now you say it.*
- Point to the *u_e* spelling pattern on the card. **Say:** *When you see the letter* u *followed by a consonant and an* e, *the letter* u *can stand for the long* u *sound, /ū/.*
- Write and read *tube*. Cover the *e*. Read *tub*, pointing out the /ŭ/ sound. Uncover the *e* and point out the *u*-consonant-*e* pattern. **Say:** *The* u-*consonant-*e *pattern makes the letter* u *stand for the /ū/ sound in* tube. *Read it with me:* tube. Repeat with the words *hug/huge* and *us/use.*

Guided Practice

BLENDING Display the words in Rows 1 and 2 below. Using Instructional Routine: Sound-by-Sound Blending, work with students to blend each word.

| 1. tune | use | globe | cube | cute |
| 2. stone | flute | mule | white | tube |

DECODING Display the sentences below. Call on individuals to blend one or more words and to read the sentences.

- Can a cute little wren sing a big tune?
- Bring me a huge plant to put in this cube.
- Show her how to use the flute.

BUILDING AND WRITING WORDS Model how to spell the word *mule* with Letter Cards. **Say:** *The letter* m *stands for the first sound /m/. The next sound is /ū/. I know that* u *followed by a consonant and* e *can stand for /ū/. The letter* l *stands for the last sound /l/. At the end I add the* e.

- Guide students to identify sounds in the following words and build them with Letter Cards: *cube, cute, flute, huge, tube, tune, use.*
- Have students write each word and read it aloud.

Apply

- Distribute copies of Practice Page 1.20D, which contains the decodable story *June Takes Pictures*. Tell students that many words in this story have the *u*-consonant-*e* pattern, which can stand for the long *u* sound. Point out that students have learned the following high-frequency words, which they will also read in the story: *around, because, show, think(s)*.

- Read aloud the first three sentences of the story as students follow along. Point out that you do not misread, add, or skip words when you read. Lead students in reading the same sentences with fluency and accuracy.

- Have students read the passage silently and then aloud. Remind them to track the words from left to right. When they come to the end of a line, they should sweep their hand down to the beginning of the next line and continue reading.

- When students have finished reading the text, choose a few sentences to review. You may want to focus on sentences that include words containing the target phonics skill. Have students read each sentence and explain in their own words what it means.

> **Fun with Words** Optional activities for engaging, hands-on practice are provided in the Resources section.

Formative Assessment and Corrective Feedback

IF a student makes an error, THEN follow this model:

Correct the error.

Guide the student to perform the task correctly by modeling.

Check for understanding by having the student repeat the task.

Reinforce: Make a note to review the skill during the student's next session.

Objectives

- Recognize and read high-frequency words.

Materials

- High-Frequency Word Cards

Formative Assessment and Corrective Feedback

IF a student makes an error, THEN follow this model:

Correct the error.

Guide the student to say the word correctly.

Check for understanding by having the student reread the word from among other randomly displayed high-frequency words.

Reinforce: Make a note to review the word during the student's next session.

High-Frequency Words: *about, by, car, could, don't, maybe, sure, there*

Teach/Model

- Display the high-frequency words. Tell students that these are useful words to know since they will see these words often. Tell them that reading will be easier if they recognize these words.

- Display the High-Frequency Word Card for *about* and say the word. Then spell the word aloud as you point to each letter. Say the word again.

- Use the word in a simple sentence that will provide context. For example: *The book was about dinosaurs.*

- Repeat the steps above with the remaining high-frequency words.

Guided Practice

Do the following for each high-frequency word:

- Display the High-Frequency Word Card. Read the word and have students repeat it.

- Note the familiar sound/spelling patterns that are shown on the back of the card. Note as well any unfamiliar and unexpected sound/spellings.

- Blend the word with students.

- Spell the word aloud, pointing to each letter.

- Have students then spell the word aloud as you point to each letter.

- Have students read the word again.

Apply

- Display the High-Frequency Word Cards in random order. Have students read the words.

- Have students write each word. Tell them to compare their writing with the word on the card and make corrections if necessary.

- Have students read each word aloud and use it in a sentence.

Phonics: Long *e* (CV, CVC*e*)

Phonemic Awareness Warm-up

- **Say:** *I'm going to change sounds to make new words. Listen:* man. *Listen as I change the /ă/ in* man *to /ā/:* mane. *Now try it with me. Change the /ă/ in* cap *to /ā/.* (cape)

- **Say:** *Let's do some more. Change /ĕ/ in* fed *to /ē/* (feed), */ĭ/ in* kit *to /ī/* (kite), */ŏ/ in* hop *to /ō/* (hope), */ŭ/ in* hug *to /ū/* (huge), */ĕ/ in* met *to /ē/* (meat), */ă/ in* pal *to /ā/* (pale), */ĭ/ in* pin *to /ī/* (pine), */ŏ/ in* glob *to /ō/* (globe), *and /ŭ/ in* cut *to /ū/* (cute).

- Say each pair of words from this activity, mixing up the order, and ask students to give "thumbs up" when they hear the word with the short vowel sound.

Teach/Model

- Display the Sound/Spelling Card for *eagle*. Name the picture and say the beginning sound. Have students repeat after you. **Say:** *Listen:* eagle, */ē/. Now you say it.* Eagle *begins with the long* e *sound, /ē/.*

- Point to the *e* spelling on the card. **Say:** *The letter* e *can stand for the /ē/ sound.*

- Display the word *me*. Point out the /ē/ spelling *e*. **Say:** *This is the word* me. *The letter* e *stands for the sound /ē/ in* me. *Read it with me:* me.

- Point to the *e_e* spelling on the card. **Say:** *When you see the letter* e *followed by a consonant and an* e, *the letter* e *can stand for the long* e *sound, /ē/.*

- Write and read *these*. Point out the /ē/ spelling *e_e*. **Say:** *This is the word* these. *The e-consonant-e pattern stands for the /ē/ sound in* these. *Read it with me:* these.

Guided Practice

BLENDING Display the words in Rows 1 and 2 below. Using Instructional Routine: Sound-by-Sound Blending, work with students to blend each word.

1. she	leg	home	these	bed
2. Eve	he	Pete	no	we

DECODING Display the sentences below. Guide students to blend one or more words and to read the sentences.

- Eve will go to the lake by car.
- She and Steve will be there by 10.
- Maybe Pete could take me at 11.

BUILDING AND WRITING WORDS Model how to build the word *theme* with Letter Cards. **Say:** *The letters* th *stand for the first sound /th/. The next sound is /ē/. I know that* e *followed by a consonant and* e *can stand for /ē/. The letter* m *stands for the last sound /m/. At the end I add the* e.

- Guide students to identify sounds in the following words and build them with Letter Cards: *we, she, me, Eve, Pete, these, Zeke*.

- Have students write each word and read it aloud.

Objectives

- Learn the sound-spelling correspondences for long *e* (CV, CVC*e*).
- Distinguish long and short vowel sounds in spoken words.
- Blend, build, and decode regularly spelled one-syllable words with _*e*, *e*_*e*.
- Read on-level text with fluency and accuracy.

Materials

- Sound/Spelling Cards
- Instructional Routine: Sound-by-Sound Blending
- Letter Cards
- Practice Page 1.21B

Formative Assessment and Corrective Feedback

IF a student makes an error, THEN follow this model:

Correct the error.

Guide the student to perform the task correctly by modeling.

Check for understanding by having the student repeat the task.

Reinforce: Make a note to review the skill during the student's next session.

Apply

- Distribute copies of Practice Page 1.21B, which contains the decodable story *Show and Tell*. Tell students that many words in this story have *e* or the *e*-consonant-*e* pattern, which can stand for the long *e* sound. Point out that students have learned the following high-frequency words, which they will also read in the story: *about, car, could, maybe*.

- Read aloud the first four sentences of the story as students follow along. Point out that you do not misread, add, or skip words when you read. Lead students in reading the same sentences with fluency and accuracy.

- Have students read the passage silently and then aloud. Remind them to track the words from left to right. When they come to the end of a line, they should sweep their hand down to the beginning of the next line and continue reading.

- When students have finished reading the text, choose a few sentences to review. You may want to focus on sentences that include words containing the target phonics skill. Have students read each sentence and explain in their own words what it means.

> **Fun with Words** Optional activities for engaging, hands-on practice are provided in the Resources section.

Phonics: Long *e* Spelled *ee, ea*

Phonemic Awareness Warm-up

- **Say:** *Let's play a game. I'll say a word. You name the sound you hear in the middle of the word. Listen: /t/ /ē/ /m/,* team. *What sound do you hear in the middle of* team? *(/ē/) Let's do another one. Listen: /b/ /e/ /d/,* bed. *What is the middle sound in* bed? *(/ě/)*

- Continue with the following words: leg (/ě/), need (/ē/), speak (/ē/), bend (/ě/), stem (/ě/), green (/ē/), cream (/ē/), trend (/ě/), please (/ē/).

Teach/Model

- Display the Sound/Spelling Card for *eagle*. Name the picture and say the beginning sound. Have students repeat after you. **Say:** *Listen:* eagle, */ē/. Now you say it.*

- Say the sound and give the spelling. **Say:** Eagle *begins with the long* e *sound, /ē/. The letters* ea *can stand for the /ē/ sound at the beginning, middle, or end of a word.*

- Write and read *bean.* Point out the /ē/ spelling *ea.* **Say:** *This is the word* bean. *The letters* ea *stand for the /ē/ sound in* bean. *Read it with me:* bean.

- Point to the *ee* spelling on the card. **Say:** *The letters* ee *can stand for the /ē/ sound.*

- Write and read *feet.* Point out the /ē/ spelling *ee.* **Say:** *This is the word* feet. *The letters* ee *stand for the /ē/ sound in* feet. *Read it with me:* feet.

Guided Practice

BLENDING Display the words in Rows 1 and 2 below. Using Instructional Routine: Sound-by-Sound Blending, work with students to blend each word.

1. greet	leak	best	feel	bead
2. clean	these	we	blend	sleep

DECODING Display the sentences below. Call on individuals to blend one or more words and to read the sentences.

- All three could meet at the beach.
- Dean will go there in a green jeep.
- We don't clean out the weeds each week.

BUILDING AND WRITING WORDS Model how to build the word *cheek* with Letter Cards. **Say:** *The letters* ch *stand for the first sound /ch/. The next sound is /ē/. I know that* ee *can stand for /ē/. The letter* k *stands for the last sound /k/.*

- Guide students to identify sounds in the following words and build them with Letter Cards: *team, feel, she, Pete, street, reach.*

- Have students write each word and read it aloud.

Objectives

- Learn the sound-spelling correspondences for long *e (ee, ea)*.
- Distinguish long and short vowel sounds in spoken words.
- Blend, build, and decode regularly spelled one-syllable words with *ee* and *ea.*
- Read on-level text with fluency and accuracy.

Materials

- Sound/Spelling Cards
- Instructional Routine: Sound-by-Sound Blending
- Letter Cards
- Practice Page 1.21C

English Language Support

Linguistic Transfer Explain to students that long vowel sounds can be spelled in different ways in English, unlike in most languages. As an example, ask a student with reading skills in Spanish to tell how the sound /ē/ (as in *rico*) is spelled in Spanish (i). Explain that this sound is always spelled with an *i* in Spanish. In English, the sound /ē/ can be spelled different ways, including *e*, *e*-consonant-*e*, *ee*, and *ea*.

Formative Assessment and Corrective Feedback

IF a student makes an error, THEN follow this model:

Correct the error.

Guide the student to perform the task correctly by modeling.

Check for understanding by having the student repeat the task.

Reinforce: Make a note to review the skill during the student's next session.

Apply

- Distribute copies of Practice Page 1.21C, which contains the decodable story *Fun at the Beach*. Tell students that many words in this story have the letters *ee* or *ea*, which can stand for the long *e* sound. Point out that students have learned the following high-frequency words, which they will also read in the story: *about, by, don't, maybe, there.*

- Read aloud the first three sentences of the story as students follow along. Point out that you do not misread, add, or skip words when you read. Lead students in reading the same sentences with fluency and accuracy.

- Have students read the passage silently and then aloud. Remind them to track the words from left to right. When they come to the end of a line, they should sweep their hand down to the beginning of the next line and continue reading.

- When students have finished reading the text, choose a few sentences to review. You may want to focus on sentences that include words containing the target phonics skill. Have students read each sentence and explain in their own words what it means.

> **Fun with Words** Optional activities for engaging, hands-on practice are provided in the Resources section.

Phonics: Final *ng, nk*

Phonemic Awareness Warm-up

- **Say:** *I'm going to say two words that sound almost alike but have one difference. Listen:* rub, run. *These words have different last sounds. The last sound in* rub *is /b/. The last sound in* run *is /n/.*

- **Say:** *Let's do some together. Say* cat, can. *What is the last sound in* cat? *(/t/) What is the last sound in* can? *(/n/)*

- **Say:** *Now let's do some more. Tell me what is different about the sounds in each pair of words:* feel, feet (/l/, /t/); beak, beam (/k/, /m/); sip, sing (/p/, /ng/); thin, think (/n/, /ngk/).

Teach/Model

- Display the Sound/Spelling Card for *ring*. Name the picture and say the ending sound /ng/.

- Repeat *ring* and give the spelling. **Say:** *The word* ring *ends with the sound /ng/. Say the word with me and listen for the sound at the end of* ring. *The letters* ng *stand for /ng/ at the end of* ring.

- Write and read *sang*. Have students repeat it. **Say:** *The letters* ng *stand for the sound at the end of* sang. *Read the word with me:* sang. Tell students that the letters *ng* blend together so closely that they make a special sound.

- Point out the second spelling on the card. Say the words *bank* and *think*. Have students repeat the words. Point to the letters on the card to connect the ending sound with the *nk* spelling.

- Write and read *sunk*. Have students repeat it. **Say:** *The letters* nk *stand for the sound /ngk/ at the end of* sunk. Have students read the word with you.

Guided Practice

BLENDING Display the words in Rows 1 and 2 below. Using Instructional Routine: Sound-by-Sound Blending, work with students to blend each word.

1. pink	think	bank	bring	link
2. week	king	bridge	junk	poke

DECODING Display the sentences below. Call on individuals to blend one or more words and to read the sentences.

- Her new car had long, pink stripes.

- Be sure to put that ring in a bank.

- Could we hang the picture over the sink?

BUILDING AND WRITING WORDS Model using Letter Cards to build the word *sink*. **Say:** *The letters* s, i, *and* nk *stand for the sounds /s/ /ĭ/ /ngk/ in* sink. Write the word. Repeat for the word *blink*. Point out that *sink* and *blink* belong to the same word family because they end with the same letters (-*ink*) and sounds (/ĭ/ /ngk/).

- Guide students to identify sounds in other words in the -*ink* word family and build them with Letter Cards: *link, pink, rink, wink, think, drink.*

- Have students write each word and read it aloud.

- Learn the sound-spelling correspondences for final *ng* and *nk*.
- Isolate final sounds in spoken single-syllable words.
- Blend, build, and decode regularly spelled one-syllable words with final *ng* and *nk*.
- Read on-level text with fluency and accuracy.

Materials
- Sound/Spelling Cards
- Instructional Routine: Sound-by-Sound Blending
- Letter Cards
- Practice Page 1.21D

Formative Assessment and Corrective Feedback

IF a student makes an error, THEN follow this model:

Correct the error.

Guide the student to perform the task correctly by modeling.

Check for understanding by having the student repeat the task.

Reinforce: Make a note to review the skill during the student's next session.

Apply

- Distribute copies of Practice Page 1.21D, which contains the decodable story *King Ming Sings*. Tell students that many words in this story end with *ng* or *nk*. Point out that students have learned the following high-frequency words, which they will also read in the story: *could, don't, maybe, sure.*

- Read aloud the first three sentences of the story as students follow along. Point out that you do not misread, add, or skip words when you read. Lead students in reading the same sentences with fluency and accuracy.

- Have students read the passage silently and then aloud. Remind them to track the words from left to right. When they come to the end of a line, they should sweep their hand down to the beginning of the next line and continue reading.

- When students have finished reading the text, choose a few sentences to review. You may want to focus on sentences that include words containing the target phonics skill. Have students read each sentence and explain in their own words what it means.

> **Fun with Words** Optional activities for engaging, hands-on practice are provided in the Resources section.

High-Frequency Words: *first, food, ground, right, sometimes, these, under, your*

Teach/Model

- Display the high-frequency words. Tell students that these are useful words to know since they will see these words often. Tell them that reading will be easier if they recognize these words.

- Display the High-Frequency Word Card for *first* and say the word. Then spell the word aloud as you point to each letter. Say the word again.

- Use the word in a simple sentence that will provide context. For example: *Casey was the first student in line.*

- Repeat the steps above with the remaining high-frequency words.

Guided Practice

Do the following for each high-frequency word:

- Display the High-Frequency Word Card. Read the word and have students repeat it.

- Note the familiar sound/spelling patterns that are shown on the back of the card. Note as well any unfamiliar and unexpected sound/spellings.

- Blend the word with students.

- Spell the word aloud, pointing to each letter.

- Have students then spell the word aloud as you point to each letter.

- Have students read the word again.

Apply

- Display the High-Frequency Word Cards in random order. Have students read the words.

- Have students write each word. Tell them to compare their writing with the word on the card and make corrections if necessary.

- Have students read each word aloud and use it in a sentence.

Objectives

- Recognize and read high-frequency words.

Materials

- High-Frequency Word Cards

Formative Assessment and Corrective Feedback

IF a student makes an error, THEN follow this model:

Correct the error.

Guide the student to say the word correctly.

Check for understanding by having the student reread the word from among other randomly displayed high-frequency words.

Reinforce: Make a note to review the word during the student's next session.

Objectives

- Isolate and substitute the final sounds in spoken single-syllable words.

English Language Support

It's important for English learners to understand the meaning of words they are using for skills practice. Use visuals, gestures, and context sentences to support student understanding.

Formative Assessment and Corrective Feedback

IF a student makes an error, THEN follow this model:

Correct the error.

Guide the student to perform the task correctly by modeling.

Check for understanding by having the student repeat the task.

Reinforce: Make a note to review the skill during the student's next session.

Teach/Model

- **Say:** *Today we're going to change the last sound in a word to make a new word. For example, the word* bag *ends with the /g/ sound. The last sound in* bag *is /g/.*
- Say the word *bag*, emphasizing the /g/ sound. **Say:** *Listen:* bag.
- **Say:** *Now I'll change the /g/ sound in* bag *to /th/. Listen: /b/ /ă/ /th/,* bath. *Say it with me:* bath. *I changed the last sound /g/ in* bag *to /th/ and made the word* bath.
- **Say:** *Now I'll change the /g/ sound in* bag *to /ch/. Listen: /b/ /ă/ /ch/,* batch. *Say it with me:* batch. *I changed the last sound /g/ in* bag *to /ch/ and made the word* batch. *Let's keep going.*

Guided Practice

- **Say:** *We're going to change the last sounds in words to make new words. For example, what is the last sound in* feed? *(/d/) Good. Now let's change the last sound in* feed *to /t/. What is the word? (*feet*) Good! Now let's change the last sound in* feet *to /l/. What is the word? (*feel*) Let's try some more.*
- Continue with the words shown below.

Change the . . .	Result
/ng/ in sing to /ngk/	sink
/th/ in with to /l/	will
/b/ in cube to /t/	cute
/sh/ in crash to /b/	crab
/ngk/ in think to /ng/	thing
/l/ in hole to /z/	hose
/k/ in peak to /ch/	peach
/j/ in page to /s/	pace

Apply

Have students practice substituting final phonemes, using the words below. **Say:**

- *Change the /ng/ in* sting *to /k/. What is the word? (*stick*)
- *Change the /th/ in* teeth *to /ch/. What is the word? (*teach*)
- *Change the /n/ in* spine *to /s/. What is the word? (*spice*)
- *Change the /sh/ in* rash *to /ng/. What is the word? (*rang*)
- *Change the /m/ in* steam *to /p/. What is the word? (*steep*)
- *Change the /dge/ in* budge *to /k/. What is the word? (*buck*)
- *Change the last sound in* rip *to /j/. What is the word? (*ridge*)
- *Change the last sound in* stone *to /v/. What is the word? (*stove*)
- *Change the last sound in* wish *to /ngk/. What is the word? (*wink*)
- *Change the last sound in* shape *to /d/. What is the word? (*shade*)

Phonics: Long *a* Spelled *ai, ay*

Phonemic Awareness Warm-up

- **Say:** *I'll change the sound at the end of a word. Listen:* wait. *The middle sound is /ā/. The last sound is /t/. Now I'll change the last sound. Listen:* wait, wail. *The last sound is /l/. Listen again:* wait, ways. *Now the last sound is /z/.*

- **Say:** *Listen as I change another word:* Gail. *I hear /ā/ in the middle and /l/ at the end. How can we change the last sound? Listen:* Gail, gain, gate. *Now you change the last sound in each word I say to make new words. Listen:* Jade (jail, Jane); raise (raid, rain); maid (mail, make).

- Repeat some of the words from the activity. Have students say the initial, medial, and final sounds in each word.

Teach/Model

- Display the Sound/Spelling Card for *acorn*. Name the picture and say the beginning sound. Have students repeat after you. **Say:** *Listen:* acorn, /ā/. *Now you say it.* Remind students that they learned about the long vowel sound /ā/ in an earlier lesson.

- Write and read *bake*. Say the vowel sound and point out the spelling for /ā/ students have already learned. Point to *a_e* on the card.

- Write and read *pain*. Point out the *ai* spelling for long *a*. Explain that in a vowel pair, or vowel team, two letters stand for one sound. **Say:** *This is the word* pain. *The letters* ai *stand for the /ā/ sound. Read the word with me:* pain.

- Write and read *day*. Point out the *ay* spelling for long *a*. **Say:** *This is the word* day. *The letters* ay *stand for the /ā/ sound. Read the word with me:* day.

Guided Practice

BLENDING Display the words in Rows 1 and 2 below. Using Instructional Routine: Sound-by-Sound Blending, work with students to blend each word.

1. clay	day	hay	rain	pail
2. shade	peach	braid	while	huge

DECODING Display the sentences below. Call on individuals to blend one or more words and to read the sentences.

- We sailed under the bridge into the bay.
- These pails may be full of green paint.
- Did it rain on your first day on the trail?

BUILDING AND WRITING WORDS Model how to spell the word *main*. **Say:** *The letter* m *stands for the first sound. The next sound is /ā/. The vowel pair* ai *stands for /ā/. The letter* n *stands for the last sound, /n/.* Repeat for the words *rain* and *chain*. Point out that *main, rain,* and *chain* belong to the same word family because they end with the same letters (*-ain*) and sounds (/ā/ /n/). Repeat with the phonogram *-ay,* using *day* and *bay*.

- Guide students to identify sounds in the following words and build them with Letter Cards: *gain, brain, stain, sprain, may, pay, way, play, spray.*

- Have students write each word and read it aloud.

Objectives

- Learn the sound-spelling correspondences for long *a (ai, ay)*.
- Blend sounds in spoken single-syllable words with /ā/.
- Blend and decode regularly spelled one-syllable words with *ai* and *ay*.
- Read on-level text with fluency and accuracy.

Materials

- Sound/Spelling Cards
- Instructional Routine: Sound-by-Sound Blending
- Letter Cards
- Practice Page 1.22C

English Language Support

Linguistic Transfer Students with reading skills in Spanish may tend to use the letter *e* to represent the long *a* sound in English because the letter *e* in Spanish stands for the sound /ā/. Explain to students that in English, the /ā/ sound is usually spelled with the letter *a* plus another letter, such as *i* or *y*, as in *wait, train, mail, play, gray,* and *day.* Provide additional example words for practice, and use each word in a brief sentence to reinforce meaning.

Formative Assessment and Corrective Feedback

IF a student makes an error, THEN follow this model:

Correct the error.

Guide the student to perform the task correctly by modeling.

Check for understanding by having the student repeat the task.

Reinforce: Make a note to review the skill during the student's next session.

- Distribute copies of Practice Page 1.22C, which contains the decodable story *Fay Trains Tank.* Tell students that many words in this story have the letters *ai* or *ay*, which stand for the long *a* sound. Point out that students have learned the following high-frequency words, which they will also read in the story: *first, food, ground.*

- Read aloud the first four sentences of the story as students follow along. Point out that you do not misread, add, or skip words when you read. Lead students in reading the same sentences with fluency and accuracy.

- Have students read the passage silently and then aloud. Remind them to track the words from left to right. When they come to the end of a line, they should sweep their hand down to the beginning of the next line and continue reading.

- When students have finished reading the text, choose a few sentences to review. You may want to focus on sentences that include words containing the target phonics skill. Have students read each sentence and explain in their own words what it means.

Fun with Words Optional activities for engaging, hands-on practice are provided in the Resources section.

Phonics: Contractions with *'ll, 'd*

Phonemic Awareness Warm-up

- **Say:** *I will say two words. Listen closely:* cab, cat. *The last sounds in* cab *and* cat *are different. The last sound in* cab *is /b/. The last sound in* cat *is /t/. Listen:* braid. *What is the last sound?* (/d/) *Now you listen and change the last sound in each word to /d/:* pain (paid); reef (reed); beam (bead); cone (code); fresh (Fred).

- **Say:** *Listen to two words and tell how the second word is different from the first word:* can, can't. (The /t/ sound has been added to the end of *can* to make *can't*.)

Teach/Model

- **Say:** *Remember, a contraction is formed by combining two words into one shorter word. A special mark called an apostrophe takes the place of missing letters.*

- Use Letter Cards to build the words *I will*. Read the words. Model forming the contraction *I'll*. Make an apostrophe card. **Say:** *The contraction* I'll *is a short way to say* I will. *To make the contraction* I'll, *I replace the letters* wi *in* will *with an apostrophe.* Display the *I* and *ll* cards. Add the apostrophe card between them. Use *I'll* in a sentence: *I'll be gone for three hours.* Repeat with the contraction *she'll*.

- Use Letter Cards to build the words *I would*. Read the words. Model forming the contraction *I'd*. **Say:** *The contraction* I'd *is a short way to say* I would. *To make the contraction* I'd, *I replace the letters* w, o, u, *and* l *in* would *with an apostrophe.* Display the *I* and *d* cards. Add the apostrophe card between them. Use *I'd* in a sentence: *I'd rather read a book.* Repeat with the contraction *he'd*.

Guided Practice

BLENDING Display the words in Rows 1 and 2 below. Using Instructional Routine: Sound-by-Sound Blending, work with students to blend each word.

1. we'd	he'll	that'll	it'll	she'd
2. sink	tray	cream	thing	chain

DECODING Display the sentences below. Call on individuals to blend one or more words and to read the sentences.

- He'll wait right here for her.
- Did she say she'd bring food?
- We'll be fine if we stay in.

BUILDING AND WRITING WORDS Model using Letter Cards to build the word *we'll*. **Say:** We'll *is a contraction for* we will. *I will build the words* we *and* will. *Then I will replace the letters* w *and* i *in* will *with an apostrophe.*

- Guide students to identify sounds in the following words and build them with Letter Cards: *he'll, she'll, we'd, it'd*. Remind students to put an apostrophe in each contraction.

- Have students write each contraction and read it aloud.

- Blend, build, and decode contractions with *'ll* and *'d*.
- Isolate and substitute final sounds in spoken words.
- Review how to use apostrophes when writing contractions.
- Read on-level text with fluency and accuracy.

Materials

- Instructional Routine: Sound-by-Sound Blending
- Letter Cards
- Practice Page 1.22D

Formative Assessment and Corrective Feedback

IF a student makes an error, THEN follow this model:

Correct the error.

Guide the student to perform the task correctly by modeling.

Check for understanding by having the student repeat the task.

Reinforce: Make a note to review the skill during the student's next session.

Apply

- Distribute copies of Practice Page 1.22D, which contains the decodable story *A Fine Meal*. Tell students that many words in this story are contractions with *'ll* and *'d*. Point out that students have learned the following high-frequency words, which they will also read in the story: *food, these, under, your*.

- Read aloud the first four sentences of the story as students follow along. Point out that you do not misread, add, or skip words when you read. Lead students in reading the same sentences with fluency and accuracy.

- Have students read the passage silently and then aloud. Remind them to track the words from left to right. When they come to the end of a line, they should sweep their hand down to the beginning of the next line and continue reading.

- When students have finished reading the text, choose a few sentences to review. You may want to focus on sentences that include words containing the target phonics skill. Have students read each sentence and explain in their own words what it means.

> **Fun with Words** Optional activities for engaging, hands-on practice are provided in the Resources section.

High-Frequency Words: *done, great, laugh, paper, soon, talk, were, work*

Teach/Model

- Display the high-frequency words. Tell students that these are useful words to know since they will see these words often. Tell them that reading will be easier if they recognize these words.

- Display the High-Frequency Word Card for *done* and say the word. Then spell the word aloud as you point to each letter. Say the word again.

- Use the word in a simple sentence that will provide context. For example: *She had done her homework.*

- Repeat the steps above with the remaining high-frequency words.

Guided Practice

Do the following for each high-frequency word:

- Display the High-Frequency Word Card. Read the word and have students repeat it.

- Note the familiar sound/spelling patterns that are shown on the back of the card. Note as well any unfamiliar and unexpected sound/spellings.

- Blend the word with students.

- Spell the word aloud, pointing to each letter.

- Have students then spell the word aloud as you point to each letter.

- Have students read the word again.

Apply

- Display the High-Frequency Word Cards in random order. Have students read the words.

- Have students write each word. Tell them to compare their writing with the word on the card and make corrections if necessary.

- Have students read each word aloud and use it in a sentence.

Objectives

- Recognize and read high-frequency words.

Materials

- High-Frequency Word Cards

Formative Assessment and Corrective Feedback

IF a student makes an error, THEN follow this model:

Correct the error.

Guide the student to say the word correctly.

Check for understanding by having the student reread the word from among other randomly displayed high-frequency words.

Reinforce: Make a note to review the word during the student's next session.

Phonics: Long *o* Spelled *oa, ow*

Objectives

- Learn the sound-spelling correspondences for long *o* (*oa, ow*).
- Substitute medial sounds in spoken words.
- Blend and decode regularly spelled one-syllable words with *oa* and *ow*.
- Read on-level text with fluency and accuracy.

Materials

- Sound/Spelling Cards
- Instructional Routine: Sound-by-Sound Blending
- Letter Cards
- Practice Page 1.23B

Phonemic Awareness Warm-up

- **Say:** *I'll change the middle vowel sound in a word. Listen:* bait. *The middle sound is /ā/. Listen again:* boat. *The middle sound is /ō/. Now let's do it. Listen:* Kate, coat. *What word has the /ō/ sound/?* (coat) *Now change the middle sound in each word to the /ō/ sound:* raid (road); gate (goat); taste (toast); main (moan); fame (foam).
- Repeat some of the words from the activity. Have students say the medial vowel sound in each word.

Teach/Model

- Display the Sound/Spelling Card for *ocean*. Name the picture and say the beginning sound. Have students repeat after you. **Say:** *Listen:* ocean, /ō/. *Now you say it.* Remind students that they learned about the long vowel sound /ō/ in an earlier lesson.
- Write and read *hope.* Say the vowel sound and point out the spelling for /ō/ students have already learned. Point to *o_e* on the card.
- Write and read *boat.* Point out the *oa* spelling for long *o.* Explain that in a vowel pair, or vowel team, two letters stand for one sound. **Say:** *This is the word* boat. *The letters* oa *together stand for the /ō/ sound. Read the word with me:* boat. Repeat with the words *float* and *coast.*
- Write and read *snow.* Point out the *ow* spelling for long *o.* **Say:** *This is the word* snow. *The letters* ow *stand for the /ō/ sound in* snow. *Read the word with me:* snow. Repeat with the words *grow* and *mow.*

Guided Practice

BLENDING Display the words in Rows 1 and 2 below. Using Instructional Routine: Sound-by-Sound Blending, work with students to blend each word.

| 1. road | snow | boat | load | goat |
| 2. plain | row | hope | crow | stay |

DECODING Display the sentences below. Call on individuals to blend one or more words and to read the sentences.

- Soon snow was all over the roads.
- They had to work to row the boat.
- Coach helped me make a great throw.

BUILDING AND WRITING WORDS Model how to spell the word *low.* **Say:** *The letter* l *stands for the first sound. The next sound is /ō/. The vowel pair* ow *stands for /ō/.* Repeat for the words *mow* and *row.* Point out that *low, mow,* and *row* belong to the same word family because they end with the same letters (*-ow*) and sound (/ō/). Repeat with the phonogram *-oat,* using the words *oat* and *boat.*

- Guide students to identify sounds in the following words and build them with Letter Cards: *flow, snow, throw, boat, float, goat, throat.*
- Have students write each word and read it aloud.

Apply

- Distribute copies of Practice Page 1.23B, which contains the decodable story *Which Boat?* Tell students that many words in this story have the letters *oa* or *ow*, which can stand for the long *o* sound. Point out that students have learned the following high-frequency words, which they will also read in the story: *great, soon, were.*

- Read aloud the first two sentences of the story as students follow along. Point out that you do not misread, add, or skip words when you read. Lead students in reading the same sentences with fluency and accuracy.

- Have students read the passage silently and then aloud. Remind them to track the words from left to right. When they come to the end of a line, they should sweep their hand down to the beginning of the next line and continue reading.

- When students have finished reading the text, choose a few sentences to review. You may want to focus on sentences that include words containing the target phonics skill. Have students read each sentence and explain in their own words what it means.

> **Fun with Words** Optional activities for engaging, hands-on practice are provided in the Resources section.

English Language Support

Linguistic Transfer Point out to Spanish speakers that the /ō/ sound is the same in Spanish as in English. Encourage students to share words they know in both Spanish and English with the /ō/ sound.

Formative Assessment and Corrective Feedback

IF a student makes an error, THEN follow this model:

Correct the error.

Guide the student to perform the task correctly by modeling.

Check for understanding by having the student repeat the task.

Reinforce: Make a note to review the skill during the student's next session.

Phonics: Contractions with *'ve, 're*

Objectives

- Blend and decode contractions with *'ve* and *'re*.
- Review how to use apostrophes when writing contractions.
- Read on-level text with fluency and accuracy.

Materials

- Instructional Routine: Sound-by-Sound Blending
- Letter Cards
- Practice Page 1.23C

Phonemic Awareness Warm-up

- **Say:** *I will say two words and tell how the second word is different. Listen closely. My words are* we *and* we'll. *An /l/ sound has been added to* we *to make* we'll. *Now listen and tell how these words are different:* I, I've; you, you're; we, we're; we, we've.

- **Say:** *Listen and add a /v/ sound to each word:* I (I've); you (you've); we (we've). *Now listen and add an /r/ sound to each word:* you (you're); we (we're).

Teach/Model

- **Say:** *Remember, a contraction is formed by combining two words into one shorter word. A special mark called an apostrophe takes the place of missing letters.*

- Use Letter Cards to build the words *we are*. Read the words. Model forming the contraction *we're*. Make an apostrophe card. **Say:** *The contraction* we're *is a short way to say* we are. *To make the contraction* we're, *I replace the letter* a *in* are *with an apostrophe.* Display the *w, e, r, e* cards. Add the apostrophe card between the first *e* and the *r*. Read the word. Use *we're* in a sentence: *We're done with our work.* Repeat with the contractions *they're* and *you're*.

- Use Letter Cards to build the words *we have*. Read the words. Model forming the contraction *we've*. **Say:** *The contraction* we've *is a short way to say* we have. *To make the contraction* we've, *I replace the letters* h *and* a *in* have *with an apostrophe.* Display the *w, e, v, e* cards. Add the apostrophe card between the first *e* and the *v*. Read the word. Use *we've* in a sentence: *We've cleaned our room.* Repeat with the contractions *they've* and *you've*.

Guided Practice

BLENDING Display the words in Rows 1 and 2 below. Using Instructional Routine: Sound-by-Sound Blending, work with students to blend each word.

| 1. we're | you've | they've | you're | I've |
| 2. low | she'd | load | that'll | plain |

DECODING Display the sentences below. Call on individuals to blend one or more words and to read the sentences.

- I've got work to do.
- They're out of paper.
- We've had a great time.

BUILDING AND WRITING WORDS Model using Letter Cards to build the word *I've*. **Say:** I've *is a contraction for* I have. *I will build the words* I *and* have. *Then to make the contraction, I will replace the letters* ha *in* have *with an apostrophe.*

- Guide students to build the following words with Letter Cards: *we're, they've, you're, we've*. Remind students to put an apostrophe in each contraction.

- Have students write each contraction and read it aloud.

Apply

- Distribute copies of Practice Page 1.23C, which contains the decodable story *A Great Time at Gram's*. Tell students that many words in this story are contractions with *'ve* and *'re*. Point out that students have learned the following high-frequency words, which they will also read in the story: *done, great, laugh, paper*.

- Read aloud the first four sentences of the story as students follow along. Point out that you do not misread, add, or skip words when you read. Lead students in reading the same sentences with fluency and accuracy.

- Have students read the passage silently and then aloud. Remind them to track the words from left to right. When they come to the end of a line, they should sweep their hand down to the beginning of the next line and continue reading.

- When students have finished reading the text, choose a few sentences to review. You may want to focus on sentences that include words containing the target phonics skill. Have students read each sentence and explain in their own words what it means.

Fun with Words Optional activities for engaging, hands-on practice are provided in the Resources section.

Formative Assessment and Corrective Feedback

IF a student makes an error, THEN follow this model:

Correct the error.

Guide the student to perform the task correctly by modeling.

Check for understanding by having the student repeat the task.

Reinforce: Make a note to review the skill during the student's next session.

Objectives

- Recognize and read high-frequency words.

Materials

- High-Frequency Word Cards

Formative Assessment and Corrective Feedback

IF a student makes an error, THEN follow this model:

Correct the error.

Guide the student to say the word correctly.

Check for understanding by having the student reread the word from among other randomly displayed high-frequency words.

Reinforce: Make a note to review the word during the student's next session.

High-Frequency Words: *door, more, mother, old, try, use, want, wash*

Teach/Model

- Display the high-frequency words. Tell students that these are useful words to know since they will see these words often. Tell them that reading will be easier if they recognize these words.

- Display the High-Frequency Word Card for *door* and say the word. Then spell the word aloud as you point to each letter. Say the word again.

- Use the word in a simple sentence that will provide context. For example: *He opened the door and went outside.*

- Repeat the steps above with the remaining high-frequency words.

Guided Practice

Do the following for each high-frequency word:

- Display the High-Frequency Word Card. Read the word and have students repeat it.

- Note the familiar sound/spelling patterns that are shown on the back of the card. Note as well any unfamiliar and unexpected sound/spellings.

- Blend the word with students.

- Spell the word aloud, pointing to each letter.

- Have students then spell the word aloud as you point to each letter.

- Have students read the word again.

Apply

- Display the High-Frequency Word Cards in random order. Have students read the words.

- Have students write each word. Tell them to compare their writing with the word on the card and make corrections if necessary.

- Have students read each word aloud and use it in a sentence.

Phonological Awareness: Combine and Segment Syllables

Teach/Model

- **Say:** *Remember, words are made up of parts called syllables. Each word part, or syllable, has a vowel sound. Listen as I say this word:* backpack. *Now listen as I say the word in syllables:* back-pack. *The word has two vowel sounds, so it has two syllables. Now I'll put the syllables together to say the word:* backpack.

- Repeat with other two-syllable words, such as *sunshine, playground, football, bookcase,* and *sailboat.*

Guided Practice

- **Say:** *Let's do it together. Listen:* raincoat. *Say the word in syllables. Hold up one finger for each syllable you say:* rain-coat. *How many fingers did you hold up?* (2) *How many syllables does the word have?* (2) *What are the syllables?* (*rain* and *coat*) *Let's put the syllables together and say the word:* raincoat.

- Continue with the words shown below. Have students segment each word into syllables. Then have them combine the syllables to say the word.

Word	Syllables
summer	sum-mer
summertime	sum-mer-time
basket	bas-ket
basketball	bas-ket-ball
window	win-dow
windowsill	win-dow-sill

Apply

Have students practice segmenting syllables. **Say:**

- *What are the syllables in* homework? (home-work)
- *What are the syllables in* earthquake? (earth-quake)
- *What are the syllables in* carpet? (car-pet)
- *What are the syllables in* winter? (win-ter)
- *What are the syllables in* sandpaper? (sand-pa-per)

Have students practice combining syllables. **Say:**

- *Put these syllables together:* back-yard. *What is the word?* (backyard)
- *Put these syllables together:* rain-bow. *What is the word?* (rainbow)
- *Put these syllables together:* nap-kin. *What is the word?* (napkin)
- *Put these syllables together:* cac-tus. *What is the word?* (cactus)
- *Put these syllables together:* su-per-mar-ket. *What is the word?* (supermarket)

Objectives

- Combine and segment syllables in spoken words.

English Language Support

It's important for English learners to understand the meaning of the words they are using for skills practice. Use visuals, gestures, and context sentences to support student understanding.

Formative Assessment and Corrective Feedback

IF a student makes an error, THEN follow this model:

Correct the error.

Guide the student to perform the task correctly by modeling.

Check for understanding by having the student repeat the task.

Reinforce: Make a note to review the skill during the student's next session.

Phonics: Compound Words

Objectives

- Blend and segment syllables in spoken words.
- Blend, build, and decode compound words.
- Read on-level text with fluency and accuracy.

Materials

- Instructional Routine: Sound-by-Sound Blending
- Letter Cards
- Practice Page 1.24C

Phonemic Awareness Warm-up

- **Say:** *I'm going to say a word that is made up of two smaller words. Listen:* sandbox. *Now I'll take the word* sand *away from the word* sandbox. *What word is left?* (box) *Let's try another one. Listen:* beehive. *Let's take* hive *away from* beehive. *What word is left?* (bee) *Now you listen and name the leftover word:* lighthouse, light (house); snowflake, flake (snow); boxcar, car (box); waterfall, water (fall); bluebird, bird (blue); cupcake, cake (cup).

Teach/Model

- **Say:** *Sometimes two words put together can make a new, longer word called a compound word.*
- Write the words *rain* and *coat*. Read the words. Model making a compound word. **Say:** *If I put the words* rain *and* coat *together, I make the word* raincoat: rain, coat, raincoat. *Write the word* raincoat. *Explain its meaning.*
- **Say:** *I hear two vowel sounds in* raincoat. Rain *has the long a sound, and* coat *has the long o sound.* Raincoat *has two vowel sounds, so it has two syllables. Clap the syllables with me.*
- Continue with these compound words, having students repeat each smaller word and compound word after you: *seashell, backbone, mailbox, rowboat, daydream*. Then have students identify the vowel sounds in each compound word and tell how many syllables they hear. Clap the syllables together.

Guided Practice

BLENDING Display the words in Rows 1 and 2 below. Using Instructional Routine: Sound-by-Sound Blending, work with students to blend each word.

1. inside	sailboat	cupcake	sunshine
2. snowflake	beehive	we're	you've

DECODING Display the sentences below. Guide students to blend one or more words and to read the sentences.

- Mother put a cupcake in my lunchbox.
- Try the peanuts at that roadside stand.
- Do you want more homemade pancakes?

BUILDING AND WRITING WORDS Model using Letter Cards to build the word *snowflake*.
Say: *First I spell* snow. *The letter* s *stands for /s/. The letter* n *stands for /n/. The letters* ow *stand for /ō/. Then I spell* flake. *The letter* f *stands for the /f/ sound. The a_e pattern stands for /ā/, and the letter* k *stands for /k/.*

- Guide students to identify sounds and spell the smaller words in these compound words: *rowboat, roadway, rainbow, doghouse, seaweed*.
- Have students write each compound word and read it aloud.

Apply

- Distribute copies of Practice Page 1.24C, which contains the decodable story *Run, Flapjack!* Tell students that many words in this story are compound words. Point out that students have learned the following high-frequency words, which they will also read in the story: *door, old, try.*

- Read aloud the first three sentences of the story as students follow along. Point out that you do not misread, add, or skip words when you read. Lead students in reading the same sentences with fluency and accuracy.

- Have students read the passage silently and then aloud. Remind them to track the words from left to right. When they come to the end of a line, they should sweep their hand down to the beginning of the next line and continue reading.

- When students have finished reading the text, choose a few sentences to review. You may want to focus on sentences that include words containing the target phonics skill. Have students read each sentence and explain in their own words what it means.

> **Fun with Words** Optional activities for engaging, hands-on practice are provided in the Resources section.

Formative Assessment and Corrective Feedback

IF a student makes an error, THEN follow this model:

Correct the error.

Guide the student to perform the task correctly by modeling.

Check for understanding by having the student repeat the task.

Reinforce: Make a note to review the skill during the student's next session.

Phonics: Short Vowel *ea*

Phonemic Awareness Warm-up

- **Say:** *I'll say a word and you say the vowel sound you hear in the word. Listen:* bread. *Do you hear the vowel sound? The vowel sound is /ĕ/. Now let's listen for /ĕ/ in a word with more than one syllable:* heavy. *How many syllables do you hear?* (2) *What vowel sound do you hear in the first syllable?* (/ĕ/) *Now listen to some more words. Count the number of syllables in each word. Say which syllable has the /ĕ/ sound:* breakfast, ready, instead, feather, healthy.

Teach/Model

- Display the Letter Cards *h, ea, d.* Read the word and say the middle vowel sound /ĕ/. Have students repeat after you. **Say:** *Listen:* head, /ĕ/. *Now you say it.*

- Repeat *head* and give the spelling. **Say:** *The word* head *has the vowel sound /ĕ/. Say the word with me and listen for the sound in the middle of the word. The letters* ea *stand for the sound /ĕ/ in the middle of the word* head.

- Write the word *head.* Say the word and have students repeat it after you. **Say:** *This is the word* head. *The letters* ea *stand for the /ĕ/ sound in* head. *Read the word with me:* head.

Guided Practice

BLENDING Display the words in Rows 1 and 2 below. Using Instructional Routine: Sound-by-Sound Blending, work with students to blend each word.

1. bread	head	dead	spread	thread
2. throw	meant	throat	health	sailboat

DECODING Display the sentences below. Guide students to blend one or more words and to read the sentences.

- Spread more jam on your bread.
- Will Mother wash the heavy plate instead?
- We read about an old man who hid his wealth.

BUILDING AND WRITING WORDS Model how to build the word *spread* with Letter Cards. **Say:** *The letters* s, p, *and* r *stand for the sounds /s/ /p/ /r/ at the beginning. The next sound is /ĕ/. I know that* ea *stands for /ĕ/ in* spread. *The last sound is /d/. The letter* d *stands for the sound.*

- Guide students to identify sounds in the following words and build them with Letter Cards: *head, bread, health, read, thread, wealth.*

- Have students write each word and read it aloud.

Objectives

- Learn the sound-spelling correspondence for /ĕ/ spelled *ea.*
- Segment syllables in spoken words with /ĕ/ spelled *ea.*
- Blend, build, and decode regularly spelled one-syllable words with /ĕ/ spelled *ea.*
- Read on-level text with fluency and accuracy.

Materials

- Instructional Routine: Sound-by-Sound Blending
- Letter Cards
- Practice Page 1.24D

Apply

- Distribute copies of Practice Page 1.24D, which contains the decodable story *The* Fishtail. Tell students that several words in this story have the letters *ea*, which can stand for the short *e* sound. Point out that students have learned the following high-frequency words, which they will also read in the story: *more, mother, old, want.*

- Read aloud the first three sentences of the story as students follow along. Point out that you do not misread, add, or skip words when you read. Lead students in reading the same sentences with fluency and accuracy.

- Have students read the passage silently and then aloud. Remind them to track the words from left to right. When they come to the end of a line, they should sweep their hand down to the beginning of the next line and continue reading.

- When students have finished reading the text, choose a few sentences to review. You may want to focus on sentences that include words containing the target phonics skill. Have students read each sentence and explain in their own words what it means.

> **Fun with Words** Optional activities for engaging, hands-on practice are provided in the Resources section.

English Language Support

Linguistic Transfer Some English learners, including speakers of Spanish, Korean, Vietnamese, and Tagalog, may need extra practice with the /ĕ/ sound. Have students listen carefully as you say words with the /ĕ/ sound: *bread, head, health, read, spread, thread, wealth.* Have students repeat each word, vocalize the middle sound, and say the whole word again. Use each word in a brief sentence to reinforce meaning.

Formative Assessment and Corrective Feedback

IF a student makes an error, THEN follow this model:

Correct the error.

Guide the student to perform the task correctly by modeling.

Check for understanding by having the student repeat the task.

Reinforce: Make a note to review the skill during the student's next session.

Objectives

- Decode words with patterns and digraphs for long vowels *a, e, o, u;* short vowel *ea;* and final *nk, ng;* contractions; and compound words.
- Recognize and read high-frequency words.
- Read on-level text with purpose and understanding.
- Read on-level text orally with accuracy, appropriate rate, and expression on successive readings.
- Use context to confirm or self-correct word recognition and understanding, rereading as necessary.

Materials

- High-Frequency Word Cards
- Instructional Routine: High-Frequency Words
- Practice Page 1.25

Cumulative Review/Fluency

Teach/Model

REVIEW

- Remind students they have learned long vowel sounds spelled CV, CVC*e, ai, ay, ee, ea, oa,* and *ow;* the short *e* sound spelled *ea;* and sounds for *nk* and *ng.* Display the vowel pairs and final consonants and review the sound for each.
- Remind students they have learned sounds for *'ll, 'd, 're,* and *'ve* in contractions and identified the sounds in the words that make up compounds. Display the endings and review the sound for each.
- Display these sentences:

    Will the stream carry the rowboat right to the sea?

    Eve wrote a cute song to mail to her mother.

    We've read about the free play in the paper.

- Point to the high-frequency words *carry, right, mother, about,* and *paper* and read each one. Remind students that they know these words. Use the High-Frequency Word Cards and Instructional Routine: High-Frequency Words to review these words.

MODEL FLUENCY

- Explain that good readers don't skip hard parts. They take their time, go back, and correct themselves. That way, they understand the words they are reading and what the words mean.
- Read the sentences, pointing to each word as you read it slowly. Read the following sentence with an error: **Say:** *Eve wrote a cute son to mail to her mother.* Point to the word *song.* **Say:** *I read this word as* son, *but that doesn't make sense. I'm going to try again: /s/ /ŏ/ /ng/,* song. *The letters* ng *stand for the /ng/ sound, not the /n/ sound. I also looked for clues in the text. Eve couldn't write a* son, *but she could write a* song. *Now it makes sense.*
- Reread the sentences with no mistakes. Model reading with expression and at a natural rate. Point out that you read aloud in a natural way: not too slowly and not too quickly. Note that your voice rose up at the end of the question.

Guided Practice

- Tell students they will practice reading. Display the following sentences:

    They think she'll wait to talk to Pete first.

    Show me the way to go around the sea.

    I've read that huge old toads sleep under those grapevines!

- Guide students in reading the sentences aloud. Coach them to sound out each word. Have students go back to any word they read incorrectly. Remind them that sometimes letters can be pronounced in more than one way, and have them sound out the word again. Guide students to look for context clues in surrounding text to help them figure out the word.
- Guide students to read the text again. Coach them to read at a natural rate and to use expression when reading questions or exclamations.

- Have students read aloud the practice text on Practice Page 1.25.

- Explain that the main purpose of reading the text is to practice their reading skills.

- Coach students to use decoding skills and context to self-correct any mistakes they make during reading. They should read the text several times until they are able to read smoothly and accurately with expression and at a natural rate.

- When students have finished the fluency practice, choose a few sentences to review. Have students read each sentence and explain in their own words what it means.

- After students are able to read the text fluently, guide them to track their progress on their My Progress line graphs.

Formative Assessment and Corrective Feedback

IF a student makes an error, THEN follow this model:

Correct the error.

Guide the student to say the word correctly.

Check for understanding by having the student reread the word.

Reinforce: Make a note to review the word during the student's next session.

Objectives

- Recognize and read high-frequency words.

Materials

- High-Frequency Word Cards

Formative Assessment and Corrective Feedback

IF a student makes an error, THEN follow this model:

Correct the error.

Guide the student to say the word correctly.

Check for understanding by having the student reread the word from among other randomly displayed high-frequency words.

Reinforce: Make a note to review the word during the student's next session.

High-Frequency Words:
few, loudly, night, noise, shall, story, window, world

Teach/Model

- Display the high-frequency words. Tell students that these are useful words to know since they will see these words often. Tell them that reading will be easier if they recognize these words.
- Display the High-Frequency Word Card for *few* and say the word. Then spell the word aloud as you point to each letter. Say the word again.
- Use the word in a simple sentence that will provide context. For example: *Few people go to the beach when it rains.*
- Repeat the steps above with the remaining high-frequency words.

Guided Practice

Do the following for each high-frequency word:

- Display the High-Frequency Word Card. Read the word and have students repeat it.
- Note the familiar sound/spelling patterns that are shown on the back of the card. Note as well any unfamiliar and unexpected sound/spellings.
- Blend the word with students.
- Spell the word aloud, pointing to each letter.
- Have students then spell the word aloud as you point to each letter.
- Have students read the word again.

Apply

- Display the High-Frequency Word Cards in random order. Have students read the words.
- Have students write each word. Tell them to compare their writing with the word on the card and make corrections if necessary.
- Have students read each word aloud and use it in a sentence.

Phonemic Awareness: Substitute Vowel Sounds

Teach/Model

- **Say:** *Today we're going to change the vowel sound in a word to make a new word. The vowel sound in the word* bag *is /ă/.* Say the word bag, emphasizing the /ă/ sound. **Say:** *Listen:* bag, /ă/.

- **Say:** *Now I'll change the /ă/ sound in* bag *to /ŭ/. Listen: /b//ŭ//g/,* bug. *Say it with me:* bug. *I changed the vowel sound /ă/ in* bag *to /ŭ/ and made the word* bug.

- **Say:** *Now I'll change the /ĭ/ sound in* hid *to /är/. Listen: /h/ /är/ /d/,* hard. *Say it with me:* hard. *I changed the vowel sound /ĭ/ in* hid *to /är/ and made the word* hard. *Let's keep going.*

Guided Practice

- **Say:** *We're going to change the vowel sounds in words to make new words. What is the vowel sound in* pat? *(/ă/) Good. Now let's change the vowel sound in* pat *to /är/. What is the word? (part) Good! Now let's change the vowel sound in* part *to /ôr/. What is the word? (port) Let's try some more.*

- Continue with the words shown below.

Change the . . .	Result
/ă/ in *cat* to /är/	cart
/ŏ/ in *cod* to /ôr/	cord
/ă/ in *mat* to /är/	mart
/ŏ/ in *pot* to /ôr/	port
/ă/ in *ban* to /är/	barn
/ŏ/ in *spot* to /ôr/	sport
/ă/ in *ham* to /är/	harm
/ŏ/ in *stock* to /ôr/	stork

Apply

Have students practice substituting vowel sounds, using the words below. **Say:**

- *Change the /ă/ in* mash *to /är/. What is the word?* (marsh)
- *Change the /ī/ in* fight *to /ôr/. What is the word?* (fort)
- *Change the /är/ in* farm *to /ā/. What is the word?* (fame)
- *Change the /ā/ in* fame *to /ôr/. What is the word?* (form)
- *Change the /ă/ in* back *to /är/. What is the word?* (bark)
- *Change the /ôr/ in* cord *to /ō/. What is the word?* (code)
- *Change the vowel sound in* chart *to /ă/. What is the word?* (chat)
- *Change the vowel sound in* fake *to /ôr/. What is the word?* (fork)
- *Change the vowel sound in* hope *to /är/. What is the word?* (harp)
- *Change the vowel sound in* court *to /ī/. What is the word?* (kite)

Objectives

- Isolate and substitute the medial vowel sounds in spoken single-syllable words.

English Language Support

It's important for English learners to understand the meaning of the words they are using for skills practice. Use visuals, gestures, and context sentences to support student understanding.

Formative Assessment and Corrective Feedback

IF a student makes an error, THEN follow this model:

Correct the error.

Guide the student to perform the task correctly by modeling.

Check for understanding by having the student repeat the task.

Reinforce: Make a note to review the skill during the student's next session.

Phonics: Words with *r*-Controlled Vowel *a (ar)*

Objectives

- Learn the sound-spelling correspondence for /är/*ar*.
- Substitute medial sounds in spoken words.
- Blend, build, and decode regularly spelled one-syllable words with /är/*ar*.
- Read on-level text with fluency and accuracy.

Materials

- Sound/Spelling Cards
- Instructional Routine: Sound-by-Sound Blending
- Letter Cards
- Practice Page 1.26C

Phonemic Awareness Warm-up

- **Say:** *Listen to hear what makes one word different from a second word. Listen:* pat, part. *Say the sounds in the words with me: /p/ /ă/ /t/, /p/ /är/ /t/. The /ă/ was changed to /är/:* pat, part. *Now let's change the middle sound in* cat, /ă/, *to* /är/. *Blend these sounds: /k/ /är/ /t/. What is the new word?* (cart)
- **Say:** *Let's do some more. Change the /ī/ sound in* bike *to /är/* (bark), */ă/ in* pack *to /är/* (park), */ĭ/ in* bin *to /är/* (barn), *and /ŭ/ in* hum *to /är/* (harm).
- Guide students to blend two-syllable words with /är/. **Say:** *Say the sounds after me and then blend them to say the word: /s/ /p/ /är/ /k/ /əl/* (sparkle); */b/ /är/ /n/ /y/ /är/ /d/* (barnyard); */är/ /t/ /ĭ/ /s/ /t/* (artist).

Teach/Model

- Display the Sound/Spelling Card for *artist*. Name the picture and say the beginning sound. Have students repeat after you. **Say:** *Listen:* artist, /är/. *Now you say it.*
- Say the sound and give the spelling. **Say:** *Artist begins with the /är/ sound. The letters* ar *stand for the /är/ sound at the beginning, middle, or end of a word.*
- Write and read *farm*. **Say:** *This is the word* farm. *The letter* f *stands for the beginning sound /f/ in* farm. *The letters* ar *stand for the /är/ sound in* farm. *The letter* m *stands for the end sound /m/ in* farm. *Read the word with me: /f/ /är/, /fär/ /m/, /färm/,* farm. *Repeat with the words* barn *and* card.

Guided Practice

BLENDING Display the words in Rows 1 and 2 below. Using Instructional Routine: Sound-by-Sound Blending, work with students to blend each word.

1. car	bark	harp	march	hard
2. backyard	far	bread	starts	lunchtime

DECODING Display the sentences below. Call on individuals to blend one or more words and to read the sentences.

- We shall see a barn at the farm.
- Do the dogs in the yard bark at night?
- The band played loudly in the park.

BUILDING AND WRITING WORDS Model how to spell the word *far*. **Say:** *The letter* f *stands for the first sound. The next sound is /är/. The letters* ar *stand for /är/.* Repeat for the word *star*. Point out that *far* and *star* belong to the same word family because they end with the same letters (-*ar*) and sound (/är/).

- Guide students to identify sounds in other words in the -*ar* word family and build them with Letter Cards: *car, jar, bar, tar, scar.*
- Have students write each word and read it aloud.

Apply

- Distribute copies of Practice Page 1.26C, which contains the decodable story *Clark Shark*. Tell students that many words in this story have the letters *ar,* which stand for the /är/ sound. Point out that students have learned the following high-frequency words, which they will also read in the story: *few, loudly, shall.*

- Read aloud the first three sentences of the story as students follow along. Point out that you do not misread, add, or skip words when you read. Lead students in reading the same sentences with fluency and accuracy.

- Have students read the passage silently and then aloud. Remind them to track the words from left to right. When they come to the end of a line, they should sweep their hand down to the beginning of the next line and continue reading.

- When students have finished reading the text, choose a few sentences to review. You may want to focus on sentences that include words containing the target phonics element. Have students read each sentence and explain in their own words what it means.

Fun with Words Optional activities for engaging, hands-on practice are provided in the Resources section.

Formative Assessment and Corrective Feedback

IF a student makes an error, THEN follow this model:

Correct the error.

Guide the student to perform the task correctly by modeling.

Check for understanding by having the student repeat the task.

Reinforce: Make a note to review the skill during the student's next session.

Phonics: Words with *r*-Controlled Vowel *o* (*or, ore*)

Objectives

- Learn the sound-spelling correspondence for /ôr/*or, ore*.
- Substitute medial vowels sounds in spoken words.
- Blend, build, and decode regularly spelled one-syllable words with /ôr/ *or, ore*.
- Read on-level text with fluency and accuracy.

Materials

- Sound/Spelling Cards
- Instructional Routine: Sound-by-Sound Blending
- Letter Cards
- Practice Page 1.26D

Phonemic Awareness Warm-up

- **Say:** *Listen as I say two words. Try to hear what is different about the words. Listen: sat, sort. Say the words with me. Can you hear that the vowel sounds in the middle are different? Listen: /s/ /ă/ /t/, /s/ /ôr/ /t/.*
- **Say:** *Let's do one together. Change the /ă/ sound in* can *to /ôr/. Blend the sounds: /k/ /ôr/ /n/. What is the new word?* (corn) *Now let's do some more. Change the /ē/ in* feet *to /ôr/* (fort), *the /ă/ in* tan *to /ôr/* (torn), *and the /ĕ/ in* hen *to /ôr/* (horn).
- Guide students to blend two-syllable words with /ôr/. **Say:** *Say the sounds after me and then blend them to say the word: /ôr/ /b/ /ĭ/ /t/* (orbit); */m/ /ôr/ /n/ /ĭ/ /ng/* (morning); */s/ /t/ /ôr/ /m/ /ē/* (stormy).

Teach/Model

- Display the Sound/Spelling Card for *orange*. Name the picture and say the sound /ôr/.
- Repeat *orange* and give the spelling. **Say:** Orange *begins with the /ôr/ sound. Say the word with me and listen for the beginning sound. The letters* or *stand for /ôr/ at the beginning of the word* orange.
- Write the word *storm*. Say the word and have students repeat it after you. **Say:** *The letters* or *stand for the /ôr/ sound in the middle of* storm. *Read it with me:* storm.
- Point out the *ore* spelling on the card. Write and read the words *shore* and *more*. Have students repeat the words. Point to the letters on the card and have students say the sound /ôr/ to connect it to the *ore* spelling.
- Write and read *core*. Say the word and have students repeat it after you. **Say:** *The letters* ore *stand for the /ôr/ sound in the end of* core. *Read it with me:* core.

Guided Practice

BLENDING Display the words in Rows 1 and 2 below. Using Instructional Routine: Sound-by-Sound Blending, work with students to blend each word.

1. fork	shore	store	sore	force
2. born	hard	or	head	thorn

DECODING Display the sentences below. Call on individuals to blend one or more words and to read the sentences.

- A horse came to the window and snorted.
- The story was about a stork with a horn.
- Shall I get more corn at the store?

BUILDING AND WRITING WORDS Model how to spell the word *more*. **Say:** *The letter* m *stands for the first sound. The next sound is /ôr/. I know the letters* ore *stand for /ôr/. Repeat for the word* store. Point out that *more* and *store* belong to the same word family because they end with the same letters (-*ore*) and sound (/ôr/).

- Guide students to identify sounds in other words in the -*ore* word family and build them with Letter Cards: *core, tore, sore, wore, score, shore, snore.*
- Have students write each word and read it aloud.

Apply

- Distribute copies of Practice Page 1.26D, which contains the decodable story *A Home on the Shore*. Tell students that many words in this story have the letters *or* or *ore,* which stand for the /ôr/ sound. Point out that students have learned the following high-frequency words, which they will also read in the story: *few, story, window, world.*

- Read aloud the first two sentences of the story as students follow along. Point out that you do not misread, add, or skip words when you read. Lead students in reading the same sentences with fluency and accuracy.

- Have students read the passage silently and then aloud. Remind them to track the words from left to right. When they come to the end of a line, they should sweep their hand down to the beginning of the next line and continue reading.

- When students have finished reading the text, choose a few sentences to review. You may want to focus on sentences that include words containing the target phonics element. Have students read each sentence and explain in their own words what it means.

> **Fun with Words** Optional activities for engaging, hands-on practice are provided in the Resources section.

English Language Support

Linguistic Transfer Speakers of Spanish and most Asian languages may have difficulty with the way vowels change in English when they are followed by an *r.* Explain that in English, vowels can sound a little different before the /r/ sound. Read aloud words such as *car, star, arm, barn, for, corn, more,* and *store,* and have students chorally repeat each word, say just the vowel sound, and then say the whole word again. Use each word in a sentence to reinforce meaning.

Formative Assessment and Corrective Feedback

IF a student makes an error, THEN follow this model:

Correct the error.

Guide the student to perform the task correctly by modeling.

Check for understanding by having the student repeat the task.

Reinforce: Make a note to review the skill during the student's next session.

Objectives

- Recognize and read high-frequency words.

Materials

- High-Frequency Word Cards

Formative Assessment and Corrective Feedback

IF a student makes an error, THEN follow this model:

Correct the error.

Guide the student to say the word correctly.

Check for understanding by having the student reread the word from among other randomly displayed high-frequency words.

Reinforce: Make a note to review the word during the student's next session.

High-Frequency Words:
baby, begins, eight, follow, learning, until, years, young

Teach/Model

- Display the high-frequency words. Tell students that these are useful words to know since they will see these words often. Tell them that reading will be easier if they recognize these words.
- Display the High-Frequency Word Card for *baby* and say the word. Then spell the word aloud as you point to each letter. Say the word again.
- Use the word in a simple sentence that will provide context. For example: *The baby is learning to walk.*
- Repeat the steps above with the remaining high-frequency words.

Guided Practice

Do the following for each high-frequency word:

- Display the High-Frequency Word Card. Read the word and have students repeat it.
- Note the familiar sound/spelling patterns that are shown on the back of the card. Note as well any unfamiliar and unexpected sound/spellings.
- Blend the word with students.
- Spell the word aloud, pointing to each letter.
- Have students then spell the word aloud as you point to each letter.
- Have students read the word again.

Apply

- Display the High-Frequency Word Cards in random order. Have students read the words.
- Have students write each word. Tell them to compare their writing with the word on the card and make corrections if necessary.
- Have students read each word aloud and use it in a sentence.

Phonemic Awareness: Review: Substitute Vowel Sounds

Teach/Model

- **Say:** *Today we're going to change the vowel sound in a word to make a new word. For example, the vowel sound in the word* hat *is /ă/.* Say the word *hat, emphasizing the /ă/ sound.* **Say:** *Listen:* hat, /ă/.

- **Say:** *Now I'll change the /ă/ sound in* hat *to /ûr/. Listen: /h/ /ûr/ / /t/, hurt. Say it with me:* hurt. *I changed the vowel sound /ă/ in* hat *to /ûr/ and made the word* hurt. *Let's keep going.*

Guided Practice

- **Say:** *We're going to change the vowel sounds in words to make new words. For example, what is the vowel sound in* barn? *(/är/) Good. Now let's change the vowel sound in* barn *to /ôr/. What is the word?* (born) *Good! Now let's change the vowel sound in* born *to /ûr/. What is the word?* (burn) *Let's try some more.*

- Continue with the words shown below.

Change the . . .	Result
/ă/ in *fan* to /ûr/	fern
/ă/ in *fast* to /ûr/	first
/ĭ/ in *slip* to /ûr/	slurp
/ôr/ in *form* to /ûr/	firm
/ûr/ in *firm* to /är/	farm
/ûr/ in *stir* to /ôr/	store
/ôr/ in *store* to /är/	star

Apply

Have students practice substituting vowel sounds, using the words below. **Say:**
- *Change the /ă/ in* bath *to /ûr/. What is the word?* (birth)
- *Change the /ûr/ in* fern *to /ī/. What is the word?* (fine)
- *Change the /ĕ/ in* bed *to /ûr/. What is the word?* (bird)
- *Change the /ûr/ in* hurt *to /ē/. What is the word?* (heat)
- *Change the /ā/ in* save *to /ûr/. What is the word?* (serve)
- *Change the /ûr/ in* curve *to /ā/. What is the word?* (cave)
- *Change the vowel sound in* tune *to /ûr/. What is the word?* (turn)
- *Change the vowel sound in* stone *to /ûr/. What is the word?* (stern)
- *Change the vowel sound in* dart *to /ûr/. What is the word?* (dirt)
- *Change the vowel sound in* porch *to /ûr/. What is the word?* (perch)

Objectives

- Isolate, pronounce, and substitute vowel sounds in spoken words.

Formative Assessment and Corrective Feedback

IF a student makes an error, THEN follow this model:

Correct the error.

Guide the student to perform the task correctly by modeling.

Check for understanding by having the student repeat the task.

Reinforce: Make a note to review the skill during the student's next session.

Phonics: Words with *r*-Controlled Vowels *e, i, u (er, ir, ur)*

Objectives

- Learn the sound-spelling correspondence for /ûr/er, ir, ur.
- Blend and segment syllables in spoken words.
- Blend, build, and decode regularly spelled one-syllable words with /ûr/er, ir, ur.
- Read on-level text with fluency and accuracy.

Materials

- Sound/Spelling Cards
- Instructional Routine: Sound-by-Sound Blending
- Letter Cards
- Practice Page 1.27C

Phonological Awareness Warm-up

- **Say:** *Listen as I say a word. Then I will break the word into word parts, or syllables. Each syllable has its own vowel sound. I will clap as I say each syllable. Listen:* uphill; up (clap), hill (clap). *Uphill has two syllables, and each syllable has its own vowel sound. Now let's do some more. I'll say a word. Then clap the syllables with me and tell how many syllables you hear:* bird (1), park (1), shortcut (2), barnyard (2), snowflake (2), perch (1), chirping (2), surprised (2).

- Guide students to blend sounds to say two-syllable words. **Say:** *Each word will have two syllables. Say the sounds after me and then blend them to say the word:* /t/ /ûr/ /n/ /ĭ/ /p/ (turnip); /s/ /t/ /ûr/ /ĭ/ /ng/ (stirring); /f/ /l/ /ûr/ /ē/ (flurry).

Teach/Model

- Display the Sound/Spelling Card for *bird*. Name the picture and say the sound /ûr/. Have students repeat after you. **Say:** *Listen:* bird, */ûr/. Now you say it.*

- Say the sound and give the spelling. **Say:** Bird *has the /ûr/ sound in the middle. The letters* ir *together stand for the /ûr/ sound.*

- Write and read *shirt*. **Say:** *This is the word* shirt. *The letters* sh *stand for the /sh/ sound. The letters* ir *stand for the /ûr/ sound. The letter* t *stands for the /t/ sound. Read the word with me:* /sh/ /ûr/ /t/, shirt.

- Point out the *er* and *ur* spellings on the card. Say the words *fern* and *burn* as examples and have students repeat the words.

- Write and read *her*. Point to the *er* spelling of /ûr/. **Say:** *This is the word* her. *The letters* er *stand for the /ûr/ sound in* her. *Read it with me:* her. *Repeat with the word* turn.

Guided Practice

BLENDING Display the words in Rows 1 and 2 below. Using Instructional Routine: Sound-by-Sound Blending, work with students to blend each word.

| 1. herd | skirt | turn | perch | girl |
| 2. curl | shore | clerk | shark | thirst |

DECODING Display the sentences below. Call on individuals to blend one or more words and to read the sentences.

- Meg is a young girl with many curls.
- Did the baby fall and hurt her arm?
- The bird perched in the fir until sunset.

BUILDING AND WRITING WORDS Model how to build the word *perch* with Letter Cards. **Say:** *The letter* p *stands for the first sound, /p/. The next sound is /ûr/. I know that* er *can stand for /ûr/. The last sound I hear is /ch/. The letters* ch *stand for /ch/.*

- Guide students to identify sounds in the following words and build them with Letter Cards: *dirt, her, shirt, first, turn, clerk, curl.*
- Have students write each word and read it aloud.

Apply

- Distribute copies of Practice Page 1.27C, which contains the decodable story *What Can Birds Do?* Tell students that many words in this story have the letters *er, ir,* or *ur,* which can stand for the /ûr/ sound. Point out that students have learned the following high-frequency words, which they will also read in the story: *baby, begins, young.*

- Read aloud the first three sentences of the story as students follow along. Point out that you do not misread, add, or skip words when you read. Lead students in reading the same sentences with fluency and accuracy.

- Have students read the passage silently and then aloud. Remind them to track the words from left to right. When they come to the end of a line, they should sweep their hand down to the beginning of the next line and continue reading.

- When students have finished reading the text, choose a few sentences to review. You may want to focus on sentences that include words containing the target phonics element. Have students read each sentence and explain in their own words what it means.

Fun with Words Optional activities for engaging, hands-on practice are provided in the Resources section.

English Language Support

Linguistic Transfer Speakers of Spanish and most Asian languages may have difficulty with the way vowels change in English when they are followed by an *r*. Explain that in English, vowels can sound a little different before the /r/ sound. Read aloud words such as *fern, her, perch, bird, dirt, stir, fur, burn,* and *hurt,* and have students chorally repeat each word, say just the vowel sound, and then say the whole word again. Use each word in a sentence to reinforce meaning.

Formative Assessment and Corrective Feedback

IF a student makes an error, THEN follow this model:

Correct the error.

Guide the student to perform the task correctly by modeling.

Check for understanding by having the student repeat the task.

Reinforce: Make a note to review the skill during the student's next session.

Objectives

- Recognize and read high-frequency words.

Materials

- High-Frequency Word Cards

Formative Assessment and Corrective Feedback

IF a student makes an error, THEN follow this model:

Correct the error.

Guide the student to say the word correctly.

Check for understanding by having the student reread the word from among other randomly displayed high-frequency words.

Reinforce: Make a note to review the word during the student's next session.

High-Frequency Words:
again, along, began, boy, father, house, nothing, together

Teach/Model

- Display the high-frequency words. Tell students that these are useful words to know since they will see these words often. Tell them that reading will be easier if they recognize these words.
- Display the High-Frequency Word Card for *again* and say the word. Then spell the word aloud as you point to each letter. Say the word again.
- Use the word in a simple sentence that will provide context. For example: *She called my name, and then she called it again.*
- Repeat the steps above with the remaining high-frequency words.

Guided Practice

Do the following for each high-frequency word:

- Display the High-Frequency Word Card. Read the word and have students repeat it.
- Note the familiar sound/spelling patterns that are shown on the back of the card. Note as well any unfamiliar and unexpected sound/spellings.
- Blend the word with students.
- Spell the word aloud, pointing to each letter.
- Have students then spell the word aloud as you point to each letter.
- Have students read the word again.

Apply

- Display the High-Frequency Word Cards in random order. Have students read the words.
- Have students write each word. Tell them to compare their writing with the word on the card and make corrections if necessary.
- Have students read each word aloud and use it in a sentence.

Phonics: Vowel Digraph *oo*

Objectives

- Learn the sound-spelling correspondence for /o͞o/oo.
- Segment spoken words into syllables and determine the number of syllables in each word.
- Blend, build, and decode regularly spelled one-syllable words with /o͞o/oo.
- Read on-level text with fluency and accuracy.

Materials

- Sound/Spelling Cards
- Instructional Routine: Sound-by-Sound Blending
- Letter Cards
- Practice Page 1.28B

Phonological Awareness Warm-up

- Guide students to listen for syllables and clap to count them. **Say:** *Let's practice breaking words into syllables. Remember that each syllable has its own vowel sound. I will clap as I say each syllable. Listen:* butter *(2 claps),* book *(1 clap).* Butter *has two syllables;* book *has one syllable. Now let's do it together. Clap each time you hear a syllable. Listen:* look *(1 clap),* yellow *(2 claps). How many syllables does* look *have? (1) How many syllables does* yellow *have? (2) Now you do some. Listen:* sport *(1 clap),* cookbook *(2 claps),* bookstore *(2 claps).*

Teach/Model

- Display the Sound/Spelling Card for *cook*. Name the picture and say the vowel sound. Have students repeat after you. **Say:** *Listen:* cook, /o͞o/. *Now you say it.*
- Say the sound and give the spelling. **Say:** Cook *has the /o͞o/ sound in the middle. The letters* oo *together stand for the /o͞o/ sound. This sound is usually found in the middle of words.*
- Write and read *foot*. **Say:** *This is the word* foot. *The letter* f *stands for the /f/ sound at the beginning. The letters* oo *stand for the /o͞o/ sound in the middle. The letter* t *stands for the /t/ sound at the end. Read the word with me:* foot.
- Write and read these words: *hook, hood, stood*. Point out that the letters *oo* stand for the /o͞o/ sound in these words. Have students read the words with you.

Guided Practice

BLENDING Display the words in Rows 1 and 2 below. Using Instructional Routine: Sound-by-Sound Blending, work with students to blend each word.

1. hood	stood	shook	foot	look
2. term	took	bird	good	hurt

DECODING Display the sentences below. Call on individuals to blend one or more words and to read the sentences.

- Will the boy get a look at the book?
- My good coat with the hood is at the house.
- He got his foot wet in the brook again!

BUILDING AND WRITING WORDS Model how to build the word *shook* with Letter Cards. **Say:** *The letters* sh *stands for the first sound, /sh/. The next sound I hear is /o͞o/. I know that* oo *can stand for /o͞o/. The last sound is /k/. The letter* k *stands for /k/.*

- Guide students to identify sounds in the following words and build them with Letter Cards: *hood, stood, wood, foot, brook*.
- Have students write each word and read it aloud.

English Language Support

Linguistic Transfer Speakers of Spanish, Vietnamese, Cantonese or Mandarin, or Tagalog may have difficulty with the vowel sound in *book*. Explain that English has more vowel sounds than most languages and that it takes a long time to learn them all. Read aloud words such as *book, foot, good, wood, hook,* and *stood,* and have students chorally repeat each word after you, say just the middle sound, and then say the whole word again. Use each word in a sentence to reinforce meaning.

Formative Assessment and Corrective Feedback

IF a student makes an error, THEN follow this model:

Correct the error.

Guide the student to perform the task correctly by modeling.

Check for understanding by having the student repeat the task.

Reinforce: Make a note to review the skill during the student's next session.

- Distribute copies of Practice Page 1.28B, which contains the decodable story *Brook's Plants.* Tell students that many words in this story have the letters *oo,* which can stand for the /o͞o/ sound. Point out that students have learned the following high-frequency words, which they will also read in the story: *again, along, together.*

- Read aloud the first three sentences of the story as students follow along. Point out that you do not misread, add, or skip words when you read. Lead students in reading the same sentences with fluency and accuracy.

- Have students read the passage silently and then aloud. Remind them to track the words from left to right. When they come to the end of a line, they should sweep their hand down to the beginning of the next line and continue reading.

- When students have finished reading the text, choose a few sentences to review. You may want to focus on sentences that include words containing the target phonics element. Have students read each sentence and explain in their own words what it means.

> **Fun with Words** Optional activities for engaging, hands-on practice are provided in the Resources section.

Phonics: Syllable Pattern CVC

Phonological Awareness Warm-up

- **Say:** *Listen as I say and clap each syllable in this word:* window. *I hear the vowel sound /ĭ/ in the first syllable and the vowel sound /ō/ in the second syllable. There are two vowel sounds, so there are two syllables in* window. *Say and clap the syllables with me:* win-dow, window. *Now you clap the syllables, say the vowel sounds, and tell the number of syllables in these words:* sunset (sun-set, 2 claps; /ŭ/ /ĕ/; 2 syllables), insect (in-sect, 2 claps; /ĭ/ /ĕ/; 2 syllables).

Teach/Model

- Write the word *yellow* and read the word. Have students repeat the word with you and clap for each of the two syllables in the word. Tell them that if they see a longer word that they do not recognize right away, they can try to break it into syllables.

- Point to the two consonants together in the middle of *yellow*. **Say:** *Words are often divided into syllables between two consonants.* Draw a line between the two *l*s to show where the syllable break is.

- **Say:** *Remember each syllable must have a vowel sound. This can help them know how many syllables a word has.* Cover *low* and read the first syllable with students, *yel*. Point out that this syllable has the short *e* sound.

- Uncover *low* and cover *yel*. Remind students that they have learned that *ow* can stand for the long *o* sound. Have them read the syllable with you: *low*.

- Repeat the activity with these words: *pil/low, rab/bit, vel/vet*.

- To reinforce syllables, use Instructional Routine: Syllable Division VCCV Pattern to divide the word *napkin* into syllables.

Guided Practice

BLENDING Display the words in Rows 1 and 2 below. Using Instructional Routine: Sound-by-Sound Blending, work with students to blend each word.

1. fellow	bookshop	basket	sister	window
2. turn	hook	shirt	rabbit	insect

DECODING Display the sentences below. Call on individuals to blend one or more words and to read the sentences.

- Winter began with a big snowstorm.
- Summer is best for a picnic together.
- Did my father make batter for pancakes?

BUILDING AND WRITING WORDS Model how to build the word *picnic* with Letter Cards. **Say:** *I know this word has two syllables. The first syllable is* pic. *The letter* p *stands for /p/, the letter* i *stands for /ĭ/, and the letter* c *stands for /k/. The second syllable is* nic. *The letter* n *stands for /n/, the letter* i *stands for /ĭ/, and the letter* c *stands for /k/.*

- Guide students to identify sounds in the following words and build them with Letter Cards: *tennis, hollow, laptop, mascot, hiccup, cobweb*.

- Have students write each word and read it aloud.

Objectives

- Segment words into syllables and determine the number of syllables.
- Use knowledge that every syllable has a vowel sound to count syllables in words.
- Blend, build, and decode two-syllable words with the CVC pattern.
- Read on-level text with fluency and accuracy.

Materials

- Instructional Routine: Sound-by-Sound Blending
- Instructional Routine: Syllable Division VCCV Pattern
- Letter Cards
- Practice Page 1.28C

Formative Assessment and Corrective Feedback

IF a student makes an error, THEN follow this model:

Correct the error.

Guide the student to perform the task correctly by modeling.

Check for understanding by having the student repeat the task.

Reinforce: Make a note to review the skill during the student's next session.

Apply

- Distribute copies of Practice Page 1.28C, which contains the decodable story *Bandit's Big Problems*. Tell students that many words in this story have two syllables with the CVC pattern. Point out that students have learned the following high-frequency words, which they will also read in the story: *again, began, house, together.*

- Read aloud the first four sentences of the story as students follow along. Point out that you do not misread, add, or skip words when you read. Lead students in reading the same sentences with fluency and accuracy.

- Have students read the passage silently and then aloud. Remind them to track the words from left to right. When they come to the end of a line, they should sweep their hand down to the beginning of the next line and continue reading.

- When students have finished reading the text, choose a few sentences to review. You may want to focus on sentences that include words containing the target phonics element. Have students read each sentence and explain in their own words what it means.

Fun with Words Optional activities for engaging, hands-on practice are provided in the Resources section.

High-Frequency Words:
almost, country, covers, earth, kinds, ready, soil, warms

Teach/Model

- Display the high-frequency words. Tell students that these are useful words to know since they will see these words often. Tell them that reading will be easier if they recognize these words.
- Display the High-Frequency Word Card for *almost* and say the word. Then spell the word aloud as you point to each letter. Say the word again.
- Use the word in a simple sentence that will provide context. For example: *Grace almost forgot to take her lunch with her.*
- Repeat the steps above with the remaining high-frequency words.

Guided Practice

Do the following for each high-frequency word:

- Display the High-Frequency Word Card. Read the word and have students repeat it.
- Note the familiar sound/spelling patterns that are shown on the back of the card. Note as well any unfamiliar and unexpected sound/spellings.
- Blend the word with students.
- Spell the word aloud, pointing to each letter.
- Have students then spell the word aloud as you point to each letter.
- Have students read the word again.

Apply

- Display the High-Frequency Word Cards in random order. Have students read the words.
- Have students write each word. Tell them to compare their writing with the word on the card and make corrections if necessary.
- Have students read each word aloud and use it in a sentence.

Phonics: Vowel Digraphs/Spelling Patterns
oo, ou, ew, ue, u, u_e

Objectives

- Learn the sound-spelling correspondence for /o͞o/*oo, ou, ew, ue, u, u_e.*
- Segment spoken words into syllables.
- Blend, build, and decode regularly spelled one-syllable words with /o͞o/ *oo, ou, ew, ue, u, u_e.*
- Read on-level text with fluency and accuracy.

Materials

- Sound/Spelling Cards
- Instructional Routine: Sound-by-Sound Blending
- Letter Cards
- Practice Page 1.29B

Phonological Awareness Warm-up

- **Say:** *I'll say a word. You'll clap once for each word part, or syllable, you hear in the word. Listen as I say the word* rooster *and clap:* roo-ster. *Now let's do it together. Listen:* roo-ster. *Let's say and clap the syllables:* roo-ster.

- **Say:** *Now you do it:* rooster (roo-ster), classroom (class-room), doctor (doc-tor), winter (win-ter), princess (prin-cess), sunset (sun-set).

Teach/Model

- Display the Sound/Spelling Card for *moon.* Name the picture and say the vowel sound. Have students repeat after you. **Say:** *Listen:* moon, /o͞o/. *Now you say it.*

- Say the sound and give the spelling. **Say:** Moon *has the /o͞o/ sound. The letters* oo *together stand for the /o͞o/ sound.* Remind students that they have learned that the letters *oo* can stand for the /o͞o/ sound as in *book* and *look.* Reinforce that *oo* in words such as *moon* stands for a different sound.

- Write and read *boot.* Point out the /o͞o/ spelling *oo.* **Say:** *This is the word* boot. *The letters* oo *stand for the /o͞o/ sound in* boot. *Read the word with me:* boot.

- Repeat the routine with the words *soup, new, blue, truth,* and *flute* and the *ou, ew, ue, u,* and *u_e* spellings for the /o͞o/ sound.

Guided Practice

BLENDING Display the words in Rows 1 and 2 below. Using Instructional Routine: Sound-by-Sound Blending, work with students to blend each word.

1. cool	grew	soup	broom	flew
2. true	due	tuna	rude	rule

DECODING Display the sentences below. Call on individuals to blend one or more words and to read the sentences.

- At noon we will have new kinds of soup.
- As a rule, the soil here warms up in June.
- Is it true Duke is ready to catch tuna?

BUILDING AND WRITING WORDS Model how to build the word *cool* with Letter Cards.
Say: *The letter* c *stands for the first sound, /k/. The next sound I hear is /o͞o/. I know that* oo *can stand for /o͞o/. The last sound is /l/. The letter* l *stands for /l/.*

- Guide students to identify sounds in the following words and build them with Letter Cards: *broom, group, grew, truth, rude, glue.*
- Have students write each word and read it aloud.

Apply

- Distribute copies of Practice Page 1.29B, which contains the decodable story *Blue Sue and Red Ruth*. Tell students that many words in this story have the letters *oo, ou, ew, ue, u,* or *u_e*, which can stand for the /o͞o/ sound. Point out that students have learned the following high-frequency words, which they will also read in the story: *covers, ready, soil, warms.*

- Read aloud the first five sentences of the story as students follow along. Point out that you do not misread, add, or skip words when you read. Lead students in reading the same sentences with fluency and accuracy.

- Have students read the passage silently and then aloud. Remind them to track the words from left to right. When they come to the end of a line, they should sweep their hand down to the beginning of the next line and continue reading.

- When students have finished reading the text, choose a few sentences to review. You may want to focus on sentences that include words containing the target phonics element. Have students read each sentence and explain in their own words what it means.

Fun with Words Optional activities for engaging, hands-on practice are provided in the Resources section.

English Language Support

Linguistic Transfer Point out to Spanish speakers that the /o͞o/ sound is the same in Spanish as in English. Encourage students to share words they know in both Spanish and English with the /o͞o/ sound.

Formative Assessment and Corrective Feedback

IF a student makes an error, THEN follow this model:

Correct the error.

Guide the student to perform the task correctly by modeling.

Check for understanding by having the student repeat the task.

Reinforce: Make a note to review the skill during the student's next session.

Objectives

- Recognize and read high-frequency words.

Materials

- High-Frequency Word Cards

Formative Assessment and Corrective Feedback

IF a student makes an error, THEN follow this model:

Correct the error.

Guide the student to say the word correctly.

Check for understanding by having the student reread the word from among other randomly displayed high-frequency words.

Reinforce: Make a note to review the word during the student's next session.

High-Frequency Words:
buy, city, family, myself, party, please, school, seven

Teach/Model

- Display the high-frequency words. Tell students that these are useful words to know since they will see these words often. Tell them that reading will be easier if they recognize these words.
- Display the High-Frequency Word Card for *buy* and say the word. Then spell the word aloud as you point to each letter. Say the word again.
- Use the word in a simple sentence that will provide context. For example: *She can buy that pair of gloves for $10.*
- Repeat the steps above with the remaining high-frequency words.

Guided Practice

Do the following for each high-frequency word:

- Display the High-Frequency Word Card. Read the word and have students repeat it.
- Note the familiar sound/spelling patterns that are shown on the back of the card. Note as well any unfamiliar and unexpected sound/spellings.
- Blend the word with students.
- Spell the word aloud, pointing to each letter.
- Have students then spell the word aloud as you point to each letter.
- Have students read the word again.

Apply

- Display the High-Frequency Word Cards in random order. Have students read the words.
- Have students write each word. Tell them to compare their writing with the word on the card and make corrections if necessary.
- Have students read each word aloud and use it in a sentence.

Phonics: Vowel Combinations
ou, ow, oi, oy, au, aw

Objectives

- Learn the sound-spelling correspondence for /ou/*ou, ow;* /oi/*oi, oy;* /aw/*au, aw.*
- Add individual sounds to spoken words to make new words.
- Blend, build, and decode regularly spelled one-syllable words with /ou/*ou, ow;* /oi/*oi, oy;* /aw/*au, aw.*
- Read on-level text with fluency and accuracy.

Materials

- Sound/Spelling Cards
- Instructional Routine: Sound-by-Sound Blending
- Letter Cards
- Practice Page 1.30B

Phonemic Awareness Warm-up

- Have students add a sound to the beginning of a word to make a new word. **Say:** *Listen. The word is* round. *Add /g/ to the beginning, and the new word is* ground. *Now you do it.* Loud. *Add /k/ to the beginning.* (cloud) Out. *Add /sh/ to the beginning.* (shout) Owl. *Add /f/ to the beginning.* (fowl) Round. *Add /f/ to the beginning.* (frowned)

Teach/Model

- Display the Sound/Spelling Card for *owl.* Name the picture and say the vowel sound. Have students repeat after you. **Say:** *Listen:* owl, */ou/. Now you say it.*
- Say the sound and give the spelling. **Say:** Owl *has the /ou/ sound. The letters* ow *together can stand for the /ou/ sound at the beginning, middle, or end of a word.*
- Write and read *down.* Point out the *ow.* **Say:** *This is the word* down. *The letters* ow *stand for the /ou/ sound in* down. *Read the word with me:* down.
- Point out the *ou* on the card. **Say:** *The letters* ou *can also stand for the /ou/ sound.* Say the words *loud, cloud,* and *ground* as examples and have students repeat each word.
- Write and read *loud.* Point out the *ou.* **Say:** *This is the word* loud. *The letters* ou *stand for the /ou/ sound in* loud. *Read the word with me:* loud.
- Repeat the routine using the Sound/Spelling Card for *boy* and the words *boy, toy, coin,* and *point* to introduce /oi/*oi, oy.*
- Repeat the routine the Sound/Spelling Card for *saw* and the words *saw, draw, sauce,* and *haul* to introduce /aw/*au, aw.*

Guided Practice

BLENDING Display the words in Rows 1, 2, and 3 below. Using Instructional Routine: Sound-by-Sound Blending, work with students to blend each word.

1. cow	shout	joy	coin	draw
2. haul	snow	toy	frown	stew
3. claw	cloud	group	point	cause

DECODING Display the sentences below. Call on individuals to blend one or more words and to read the sentences.

- Please don't shout out loud at school.
- Paul joined the party on the lawn.
- Where did Joy buy a brown cow?

BUILDING AND WRITING WORDS Model how to build the word *pouch* with Letter Cards. **Say:** *The letter* p *stands for the /p/ sound in this word. The next sound is /ou/. I know that* ou *can stand for /ou/. The last sound is /ch/. The letters* ch *stand for the sound /ch/.*

- Guide students to identify sounds in the following words and build them with Letter Cards: *town, scout, spoil, joy, pause, yawn.*
- Have students write each word and read it aloud.

Apply

English Language Support

Linguistic Transfer Speakers of Spanish may have difficulty with the vowel sounds in *now* and *saw*. Explain that English has more vowel sounds than most languages and that it takes a long time to learn them all. For the /ou/ vowel sound, read aloud words such as *now, cow, how, shout, loud, house,* and *down,* and have students chorally repeat each word after you, vocalize the vowel sound, and then say the whole word again. Use each word in a sentence to reinforce meaning. Repeat for the /aw/ vowel sound using the words *saw, paw, law, raw, cause, haul,* and *sauce*.

Formative Assessment and Corrective Feedback

IF a student makes an error, THEN follow this model:

Correct the error.

Guide the student to perform the task correctly by modeling.

Check for understanding by having the student repeat the task.

Reinforce: Make a note to review the skill during the student's next session.

- Distribute copies of Practice Page 1.30B, which contains the decodable story *Dawn's Toys.* Tell students that many words in this story have the letters *ou, ow, oi, oy, au,* or *aw.* Point out that students have learned the following high-frequency words, which they will also read in the story: *buy, city, please.*

- Read aloud the first four sentences of the story as students follow along. Point out that you do not misread, add, or skip words when you read. Lead students in reading the same sentences with fluency and accuracy.

- Have students read the passage silently and then aloud. Remind them to track the words from left to right. When they come to the end of a line, they should sweep their hand down to the beginning of the next line and continue reading.

- When students have finished reading the text, choose a few sentences to review. You may want to focus on sentences that include words containing the target phonics element. Have students read each sentence and explain in their own words what it means.

Fun with Words Optional activities for engaging, hands-on practice are provided in the Resources section.

Cumulative Review/Fluency

Teach/Model

REVIEW

- Remind students they have learned *r*-controlled vowel sounds spelled *ar, or, ore, er, ir, ur;* the vowel sound /o͞o/ spelled *oo;* the vowel sound /o͞o/ spelled *oo, ou, ew, ue, u, u_e;* the vowel sound /ou/ spelled *ou, ow;* the vowel sound /oi/ spelled *oi, oy;* and the vowel sound /aw/ spelled *au, aw.* Display the letters and review the sounds.

- Remind students they have learned the syllable pattern CVC. Display the example words *rabbit* and *velvet* and review the syllables in each.

- Display these sentences:

    Dawn and her family took a basket of food to the park.

    The food was for a picnic.

    Drew got hurt again.

    He was digging in the soil on the farm.

    Why do the groups count and sort nouns and verbs together?

- Point to the high-frequency words *family, again,* and *together* and read each one. Remind students that they know these words. Use the High-Frequency Word Cards and Instructional Routine: High-Frequency Words to review these words.

MODEL FLUENCY

- Explain that good readers don't skip hard parts. They take their time, go back, and correct themselves. That way, they understand the words they are reading and what the words mean.

- Read the sentences, pointing to each word as you read it slowly. Read the following sentence with an error: **Say:** *He was digging in the soil on the fame.* Point to the word *farm.* **Say:** *I read this word with a long a sound as fame, but that doesn't make sense. I'm going to try again: /f/ /är/ /m/, farm. The letters ar stand for the /är/ sound, not the /ā/ sound. I also looked for clues in the text. Soil is something you would dig in on a farm. Now it makes sense.*

- Reread the sentences with no mistakes. Model reading with expression and at a natural rate. Point out that you read aloud in a natural way: not too slowly and not too quickly. Note that your voice rose up at the end of the question.

Guided Practice

- Tell students they will practice reading. Display the following sentences:

    Don't frown if your soup starts to boil too much and burn!

    The star of the party was the girl who wore the blue shirt.

    The dentist was ready to take a look at that tooth in Paul's mouth.

- Guide students in reading the sentences aloud. Coach them to sound out each word. Have students go back to any word they read incorrectly. Remind them that sometimes letters can be pronounced in more than one way, and have them sound out the word again. Guide students to look for context clues in surrounding text to help them figure out the word.

- Guide students to read the text again. Coach them to read at a natural rate and to use expression when reading exclamations.

Objectives

- Decode words with *r*-controlled vowels *ar, or, ore, er, ir, ur;* vowel digraphs *oo, ou, ew, ue, u, u_e;* vowel combinations *ou, ow, oi, oy, au, aw;* and syllable pattern CVC.
- Recognize and read high-frequency words.
- Read on-level text with purpose and understanding.
- Read on-level text orally with accuracy, appropriate rate, and expression on successive readings.
- Use context to confirm or self-correct word recognition and understanding, rereading as necessary.

Materials

- High-Frequency Word Cards
- Instructional Routine: High-Frequency Words
- Practice Page 1.31

Formative Assessment and Corrective Feedback

IF a student makes an error, THEN follow this model:

Correct the error.

Guide the student to say the word correctly.

Check for understanding by having the student reread the word.

Reinforce: Make a note to review the word during the student's next session.

Apply

- Have students read aloud the practice text on Practice Page 1.31.
- Explain that the main purpose of reading the text is to practice their reading skills.
- Coach students to use decoding skills and context to self-correct any mistakes they make during reading. They should read the text several times until they are able to read smoothly and accurately with expression and at a natural rate.
- When students have finished the fluency practice, choose a few sentences to review. Have students read each sentence and explain in their own words what it means.
- After students are able to read the text fluently, guide them to track their progress on their My Progress graphs.

High-Frequency Words:
above, bear, even, pushed, studied, surprised, teacher, toward

Teach/Model

- Display the high-frequency words. Tell students that these are useful words to know since they will see these words often. Tell them that reading will be easier if they recognize these words.
- Display the High-Frequency Word Card for *above* and say the word. Then spell the word aloud as you point to each letter. Say the word again.
- Use the word in a simple sentence that will provide context. For example: *The balloon floated high above the ground.*
- Repeat the steps above with the remaining high-frequency words.

Guided Practice

Do the following for each high-frequency word:

- Display the High-Frequency Word Card. Read the word and have students repeat it.
- Note the familiar sound/spelling patterns that are shown on the back of the card. Note as well any unfamiliar and unexpected sound/spellings.
- Blend the word with students.
- Spell the word aloud, pointing to each letter.
- Have students then spell the word aloud as you point to each letter.
- Have students read the word again.

Apply

- Display the High-Frequency Word Cards in random order. Have students read the words.
- Have students write each word. Tell them to compare their writing with the word on the card and make corrections if necessary.
- Have students read each word aloud and use it in a sentence.

Objectives

- Recognize and read high-frequency words.

Materials

- High-Frequency Word Cards

Formative Assessment and Corrective Feedback

IF a student makes an error, THEN follow this model:

Correct the error.

Guide the student to say the word correctly.

Check for understanding by having the student reread the word from among other randomly displayed high-frequency words.

Reinforce: Make a note to review the word during the student's next session.

Phonological Awareness: Segment Syllables

Objectives

- Segment syllables in spoken words.

Formative Assessment and Corrective Feedback

IF a student makes an error, THEN follow this model:

Correct the error.

Guide the student to perform the task correctly by modeling.

Check for understanding by having the student repeat the task.

Reinforce: Make a note to review the skill during the student's next session.

Teach/Model

- **Say:** *Remember, words are made up of parts called syllables. Each word part, or syllable, has a vowel sound. I'm going to say a word and clap each syllable in the word as I say it. Listen:* shout (clap), ed (clap). *The word has two vowel sounds, and I clapped twice, so the word* shouted *has two syllables.*
- Repeat with other multisyllabic words, such as *family, planted,* and *working.*

Guided Practice

- **Say:** *Let's do it together. I want you to say the word with me and clap each syllable as you say it. Then we'll count the syllables we said and clapped. Listen:* drawing. *Say the word and clap each syllable:* draw (clap), ing (clap). *How many times did you clap?* (2) *How many syllables does the word* drawing *have?* (2)
- Continue with the words shown below. Have students segment each word, clapping and counting the syllables.

Word	Syllables/Number of Claps
greeted	2
wanted	2
universe	3
flying	2
magical	3
rested	2
standing	2
unloaded	3

Apply

- **Say:** *Today we're going to work in pairs. I'm going to say a word that has two syllables. Clap each time I say a syllable. Then I want the first person in the pair to say the first syllable in the word. I want the second person to say the second syllable. Are you ready? Let's go!*

Word	First Syllable	Second Syllable
winter	win-	-ter
teaching	teach-	-ing
happen	hap-	-pen
painted	paint-	-ed
showing	show-	-ing
hammer	ham-	-mer
waited	wait-	-ed
awful	aw-	-ful
needed	need-	-ed
willow	wil-	-low

Phonics: Base Words and Inflections
-ed, -ing (CVCe, CVC)

Objectives

- Segment syllables in spoken words.
- Blend, build, and decode regularly spelled one- and two-syllable words with inflectional endings -ed and -ing.
- Recognize spelling changes in CVCe and CVC base words with inflectional endings -ed and -ing.
- Read on-level text with fluency and accuracy.

Materials

- Instructional Routine: Sound-by-Sound Blending
- Letter Cards
- Practice Page 1.32C

Phonological Awareness Warm-up

- **Say:** *I'll say some words and clap their syllables. Listen:* bike. Bike *has one syllable. Now listen:* biking. Biking *has two syllables,* bike *and* -ing. *Listen and say* shrugged. Shrugged *has one syllable,* shrugged.

- **Say:** *Let's do one together. Listen:* barking. *How many syllables do you hear in* barking? (2) *Now let's do some more. I'll say a word. Then you tell me how many syllables you hear in the word:* parking (2), parked (1), showed (1), showing (2), studying (3), pushed (1), pushing (2), traded (2), grabbed (1), treated (2).

Teach/Model

- Write the word *bike*. Read the word and have students repeat the word after you. **Say:** *To add* -ed *or* -ing *to a word that ends with* e, *we first need to drop the final* e. *Then we add the ending.* Erase the *e* at the end of *bike*. Add *-ed*. Read the word *biked* and have students read it. Then change the *-ed* to *-ing* and repeat.

- Write the word *hop*. Read the word and have students repeat the word after you. Add *-ed* to *hop*. **Say:** *If we add* -ed *to* hop, *we get the word* hoped *with a long* o *sound. How can we add* -ed *and get the word* hopped? *Let's see.*

- Write the word *hop* again. **Say:** *To add* -ed *or* -ing *to a word that ends with a single consonant, we first need to double the final consonant. Then we add the ending.* Add another *p* to *hop* and then add *-ed*. Read the word *hopped* and have students read it. Show them how to add *-ing* to the word *hop*.

Guided Practice

BLENDING Display the words in Rows 1 and 2 below. Using Instructional Routine: Sound-by-Sound Blending, work with students to blend each word.

1. hop	hopping	hopped	bike	biking
2. biked	running	hoped	using	jumped

DECODING Display the sentences below. Call on individuals to blend one or more words and to read the sentences. Have students break two-syllable words into syllables to read the words.

- I noticed a bear swimming in the lake!
- The teacher was smiling as we petted the dog.
- Was Sam surprised when the girl waved at him?

BUILDING AND WRITING WORDS Model how to spell the word *winning*. **Say:** *I know this word has two syllables. The first syllable is* win. *The letter* w *stands for /w/, the letter* i *stands for /ĭ/, and the letter* n *stands for /n/. The second syllable is the ending* –ing. *To keep the short sound in* win, *when I add the* –ing, *I must add another* n. *Now I can add the syllable* ing. *Let's spell it together:* w, i, n, n, i, n, g.

- Guide students to break the following words into syllables, identify the sounds, and build them with Letter Cards: *tagged, gazing, used, grinned, pausing, clapping.*

- Have students write each word and read it aloud.

English Language Support

Linguistic Transfer Past-tense endings can be challenging for many English learners as their first language either lacks such endings or has less variation in the way such endings are pronounced. Explain that in English, the ending -ed can be pronounced in three ways: /ed/ *wanted, needed;* /d/ *nodded, waved;* /t/ *reached, walked.* Paying attention to these endings can help students be clear and effective when writing and speaking. Have them practice using past-tense forms when telling stories.

Formative Assessment and Corrective Feedback

IF a student makes an error, THEN follow this model:

Correct the error.

Guide the student to perform the task correctly by modeling.

Check for understanding by having the student repeat the task.

Reinforce: Make a note to review the skill during the student's next session.

- Distribute copies of Practice Page 1.32C, which contains the decodable story *Miss Joy's Game.* Tell students that many words in this story end with -ed or -ing. Point out that students have learned the following high-frequency words, which they will also read in the story: *above, surprised, teacher.*

- Read aloud the first three sentences of the story as students follow along. Point out that you do not misread, add, or skip words when you read. Lead students in reading the same sentences with fluency and accuracy.

- Have students read the passage silently and then aloud. Remind them to track the words from left to right. When they come to the end of a line, they should sweep their hand down to the beginning of the next line and continue reading.

- When students have finished reading the text, choose a few sentences to review. You may want to focus on sentences that include words containing the target phonics elements. Have students read each sentence and explain in their own words what it means.

> **Fun with Words** Optional activities for engaging, hands-on practice are provided in the Resources section.

Phonics: Long *e* Spelling Patterns *y, ie*

Objectives

- Learn the sound-spelling correspondences for long *e* (*y, ie*).
- Isolate and substitute medial vowel sounds.
- Blend, build, and decode regularly spelled one- and two-syllable words with *y* and *ie*.
- Read on-level text with fluency and accuracy.

Materials

- Sound/Spelling Cards
- Instructional Routine: Sound-by-Sound Blending
- Letter Cards
- Practice Page 1.32D

Phonological Awareness Warm-up

- Guide students to change the sound they hear in the middle of each word to /ē/. **Say:** *Listen:* filled. *The middle sound in* filled *is* /ĭ/. *Now, change the middle sound to* /ē/. *The new word is* field. *Let's do one together. Listen:* nice. *What is the middle sound you hear?* (/ī/) *Change* /ī/ *to* /ē/. *What is the new word?* (niece) *Let's do some more:* shelled (shield), yelled (yield), pass (piece), sage (siege), graph (grief).

- Guide students to segment syllables. **Say:** *Listen:* baby. *I hear two syllables in* baby. *The second syllable is* /ē/. *Now listen:* babies. *I still hear two syllables. You listen and tell how many syllables you hear in each word:* city, cities, story, stories, copy, copies, study, studies, hurry, hurries.

Teach/Model

- Display the Sound/Spelling Card for *eagle*. Review the long *e* sound. Name the picture and say the sound. Have students repeat after you.

- Write the word *bunny*. Point out that the letter *y* on the card stands for the /ē/ sound. **Say:** *The word* bunny *ends with the* /ē/ *sound. Say the word with me and listen for the sound at the end of* bunny. *The letter* y *stands for the* /ē/ *sound at the end of* bunny.

- Write the word *bunnies*. Say the word and have students repeat it after you. Circle the letters *ie* and say /ē/. **Say:** *The letters* ie *stand for the* /ē/ *sound in* bunnies. *Read the word with me:* bunnies.

- Write and read the word *brief*. Point out that the letters *ie* stand for the /ē/ sound. **Say:** *The letters* ie *stand for the* /ē/ *sound in* brief. *Read the word with me:* brief.

Guided Practice

BLENDING Display the words in Rows 1 and 2 below. Using Instructional Routine: Sound-by-Sound Blending, work with students to blend each word.

1. cities	study	field	niece	body
2. choice	sunny	used	furry	hopped

DECODING Display the sentences below. Call on individuals to blend one or more words and to read the sentences.

- Heavy snow is heading toward the cities.
- What lucky teacher led the field trip on a sunny day?
- Even my niece was surprised by the big furry puppies!

BUILDING AND WRITING WORDS Model how to build the word *party* with Letter Cards. **Say:** *The first syllable is* par. *The letter* p *stands for the* /p/ *sound, and the letters* ar *stand for the* /är/ *vowel sound. The second syllable is* ty. *The letter* t *stands for the* /t/ *sound. The last sound is* /ē/. *I know that* y *can stand for* /ē/ *at the end of a two-syllable word.*

- Guide students to break the following words into syllables, identify the sounds, and build them with Letter Cards: *dirty, puppy, sleepy, penny, pennies, brief, parties.*

- Have students write each word and read it aloud.

English Language Support

Linguistic Transfer Explain to students that long vowel sounds can be spelled in different ways in English, unlike in most languages. As an example, ask a student with reading skill in Spanish to tell how the sound /ē/ (as in *rico*) is spelled in Spanish (*i*). Explain that this sound is always spelled with an *i* in Spanish. In English, the sound /ē/ can be spelled different ways, including *e, e-consonant-e, ee, ea, y,* and *ie*.

Formative Assessment and Corrective Feedback

IF a student makes an error, THEN follow this model:

Correct the error.

Guide the student to perform the task correctly by modeling.

Check for understanding by having the student repeat the task.

Reinforce: Make a note to review the skill during the student's next session.

- Distribute copies of Practice Page 1.32D, which contains the decodable story *Carly and Mom Go Camping*. Tell students that many words in this story have the letters *ie* or *y*, which can stand for the long *e* sound. Point out that students have learned the following high-frequency words, which they will also read in the story: *pushed, surprised, toward.*

- Read aloud the first two sentences of the story as students follow along. Point out that you do not misread, add, or skip words when you read. Lead students in reading the same sentences with fluency and accuracy.

- Have students read the passage silently and then aloud. Remind them to track the words from left to right. When they come to the end of a line, they should sweep their hand down to the beginning of the next line and continue reading.

- When students have finished reading the text, choose a few sentences to review. You may want to focus on sentences that include words containing the target phonics element. Have students read each sentence and explain in their own words what it means.

> **Fun with Words** Optional activities for engaging, hands-on practice are provided in the Resources section.

High-Frequency Words:
always, different, enough, happy, high, near, once, stories

- Recognize and read high-frequency words.

- High-Frequency Word Cards

Teach/Model

- Display the high-frequency words. Tell students that these are useful words to know since they will see these words often. Tell them that reading will be easier if they recognize these words.
- Display the High-Frequency Word Card for *always* and say the word. Then spell the word aloud as you point to each letter. Say the word again.
- Use the word in a simple sentence that will provide context. For example: *The sun always rises in the east and sets in the west.*
- Repeat the steps above with the remaining high-frequency words.

Formative Assessment and Corrective Feedback

IF a student makes an error, THEN follow this model:

Correct the error.

Guide the student to say the word correctly.

Check for understanding by having the student reread the word from among other randomly displayed high-frequency words.

Reinforce: Make a note to review the word during the student's next session.

Guided Practice

Do the following for each high-frequency word:

- Display the High-Frequency Word Card. Read the word and have students repeat it.
- Note the familiar sound/spelling patterns that are shown on the back of the card. Note as well any unfamiliar and unexpected sound/spellings.
- Blend the word with students.
- Spell the word aloud, pointing to each letter.
- Have students then spell the word aloud as you point to each letter.
- Have students read the word again.

Apply

- Display the High-Frequency Word Cards in random order. Have students read the words.
- Have students write each word. Tell them to compare their writing with the word on the card and make corrections if necessary.
- Have students read each word aloud and use it in a sentence.

Formative Assessment and Corrective Feedback

IF a student makes an error, THEN follow this model:

Correct the error.

Guide the student to perform the task correctly by modeling.

Check for understanding by having the student repeat the task.

Reinforce: Make a note to review the skill during the student's next session.

Phonological Awareness: Segment and Identify Syllables

Teach/Model

- **Say:** *Remember, words are made up of parts called syllables, and each syllable has a vowel sound. I'll say a word and then I'll clap for each syllable in the word as I say it. Listen:* shortest, short (clap), est (clap). *I clapped twice, once for the syllable* short *and once for the syllable* est. *The word* shortest *has two syllables—*short-est.

- Repeat with other words, such as *tighter, slapping, longest, taller, bedtime,* and *worked.*

Guided Practice

- **Say:** *Let's do it together. I want you to say the word with me and then clap for each syllable as we say it. Then we'll count the syllables we said and clapped. Listen:* stronger. *Say the word and clap each syllable:* stronger, strong (clap), er (clap). *How many times did we clap?* (2) *What syllables did we say?* (strong *and* er) *How many syllables does the word* stronger *have?* (2)

- Continue with the words shown below. Have students segment each word, clapping for, identifying, and counting the syllables.

Word	Syllables	Number of Claps/Syllables
tallest	tall-est	2
faster	fast-er	2
midnight	mid-night	2
strongest	strong-est	2
swimming	swim-ming	2
smiled	smiled	1
windier	wind-i-er	3
happiest	hap-pi-est	3

Apply

- **Say:** *Today I'm going to say some words with endings. I will say a word. You say the word and then say the syllables in the word. If the word has the ending* -er *or* -est, *stomp your feet. If the word has some other ending, keep your feet still.*

Word	Syllables	Response
longest	long-est	stomp
writing	writ-ing	(none)
slower	slow-er	stomp
stopped	stopped	(none)
quickest	quick-est	stomp
smarter	smart-er	stomp
funniest	fun-ni-est	stomp
copied	cop-ied	(none)
easier	eas-i-er	stomp
grabbing	grab-bing	(none)
silliest	sil-li-est	stomp
sunnier	sun-ni-er	stomp

Phonics: Base Words and Inflections
-er, -est (change y to i)

Phonological Awareness Warm-up

- **Say:** *I'll say a word and clap its syllables. Listen:* faster. Faster *has two syllables,* fast *and* er. *Listen and say* fastest. Fastest *has two syllables, too,* fast *and* est. *Let's do some others. I'll say a word. Clap the syllables with me and tell how many syllables you hear. Listen:* harder (2), hardest (2). *Now you listen and clap. Tell me how many syllables you hear:* busier (3), jumpy (2), sillier (3), silliest (3), colder (2), chillier (3).

Teach/Model

- Write the word *happy*. Read the word and have students repeat the word after you.
  Say: *The base word* happy *can have the ending* -er *added to show you are comparing two things. Listen:* happier. *Now you say it. The word* happy *can have the ending* -est *added to show you are comparing more than two things. Listen:* happiest. *Now you say it.*
- Write the word *happy* again. **Say:** *The word* happy *ends with* y. *To write the word* happier, *I change the* y *to* i *and add* -er. *Erase the* y *and write* i *and* -er. **Say:** *This is the word* happier. *Read the word with me:* happier.
- Write the word *happy* again. **Say:** *To write the word* happiest, *I change the* y *to* i *and add* -est. *Erase the* y *and write* i *and* -est. **Say:** *This is the word* happiest. *Read the word with me:* happiest.

Guided Practice

BLENDING Display the words in Rows 1 and 2 below. Using Instructional Routine: Sound-by-Sound Blending, work with students to blend each word.

| 1. sillier | silliest | grumpier | grumpiest | funnier |
| 2. funniest | windier | sunny | fanciest | chilly |

DECODING Display the sentences below. Call on individuals to blend one or more words and to read the sentences. Have students break two-syllable words into syllables to read the words.

- Who always makes the funniest faces?
- Sally is happy to go, but Ellie is happier.
- It is chillier and windier on top of a high hill.

BUILDING AND WRITING WORDS Model how to spell the word *fanciest*. Say: *The letter* f *stands for /f/, the letter* a *for /ă/, the letter* n *for /n/, and the letter* c *for /s/. Then comes* i *in place of* y *followed by the ending* -est: fanciest.

- Guide students to break the following words into syllables, identify the sounds, and build them with Letter Cards: *dirtier, trickiest, fancier, bumpiest, sillier.*
- Have students write each word and read it aloud.

Objectives

- Segment words into syllables and determine the number of syllables in each word.
- Blend, build, and decode regularly spelled two-syllable words with inflectional endings -er and -est.
- Learn to change y to i when adding inflectional endings -er and -est.
- Read on-level text with fluency and accuracy.

Materials

- Instructional Routine: Sound-by-Sound Blending
- Letter Cards
- Practice Page 1.33C

Formative Assessment and Corrective Feedback

IF a student makes an error, THEN follow this model:

Correct the error.

Guide the student to perform the task correctly by modeling.

Check for understanding by having the student repeat the task.

Reinforce: Make a note to review the skill during the student's next session.

Apply

- Distribute copies of Practice Page 1.33C, which contains the decodable story *Races at the Park*. Tell students that many words in this story end with *-er* or *-est*. Point out that students have learned the following high-frequency words, which they will also read in the story: *different, enough, happy*.

- Read aloud the first two sentences of the story as students follow along. Point out that you do not misread, add, or skip words when you read. Lead students in reading the same sentences with fluency and accuracy.

- Have students read the passage silently and then aloud. Remind them to track the words from left to right. When they come to the end of a line, they should sweep their hand down to the beginning of the next line and continue reading.

- When students have finished reading the text, choose a few sentences to review. You may want to focus on sentences that include words containing the target phonics element. Have students read each sentence and explain in their own words what it means.

> **Fun with Words** Optional activities for engaging, hands-on practice are provided in the Resources section.

Phonics: Syllable -le

Phonological Awareness Warm-up

- **Say:** *I'll say a word and clap its syllables. Listen:* table. *Table has two syllables,* ta-ble. *Listen and say* scribble. *Scribble has two syllables:* scrib-ble. *Now let's do some more. I'll say a word. Clap the syllables with me and tell how many syllables you hear. Listen:* bumble (2). *Now you listen and clap. Tell me how many syllables you hear:* scramble (2), simple (2), nibble (2), tumble (2), fable (2).

Teach/Model

- Display the Sound/Spelling Card for *table*. Name the picture and say the end sounds /əl/.

- Repeat *table* and give the spelling. **Say:** *The word* table *ends with /əl/. Say the word with me and listen for the sounds at the end of* table. *The letters* le *stand for /əl/ at the end of the word* table.

- Remind students that they can use syllables to help them read a longer word. Cover *ble* in *table* and read the first syllable with students, *ta*. **Say:** *What vowel sound do you hear in this syllable?* (/ā/) *Then cover* ta *and read the second syllable with students,* ble. **Say:** *These letters stand for the sounds /b/ /əl/.*

- Review that counting vowel sounds can help students determine the number of syllables in a word. **Say:** *How many vowel sounds did you hear in* table? (2) *How many syllables are in the word?* (2) *Read the word with me:* table.

- Write the word *wiggle*. Say the word and have students repeat it after you. **Say:** *The letters* le *stand for the sounds at the end of* wiggle. *How many syllables do you hear in the word* wiggle? (2) *Break the word into sounds and syllables and read the word with me: /w/ /ĭ/ /g/ /g/ /əl/,* wig-gle, wiggle.

Guided Practice

BLENDING Display the words in Rows 1 and 2 below. Using Instructional Routine: Sound-by-Sound Blending, work with students to blend each word.

1. handle	sample	scribble	puddle	candle
2. babble	giggle	nibble	little	wiggle

DECODING Display the sentences below. Call on individuals to blend one or more words and to read the sentences. Have students break two-syllable words into syllables to read the words.

- Once Roy jumped in the middle of a puddle.

- They got a sample of each different pebble.

- Do babies always giggle as they tumble?

BUILDING AND WRITING WORDS Model how to spell the word *paddle*. **Say:** *I know this word has two syllables. The first syllable is* pad. *The letter* p *stands for /p/, the letter* a *stands for /ă/, and the letter* d *twice stands for /d/. The second syllable is* le. *The letters* le *stand for /əl/.*

- Guide students to break following words into syllables, identify the sounds, and build them with Letter Cards: *wrinkle, bottle, crumple, jiggle, tangle, fiddle, grumble.*

- Have students write each word and read it aloud.

Objectives

- Use knowledge that every syllable has a vowel sound to count syllables in words.
- Decode two-syllable words by breaking them into syllables.
- Blend, build, and decode two-syllable words with the syllable -le.
- Read on-level text with fluency and accuracy.

Materials

- Sound/Spelling Cards
- Instructional Routine: Sound-by-Sound Blending
- Letter Cards
- Practice Page 1.33D

English Language Support

It is important for English learners to understand the meanings of the words they are using for skills practice. Use visuals, gestures, and context sentences to support student understanding.

Formative Assessment and Corrective Feedback

IF a student makes an error, THEN follow this model:

Correct the error.

Guide the student to perform the task correctly by modeling.

Check for understanding by having the student repeat the task.

Reinforce: Make a note to review the skill during the student's next session.

Apply

- Distribute copies of Practice Page 1.33D, which contains the decodable story *Bobble, Baffle, and Bubble.* Tell students that many words in this story end with the syllable *-le.* Point out that students have learned the following high-frequency words, which they will also read in the story: *always, happy, high, near.*

- Read aloud the first four sentences of the story as students follow along. Point out that you do not misread, add, or skip words when you read. Lead students in reading the same sentences with fluency and accuracy.

- Have students read the passage silently and then aloud. Remind them to track the words from left to right. When they come to the end of a line, they should sweep their hand down to the beginning of the next line and continue reading.

- When students have finished reading the text, choose a few sentences to review. You may want to focus on sentences that include words containing the target phonics element. Have students read each sentence and explain in their own words what it means.

Fun with Words Optional activities for engaging, hands-on practice are provided in the Resources section.

High-Frequency Words:
across, ball, cried, head, heard, large, second, should

Teach/Model

- Display the high-frequency words. Tell students that these are useful words to know since they will see these words often. Tell them that reading will be easier if they recognize these words.
- Display the High-Frequency Word Card for *across* and say the word. Then spell the word aloud as you point to each letter. Say the word again.
- Use the word in a simple sentence that will provide context. For example: *The ball rolled across the room.*
- Repeat the steps above with the remaining high-frequency words.

Guided Practice

Do the following for each high-frequency word:

- Display the High-Frequency Word Card. Read the word and have students repeat it.
- Note the familiar sound/spelling patterns that are shown on the back of the card. Note as well any unfamiliar and unexpected sound/spellings.
- Blend the word with students.
- Spell the word aloud, pointing to each letter.
- Have students then spell the word aloud as you point to each letter.
- Have students read the word again.

Apply

- Display the High-Frequency Word Cards in random order. Have students read the words.
- Have students write each word. Tell them to compare their writing with the word on the card and make corrections if necessary.
- Have students read each word aloud and use it in a sentence.

Objectives

- Recognize and read high-frequency words.

Materials

- High-Frequency Word Cards

Formative Assessment and Corrective Feedback

IF a student makes an error, THEN follow this model:

Correct the error.

Guide the student to say the word correctly.

Check for understanding by having the student reread the word from among other randomly displayed high-frequency words.

Reinforce: Make a note to review the word during the student's next session.

Objectives

- Isolate and delete the initial or final sounds in spoken words.

Formative Assessment and Corrective Feedback

IF a student makes an error, THEN follow this model:

Correct the error.

Guide the student to perform the task correctly by modeling.

Check for understanding by having the student repeat the task.

Reinforce: Make a note to review the skill during the student's next session.

Phonemic Awareness: Delete Phonemes

Teach/Model

- **Say:** *Today we're going to take away the first or last sounds in words to make new words. For example, the word* sticky *ends with the /ē/ sound. If I take away the ending /ē/ sound, what word do I get? I get the word* stick.
- Say the word *sticky*, emphasizing the /ē/ sound. **Say:** *Listen:* sticky. Then say the word *stick*. **Say:** *Listen:* stick.
- **Say:** *The word* make *begins with the /m/ sound. If I take away the beginning /m/ sound, what word do I get? I get the word* ache.
- Say the word *make*, emphasizing the /m/ sound. **Say:** *Listen:* make. Then say the word *ache*. **Say:** *Listen:* ache.

Guided Practice

- **Say:** *We're going to change the first or last sounds in words to make new words. For example, what is the last sound in* goat? *(/t/) Let's take away the /t/ sound in* goat. *What is the new word?* (go) *Good! Now what is the first sound in* goat? *(/g/) Let's take away the /g/ sound in* goat. *What is the new word?* (oat) *Good! Let's try some more.*
- Continue with the words shown below.

Word	Minus Last Sound	New Word
cart	/t/	car
sheep	/p/	she
whine	/n/	why
funny	/ē/	fun

Word	Minus First Sound	New Word
meet	/m/	eat
cup	/k/	up
rice	/r/	ice
tape	/t/	ape

Apply

Have students practice deleting initial or final phonemes, using the words below. **Say:**

- *Take away the last sound in* wake. *What is the new word?* (way)
- *Take away the last sound in* light. *What is the new word?* (lie)
- *Take away the last sound in* roam. *What is the new word?* (row)
- *Take away the last sound in* hump. *What is the new word?* (hum)
- *Take away the last sound in* tent. *What is the new word?* (ten)
- *Take away the first sound in* wink. *What is the new word?* (ink)
- *Take away the first sound in* gate. *What is the new word?* (ate)
- *Take away the first sound in* dear. *What is the new word?* (ear)
- *Take away the first sound in* pants. *What is the new word?* (ants)
- *Take away the first sound in* spine. *What is the new word?* (pine)

Phonics: Words with Long *i* Spelling Patterns *igh, y, ie*

Phonemic Awareness Warm-up

- Guide students to listen for and delete the final sounds in words. **Say:** *I'll say a word and then I'll take away the sound at the end of the word. Listen:* might. *What is the sound at the end of* might? *(/t/) Now listen:* my. *I took away the /t/ sound and made the new word* my.

- **Say:** *Let's do one together. Say* like. *Now say* lie. *What sound did you take away from* like *to make the word* lie? *(/k/)*

- **Say:** *Let's do some more. Take away the last sound in each of these words:* safe (say), past (pass), shine (shy), week (we), pint (pine), size (sigh).

Teach/Model

- Display the Sound/Spelling Card for *ice cream*. Name the picture and say the sound. Have students repeat after you. **Say:** *Listen:* ice cream, /ī/. *Now you say it.*

- Say the sound and give the spelling. **Say:** Ice cream *begins with the long i sound, /ī/. You can hear the /ī/ sound at the beginning, middle, or end of a word.*

- Write and read *high*. Point out the *igh* spelling in the word and on the card. **Say:** *This is the word* high. *The letters* igh *stand for the /ī/ sound in* high. *Read the word with me:* high.

- Write and read *fly*. Point out the *y* spelling in the word and on the card. **Say:** *This is the word* fly. *The letter* y *stands for the /ī/ sound in* fly. *Read the word with me:* fly.

- Write and read *pie*. Point out the *ie* spelling in the word and on the card. **Say:** *This is the word* pie. *The letters* ie *stand for the /ī/ sound in* pie. *Read the word with me:* pie.

Guided Practice

BLENDING Display the words in Rows 1 and 2 below. Using Instructional Routine: Sound-by-Sound Blending, work with students to blend each word.

1. high	my	dries	sight	lie
2. try	bright	fly	tie	cries

DECODING Display the sentences below. Call on individuals to blend one or more words and to read the sentences.

- The ball flies high into the sky.
- My second race ended in a tie.
- At night the lights should be bright.

BUILDING AND WRITING WORDS Model how to spell the word *night*. Say: *The letter* n *stands for first sound. The next sound is /ī/. I know the letters* igh *stand for /ī/ in this word. The last sound is /t/. The letter* t *stands for /t/.* Repeat for the word *bright*. Point out that *night* and *bright* belong to the same word family because they end with the same letters (-ight) and sounds (/ī/ /t/).

- Guide students to identify sounds in the following words and build them with Letter Cards: *fight, light, sight, tight, by, my, fly, sky, try, why.*

- Have students write each word and read it aloud.

Objectives

- Learn the sound-spelling correspondence for long *i* (*igh, y, ie*).
- Isolate and delete final phonemes in spoken words.
- Blend, build, and decode regularly spelled one-syllable words with *igh, y,* and *ie*.
- Read on-level text with fluency and accuracy.

Materials

- Sound/Spelling Cards
- Instructional Routine: Sound-by-Sound Blending
- Letter Cards
- Practice Page 1.34C

Formative Assessment and Corrective Feedback

IF a student makes an error, THEN follow this model:

Correct the error.

Guide the student to perform the task correctly by modeling.

Check for understanding by having the student repeat the task.

Reinforce: Make a note to review the skill during the student's next session.

Apply

- Distribute copies of Practice Page 1.34C, which contains the decodable story *Ty and Ike*. Tell students that many words in this story have the spelling patterns *igh, y,* or *ie,* which can stand for the long *i* sound. Point out that students have learned the following high-frequency words, which they will also read in the story: *across, heard, large, should.*

- Read aloud the first four sentences of the story as students follow along. Point out that you do not misread, add, or skip words when you read. Lead students in reading the same sentences with fluency and accuracy.

- Have students read the passage silently and then aloud. Remind them to track the words from left to right. When they come to the end of a line, they should sweep their hand down to the beginning of the next line and continue reading.

- When students have finished reading the text, choose a few sentences to review. You may want to focus on sentences that include words containing the target phonics element. Have students read each sentence and explain in their own words what it means.

> **Fun with Words** Optional activities for engaging, hands-on practice are provided in the Resources section.

Phonics: Base Words and Inflections -ed, -ing, -er, -est, -es

Phonological Awareness Warm-up

- **Say:** *I'm going to say a word. Listen:* jump. *The word* jump *has one syllable. Now listen to the next word:* jumping. *How many syllables do you hear in the word* jumping? *There are two syllables,* jump *and* ing. *Let's do some together. Now listen:* surprising. *How many syllables do you hear in this word?* (3) *There are three syllables in* surprising. *Let's do some more. Tell me how many syllables you hear in each word:* closed (1), babies (2), running (2), faster (2), biggest (2), passes (2), studying (3).

Teach/Model

- Write and read *pet, petted,* and *petting.* **Say:** *Say the words with me and listen for the endings.* Circle the endings *-ed* and *-ing* that were added to the word *pet.* **Say:** *To keep the short vowel sound in* pet, *we must double the final consonant when we add the ending* -ed *or* -ing. Read the words together. Have students identify the base word in each word and underline it (*pet*). Repeat to review dropping final *e* when adding *-ed* and *-ing* using the example words *like, liked,* and *liking.*

- Write and read *big, bigger,* and *biggest.* **Say:** *Say the words with me and listen for the endings.* Circle the endings *-er* and *-est* that were added to the word *big.* **Say:** *To keep the short vowel sound in* big, *we must double the final consonant when we add the ending* -er *or* -est. Read the words together. Have students identify the base word in each word and underline it (*big*).

- Write and read *wishes.* Say the word and have students repeat it after you. Circle the ending *-es.* **Say:** *Add* -es *to the word* wish *to make the word* wishes. *Read the word with me:* wishes.

Guided Practice

BLENDING Display the words in Rows 1 and 2 below. Using Instructional Routine: Sound-by-Sound Blending, work with students to blend each word.

1. faster	running	largest	cried	splashes
2. liked	thinner	playing	tries	hoped

DECODING Display the sentences below. Call on individuals to blend one or more words and to read the sentences. Have students break two-syllable words into syllables to read the words.

- The ball kept rolling for a while before it stopped.
- We jumped because we heard the loudest, strangest noise.
- Is Ann or Jan faster when she dashes across the finish line?

BUILDING AND WRITING WORDS Model how to spell the word *winning.* **Say:** *I hear two syllables in* winning. *In the first syllable, the letter* w *stands for /w/, the letter* i *stand for /i/, and the letter* n *stands for /n/. To keep the short sound in* win, *when I add the ending* –ing, *I must add another* n. *Now I can add the other syllable* ing.

- Guide students to break the following words into syllables, identify the sounds, and build them with Letter Cards: *closest, hotter, wishes, stepping, palest, catches.*
- Have students write each word and read it aloud.

Session 1.34D

Objectives
- Blend sounds in spoken words with inflectional endings *-ed, -ing, -er, -est,* and *-es.*
- Blend, build, and decode regularly spelled one- and two-syllable words with inflectional endings *-ed, -ing, -er, -est,* and *-es.*
- Read on-level text with fluency and accuracy.

Materials
- Instructional Routine: Sound-by-Sound Blending
- Letter Cards
- Practice Page 1.34D

English Language Support

Linguistic Transfer Many English learners, including speakers of Spanish, Hmong, Haitian Creole, and Korean, may have trouble with the /ng/ sound in words with the *-ing* ending. Model pronouncing the sound, and have students practice pronouncing words such as these: *running, reading, looking, riding, eating, smiling, crying, hopping.* Use each word in a brief sentence to reinforce meaning.

Formative Assessment and Corrective Feedback

IF a student makes an error, THEN follow this model:

Correct the error.

Guide the student to perform the task correctly by modeling.

Check for understanding by having the student repeat the task.

Reinforce: Make a note to review the skill during the student's next session.

Apply

- Distribute copies of Practice Page 1.34D, which contains the decodable story *Benches! Benches!* Tell students that many words in this story end with *-ed, -ing, -er, -est,* or *-es.* Point out that students have learned the following high-frequency words, which they will also read in the story: *ball, heard, second, should.*

- Read aloud the first six sentences of the story as students follow along. Point out that you do not misread, add, or skip words when you read. Lead students in reading the same sentences with fluency and accuracy.

- Have students read the passage silently and then aloud. Remind them to track the words from left to right. When they come to the end of a line, they should sweep their hand down to the beginning of the next line and continue reading.

- When students have finished reading the text, choose a few sentences to review. You may want to focus on sentences that include words containing the target phonics elements. Have students read each sentence and explain in their own words what it means.

Fun with Words Optional activities for engaging, hands-on practice are provided in the Resources section.

High-Frequency Words:
beautiful, caught, friendship, idea, listen, minute, thought, took

Teach/Model

- Display the high-frequency words. Tell students that these are useful words to know since they will see these words often. Tell them that reading will be easier if they recognize these words.
- Display the High-Frequency Word Card for *beautiful* and say the word. Then spell the word aloud as you point to each letter. Say the word again.
- Use the word in a simple sentence that will provide context. For example: *In summer the garden has many beautiful flowers.*
- Repeat the steps above with the remaining high-frequency words.

Guided Practice

Do the following for each high-frequency word:

- Display the High-Frequency Word Card. Read the word and have students repeat it.
- Note the familiar sound/spelling patterns that are shown on the back of the card. Note as well any unfamiliar and unexpected sound/spellings.
- Blend the word with students.
- Spell the word aloud, pointing to each letter.
- Have students then spell the word aloud as you point to each letter.
- Have students read the word again.

Apply

- Display the High-Frequency Word Cards in random order. Have students read the words.
- Have students write each word. Tell them to compare their writing with the word on the card and make corrections if necessary.
- Have students read each word aloud and use it in a sentence.

Objectives

- Recognize and read high-frequency words.

Materials

- High-Frequency Word Cards

Formative Assessment and Corrective Feedback

IF a student makes an error, THEN follow this model:

Correct the error.

Guide the student to say the word correctly.

Check for understanding by having the student reread the word from among other randomly displayed high-frequency words.

Reinforce: Make a note to review the word during the student's next session.

Objectives

- Learn suffixes *-ful, -ly,* and *-y.*
- Segment syllables in spoken words.
- Blend, build, and decode regularly spelled words with suffixes *-ful, -ly,* and *-y.*
- Read on-level text with fluency and accuracy.

Materials

- Instructional Routine: Sound-by-Sound Blending
- Letter Cards
- Practice Page 1.35B

Phonics: Suffixes *-ful, -ly, -y*

Phonological Awareness Warm-up

- **Say:** *I'm going to say a word and clap to show how many syllables are in the word. Listen:* rabbit. Rab-bit. *This word has two syllables. Clap with me.* (2 claps) *Now you try. Help me clap the syllables in* winter. Win-ter. (2 claps) Continue with these words: yellow (2 claps), thankful (2 claps), funny (2 claps).

Teach/Model

- Write *-ful, -ly,* and *-y.* Point to and read each, and have students repeat. **Say:** *A suffix is a word part added to the ends of some words to make new words. The suffix* -ful *can mean "full of." The suffix* -ly *can mean "like." The suffix* -y *can mean "full of" or "like." When you add a suffix, you also add a syllable.*

- Write and read *help* and *helpful.* Point out the suffix *-ful.* **Say:** *The suffix* -ful *can be added to* help. *Read the word with me:* helpful. *If you are helpful, you do many things that help others. How many vowel sounds do you hear in* helpful? (2) *What are they?* (/ĕ/, /ŭ/) *So how many syllables are there in* helpful? (2)

- Write and read *sad* and *sadly.* Point out the suffix *-ly.* **Say:** *The suffix* -ly *can be added to* sad. *Read the word with me:* sadly. *If you talk sadly, you talk like you are sad. How many vowel sounds do you hear in* sadly? (2) *What are they?* (/ă/, /ē/) *So how many syllables are there in* sadly? (2)

- Write and read *snow* and *snowy.* Point out the suffix *-y.* **Say:** *The suffix* -y *can be added to* snow. *Read the word with me:* snowy. *If there is lots of snow on the ground or in the air, you might say that it is snowy outside. How many vowel sounds do you hear in* snowy? (2) *What are they?* (/ō/, /ē/) *So how many syllables are there in* snowy? (2)

Guided Practice

BLENDING Display the words in Rows 1 and 2 below. Using Instructional Routine: Sound-by-Sound Blending, work with students to blend each word.

| 1. peaceful | slowly | cloudy | safely | restful |
| 2. tricky | quickly | joyful | windy | gladly |

DECODING Display the sentences below. Call on individuals to blend one or more words and to read the sentences. Have students break two-syllable words into syllables to read the words.

- Jess caught the puppy and took it safely home.
- Rick was thankful for his friendship with Cal.
- A snowy, windy day can be beautiful.

BUILDING AND WRITING WORDS Model how to spell the word *windy.* **Say:** *I hear two syllables in* windy—wind-y. *In the first syllable, the letter* w *stands for the first sound,* /w/. *The next sound I hear is* /ĭ/. *The letter* i *stands for* /ĭ/. *Then comes* n *for* /n/, d *for* /d/. *The other syllable I hear is a suffix and the sound is* /ē/. *The letter* y *stands for* /ē/.

- Guide students to break the following words into syllables, identify the sounds, and build them with Letter Cards: *quickly, harmful, dusty, neatly, graceful, sunny.*

- Have students write each word and read it aloud.

Apply

- Distribute copies of Practice Page 1.35B, which contains the decodable story *Jake's Beans.* Tell students that many words in this story have the suffixes *-ful, -ly,* and *-y*. Point out that students have learned the following high-frequency words, which they will also read in the story: *idea, minute, thought.*

- Read aloud the first three sentences of the story as students follow along. Point out that you do not misread, add, or skip words when you read. Lead students in reading the same sentences with fluency and accuracy.

- Have students read the passage silently and then aloud. Remind them to track the words from left to right. When they come to the end of a line, they should sweep their hand down to the beginning of the next line and continue reading.

- When students have finished reading the text, choose a few sentences to review. You may want to focus on sentences that include words containing the target phonics elements. Have students read each sentence and explain in their own words what it means.

> **Fun with Words** Optional activities for engaging, hands-on practice are provided in the Resources section.

English Language Support

It is important for English learners to understand the meanings of the words they are using for skills practice. Use visuals, gestures, and context sentences to support student understanding.

Formative Assessment and Corrective Feedback

IF a student makes an error, THEN follow this model:

Correct the error.

Guide the student to perform the task correctly by modeling.

Check for understanding by having the student repeat the task.

Reinforce: Make a note to review the skill during the student's next session.

Phonics: Long Vowel Spelling Patterns *a, e, i, o, u*

Objectives

- Learn the sound-spelling correspondences for long vowel sounds *(a, e, i, o, u)*.
- Isolate and delete final sounds in spoken words.
- Blend, build, and decode regularly spelled one- and two-syllable words with long vowel sounds spelled *a, e, i, o,* or *u*.
- Read on-level text with fluency and accuracy.

Materials

- Sound/Spelling Cards
- Instructional Routine: Sound-by-Sound Blending
- Letter Cards
- Practice Page 1.35C

Phonemic Awareness Warm-up

- Guide students to listen for and delete the final sounds in words. **Say:** *Listen:* sight, /s/ /ī/ /t/. *What is the last sound?* (/t/) *If I take away /t/, the word is /s/ /ī/,* sigh. *Now you do it. What is the last sound in* sunny? (/ē/) *Take it away. What is left?* (sun) Continue with *goat* (go), *tube* (too), *bean* (be), *hide* (hi), and *wade* (way).

- Guide students to distinguish long and short vowel sounds. **Say:** *If a word has long vowel sound, give a "thumbs up."* Say the following word pairs, emphasizing the vowel sounds: *cap/cape, met/meet, hope/hop, bite/bit, cut/cute.*

Teach/Model

- Display the Sound/Spelling Card for *acorn.* Name the picture and say the /ā/ sound.

- Repeat *acorn* and give the spelling. **Say:** Acorn *begins with the /ā/ sound. Say the word with me and listen for the beginning sound. The letter* a *can stand for the /ā/ sound at the beginning, middle, or end of a word.*

- Write and read *fable.* Say the word and have students repeat it after you. **Say:** *The letter* a *stands for the /ā/ sound in* fable. *Read it with me:* fable.

- Repeat the routine using the Sound/Spelling Card for *eagle* and the word *be* to introduce the /ē/ sound spelled *e,* the Sound/Spelling Card for *ice cream* and the word *kind* to introduce the /ī/ sound spelled *i,* the Sound/Spelling Card for *ocean* and the word *go* to introduce the /ō/ sound spelled *o,* and the Sound/Spelling Card for *uniform* and the word *flu* to introduce the /ū/ sound spelled *u.*

Guided Practice

BLENDING Display the words in Rows 1 and 2 below. Using Instructional Routine: Sound-by-Sound Blending, work with students to blend each word.

1. fold	she	find	baby	flu
2. table	no	we	hi	unit

DECODING Display the sentences below. Call on individuals to blend one or more words and to read the sentences.

- He thought he saw a wild pony.
- Should babies listen to beautiful music?
- Climbing that cliff is a crazy idea!

BUILDING AND WRITING WORDS Model how to spell the word *both.* **Say:** *The letter* b *stands for the first sound, /b/. The next sound I hear is /ō/. I know the letter* o *can stand for /ō/. The last sound is /th/. The letters* th *stand for the /th/ sound.*

- Guide students to build the following words with Letter Cards: *she, lazy, kind, cold, flu, climb, stroll.*
- Have students write each word and read it aloud.

Apply

- Distribute copies of Practice Page 1.35C, which contains the decodable story *Paige's Stew*. Tell students that many words in this story have long vowel sounds spelled *a, e, i, o,* or *u*. Point out that students have learned the following high-frequency words, which they will also read in the story: *friendship, idea, thought.*

- Read aloud the first two sentences of the story as students follow along. Point out that you do not misread, add, or skip words when you read. Lead students in reading the same sentences with fluency and accuracy.

- Have students read the passage silently and then aloud. Remind them to track the words from left to right. When they come to the end of a line, they should sweep their hand down to the beginning of the next line and continue reading.

- When students have finished reading the text, choose a few sentences to review. You may want to focus on sentences that include words containing the target phonics element. Have students read each sentence and explain in their own words what it means.

> **Fun with Words** Optional activities for engaging, hands-on practice are provided in the Resources section.

IF a student makes an error, THEN follow this model:

Correct the error.

Guide the student to perform the task correctly by modeling.

Check for understanding by having the student repeat the task.

Reinforce: Make a note to review the skill during the student's next session.

Session 1.36A

Objectives

- Recognize and read high-frequency words.

Materials

- High-Frequency Word Cards

Formative Assessment and Corrective Feedback

IF a student makes an error, THEN follow this model:

Correct the error.

Guide the student to say the word correctly.

Check for understanding by having the student reread the word from among other randomly displayed high-frequency words.

Reinforce: Make a note to review the word during the student's next session.

High-Frequency Words: *brothers, everyone, field, loved, most, only, people, sorry*

Teach/Model

- Display the high-frequency words. Tell students that these are useful words to know since they will see these words often. Tell them that reading will be easier if they recognize these words.
- Display the High-Frequency Word Card for *brothers* and say the word. Then spell the word aloud as you point to each letter. Say the word again.
- Use the word in a simple sentence that will provide context. For example: *Jason has two brothers and one sister.*
- Repeat the steps above with the remaining high-frequency words.

Guided Practice

Do the following for each high-frequency word:

- Display the High-Frequency Word Card. Read the word and have students repeat it.
- Note the familiar sound/spelling patterns that are shown on the back of the card. Note as well any unfamiliar and unexpected sound/spellings.
- Blend the word with students.
- Spell the word aloud, pointing to each letter.
- Have students then spell the word aloud as you point to each letter.
- Have students read the word again.

Apply

- Display the High-Frequency Word Cards in random order. Have students read the words.
- Have students write each word. Tell them to compare their writing with the word on the card and make corrections if necessary.
- Have students read each word aloud and use it in a sentence.

Phonics: Syllabication (CV)

Objectives

- Segment words into syllables and determine the number of syllables.
- Use knowledge that every syllable has a vowel sound to count syllables in words.
- Blend, build, and decode two-syllable words with the CV pattern.
- Read on-level text with fluency and accuracy.

Materials

- Instructional Routine: Sound-by-Sound Blending
- Letter Cards
- Practice Page 1.36B

Phonological Awareness Warm-up

- **Say:** *I'll say some words and clap their syllables. Listen:* hotel. Hotel *has two syllables. Now listen:* lazy. Lazy *has two syllables. Let's do one together. Listen:* secret. *How many syllables do you hear in the word* secret? (2) *Now let's do some more. I'll say a word. Then you tell me how many syllables you hear:* final (2), stopped (1), joyful (2), acorn (2), wavy (2), snowy (2), zebra (2), loud (1).

Teach/Model

- Say the word *lady*. Have students repeat after you. **Say:** *Listen:* lady. *I hear two syllables in* lady. *Now you say it. Let's clap the syllables together.*

- Write and read *lady*. Point out that each syllable has a vowel sound. Remind students they can figure out how many syllables a word has by counting its vowel sounds. **Say:** *What vowel sounds do you hear in* lady? (/ā/, /ē/) *How many vowel sounds do you hear?* (2) *Two vowel sounds mean that this word has how many syllables?* (2)

- Help students identify and label the consonant-vowel pattern in *lady*. Write C over the *l* and V over the *a*. Say the first syllable together, /l/ /ā/. Write C over the *d* and V over the *y* (a vowel). Say the second syllable together, /d/ /ē/. Say the word together.

- Point to the first CV pattern. **Say:** *When you see a consonant-vowel pattern, divide the word into syllables after each consonant and vowel.* Draw a line dividing *la/dy* and the CV/CV letter pattern.

- Point out that a CV pattern usually indicates a long vowel sound, such as /ā/ in *lady*. Repeat the steps with *tiger* and *music*. Guide students to identify the vowel sounds, count the syllables, and read each word using the CV pattern.

Guided Practice

BLENDING Display the words in Rows 1 and 2 below. Using Instructional Routine: Sound-by-Sound Blending, work with students to blend each word.

1. music	siren	hotel	lady	even
2. baby	zebra	tiny	motor	pupil

DECODING Display the sentences below. Call on individuals to blend one or more words and to read the sentences.

- The brothers made a tiny robot.

- Everyone loved the baby zebra!

- Are people listening to the music?

BUILDING AND WRITING WORDS Model how to build the word *robot* with Letter Cards. **Say:** *I know this word has two syllables. The first syllable is* ro. *The letter* r *stands for /r/ and the letter* o *stands for /ō/. The second syllable is* bot. *The letter* b *stands for /b/, the letter* o *stands for /ŏ/, and the letter* t *stands for /t/.*

- Guide students to break the following words into syllables, identify the sounds, and build them with Letter Cards: *pilot, frozen, favor, secret, unit, minus, label.*

- Have students write each word and read it aloud.

Formative Assessment and Corrective Feedback

IF a student makes an error, THEN follow this model:

Correct the error.

Guide the student to perform the task correctly by modeling.

Check for understanding by having the student repeat the task.

Reinforce: Make a note to review the skill during the student's next session.

Apply

- Distribute copies of Practice Page 1.36B, which contains the decodable story *Katy Ant*. Tell students that many words in this story have two syllables with the CV pattern in the first syllable. Point out that students have learned the following high-frequency words, which they will also read in the story: *everyone, only*.

- Read aloud the first four sentences of the story as students follow along. Point out that you do not misread, add, or skip words when you read. Lead students in reading the same sentences with fluency and accuracy.

- Have students read the passage silently and then aloud. Remind them to track the words from left to right. When they come to the end of a line, they should sweep their hand down to the beginning of the next line and continue reading.

- When students have finished reading the text, choose a few sentences to review. You may want to focus on sentences that include words containing the target phonics elements. Have students read each sentence and explain in their own words what it means.

> **Fun with Words** Optional activities for engaging, hands-on practice are provided in the Resources section.

Phonics: Prefixes *un-*, *re-*

Phonological Awareness Warm-up

- **Say:** *I'm going to say some words and clap their syllables. Listen:* undo, un-do. Undo *has two syllables. Now listen:* replay, re-play. Replay *has two syllables. Let's do one together. Listen:* untie. *How many syllables do you hear in the word* untie? (2) *Now let's do some more. I'll say a word. Then you tell me how many syllables you hear in the word:* unplug (2), reset (2), play (1), tie (1), return (2), unwind (2), reseal (2), lock (1).

Teach/Model

- Explain that a prefix is a word part added to the beginning of a word to make a new word. Write and read the prefixes *un-* and *re-*. Then write and read the word *zip*. **Say:** *The prefix* un- *can be added to* zip *to make the new word* unzip. *The prefix* re- *can be added to* zip *to make the new word* rezip.

- Write and read *unzip*. **Say:** *The word* unzip *begins with the prefix* un-. *Say the word with me and listen for the beginning sounds. The letters* u *and* n *stand for* /ŭ/ /n/ *at the beginning of* unzip. *If you unzip your coat, you do the opposite of zipping it. Read the word with me:* unzip.

- Write and read *rezip*. **Say:** *The word* rezip *begins with the prefix* re-. *Say the word with me and listen for the beginning sounds. The letters* r *and* e *stand for* /r/ /ē/ *at the beginning of* rezip. *If you rezip your coat, you zip it again. Read the word with me:* rezip.

Guided Practice

BLENDING Display the words in Rows 1 and 2 below. Using Instructional Routine: Sound-by-Sound Blending, work with students to blend each word.

1. unpack	reset	unlock	unplug	relock
2. replay	unfit	rework	rewind	unwrap

DECODING Display the sentences below. Call on individuals to blend one or more words and to read the sentences. Have students break two-syllable words into syllables to read the words.

- Cody loved to reread his books.
- Everyone likes to unwrap gifts.
- People unpack and then repack their bags.

BUILDING AND WRITING WORDS Model how to spell the word *unload*. **Say:** *I know this word has two syllables. The first syllable is the prefix* un-. *The letters* u *and* n *stand for the sounds* /ŭ/ /n/ *in the prefix* un-. *The next syllable is* load. *The first sound I hear in this syllable is* /l/. *The letter* l *stands for* /l/. *The next sound I hear is* /ō/. *The letters* oa *stand for* /ō/. *The last sound is* /d/. *The letter* d *stands for* /d/.

- Guide students to break the following words into syllables, identify the sounds, and build them with Letter Cards: *unpack, relock, unwind, repaint, unplug, rethink.*

- Have students write each word and read it aloud.

Session 1.36C

Objectives

- Learn prefixes *un-* and *re-*.
- Segment syllables in words with prefixes *un-* and *re-*.
- Blend, build, and decode regularly spelled words with prefixes *un-* and *re-*.
- Read on-level text with fluency and accuracy.

Materials

- Instructional Routine: Sound-by-Sound Blending
- Letter Cards
- Practice Page 1.36C

English Language Support

Linguistic Transfer Students with substantial reading skill in Spanish should be encouraged to transfer their knowledge of prefixes to English. The Spanish prefixes *in-* and *re-* are similar to the English prefixes *un-* and *re-*. Have students work in mixed proficiency groups to identify examples of words with these prefixes in Spanish and English.

Formative Assessment and Corrective Feedback

IF a student makes an error, THEN follow this model:

Correct the error.

Guide the student to perform the task correctly by modeling.

Check for understanding by having the student repeat the task.

Reinforce: Make a note to review the skill during the student's next session.

- Distribute copies of Practice Page 1.36C, which contains the decodable story *Sadie's New Home.* Tell students that many words in this story have the prefixes *un-* and *re-*. Point out that students have learned the following high-frequency words, which they will also read in the story: *everyone, loved, people.*

- Read aloud the first four sentences of the story as students follow along. Point out that you do not misread, add, or skip words when you read. Lead students in reading the same sentences with fluency and accuracy.

- Have students read the passage silently and then aloud. Remind them to track the words from left to right. When they come to the end of a line, they should sweep their hand down to the beginning of the next line and continue reading.

- When students have finished reading the text, choose a few sentences to review. You may want to focus on sentences that include words containing the target phonics elements. Have students read each sentence and explain in their own words what it means.

Fun with Words Optional activities for engaging, hands-on practice are provided in the Resources section.

Cumulative Review/Fluency

Teach/Model

REVIEW

- Remind students they have learned the long *e* vowel sound spelled *y* and *ie;* the long *i* vowel sound spelled *igh, y,* and *ie;* and the long vowel sounds spelled *a, e, i, o,* and *u.* Display the letters and review the sounds.

- Remind students they have learned sounds for the endings *-ed, -ing, -er, -est,* and *-es;* the suffixes *-ful, -ly,* and *-y;* the prefixes *un-* and *re-;* and the syllable *-le.* Display the word parts and review the sounds.

- Remind students they have learned the syllable pattern CV. Display the example words *lady* and *music* and review the syllables in each.

- Display these sentences:

    One cold, windy night Nellie heard a little kitten crying loudly!

    Why are the brothers always happiest when riding their ponies?

    Helpful people should try to reuse paper, cans, and glass bottles.

- Point to the high-frequency words *always, brothers, heard, people,* and *should* and read each one. Remind students that they know these words. Use the High-Frequency Word Cards and Instructional Routine: High-Frequency Words to review these words.

MODEL FLUENCY

- Explain that good readers don't skip hard parts. They take their time, go back, and correct themselves. That way, they understand the words they are reading and what the words mean.

- Read the sentences, pointing to each word as you read it slowly. Read the following sentence with an error: **Say:** *One cold, wīndy night Nellie heard a little kitten crying loudly!* Point to the word *windy.* **Say:** *I read this word with a long* i *sound as* wīndy, *but that doesn't make sense. I'm going to try again: /w/ /ĭ/ /n/ /d/ /ē/,* windy. *The letter* i *stands for the /ĭ/ sound, not the /ī/ sound. I also looked for clues in the text. A night is more likely to be wĭndy than wīndy. Now it makes sense.*

- Reread the sentences with no mistakes. Model reading with expression and at a natural rate. Point out that you read aloud in a natural way: not too slowly and not too quickly. Note that you used your voice to show emphasis and excitement when reading the exclamation. Note that your voice rose up at the end of the question.

Guided Practice

- Tell students they will practice reading. Display the following sentences:

    Did Katy have a fever and a painful sore throat when she caught the flu?

    Toby quickly unwrapped the pie and pushed it across the table to everyone.

    The playing field got muddier and messier as people chased the ball.

- Guide students in reading the sentences aloud. Coach them to sound out each word. Have students go back to any word they read incorrectly. Remind them that sometimes letters can be pronounced in more than one way, and have them sound out the word again. Guide students to look for context clues in surrounding text to help them figure out the word.

- Guide students to read the text again. Coach them to read at a natural rate and to use expression when reading questions or exclamations.

Objectives

- Decode words with long *e* patterns *y, ie;* long *i* patterns *igh, y, ie;* long vowels *a, e, i, o, u;* inflections *-ed, -ing, -er, -est, -es* with and without spelling changes; suffixes *-ful, -ly, -y;* prefixes *un-, re-;* syllable *-le;* and syllable pattern CV.
- Recognize and read high-frequency words.
- Read on-level text with purpose and understanding.
- Read on-level text orally with accuracy, appropriate rate, and expression on successive readings.
- Use context to confirm or self-correct word recognition and understanding, rereading as necessary.

Materials

- High-Frequency Word Cards
- Instructional Routine: High-Frequency Words
- Practice Page 1.37

Formative Assessment and Corrective Feedback

IF a student makes an error, THEN follow this model:

Correct the error.

Guide the student to say the word correctly.

Check for understanding by having the student reread the word.

Reinforce: Make a note to review the word during the student's next session.

- Have students read aloud the practice text on Practice Page 1.37.

- Explain that the main purpose of reading the text is to practice their reading skills.

- Coach students to use decoding skills and context to self-correct any mistakes they make during reading. They should read the text several times until they are able to read smoothly and accurately with expression and at a natural rate.

- When students have finished the fluency practice, choose a few sentences to review. Have students read each sentence and explain in their own words what it means.

- After students are able to read the text fluently, guide them to track their progress on their My Progress graphs.

Tracking Student Progress

The My Progress graph helps students track their progress over time as they read text of increasing difficulty

Distribute copies of the graph to students. Each time a student masters reading the Practice Page text for a Cumulative Review/Fluency session, have the student track that achievement on the graph as follows:

1. Below the horizontal axis of the graph are places for the student to record the date on which he or she has successfully completed each Cumulative Review/Fluency Practice Page. Guide students to write the date, starting with the first available date line on the left.

2. Find the session number of the Cumulative Review/Fluency Practice Page on the vertical axis of the graph. Then find the point on the graph where the line from that Practice Page intersects the line representing the date on which the passage was read. Have the student draw a star, checkmark, or other symbol of their choice to note the achievement.

3. Have the student draw a line connecting each symbol to the next as he or she progresses over time.

Celebrate and Share Student Progress

Explain to students that the rising line on the graph represents their progress as they read harder and harder text. Encourage students to show their graphs to their families and celebrate their achievements.

My Progress Graph

Name _____

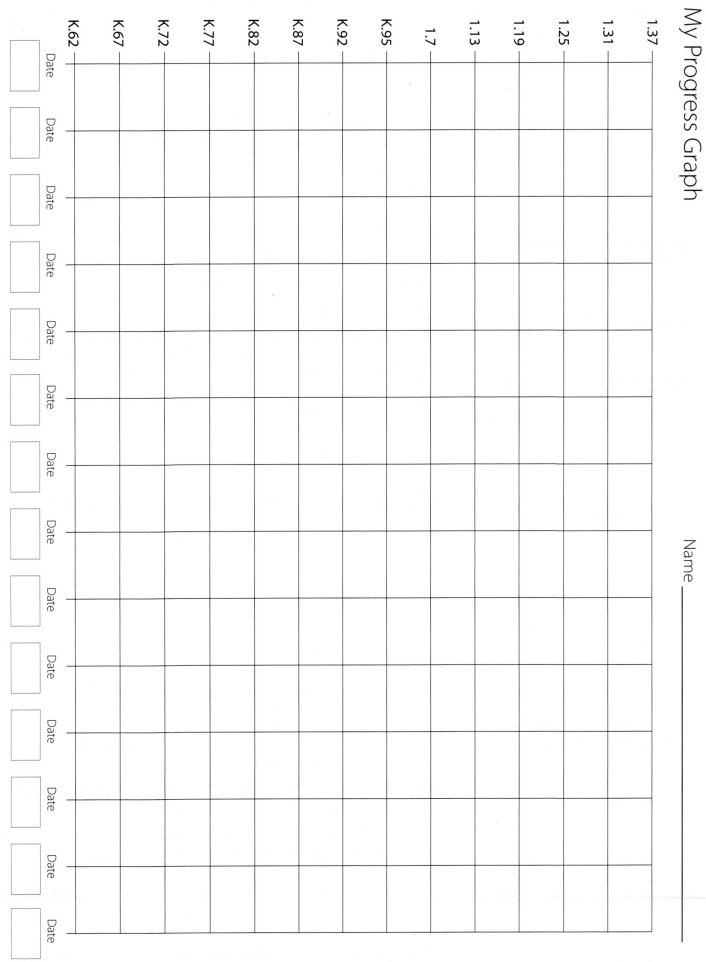

	Date	Date	Date	Date	Date	Date	Date	Date	Date	Date	Date	Date	Date	Date
1.37														
1.31														
1.25														
1.19														
1.13														
1.7														
K.95														
K.92														
K.87														
K.82														
K.77														
K.72														
K.67														
K.62														

Fun with Letters

CAPITAL CONCENTRATION: Upper- and Lowercase Letters

Objectives

- Identify and name the upper- and lowercase letters of the alphabet.

Materials

- Letter Cards

Group Size

- 2 to 4 students

Steps

1. From the Letter Cards, create one set per group of 52 cards, consisting of an uppercase and lowercase version of each letter of the alphabet.

2. Arrange the cards face down in a grid pattern.

3 The first player turns two cards face up and says the name of each letter. If the letters match, that player takes the cards and sets them aside. If the letters do not match, the player turns the cards back over. Play then continues with the next player.

4. At the end of the game, the player with the most cards wins.

Extension Activity

Students may also play individually, sorting through the cards to match letters on their own.

SCAVENGER HUNT: Letter Names

Objectives

- Identify and name upper- and lowercase letters of the alphabet.

Materials

- Letter Cards

Group Size

- 1 to 4 students

Steps

1. Choose a letter of the alphabet and give each student a letter card for that letter. Say the letter's name and have students repeat it.

2. Tell students to find other examples of the letter in the classroom. Encourage students to look at books, signs, or other print in the environment.

3. When students have found an example, have them hold their cards next to the example to make sure they match. Have students say the letter's name again.

Extension Activity

Have students search for objects around the classroom or through a collection of items you have gathered that begin with the target letter.

Fun with Sounds

RHYMES AND CHANTS: Phonological Awareness

BIRTHDAY HOP

For the following rhyme, have students hop forward when they hear their birth month and backward when they hear the date.

> Apples, peaches, pears, and plums
>
> Tell me when your birthday comes.
>
> January, February, March, ...
>
> First, second, third, ...

ECHO CHANTS

For the following chants, say a line and have students repeat it after you. Encourage students to keep time by clapping their hands once for each syllable.

> A sailor went to sea, sea, sea
>
> To see what he could see, see, see.
>
> But all that he could see, see, see
>
> Was the bottom of the deep blue sea, sea, sea.
>
> Two, four, six, eight
>
> Meet me at the garden gate.
>
> If you're late, I won't wait.
>
> Two, four, six, eight.

NAME BINGO

Guide students to sing the lyrics below (to the tune of "Bingo"), replacing syllables with claps as shown. Then repeat, replacing the name *Fernando* with the names of students in the group.

> There was a class that had a child
>
> Fernando was his name, oh!
>
> Fer-nan-do! Fer-nan-do! Fer-nan-do!
>
> Fernando was his name, oh!
>
> There was a class that had a child
>
> Fernando was his name, oh!
>
> CLAP-nan-do! CLAP-nan-do! CLAP-nan-do!
>
> Fernando was his name, oh!
>
> There was a class that had a child
>
> Fernando was his name, oh!
>
> CLAP-CLAP-do! CLAP-CLAP-do! CLAP-CLAP-do!
>
> Fernando was his name, oh!
>
> There was a class that had a child
>
> Fernando was his name, oh!
>
> CLAP-CLAP-CLAP! CLAP-CLAP-CLAP! CLAP-CLAP-CLAP!
>
> Fernando was his name, oh!

Objectives

- Demonstrate understanding of spoken words, syllables, and sounds.

Group Size

- Any size

English Language Support

Make sure each word used is in students' oral vocabulary. You might want to use each word in a sentence to reinforce meaning. See also the Spanish rhymes at the end of this activity.

RHYMES AND CHANTS: Phonological Awareness, continued

SPANISH-LANGUAGE RHYMES

Phonological awareness in students' first language can transfer to English and help develop readiness for English reading. You may want to use Spanish rhymes and chants, like those shown here, with Spanish-dominant English learners. Have students clap along with the syllables.

Caracol

Aquel caracol

que iba por el sol

en cada ramita

llevaba una flor.

Cinco lobitos

Cinco lobitos,

tiene la loba,

cinco lobitos

detrás de la cola.

Dos fueron por leche,

dos fueron por pan.

El más regordete

se quedó a merendar.

La hormiguita

Era una hormiguita

que de su hormiguero

salió calladita,

se metió en un granero,

se robó un triguito

y arrancó ligero.

   Salió otra hormiguita

del mismo hormiguero

y muy calladita,

se metió al granero,

se robó un triguito

y arrancó ligero.

   Salió otra hormiguita...

Fun with Sounds

ELKONIN BOXES: Blend and Segment Phonemes

Steps

1. Distribute a copy of Activity Template: Elkonin Boxes and three counters to each student.

2. For each target word draw a picture in the picture frame or on a self-stick note that you place in the picture frame. Suggested target words: fish, mop, nose, hat, dog, dish, sun, pen, cat, cane, bat, kite, foot, feet, cup, bed.

3. Point to the first picture and have students name it. Repeat the name and explain that the three boxes under the picture stand for each sound in the word. Model the following steps for segmenting and blending the word's sounds. The word *fish* is used here as an example:

   - Say /f/ and move a counter into the first box.
   - Say /i/ and move a counter into the second box.
   - Say /sh/ and move a counter into the third box.
   - Blend the sounds slowly as you point to each box: /fff/ /iii/ /ssshhh/.
   - Blend the word again quickly tracing your finger from left to right below each box: /fish/.

4. Guide students to segment and blend the names of the remaining pictures.

Extension Activity

A variation of this activity is to have students move a counter representing a given sound into an initial, medial, or final box, depending upon the sound's position in a word. For example, tell students to listen for the /m/ sound in *man* and say the word slowly. As they repeat the word, have students move a counter into the first, middle, or final box, depending on the sound's location.

Objectives

- Blend and segment phonemes in one-syllable words.

Materials

- Elkonin Boxes
- Counters

Group Size

- 1 to 4 students

English Language Support

Make sure each word used is in students' oral vocabulary. You might want to use each word in a sentence to reinforce meaning.

Elkonin Boxes

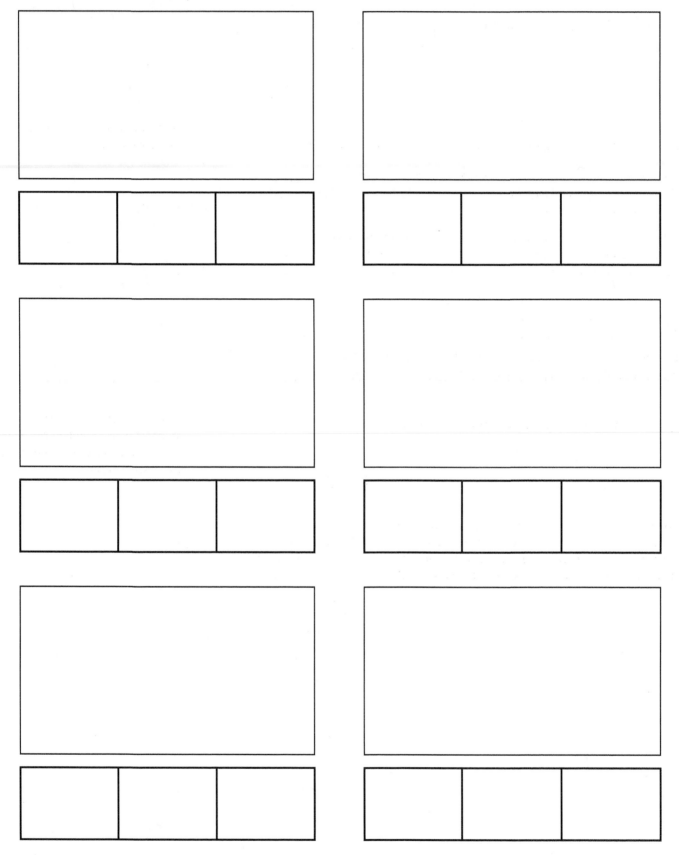

Fun with Words

WORDSCOPE: Blending

Steps

1. Distribute a copy of Activity Template: Wordscope to each student.

2. Have students cut out the box and the strips. Then have them cut slits in the box on the dotted lines.

3. Choose a phonogram and tell students to write it in the box. Suggested phonograms: *an, ap, at, ed, en, in, ip, og, op, up.*

4. Choose several consonants that could be added before the phonogram to create a word. For example, if the phonogram is *an,* you could choose the consonants *c, f, m, p,* and so on. Display the letters for students and have them write one of the letters in each square of the strip.

5. Model how to thread and pull the strip through the slit. Show students how to align a letter on the strip with the phonogram in the box and point out that, together, these form a word. Slowly blend the consonant and the phonogram. Then read the word quickly. Have students pull the strip to blend and read all the words.

6. Guide students to create additional Wordscopes using different phonograms.

Objectives

- Blend onset and rimes of one-syllable words.

Materials

- Wordscope
- Scissors

Group Size

- 1 to 2 students

English Language Support

Make sure each phonogram or word used is in students' oral vocabulary. You might want to use each word in a sentence to reinforce meaning.

Wordscope

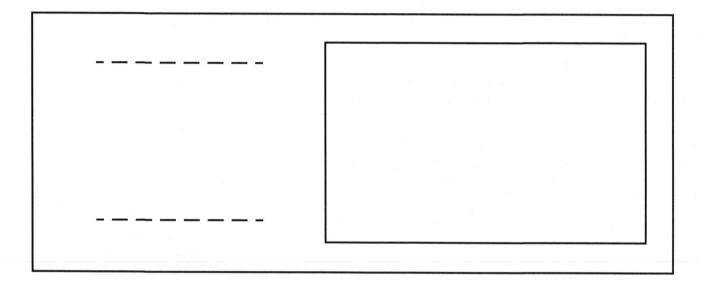

Fun with Words

MY WORD BUILDER

Steps

1. Use Activity Template: Word Builder Cards to create a set of cards for each student.

2. Distribute a sheet of construction paper or tag board to each student. Model for students how to create their own Word Builders using the following steps:

   • In the landscape position, draw a line 1 inch from the bottom.
   • Fold the paper along the line to create a flap.
   • Staple the ends of the flap to create a pocket that will hold the Word Builder Cards.

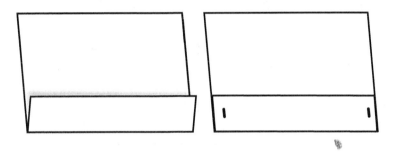

3. Have students mark the left end of the Word Builder with a marker or a sticker to help them remember where the first letter of a word belongs.

4. Model the following steps for building and blending words. The word *fish* is used here as an example:

   • Hold up the card for *f*. Say /f/ as you place the card into the Word Builder on the far left.
   • Hold up the card *i* and say /ĭ/ as you place it in the middle of the Word Builder.
   • Slide the *i* next to the *f*, and blend the sounds slowly as you point to each letter: /fffĭĭĭ/.
   • Hold up the card for *sh*, and say /sh/. Place the card on the far right.
   • Slide the *sh* next to the *f* and *i*. Blend all three sounds slowly as you point to the cards: /fffĭĭĭssshhh/.
   • Blend the word again quickly, tracing your finger from left to right below the word: /fĭsh/.

5. Guide students as they practice building and blending words until they can follow the steps easily.

Objectives

• Build and blend one-syllable words.

Materials

• Word Builder Cards
• Construction paper or tag board
• Scissors
• Stapler

Group Size

• 1 to 4 students

English Language Support

Make sure each word used is in students' oral vocabulary. You might want to use each word in a sentence to reinforce meaning.

Word Builder Cards (page 1)

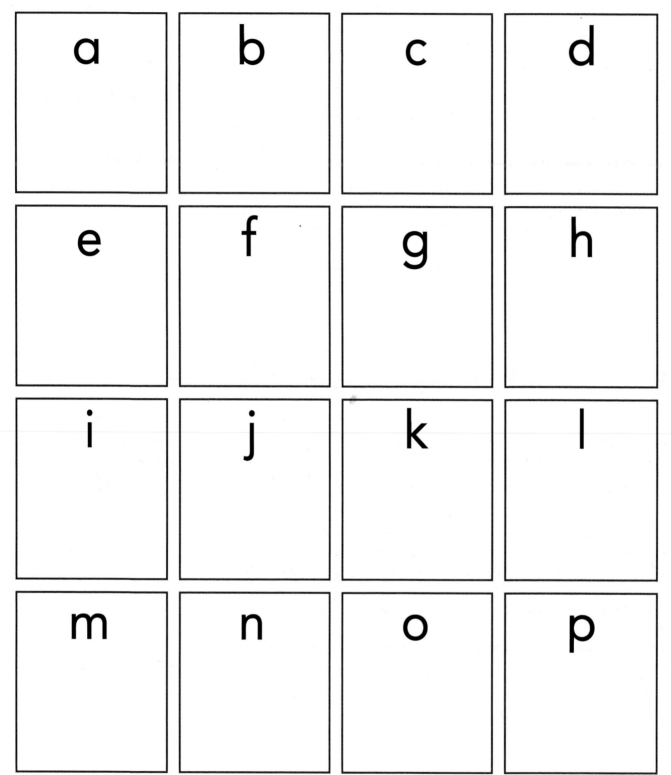

Word Builder Cards (page 2)

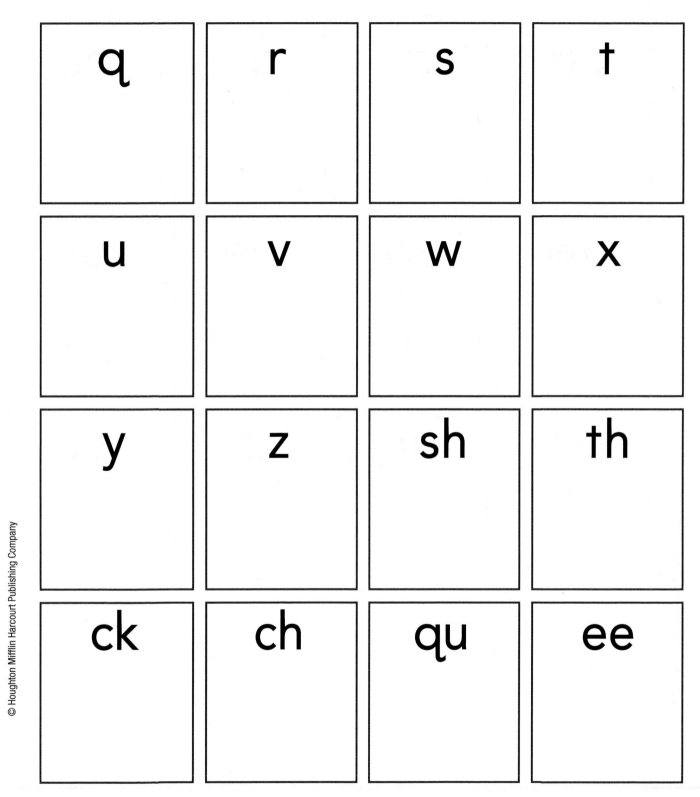

q	r	s	t
u	v	w	x
y	z	sh	th
ck	ch	qu	ee

Word Builder Cards (page 3)

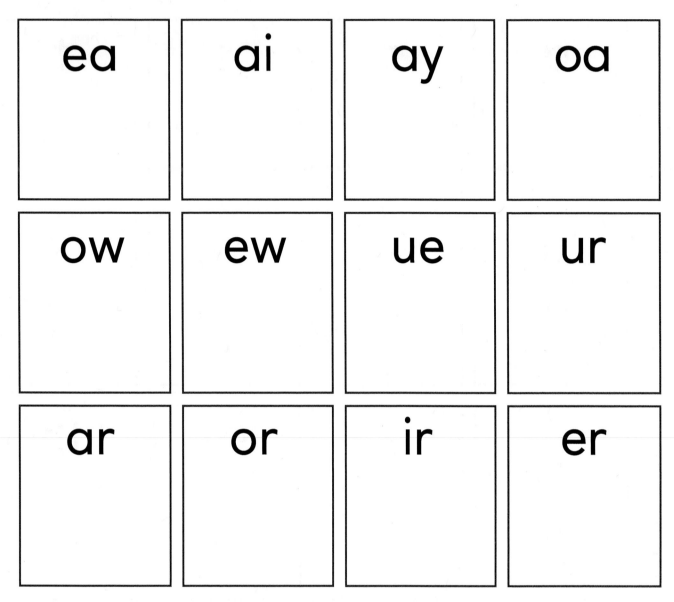

ea	ai	ay	oa
ow	ew	ue	ur
ar	or	ir	er

Fun with Words

TIC-TAC-GO!: Long Vowels *a, e, i, o, u*

Steps

1. Create a set of 27 word cards using Activity Template: Word Cards. You may wish to use the following words:

like	bike	bake	cake	make	mite	kite	site	no
go	slow	hope	cape	cute	meet	sit	kit	cup
luck	cap	bat	set	sod	cot	sat	pet	let

2. Distribute a set of cards to each student group. Have students stack the cards face down. Then have each student decide whether he or she will write "X"s or "O"s to play the game.

3. Students take turns drawing a card, reading the word aloud, and telling whether the vowel sound is long or short.

4. If the vowel sound is long, the student marks an "X" or an "O" in a space on the game board. Play then moves to the next student.

5. The first student to mark three "X"s or "O"s in a row wins. These can run horizontally, vertically, or diagonally.

Extension Activity

Have students play on an oversized board, created on the ground or floor with masking tape or chalk.

Objective

- Recognize and read words with long vowels.

Materials

- Word cards
- Tic-Tac-Go! board

Group Size

- 2 students

English Language Support

Make sure each word used is in students' oral vocabulary. You might want to use each word in a sentence to reinforce meaning.

Tic-Tac-Go!

Word Cards

Alphafriends

Purpose: Use this routine to review sound/letter correspondences.

1	• Display the front of the **Alphafriend Card.** • Review the card name and sound with students.	**What's the name of this Alphafriend Card?** *Bennie Bear* **What first sound do you hear in the words** ***Bennie Bear?*** */b/* **What's the sound?** */b/*
2	• Turn the card over to display the picture and letter side. • Connect the sound to the letter.	**We spell the sound /b/ with the letter *b*.**
3	• Have students repeat the sound and spelling three or more times as you point to the spelling.	**What's the sound?** */b/, /b/, /b/* **What's the spelling?** *b, b, b*
4	• Review the sound and letter connection.	**What is the sound for this Alphafriend Card?** */b/* **Bennie Bear has a letter. What is it?** *b* **The letter *b* stands for the /b/ sound. When you remember Bennie Bear, it will help you remember the /b/ sound.** **When you hear the /b/ sound, you can check the Bennie Bear card to see what spelling to use. The spelling you use for the /b/ sound is *b*.**

Sound/Spelling Cards, Kindergarten

Purpose: Use these routines to teach and review sound/symbol correspondences.

Introduce

1	• Display the front of the **Sound/Spelling Card.**	
2	• Say the name and sound as you point to the picture. Explain the picture if needed.	**This is Bennie Bear. The first sound we hear in the words** *Bennie Bear* **is /b/.**
3	• Guide students to name the picture and the initial sound.	**Now you say it. What name?** *Bennie Bear* **What sound?** */b/*
4	• Repeat the sound three times. • Have students repeat the sound three times.	**Listen. What sound?** **/b/ /b/ /b/** **Now you say it.** */b/ /b/ /b/*
5	• Show the letter. Point to and name the spelling. • Have students name the spelling three times.	**Listen. What spelling?** ***b b b*** **Now you say it. What spelling?** ***b b b***
6	• Write a word with the target sound.	bat
7	• Read the word. Point out the target sound.	**Look.** *Bat* **starts with** **b/b/.** ***Bat.***
8	• Read the word again, and have students read it with you. Then repeat with two or more example words.	**Listen:** ***bat.*** **Now you say it.** *bat*
9	• Repeat with alternative spellings of the sound, if appropriate.	

Review

1	• Touch the picture on the card.	**What is the picture on the card?** *Bennie Bear*
2	• Have students identify the first sound in the name of the picture.	**What is the first sound you hear in** ***bear?*** */b/*
3	• Point to the spelling on the card.	**What is the spelling?** *b*

Sound/Spelling Cards, Grade 1–3

Purpose: Use these routines to teach and review sound/symbol correspondences.

Introduce

1	• Display the **Sound/Spelling Card.**	
2	• Point to the picture. Say the name of the object shown and the initial sound.	**This is a mouse. The first sound we hear in** *mouse* **is /m/.**
3	• Guide students to name the object and the initial sound.	**What is this?** *mouse* **What is the first sound you hear in the word** *mouse?* /m/
4	• Repeat the sound three times. • Have students repeat the sound.	**Listen. What sound?** /m/ /m/ /m/ **Now you say it.** /m/ /m/ /m/
5	• Discuss the letters. Point to and name the spelling. • Have students name the spelling three times.	**Listen. What spelling?** *m m m* **Now you say it.** *m m m*
6	• Write a word with the target sound.	mat
7	• Read the word. Point out the target sound.	**Look.** *Mat* **starts with** *m*/m/. *Mat.*
8	• Read the word again, and have students read it with you. Then repeat with two or more example words.	**Listen:** *mat.* **Now you say it.** *mat*

Review

1	• Touch the picture on the card.	**What is the picture on the card?** *mouse*
2	• Have students identify the first sound in the name of the object.	**What is the first sound you hear in** *mouse?* /m/
3	• Point to the spelling on the card.	**What is the spelling?** *m*

Sound-by-Sound Blending

Purpose: Use this routine to teach students a strategy for decoding unfamiliar decodable words using the English sound/spelling system.

1	• Write or display the **Letter Card(s)** for the first sound in the word.	**m**
2	• Point to the letter(s) as you say the sound, and have students repeat it with you.	**Listen: /m/.** **Now you say it.** /m/
3	• Write or display the **Letter Card** for the next sound in the word and repeat the procedure.	**Listen: /ă/. Now you say it.** /ă/ **m** **a**
4	• Sweep your hand below the letters, and blend the sounds. • Have students blend the sounds with you.	**Blend the two sounds together.** **Listen: /m/ /ă/.** **Now you say it.** /m/ /ă/ **m a**
5	• Repeat the process for the remaining sounds, one at a time.	**Listen: /t/.** **Now you say it.** /t/ **m a t**
6	• Model reading the entire word. Sweep your hand below the letters, and blend the sounds. • Have students blend the sounds to read the word.	**Blend all of the sounds together. Listen: /m/ /ă/ /t/,** ***mat.*** **Now you say it.** /m/ /ă/ /t/, *mat* **m a t**
7	• Ask students to tell if the target word sounds like a real word. • Have them use the word in a sentence.	**Does *mat* sound like a word you know?** *Yes.* **Now use the word *mat* in a sentence.** *Possible response: I wipe my feet on the mat.*

Vowel-First Blending

Purpose: Use this routine to provide additional support to students who have difficulty with the other types of blending and need to focus on using vowel sounds.

1	• Display the **Letter Card** for the vowel in the word. • Point to the spelling as you say the sound. • Have students repeat the sound with you.	**Listen: /ôr/.** **Now you say it.** /ôr/ **or**
2	• Explain that when you see this spelling as you read, you will remember to say that sound.	**When I see these two letters together, I'll say /ôr/.**
3	• Display the **Letter Card** for the first sound in the word. • Point to the spelling as you say the sound. • Have students repeat the sound with you.	**Listen: /f/.** **Now you say it.** /f/ **f**
4	• Place the cards next to each other in order. • Sweep your hand below the cards, and blend the sounds. • Have students blend the sounds with you.	**Listen: /f/ /ôr/, *for*.** **Now you say it.** /f/ /ôr/, for **f** | **or**
5	• Repeat the process for the remaining sounds, one at a time.	**Listen: /k/.** **Now you say it.** /k/ **k**
6	• Sweep your hand below the cards, and blend the sounds. • Have students blend the sounds with you.	**Listen: /f/ /ôr/ /k/, *fork*.** **Now you say it.** /f/ /ôr/ /k/, fork **f** | **or** | **k**
7	• Ask students to tell if the target word sounds like a real word. • Have them use the word in a sentence.	**Does *fork* sound like a word you know?** *Yes.* **Now use the word *fork* in a sentence.** *Possible response: I eat pasta with a fork.*

Vowel-First Blending

Sounds in Sequence Dictation (Single-Syllable Words)

Purpose: Use this routine to give students a strategy to spell single-syllable words.

1	• Review the **Sound/Spelling Card.** • Tell students they will be spelling words with this sound/spelling.	**What is the sound for this spelling?** */m/* m
2	• Say the target word and use it in a sentence.	**We are going to spell the word *mat*.** ***I wipe my feet on the mat.***
3	• Say the word slowly with students.	**Say the word with me. Listen carefully to hear all the sounds: /m/ /ă/ /t/.**
4	• Segment the first sound in the word with students.	**Watch my mouth: /m/ /ă/ /t/.** **What's the first sound?** */m/* **Write the spelling for /m/.** *m*
5	• Repeat with remaining sounds.	**Watch my mouth: /m/ /ă/ /t/. What's the next sound?** */ă/* **Write the spelling for /ă/.** *a* **Watch my mouth: /m/ /ă/ /t/. What's the next sound?** */t/* **Write the spelling for /t/.** *t*
6	• Display the target word. • Have students check their spelling.	**What word did we spell?** *mat* **Did you write *mat* with the letters *m-a-t*?**
7	• Have students write the decodable sentence.	**Now write this sentence: *I sit on my mat*.**
8	• Repeat the sentence, saying one word at a time. Remind students to write high-frequency words as whole words.	**I...sit...on...my...mat.** **Remember that you do not need to sound out the high-frequency words.**
9	• Display the sentence. • Underline the high-frequency words.	I sit on my mat. **Now proofread your sentence.**
10	• Repeat the routine with the remaining words.	**Think about the sounds as you write the words.**

Sounds in Sequence Dictation (Multi-Syllable Words)

Purpose: Use this routine to give students a strategy to spell multi-syllable words.

1	• Review the **Sound/Spelling Card.** • Tell students they will be spelling words with this sound/spelling.	**What is the sound for this spelling?** /ā/
2	• Say the target word and use it in a sentence.	**We are going to spell the word** *safely.* *Be sure to cross the street safely.*
3	• Guide students to divide the word into syllables.	**Say the word with me:** *safely.* **Now clap the syllables: safe** *(clap)* **ly** *(clap).*
4	• Segment the first sound in the first syllable with students.	**Now listen for the sounds in the first syllable: /s/ /ā/ /f/. What's the first sound?** /s/ **Write the spelling for /s/.** *s*
5	• Repeat with the remaining sounds in the first syllable. • Then continue by segmenting the sounds in the second syllable with students.	**Watch my mouth: /s/ /ā/ /f/. What's the next sound?** /ā/ **Write the spelling for /ā/.** *a* **Watch my mouth: /s/ /ā/ /f/. What's the next sound?** /f/ **Write the spelling for /f/.** *f* **What pattern stands for the /ā/ sound in safe?** *a-consonant-e* **Write the last letter to finish the pattern.** *e*
6	• Display the target word. • Have students check their spelling.	**What word did we spell?** *safely* **Check your spelling of** *safely.*
7	• Have students write the decodable sentence.	**Now write:** *Did you get home safely?*
8	• Repeat the sentence, saying one word at a time. Remind students to write high-frequency words as whole words.	**Did…you…get…home…safely?** **Remember that you do not need to sound out the high-frequency words.**
9	• Repeat with the remaining words.	**Think about the sounds as you write.**

Syllable Division: VCV Pattern

Purpose: Use this routine to help students recognize the VCV syllable pattern.

1	• Write a word with a VCV pattern, but do not read the word aloud.	moment
2	• Remind students that each syllable in a word has a vowel sound. • Have students identify the vowels. Write a *V* under each vowel.	**Look at this word. Which letters are vowels?** *o, e* moment V V
3	• Have students identify the consonant between the vowels. • Write a *C* under the consonant.	**Which consonant letter falls between the vowels?** *m* moment V C V
4	• Point out the VCV pattern. • Explain that in a VCV word, the syllables are usually divided before the consonant. • Draw a slash before the consonant. • Explain that the first syllable is an open syllable and the vowel sound is long.	**When you see a vowel-consonant-vowel pattern, divide the word into syllables before the consonant.** mo/ment v/ c v
5	• Have students sound out each syllable and blend the syllables to read the word.	**Let's blend the syllables to read the word:** /m/ /ō/ /m/ /ĕ/ /n/ /t/, *moment.* **What's the word?** *moment*
6	• Repeat the process with a VC/V word, such as *finish.* • Explain that if the word does not make sense, students should divide the word after the consonant. • Draw a slash after the consonant. Explain that this is now a closed syllable and the vowel is short. • Have students sound out each syllable and blend the syllables to read the word.	fi/nish **/f/ /ī/ /n/ /ĭ/ /sh/** v/cv **Does /f/ /ī/ /n/ /ĭ/ /sh/ make sense?** *no* fin/ish vc/v **Let's break the syllable after the consonant like this. The first syllable is now a closed syllable. The vowel sound is short.** **/f/ /ĭ/ /n/ /ĭ/ /sh/, *finish*** **Does *finish* sound like a word you know?** *yes*

Syllable Division: VCCV Pattern

Purpose: Use this routine to teach students how to read words with the VCCV syllable pattern.

1	• Write a word with a VCCV pattern, but do not read the word aloud.	napkin
2	• Remind students that each syllable in a word has a vowel sound. • Have students identify the vowels in the word. • Write a *V* under each vowel.	**Look at this word. Which letters are vowels?** *a, i* nap kin V V
3	• Have students identify the consonants between the vowels. • Write a *C* under each consonant.	**Which letters are consonants that fall between the vowels?** *p, k* nap kin VC CV
4	• Point out the VCCV pattern. • Explain that when dividing a VCCV word, the syllables are divided between the two consonants. • Draw a slash between the two consonants in the word and between the *C*'s in the VCCV pattern.	**When you see a vowel-consonant-consonant-vowel pattern, divide the word into syllables between the two consonants.** nap/kin vc/cv
5	• Have students sound out each syllable and blend the syllables to read the word.	**Let's blend the syllables to read the word: /n/ /ă/ /p/ /k/ /ĭ/ /n/.** **What's the word?** *napkin*
6	• If students have difficulty reading the syllables correctly, remind them that each syllable has a CVC pattern, so the vowels are short.	***Nap* has a short *a* sound. *Kin* has a short *i* sound. When you put the two syllables together, you get *napkin*.**

Choral Reading

Purpose: Use this routine to provide students with opportunities to build fluency.

1	• Have students turn to the appropriate page in the text.	**We will read together. Be sure you are on the page that we will be reading.**
2	• Read the text aloud with students.	**As I read the text, you will read along with me.**
3	• Model accuracy, appropriate rate and phrasing, and expression.	**Listen to how my voice sounds as I read. Try to make your voice match mine.**

Echo Reading

Purpose: Use this routine to provide students with opportunities to build fluency.

1	• Have students turn to the appropriate page in the text.	**You will listen as I read. Then you will read with me. Be sure you are on the page that we will be reading. Put your finger on the beginning of the first sentence.**
2	• Read a section of the text aloud as students track the print. Model accuracy, appropriate rate and phrasing, and expression.	**As I read the text, use your finger to follow along. Listen to how my voice sounds as I read.**
3	• Reread the section. Have students track the print and read along with you as you read.	**Now read along with me. Try to make your voice match mine.**
4	• Continue the process with several more sections of the text.	

Repeated Reading

Purpose: Use this routine to provide students with opportunities to build fluency.

1	• Select a short passage for students to read.	
2	• Read the passage aloud once for comprehension. • Model accuracy, appropriate rate and phrasing, and expression.	**Listen as I read the text aloud. Pay attention to the speed at which I read and how my voice changes.**
3	• Have students whisper-read the passage aloud.	**Now using a whisper, read the passage aloud to yourself. Practice reading at a good speed and try to read all of the words correctly.**
4	• Listen to monitor students' reading. If a word is misread, read the word correctly and have the student repeat the word before continuing.	
5	• Have students reread the passage until the desired level of fluency is achieved.	

High-Frequency Words

Purpose: Use this routine to provide students with the opportunity to practice high-frequency words.

1	• Display the **High-Frequency Word Card** and say the word. • Have students repeat the word.	**This word is *kind*.** **What's the word?** *kind* **kind**
2	• Repeat the target word. • Then spell the word aloud as you write it.	**kind** **k-i-n-d**
3	• Use the word in a sentence.	**A butterfly is a *kind* of insect.**
4	• Point out familiar sound/spelling patterns that are listed on the back of the **High-Frequency Word Card.**	**In the spelling pattern *ind*, the letter *i* usually stands for the /ī/ sound. What's the vowel sound?** /ī/
5	• Blend the word with students.	**Now let's blend the sounds in the word: /k/ /ī/ /n/ /d/.**
6	• Point to the letters on the card as students spell the word aloud.	**Spell the word *kind*.** *k-i-n-d*
7	• Then repeat the spelling as you point to the letters.	**Say the word and spell it again.** *kind, k-i-n-d*
8	• Have students write the word.	**Now you write the word.**
9	• Have students compare their writing with the displayed word.	**Check that you spelled the word correctly. Make corrections if necessary.**

High-Frequency Words

Phonics/Decoding Strategy

What can you do when you come to a word you do not know?

1. Look at the letters from left to right.

2. Think about the sounds for the letters.

3. Blend the sounds to read the word.

4. Ask yourself:

   - Is it a word I know?

   - Does it make sense in what I am reading?

Research Bibliography

Archer, A. & Hughes, C. (2011). *Explicit Instruction: Effective and Efficient Teaching.* New York: Guilford Press.

August, D. & Shanahan, T. (2006). *Developing Literacy in Second Language Learners: Report of the National Literacy Panel on Language Minority Children and Youth.* Mahwah, NJ: Lawrence Erlbaum Associates, Publishers.

Ball, D. L. & Forzani, F. M. (2011, Summer). Building a Common Core for Learning to Teach, and Connecting Professional Learning to Practice. *American Educator*, 35(2), 17–21, 38–39. See also Teaching Works, http://www.teachingworks.org/.

Balmuth, M. (1992). *The Roots of Phonics: A Historical Introduction.* Baltimore, MD: York Press.

Bear, D., Invernizzi, M., Templeton, S., & Johnston, F. (2012). *Words Their Way: Word Study for Phonics, Vocabulary, and Spelling Instruction, Fifth Edition.* Boston, MA: Pearson/Allyn and Bacon.

Beck, I. (2006). *Making Sense of Phonics: The Hows and Whys.* New York, NY: Guilford Press.

Boardman, A. G., Roberts, G., Vaughn, S., Wexler, J., Murray, C. S., & Kosanovich, M. (2008). *Effective Instruction for Adolescent Struggling Readers: A Practice Brief.* Portsmouth, NH: RMC Research Corporation, Center on Instruction.

Bryson, B. (1990). *The Mother Tongue: English and How It Got That Way.* New York, NY: Avon Books.

California Department of Education (2010). *Improving Education for English Learners: Research-Based Approaches.* Sacramento, CA: California Department of Education.

Castiglioni-Spalten, M. L. & Ehri, L. (2003). Phonemic Awareness Instruction: Contribution of Articulatory Segmentation to Novice Beginners' Reading and Spelling. *Scientific Studies of Reading*, 7, 25–52.

Cheatham, Jennifer P. & Allor, J. H. (2012). The Influence of Decodability in Early Reading Text on Reading Achievement: A Review of the Evidence. *Reading and Writing*, 25, 2223–2246.

Collins, J. (2001). *Good to Great.* New York: HarperCollins Publishers.

Connor, C. M., Alberto, P. A., Compton, D. L., & O'Connor, R. E. (2014). *Improving Reading Outcomes for Students with or at Risk for Reading Disabilities.* Washington, DC: National Center for Special Education Research, Institute of Education Sciences, U.S. Department of Education.

Cunningham, J., and others (1999). Assessing Decoding from an Onset-rime Perspective. *Journal of Literacy Research*, 31, 391–414.

Ehri, L. C. (2005). Learning to Read Words: Theory, Findings, and Issues. *Scientific Studies of Reading*, 9 (2), 167–188.

Ehri, L. C. & McCormick, S. (1998). Phases of Word Learning: Implications for Instruction with Delayed and Disabled Readers. *Reading & Writing Quarterly*, 14, 135–163.

Ganske, K. (2000). *Word Journeys.* New York, NY: Guilford Press.

Hanna, P. R., Hanna, S., Hodges, R. E., & Rudorf, E. H. (1966). *Phoneme-Grapheme Correspondences as Cues to Spelling Improvement.* Washington, DC: Department of Health, Education, and Welfare.

Henry, M. (2003). *Unlocking Literacy: Effective Decoding and Spelling Instruction.* Baltimore, MD: Brookes.

Honig, B., Diamond, L., & Gutlohn, L. (2013). *Teaching Reading Sourcebook.* Novato, CA: Arena Press.

Hougen, M. C. & Smartt, S. M. (2012). *Fundamentals of Literacy Instruction and Assessment, Pre-K–6.* Baltimore, MD: Brookes.

International Reading Association (IRA); National Institute of Child Health & Human Development (NICHD). (2007). *Key Issues and Questions in English Language Learners Literacy Research.* Available at: http://www.ncela.gwu.edu/files/rcd/BE023800/Key_Issues_and_Questions.pdf

Justice, L. M. & Piasta, S. (2011). Developing Children's Print Knowledge through Adult-Child Storybook Reading Interactions: Print Referencing as an Instructional Practice. In Neuman S. B. & D. K. Dickinson (Eds.), *Handbook of Early Literacy Research, Volume 3*, 200–213. New York, NY: Guilford Press.

Kaiser, A. P., Roberts, M. Y., & McLeod, R. H. (2011). Young Children with Language Impairments: Challenges in Transition to Reading. In Neuman S. B. & D. K. Dickinson (Eds.), *Handbook of Early Literacy Research, Volume 3*, 153–171. New York, NY: Guilford Press.

Kosanovich, M. & Verhagen, C. (2012). *Building the Foundation: A Suggested Progression of Sub-Skills to Achieve the Reading Standards: Foundational Skills in the Common Core State Standards.* Portsmouth, NH: RMC Research Corporation, Center on Instruction.

Meadows Center for Preventing Education Risk. (2007). *Features of Effective Instruction*. Austin, TX: Texas Education Agency/University of Texas System.

Moats, L. C. (2000). *Speech to Print: Language Essentials for Teachers*. Baltimore, MD: Brookes.

Moats, L. C. (2008). *Spellography for Teachers: How English Spelling Works*. (LETRS Module 3.) Longmont, CO: Sopris West.

National Governors Association Center for Best Practices, Council of Chief State School Officers. (2010). *Common Core State Standards for English Language Arts, Appendix C*. Washington, DC.

National Institute of Child Health and Human Development (NICHD) (2000). *Report of the National Reading Panel: Teaching Children to Read: An Evidence-based Assessment of the Scientific Research Literature on Reading and Its Implications for Reading Instruction* (NIH Publication No. 00-4769). Washington, DC: U.S. Government Printing Office.

O'Connor, R. E. (2011). Phoneme Awareness and the Alphabetic Principle. In O'Connor, R. E. & Vadasy, P. F. (Eds.), *Handbook of Reading Interventions*, 9–26. New York, NY: Guilford Press.

Roessingh, H. & Elgie, S. (2009). Early Language and Literacy Development Among Young English Language Learners: Preliminary Insights from a Longitudinal Study. *TESL Canada Journal, 26* (2), 24–45.

Rosenshine, B. (2010). *Principles of Instruction*. Brussels, Belgium: The International Academy of Education. Available for download at: http://www.ibe.unesco.org/fileadmin/user_upload/Publications/Educational_Practices/EdPractices_21.pdf

Spear-Swerling, L. (2011). Phases in Reading Words and Phonics Interventions. In O'Connor, R. E. & Vadasy, P. F. (Eds.), *Handbook of Reading Interventions*, 63–87. New York, NY: Guilford Press.

Treiman, R., Pennington, B. F., Shriberg, L. D., & Boada R. (2008). Which Children Benefit from Letter Names in Learning Letter Sounds? *Cognition, 106,* 1322–1338.

Vaughn, S., Wanzek, J., Murray, C. S., & Roberts, G. (2012). *Intensive Interventions for Students Struggling in Reading and Mathematics: A Practice Guide*. Portsmouth, NH: RMC Research Corporation, Center on Instruction.

Venezky, R. (2001). *The American Way of Spelling*. New York, NY: Guilford Press.

Yopp, H. K. & Yopp, R. H. (2009). Phonological Awareness Is Child's Play! *Young Children, 64* (1), 12–21.

Glossary

alphabetic system   A system of written language in which letters stand for the sounds of spoken language.

automaticity   Fast, effortless word recognition resulting from extensive reading practice.

closed syllable   A syllable having one short vowel and ending in one or more consonants.

connected text   Text in the form of phrases, sentences, or paragraphs (as opposed to individual words).

consonant   A speech sound produced by a partial or complete obstruction of the air stream by any of various constrictions of the speech organs, such as /p/, /f/, /r/, /w/, and /h/. Also, the letter or character representing such a sound.

consonant blend   Two or more letters that are blended so that the sound of each letter is heard (sometimes called a consonant cluster); examples include /br/ *br*, /st/*st*, /str/*str*.

continuous blending   A method of sounding out words one sound at a time and continuously. For example, the word *mat* would be blended as follows: /m/ /a/ /t/.

CVC   A spelling pattern consisting of consonant-vowel-consonant; the vowel sound is short.

CVCe   A spelling pattern consisting of consonant-vowel-consonant-silent *e*; the vowel sound is long.

decodable text   Text in which the vast majority of words contain only previously taught letter-sound relationships.

decodable word   A word that contains only previously taught letter-sound relationships.

decoding   Determining letter-sound correspondences; constructing meaning from the graphic symbols of written language.

digraph   A pair of letters representing a single speech sound, such as the *ph* in *phone* or the *ea* in *beat*.

diphthong   A complex speech sound or glide that begins with one vowel sound and gradually changes to another vowel sound within the same syllable, such as /oi/ in *boil*.

encoding   Transcribing spoken language into written symbols; spelling.

expression   The natural sound of spoken language applied to oral reading.

fluency   The ability to read a text quickly, accurately, and with proper expression with little conscious attention to mechanics such as decoding.

formative assessment   The information gathered as a part of regular instruction which defines the specific scope of instruction.

foundational reading skills   The key skills that are essential to reading proficiency: print concepts, letter knowledge, phonological awareness, phonemic awareness, phonics, word recognition, and fluency.

grapheme   The letter or combination of letters that stand for a single sound. A grapheme can be a single letter, such as *n* or *e*, or more than one letter, such as *ck*.

guided practice   Guidance, assistance, and feedback provided to students as they learn and practice using a strategy or skill.

high-frequency words   Words that appear often in text and are key to reading comprehension. They may be words that are taught as wholes because they are irregularly spelled or because the spelling-sound correspondences have not yet been taught. Fluent readers are able to recognize and read these words automatically.

inflectional ending   An affix that changes the form of a word in number, person, mood, or tense. Examples include the *s* in *dogs*, the *ed* in *walked*, the *ing* in *reading*, and the *er* in *faster*.

linguistic transfer   The application of first language skills and knowledge to similar skills in the second language.

modeling   Demonstrating the reasoning and mental processes involved in applying a strategy; "thinking aloud."

morpheme   A meaningful linguistic unit that cannot be divided into smaller meaningful parts. For example, the word *man* and the suffix -*ed* (as in *walked*).

onset   Part of a syllable that precedes the vowel; for example, the *n* in *neck* or the *dr* in *drop*.

open syllable   A syllable that ends with a long vowel.

phoneme   The smallest sound in spoken language. English has about 41 different phonemes. The word *neck* has three phonemes: /n/, /e/, and/k/.

phonemic awareness   The understanding that spoken language consists of a series of individual sounds, some of which are grouped together to form words; involves the ability to distinguish, separate, and manipulate these sounds.

phonics   The predictable relationship between sounds of spoken language (phonemes) and letters that stand for sounds (graphemes); the science of matching sounds to letters in reading and spelling.

phonological awareness   The ability to identify elements of oral language, including phonemes, onsets, rimes, and syllables.

prefix   A word part added to the beginning of a word to change the meaning of the word, such as *pre* in *preread*.

print concepts Basic print concepts include the connection between spoken and written language; recognition of letters and words; directionality; and word spacing.

r-controlled vowel A vowel followed by the letter *r*; the sound that results is neither long nor short. Examples include: /ûr/ *er, ir, ur*; /ôr/ *or, ore*.

rate The speed (words per minute) at which a person reads connected text.

rime A vowel and any following consonants of a syllable; for example, the *eck* in *neck* or the *op* in *drop*.

root word A word part, usually of Greek or Latin origin in English, that is used to form a family of words.

segmenting Breaking words down into individual sounds.

sound-by-sound blending A cumulative method of sounding out words. For example, the word *mat* would be blended as follows: /m/, then /a/, then /ma/, then /t/, and finally /mat/. This method can provide extra support to struggling readers because it requires them to hold fewer individual sounds in short-term memory than other types of blending.

sound–letter correspondence The relationship between a spoken sound and the written letter (or letters) that represents it.

suffix A word part added to the end of a word to change the meaning of the word, such as *-less* in *helpless*.

syllable A unit of spoken language consisting of a single uninterrupted sound formed by a vowel, diphthong, or syllabic consonant alone, or by any of these sounds preceded, followed, or surrounded by one or more consonants.

think aloud A teaching technique in which the teacher uses a monologue to demonstrate thinking and reasoning processes; a method for modeling the use of a strategy or strategies.

variant vowel A vowel that represents a sound that is neither long nor short; for example: /ou/ *ow, ou*.

VCCCV A spelling pattern consisting of vowel-consonant-consonant-consonant-vowel.

VCCV A spelling pattern consisting of vowel-consonant-consonant-vowel.

VC*e* A spelling pattern consisting of vowel-consonant-silent *e*.

VCV A spelling pattern consisting of vowel-consonant-vowel.

vowel A speech sound, such as /ē/ or /ĭ/, created by the relatively free passage of breath through the larynx and oral cavity, usually forming the most prominent and central sound of a syllable.

VV A spelling pattern consisting of two or more vowels together that make different sounds (for example, *lion*).

word blending The combining of individual phonemes (sounds) to read words.

word building An activity in which the student builds and reads decodable words.

Resources: Skills Index

Phonological Awareness

Print Concepts